Dignity at Work

Human dignity, the ability to establish a sense of self-worth and self-respect and to enjoy the respect of others, is necessary for a fully realized life. Working with dignity is a fundamental part of achieving a life well-lived, yet the workplace often poses challenging obstacles because of mismanagement or managerial abuse. Defending dignity and realizing self-respect through work are key to workers' well-being. Insuring the dignity of employees is equally important for organizations as they attempt to make effective use of their human capital. In this book Randy Hodson, a sociologist of work and organizational behavior, applies ethnographic and statistical approaches to this topic, offering both a richly detailed, inside look at real examples of dignity in action, and a broader analysis of the pivotal role of dignity at work.

How do people attain and maintain dignity in the face of assaults on dignity at work? How can management within organizations help to preserve dignity and thus enhance workers' social relations, organizational integrity, and productivity? This book sheds valuable light on the mechanisms by which workers become satisfied and committed employees. Hodson's exploration of these questions includes ethnographic detail from diverse settings, ranging from automobile manufacturing, to medicine, to home-based sales and temporary clerical work. He focuses on four problems that deflate morale and create conflict: outright mismanagement and abuse, overwork, limits on autonomy, and contradictions of employee involvement. He also analyzes strategies that workers use to maintain and defend their dignity: resistance, citizenship, the creation of independent meaning systems, and the development of social relations at work.

Hodson offers a valuable picture of the causes, consequences, and patterns of workers' efforts to maintain dignity. He finds that even in workplaces where abuse is common and mismanagement makes pride in accomplishment difficult, workers still find ways to create meaning in work and to achieve self-respect. He uses his findings and analysis to reevaluate contemporary workplace theories, including those based on the traditions of Marx, Weber, Durkheim, Foucault, and feminist theories of the workplace. Hodson's conceptual model of human agency and dignity contributes broadly to our understanding of the nature of work in advanced societies.

Randy Hodson is Professor of Sociology at Ohio State University. He is the author of numerous articles and books, including the forthcoming *Worlds of Work: Building an International Sociology of Work* (with Daniel Cornfield) and *The Social Organization of Work*, third edition (with Teresa A. Sullivan).

Dignity at Work

Randy Hodson

Ohio State University

CAMBRIDGE
UNIVERSITY PRESS

PUBLISHED BY THE PRESS SYNDICATE OF THE UNIVERSITY OF CAMBRIDGE
The Pitt Building, Trumpington Street, Cambridge, United Kingdom

CAMBRIDGE UNIVERSITY PRESS
The Edinburgh Building, Cambridge CB2 2RU, UK
40 West 20th Street, New York, NY 10011-4211, USA
10 Stamford Road, Oakleigh, VIC 3166, Australia
Ruiz de Alarcón 13, 28014 Madrid, Spain
Dock House, The Waterfront, Cape Town 8001, South Africa

http://www.cambridge.org

First published 2001

Printed in the United States of America

Typeface Sabon 10/12 pt.   *System* QuarkXPress [BTS]

A catalog record for this book is available from the British Library.

Library of Congress Cataloging in Publication Data

Hodson, Randy.
    Dignity at work / Randy Hodson.
        p.   cm.
    Includes bibliographical references and index.
    ISBN 0-521-77131-5 – ISBN 0-521-77812-3 (pb.)
    1. Work. I. Title.
    HD4904. H62 2001
    306.3′6–dc21   2001018483

ISBN   0 521 77131 5   hardback
ISBN   0 521 77812 3   paperback

To workers everywhere
whose dignity can be challenged
but cannot be denied.

Contents

vii

Contents

Tables and Figures

Tables

Figures

Preface

Working with dignity is a foundation for a fully realized life. Despite many denials of dignity faced daily in the workplace, people still strive to do their best, to take pride in their work, and to defend themselves against indignities from employers, and sometimes from coworkers. New challenges are constantly being created for working with dignity by the inexorable process of technological and organizational change and by the unrelenting drive of market systems for profit maximization.

In spite of the centrality of the quest for dignity at work by billions of workers around the world, the pursuit of dignity is rarely a central focus of scholarly writings on the workplace. The challenges to workers' well-being posed by technological, organizational, and market forces are sometimes a focus. However, rarely do we consider the very serious business of how workers respond to these challenges on a daily basis in the office suite and on the shop floor. The creative and purposive activities of employees to achieve dignity at work are the central focus of this book. I hope that by considering these activities we can gain a better understanding of the daily struggle for dignity at work and the central place it occupies in workers' lives.

I rely on data from a systematic analysis of the population of organizational ethnographies. These data provide an empirical base for studying the quest for dignity. The in-depth observations offered by workplace ethnographies provide a unique source of information on organizational life that has previously been underutilized.

The inspiration for this book was provided by the work lives and the quest for dignity of many different people. These people include friends, family, acquaintances, employees at offices and factories where I have worked, visited, or toured, and the many students with whom I have discussed workplace issues including our own and other's quests for dignity at work. I hope this book will be helpful to those who read it and who may see their own struggles reflected in it.

The efforts of many people combined to make this book possible. I would like to thank the men and women in the accounts analyzed here who allowed themselves to be interviewed and who spoke candidly and eloquently about their lives at work and their struggle for dignity. I would also like to thank the ethnographers who spend so many months and years observing work life and reporting on it in clear and often moving terms.

A special thanks goes to the research staff and students of the Indiana University Sociological Research Practicum who worked on the research project in which we coded the organizational ethnographies. Their probing questions, good will, and enthusiasm resulted in the sort of collective intellectual experience that is too rare in the hurried world of university life. I would like, in particular, to thank Sandy Welsh, Sabine Rieble, Sean Creighton, and Cheryl Sorenson Jamison.

A number of people offered useful comments and constructive criticisms on the project. I am particularly indebted to Dan Cornfield, P. K. Edwards, Bill Form, Craig Jenkins, Garth Massey, Judith Stepan Norris, Vincent Roscigno, and Mike Wallace. Mary Child and the reviewers for Cambridge University Press offered excellent editorial guidance throughout the project for which I am also grateful. Finally, I am especially indebted to my wife and partner, Susan Rogers, for sage advice on all matters concerning work, life, and dignity.

This book contains new material and also represents an expansion and synthesis of some of my previous work. Earlier versions of some material have appeared in: "Is Worker Solidarity Undermined by Autonomy and Participation?" (with Sandy Welsh, Sabine Rieble, Cheryl Sorenson Jamison, and Sean Creighton) *American Sociological Review* (Vol. 58, 1993); "Worker Resistance," *Economic and Industrial Democracy* (Vol. 16, 1995); "Dignity in the Workplace under Participative Management," *American Sociological Review* (Vol. 61, 1996); "Group Relations at Work," *Work and Occupations* (Vol. 24, 1997); "Pride in Task Completion and Organizational Citizenship Behaviour," *Work and Stress* (Vol. 12, 1998); "Organizational Ethnographies," *Social Forces* (Vol. 76, 1998); *Analyzing Documentary Accounts*, Quantitative Applications in the Social Sciences, #128, (Sage 1999); "Organizational Anomie and Worker Consent," *Work and Occupations* (Vol. 26, 1999); and "Management Citizenship Behavior," *Social Problems* (Vol. 46, 1999).

Acknowledgments

Permission has been granted for selected use of material from the following:

From *Women on the Line* by Ruth Cavendish, Copyright © 1982 by Ruth Cavendish. All rights reserved. Reprinted by permission of Routledge and Kegan Paul, Boston, Massachusetts.

Part I

Dignity and Its Challenges

1

Four Faces of Working with Dignity

> She seeketh wool, and flax, and worketh willing with her hands.
> She layeth her hands to the spindle, and her hands hold the distaff.
> She perceiveth that her merchandise is good; . . . with the fruit of her
>   hands she planteth a vineyard.
> Strength and honor are her clothing; and she shall rejoice.
>
> Proverbs 31

Life demands dignity, and meaningful work is essential for dignity. Dignity is the ability to establish a sense of self-worth and self-respect and to appreciate the respect of others. Dignity is realized in the political sphere by striving toward democracy and justice. In the economic sphere, it is realized in the demand for a living wage and equal opportunity. In the workplace, dignity is realized through countless small acts of resistance against abuse and an equally strong drive to take pride in one's daily work. Even where abuse is commonplace and chaos and mismanagement make pride in accomplishment difficult, workers still find ways to create meaning in work and to work with dignity. Alternative avenues to achieving dignity sometimes involve focusing attention on peripheral tasks. Alternatively, dignity can be achieved through camaraderie and solidarity with coworkers.

Working with dignity requires purposive, considered, and creative efforts on the part of workers as they confront workplaces that deny their dignity and infringe on their well-being. Concepts appropriate to studying such creative efforts are less developed in the social sciences than are concepts for studying large-scale, impersonal structures. Yet people are highly active and creative, and the drive to realize human dignity and agency is a powerful force in every aspect of social life. A main goal of this book is to contribute to the development of social science concepts that foster a deeper understanding and appreciation of the struggle to work with dignity.

Human dignity is necessary for a fully realized life. But what is dignity? Dignity is a word more commonly used in social and political discourse

3

than in social science writings. People hope for a death with dignity. Unfairness and discrimination undermine one's dignity. There can be dignity in suffering.

Two different meanings underlie the idea of dignity (Meyer and Parent 1992:11). The first is that people have a certain inherent dignity as a consequence of being human. The second is that people earn dignity through their actions (Castel 1996). The inherent human dignity of a dying person, for example, may be reduced if their physical life is prolonged unnecessarily. Alternatively, they may be allowed to die with dignity. The inherent human dignity of a worker can be violated by mismanagement or by managerial abuse. Alternatively, dignity can be attained through noble action or through enduring great suffering. Examples include valiant soldiers, moral leaders, victims of injustice, and enduring workers of all kinds.

To defend one's dignity means to resist infringements on dignity and to insist on being treated with respect (Freeman and Rogers 1999). Thus, the dying person may refuse life support or the worker may one day curse the abusive boss and walk off the job. Resistance to abuse is an act by which one takes back one's dignity (Vredenburgh and Brender 1998). Taking specific actions that are worthy of respect is also an act of dignity. The employee who works effectively in spite of obstacles achieves dignity through work. Working with dignity thus entails *both* defending one's inherent human rights and taking actions that are worthy of respect by oneself and others.

Workers from all walks of life struggle to achieve dignity and to gain some measure of meaning and self-realization at work. The achievement of dignity at work thus depends on creative and purposive activity on the part of workers. Dignity can be achieved through taking pride in productive accomplishments, even if the accomplishments may be modest by someone else's standards. Dignity is also realized through resistance against denials of one's dignity, such as those arising from abusive bosses or bad management practices. In defending dignity and achieving self-realization, workers establish themselves as active agents with some control over their work lives. Without some minimum of control, without dignity, work becomes unbearable (de Man 1929; Marcuse 1991).

Working with dignity is an essential building block for a life well lived. The attainment of dignity at work is one of the most important challenges people face in their lives. Ensuring the dignity of employees is equally important for organizations as they attempt to make effective use of their human and social resources.

In this book four strategies that workers use to maintain and defend their dignity are analyzed: resistance, citizenship, the creation of independent meaning systems, and the development of social relations at work. We also discuss four principal challenges to working with dignity: mismanagement and abuse, overwork, limits on autonomy, and contradictions of employee involvement. These four strategies and challenges are at the heart of the analysis presented in this book.

The Quest for Dignity

The stories of workers in four different settings reflect the challenges of working with dignity and the joys that can sometimes be found when these challenges are met. Each of these stories illustrates a different aspect of the search for dignity at work. Each story is told by an ethnographer who spent six months to a year or more deeply immersed in the setting. Such accounts offer a rare opportunity to observe the face of dignity at work. The empirical base for this book rests on a systematic analysis of such workplace ethnographies. We begin with four cases that illustrate the core challenges to dignity at work.

In the first setting, employees at National Wire (a pseudonym) confront abusive conditions and a chaotic workplace resulting from chronic mismanagement (Juravich 1985). At Electrical Components Limited, the assembly work is hard and unrelenting, giving rise to chronic overwork and exhaustion (Cavendish 1982). At Pacific Hospital, the doctors and interns must defend their competence and establish their autonomy in relation to those higher in the hospital hierarchy (Bosk 1979). At American Security Bank, branch managers and their staffs struggle to increase productivity to avoid downsizing and layoffs (Smith 1990). Each of these stories reflects the challenges to working with dignity and the strategies through which dignity is attained and defended.

Mismanagement and Abuse

At National Wire production equipment is outdated and in ill repair. Worse, management makes no attempt to remedy the situation. Instead, repairs are completed on a piecemeal, emergency only basis:

> The lack of spare parts coupled with the general disrepair of the machines . . . made it impossible to keep the SELMs running for any length of time. As two weeks turned into a month this situation became maddening. . . .
>
> The machinery had three major problems. First, most of it was outdated for the kind of operation we were running, and it had been badly maintained over the years. Second,

management refused to stock either enough spare parts or the
tools necessary to repair the machines.

Third, management refused to hire or keep trained
personnel to maintain the machines. Instead, they hired a
series of young inexperienced mechanics (some better, some
worse) who, if they were lucky, managed to keep the
deteriorating equipment patched together. (Juravich 1985:37,
39, 40)

A young and inexperienced maintenance worker in this factory finds
that the adjusting screws on assembly machines are often stripped,
turning simple jobs into hours-long projects. Worn shafts, loose bear-
ings, and other points of wear are also apparent. After taking the back
plate off a machine to fill the oil reservoir, the worker is shocked to see
that the oil is full of stripped plastic ends of wire insulation, which are
being circulated throughout the whole mechanism. The accumulated
spare parts for this piece of equipment, which is the principal machine
producing the main components for the entire production floor, fit into
a cardboard container not much bigger than a shoe box hidden at the
back of a cluttered workbench.

Employees in this setting are treated with the same disrespect shown
the machines. Up to half the employees on the floor are laid off whenever orders drop, frequently two to three times a year. Because turnover
is high anyway, many of the laid-off workers have not been working long
enough to collect unemployment benefits. When the supervisor sched-
ules a meeting to announce the most recent round of layoffs, most of the
workers, who are used to this sort of treatment, do not protest, but some
of the younger workers do not take it so lightly. One young worker
throws a handful of leads into her machine and curses the supervisor. "I
was just starting to get my bills paid, and this no good [expletive] lays
me off with a one-day notice" (Juravich 1985:109).

In addition to the chaos resulting from worn-out machinery and the
uncertainty of layoffs, employees face more direct verbal abuse. One such
verbal attack humiliates and enrages a young worker and provokes an
angry response:

[Bobby] was originally called to make a small adjustment on
the depth of the machine's applicator. It was a simple
adjustment accomplished by loosening a single screw. In a
normally equipped shop it would have been a five-minute job,
but Bobby could not find the proper screwdriver. We searched
all the toolboxes, but the screwdrivers were either too large or
had been ground at the ends. Bobby asked Carroll [the

supervisor] if he could buy a screwdriver at the hardware store down the street. Carroll refused and told him to grind one of the ones we had. Bobby tried, but ended up stripping the screwhead so badly that nothing could get it out. Then Carroll came to the floor and in typical fashion chewed Bobby out in front of everybody. After Carroll left, Bobby brought the applicator over to the bench and . . . used a ten-pound copper mallet to smash a machine part that cost hundreds of dollars to replace. (Juravich 1985:135–136)

Eventually upper management makes a half-hearted attempt to improve the quality of production on the floor. They send a technician to check production standards and machine tolerances and make recommendations. The workers mock her behind her back and impersonate her walking around with her clipboard and micrometer. At lunch the workers refuse to sit with her in the cafeteria. She eventually quits and submits a blistering letter of resignation in which she condemns the workers for being uncooperative and criticizes the floor supervisors in even harsher terms.

Even in this chaotic and abusive environment, however, workers frequently apply their best efforts to the work at hand and use intelligence and initiative to facilitate production in spite of all the obstacles (Juravich 1985:51). For example, an aging stamping machine is used to place electrical terminals on both ends of sixteen-inch wire pieces that will eventually be assembled into wiring harnesses. The workers are instructed to put terminals on each wire, one end at a time, and then repeat this process ad infinitum. A middle-aged female worker, Betty, has a different method. She picks up a handful of wires and bounces them in her hand. This aligns the wires in the same direction following their natural bend. Then, still holding them as a bunch, she is able to quickly put a terminal on one end of each wire. She reverses the process and has a handful of leads correctly applied by an otherwise slow and temperamental machine. In the process she achieves meaning at work by mastering an uncertain and irregular process by being creative and productive in spite of obstacles.

Such self-motivated routines allow workers to impose a sense of order, control, and meaning on their daily lives at work. The jobs on the floor alternate between utter chaos and grinding monotony. But somehow, by imposing order and control, the workers made a life out of their situation. Such problems of abuse, chaos, and mismanagement are not unique to blue-collar production workers in factory settings. White-collar and professional workers also frequently encounter situations with these same characteristics.

Overwork

At a different workplace in a different country, the challenges are different, even though the products are similar. At Electrical Components Limited a mostly female work force assembles small electrical components. In this setting the constant, grinding pace of work sets the tone.

The physical challenges of the work and the stress are considerable. Freedom of movement is virtually nonexistent. There is no opportunity to take a short break or walk around, even a few steps. These stresses are increased by planned interdependence on the assembly line – each worker needs to complete her task quickly and correctly so that work does not stack up for others (Cavendish 1982:39).

The speed of the line is constantly being pushed to the limit. As the speed increases, the rejection rate goes up too, but the company is willing to live with this. "[T]ime-study must have calculated that it was cheaper for the firm to have more rejects and two women to mend them, than have a slower line, . . . especially as the exhausting effect of the fast line wouldn't enter their arithmetic" (Cavendish 1982:111).

In this setting, breakdowns on the line are a blessing. When the line stops the women are switched to packing or other lighter duties. After packing all day, many have aching arms and legs, but at least they have been able to move around a little and haven't had to face eight hours of automated pressure to keep up a steady pace (Cavendish 1982:39).

Work on the main line is rigidly controlled by the time clock. The close attention among the women to the details of "clocking in" and "clocking out" gives testimony to how unpleasant the work is. There is only one clock for a group of about fifty women and a lengthy queue forms at quitting time to clock out. The supervisors won't allow the women to leave the production line until quitting time, exactly 4:15, or their pay will be docked. But because of the queue at the clock, the last worker won't be able to clock out and leave until about 4:25 (Cavendish 1982:88).

Over time, a contest develops in which the women inch forward toward the clock and the supervisors try to keep them working on the line until the last minute. The contest itself takes on ulterior motives and meanings – it becomes more than just an attempt to get out of the plant a few minutes early. It also becomes a way to exert personal control over one's life in a situation where little or none is allowed. At one point the supervisors post a supervisor at the clock to keep the women from getting anywhere near it. The women respond by escalating their efforts:

> We knew pregnant women were allowed to stand at the front
> of the queue, so Maureen, who really was seven months

pregnant, barged in between him and the clock, and the rest of us followed saying we were all pregnant. The packer at the end of our line who was rather fat, lifted up her skirt to show him her stomach and we all laughed at him. (Cavendish 1982:89–90)

Such concerted actions to create personal space and resist the denial of dignity can create a sense of solidarity and camaraderie at work. But just as often, workers are divided by workplace relations and find that their competing goals place them in opposition to one another. For example, at Electrical Components Limited one senior worker is oblivious to the concerns of the other workers on the line and upholds rules (or breaks them) in a self-serving fashion in order to reduce her work load. This worker also works a second evening job as a janitor at a nearby shopping mall and never chips in with the other workers by contributing cakes or treats. The younger women consider her a tightwad and "mad for work" (Cavendish 1982:26). Her inconsiderate actions constitute as great a threat to the quality and meaning of the other women's daily lives at work as the moving assembly line, the supervisors, or the time clock.

In such grueling situations of chronic pressure and overwork, workers sometimes try to survive, not just through solidarity and mutual support, but also by shifting work to each other. Two strong-willed workers sit opposite each other, one to check the electrical circuits of the product and one to check the mechanical parts. Faulty devices are to be pulled off the line and fixed. If a faulty device comes down the line with a gauge that wouldn't register, the mechanics checker bangs it down hard on the table until the gauge moves. She then places it in the box for the electrical checker, having avoided fixing the underlying mechanical problem, which might now show up as a faulty circuit. The electrical checker reciprocates by insisting that her circuit tester shows adequate voltage even when the mechanical checker's doesn't. The two workers chat all day about their lives, children, and possessions, but basically they despise each other (Cavendish 1982:36–37). Coworker support, for the purpose of resisting management demands, improving output, or simply making life at work more bearable, is completely absent in this particular situation. Overwork has reduced work life to a dog-eat-dog ethos.

Bad supervisory practices also follow from the drive to maximize production at all costs, as even floor managers try to avoid their share of work:

[W]hen we ran out of something we'd have to shout to Eamonn three or four times before he brought something more, and it meant yelling really loud because he was usually

> sitting at the top of the line rather than wandering around. If
> you ran out of modules or transistors, your trays would pile
> up in front of you while he went to fetch more; he wouldn't
> stop the line to help you get 'down the wall', so you'd have to
> work extra hard. . . . He didn't lift up the boxes either, but left
> them on the ground, so you had to jump up every few
> minutes to change an empty box for a full one or refill a small
> box. This was very inconvenient. (Cavendish 1982:82)

At Electrical Components Limited, chronic pressure and overwork significantly undercut both good supervisory behavior and supportive coworker relations.

Challenges to Autonomy

Surgeons and medical residents at an elite medical school associated with a major university face different challenges to working with dignity. At Pacific Hospital the core challenge for the surgical staff and the medical residents is to master the formal and informal knowledge and skills of surgery and to defend autonomy over the work practices necessary to acquire, perfect, and maintain these skills.

The skills needed to perform surgery are formidable. These skills are based on both long training and years of practice. Surgery is at best an imperfectly applied science, which leaves much room for skilled or less-skilled applications. Incorrectly tied surgical knots can leave space for infection, and probes and scopes can slip and cause significant peripheral damage (Bosk 1979:37).

Because of the uncertainties of medicine and the variability of disease and the human body, substantial hands-on experience is required to master even basic techniques. Mastery of these techniques is at the core of medical training in Pacific Hospital. Two medical students are responsible for performing a myelogram (a procedure involving the removal of spinal fluid and the injection of dye in the spinal column) on a patient. The procedure does not go well, and they are forced to call in a senior physician:

> After examining Eckhardt's back [the resident physician]
> told the students, who were profusely apologizing for their
> failure, not to worry; that the problem was in Mr. Eckhardt's
> anatomy and not in their skills. He then proceeded with some
> difficulty to complete the procedure, instructing the students
> all the while.
>   The skill of housestaff with such procedures helps establish
> their authority to students. The ease with which they place

intravenous needles in the veins of the most troublesome
patients is a very common way to impress students; it serves
especially to humble senior students who are planning surgical
careers and who are often competitive with first-year
housestaff. (Bosk 1979:44)

Competence is achieved only through mastering new skills, starting
with the most basic. An intern is having trouble closing an incision.
Finally he turns to the chief observing resident and says, "I can't do it."
The resident informs him that that answer is not acceptable:

'What do you mean, you can't? Don't ever say you can't. Of
course you can.' 'No, I just can't seem to get it right.' Carl
had been forced to put in and remove stitches a number of
times, unable to draw the skin closed with the proper tension.
Mark replied, 'Really, there's nothing to it'; and, taking Carl's
hand in his own, he said, 'The trick is to keep the needle at
this angle and put the stitch through like this,' all the while
leading Carl through the task. 'Now, go on.' Mark then let
Carl struggle through the rest of the closure on his own. (Bosk
1979:45)

Having mastered some initial surgical skills, young residents are eager
to practice and perfect them and chafe at any limitations or interference.
A common complaint of first-year interns is that they are not allowed to
do enough cases and are required to just attend and watch. The longer
the interns and residents practice medicine the more they come to resent
such limitations (Bosk 1979:42–43).

Along with autonomy, however, comes responsibility. Early on, surgeons learn that they are the responsible party. The chief resident is
responsible for the patients on the surgery wing regardless of who is on
watch at the moment. During an orientation meeting for new interns,
the chief resident explains that he wants to be informed at all times:

'If anything comes up, I want to know about it. I don't care
what time it is; I want you to call. If there is a problem at
four in the morning call at four in the morning. Most likely,
I'll listen to what you tell me and fall right back to sleep. I
may even forget that you called. But call. I don't like to walk
in here in the morning and find myself surprised by what's
going on in my service. I'm ultimately responsible for what
goes on here, so call me.' He repeated this message a number
of times in a number of ways. (Bosk 1979:51–52)

Misjudgments or poorly learned skills can have extreme consequences,
possibly even the death of a patient. But some errors, and even some

mortality, are an inevitable part of the work of surgeons. Those in sub-ordinate positions, who have the least discretionary power, have the least opportunity to do significant harm. Senior surgeons, who have to make decisions involving the most complicated cases, also make the most serious errors. Mistakes of judgment may not have been incorrect in a technical sense given the information available, but a negative result forces reflection on the course of action taken or not taken. Surgeons accept this state of chronic uncertainty and self-reflection as part of what makes their work meaningful and challenging:

> It would look suspicious if you are doing major surgery and, week after week, you have no deaths and complications.
> You're going to have these, especially deaths, if you do major surgery. You can lead a long and happy life without deaths and complications, but you have to give up major surgery.
> (Bosk 1979:59)

On a daily basis, with lives hanging in the balance, surgeons have to make definitive treatment decisions to the best of their ability based on the sometimes limited information available.

Acquiring and practicing skills at the highest level allows the surgeon some protection against mishaps. But high levels of skill are also desir-able because they are rewarded with advancement opportunities. Each year more interns are admitted than there are available residency posi-tions. The least able are channeled to less prestigious surgical specialty training programs or to programs in other hospitals. Only the very best advance within the hierarchy at Pacific Hospital. Similarly, there are more first-year residents admitted than there are slots for senior resi-dences. Again, a weeding-out process occurs through channeling the less proficient toward other programs or institutions. The top positions, and the top rewards, are reserved for those who have demonstrated the highest levels of proficiency (Bosk 1979:149). This highly competitive environment further heightens the pressure to acquire skills, demand autonomy, and seek out extra opportunities for learning and extra responsibilities.

In its own way, the work at Pacific Hospital is as pressured as that at Electrical Components Limited. But at Pacific Hospital the pressure is largely internalized rather than being manifest through a supervisor's demands or the grinding pace of an assembly line. By 6:30 A.M., while most are still asleep, the surgeons are already at work moving among the preoperative patients, taking notes and discussing cases. After a final check on the patients, the surgeons, residents, and interns scrub thor-oughly and put on caps and gowns and are ready for the first surgery at precisely 8:00 A.M. Starting late is not an option. Although some days go flawlessly, each case holds the possibility of surprises and delays. Twelve-hour days of continuous work standing at the operating table without even a lunch break are not uncommon (Bosk 1979:2–3). In this setting, and in other highly skilled settings, autonomy is the foundation for dignity and meaning in work and is strongly defended against all incursions, including those from management, coworkers, senior workers, and allied professions (Abbott 1988).

Contradictions of Employee Involvement

Employees at American Security Bank are told they must work harder and smarter to avoid layoffs and branch office closings (Smith 1990). Heightened employee involvement and participation are promoted as solutions to the bank's problems by well-paid consultants who run training seminars for managers on how to motivate their workers. What is only dimly understood by some, and not at all by others, is that the bank's troubles are not caused by the workers or their motivations. The bank's troubles stem from questionable managerial decisions resulting in a history of risky high-stakes loans, many of which have turned out badly (Smith 1990:28).

The new management strategy based on heightened worker involvement, however, starts with the premise that workers hold the solution to higher productivity and a more competitive position (and, by implication, are to blame for past problems). Managers are encouraged to seek out, isolate, and "manage out" nonperformers – employees who are supposedly a drain on corporate profitability (Smith 1990:48). The consultants argue that the bank can be transformed into a leaner and more competitive organization by eliminating the bottom tier of employees through downsizing. The consultants call their solution "transforming the corporate culture," starting from the bottom up.

Transforming corporate culture means that managers must "drop old ideas and rigid structures," get involved, change their "thought process," and use "individual judgment" when managing their employees. When mid-level managers object that these ideas are vague and of little help, trainers accuse them of "getting off on a tangent." From the standpoint of a supervisor confronted with managing employees up or out, however, issues of rules, consistency, and fairness are not superfluous abstractions. As one branch manager reports, "The practicality [of micro-managing an employee's performance] is, you'd better know what you're doing" (Smith 1990:72).

The prospect of managing out employees is a particularly daunting one. The poorest performers will have to be identified, coached, and ultimately put on probation if their performance doesn't improve. These actions will, in all probability, have a demoralizing and destabilizing effect on other employees, who will fear for their own jobs. In addition, various personnel specialists and even lawyers will have to be consulted to evaluate any potential liabilities and risks for discrimination lawsuits.

Branch managers at American Security Bank strive to develop alternative strategies for implementing corporate restructuring and encouraging employee involvement. Instead of managing out their employees and increasing profitability through reducing staff, they seek to increase the productivity of their branch as a whole, thus providing legitimation for current staffing levels:

> Often organizing team or group efforts, sometimes utilizing a language of self-management, branch managers focused on managing up the performance of the unit by mobilizing their employees, individually and in groups, to work harder. . . .
>
> Managers employed a number of measures to improve the productivity of their branches: they worked on line with the tellers; managed up individual employees by pushing them to sell more products and to convert more customers to new deposit, withdrawal, and checking procedures and by pushing them to attend more and diverse training classes; [and] organized branch employees into quality circles. (Smith 1990:105)

The supervisor of the centralized records office resists pressures from upper management for layoffs by attempting to raise the productivity of his division. But he also creatively uses his detailed knowledge of local office procedures to implement new productivity measures that show improvements over baselines that have not, in fact, been measured, or even been measurable, in the past. In this way, he positions his unit to resist the more extreme demand from top management that he both increase productivity and identify and lay off the least productive employees (Smith 1990:141).

The consultants and trainers encourage managers to be opaque about the future of the bank and to obfuscate plans about corporate restructuring. Many branch managers, however, reject this strategy as undermining the trust of their employees and the stable operation of their units. Instead, they develop their own strategies for informing and involving employees and encouraging self-management:

> Norma held regular meetings with her branch employees to keep them informed of what she knew about ongoing branch closures, and what she had heard, if anything, about their

branch. She used these meetings also to point out problems
that might arise as a result of staff reduction through
redeployment and pressures on tellers to sell new products
with less time to do so. Employees as a group strategized ways
to confront these pressures. . . .

Loretta rejected that demand [for opaqueness] in another
way: when she met with her employees to assure them that
there would be no layoffs (following the orders of her
communiqué) she refused to understate the situation. She
prepared a presentation detailing the economics of the branch
and the continued pressures that employees should expect,
despite the absence of formal layoffs. (Smith 1990:107–108)

Branch managers also sometimes modified, or even subverted, clear
directives from the top. Local managers were asked to rank their employees on a bell curve in order to allocate raises and promotions. Managers
did this, but some of the more creative ones juggled the monthly rankings. Employees who the managers felt needed a motivational raise, but
who had previously been passed over by the ranking system, were moved
higher in the rankings. Employees who had received raises in the most
recent round were often passed over in spite of high current ranking.
Productive employees were thus ranked down but not enough to dis-
courage them. By manipulating the ranking rules, managers created a
more equitable distribution of raises and promotions. Equally importantly, the same employees were not allowed to consistently fall in the
bottom 15 percent of the curve, which would result in them being targeted to be managed out. The managers were thus able to motivate their
employees and avoid "shortsighted disciplinary action that would, in
their eyes, have irreparable long-term costs and consequences" (Smith
1990:131). By manipulating the rankings, managers were able to create
on paper a justification for their actions that was consistent with the new
corporate directives.

In spite of the best attempts of the branch managers to shield their
employees from layoffs, and perhaps in part because of the ultimately
provisional nature of the solutions devised, work at American Security
Bank became even more pressured over time. Tellers reported that they
were "never left alone" to do their jobs but were constantly pressured
to work on new tasks and projects (Smith 1990:106). Managers were
continuously pressured to turn their staffs into "quality salespeople" and
workers were directly or indirectly threatened with layoffs contingent on
the success of the restructuring efforts (Smith 1990:75). At American
Security Bank, the ultimate irony is that these pressures and contradictory demands on employees were driven by the need to compensate for

past blunders by top management. The imperative for restructuring was not driven by technological changes or by the necessity of meeting high standards of customer satisfaction or professional competence.

Adopting the consultants' language of heightened employee involvement, local managers and their staffs responded in a variety of creative ways to defend their right to work with dignity. These strategies included *both* defending job security and striving to increase productivity through greater effort and more intelligent procedures.

Safeguarding Dignity

People spend the better part of their adult lives at work. They know well the challenges to dignity that they face there, and many become high practitioners of the art of working with dignity, even under difficult and challenging circumstances. These practices are part of what social scientists have come to call *agency*: the active and creative performance of assigned roles in ways that give meaning and content to those roles beyond what is institutionally scripted.

Human beings act creatively and with purpose in the world. These creative and purposive actions give people a sense of power, effectiveness, and a sense of their personal dignity as creative, independent beings who are able to control their own destinies. Personal agency is realized through mastering new skills and operating effectively in one's environment. The workplace is thus a key arena for human agency and for the realization of human dignity.

The concept of job satisfaction is often used as a placeholder to describe workers' attitudes in lieu of having more situated and behaviorally relevant concepts to discuss their actual lives at work and their pursuit of dignity. The limitations of job satisfaction as an organizing concept for the study of work life have been well documented (Edwards and Scullion 1982; Hodson 1991; Scott 1985; Van Maanen and Barley 1984). These limitations include lack of specific behavioral referents, blindness to group dynamics, lack of relationship to measures of organizational productivity, and limited effectiveness in integrating the contradictory mental states that workers may simultaneously hold about their work and their jobs (Fisher 1980; Mortimer and Lorence 1989; Organ 1988).

Although the social sciences have had only partial success in developing concepts to describe and analyze workers' complex and sometimes contradictory behaviors, these behaviors are, nevertheless, the warp and woof of workers' daily lives. And it is out of these behaviors in the defense of dignity that workers construct meaningful experiences of work and of life more broadly.

The role of social science is to reveal patterns in seemingly idiosyncratic behaviors through systematic analysis. In the jargon of the social sciences, these patterns are the *structures* of behavior. An organizing goal of this book is to aid in the development of concepts appropriate for the study of working with dignity.

Behaviors involved in safeguarding dignity at work take place in at least four major arenas: *resistance, citizenship, the pursuit of meaning,* and *social relations at work*. Behaviors from each of these arenas are evidenced in each of the four workplaces described in this chapter. These domains include both reactive and proactive behaviors. They also include behavioral agendas that can be largely tangential to the main productive activity of the workplace. These four behavioral domains are listed in the first column of Table 1.1, which serves as a roadmap for our exploration of working with dignity.

First, in safeguarding dignity workers engage in active and passive *resistance* to abuse, overwork, and exploitation. The study of resistance has all too often been seen as a specialized and somewhat esoteric subfield in the social sciences, but it must be more fully incorporated into mainstream social science if we are to understand adequately the manner in which workers safeguard their dignity at work. The episode of machine wrecking in response to management abuse reported in the ethnography of the wiring harness factory discussed previously provides a clear example of resistance in defense of dignity. Most resistance, however, is much more subtle and subdued. Workplace resistance more typically relies on small-scale actions involving a subtle withdrawal of cooperation or a banking of enthusiasm.

Second, under better circumstances, and sometimes even simultaneously with abuse and overwork, workers are actively engaged in trying to perform their jobs in a successful and efficient manner. Creative and

Table 1.1. *Dignity at Work*

Safeguarding Dignity	Denials of Dignity
Resistance to attacks	Mismanagement and abuse
Organizational citizenship	Overwork
Independent meaning systems	Constraints on autonomy
Group relations	Contradictions of employee involvement

purposive activities oriented toward helping production successfully take place that are above and beyond organizational requirements have been labeled *citizenship* behaviors by organizational researchers (Schnake 1991). The actions of the branch managers and their staffs at American Security Bank in pursuit of organizational effectiveness, even in the face of a history of corporate mismanagement, provide an excellent example of organizational citizenship. Taking pride in one's work is a widespread and possibly universal phenomenon (although sometimes it is pushed far below the surface) (Krecker 1995; Veblen 1914).

Third, workers engage in a variety of meaningful activities during the workday in addition to resistance and citizenship that may be only tangentially related to management demands and organizational agendas. Such behaviors constitute significant side games at work whose rationale is the *attainment of meaning* outside the institutionally scripted flow of organizational activity. In the wiring harness factory, workers try to bring order and at least some sense of control and mastery to their circumstances through activities unassociated with production. Sometimes these activities build on normal daily events, making them into stabilizing routines:

> [O]ne of the older women on the floor had a routine she followed religiously. Every day at morning coffeebreak she went to the corner store and bought a newspaper. She brought it to her table and then went to the bathroom for a paper towel that she spread on her table. She then proceeded to eat half of her sandwich, no more, no less, every working day. There were numerous other examples of women 'setting up' their meager possessions – radio, cigarettes, and coffee cup – in similar fashion. (Juravich 1985:56)

Although both resistance and citizenship provide important sources of meaning for workers, independent agendas oriented toward creating personal meaning at work are also extremely important in the daily lives of countless employees across a wide range of organizations and occupations.

Fourth and finally, the *social aspects of work life* defined by relations with coworkers must be fully incorporated in any meaningful analysis of working with dignity. Social aspects of work include social diversions, friendships, and other activities whose purpose is to provide meaning in a world too often offering too little of it. Coworkers provide the social fabric that is often crucial for meaning at work. Coworkers also provide a significant line of both formal and informal defense against managerial fiat. As trade unionists have known since the beginning of industrial society, there is power in numbers. The previously discussed episode at

Electrical Components Limited in which the line workers conspired against the floor supervisors over queuing at the time clock illustrates well the importance of social support, solidarity, and mutual defense for safeguarding dignity at work.

Coworker relations, however, can also constitute significant challenges to dignity. The chronic hostility and interference between the electrical checker and the mechanical checker reported at Electrical Components Limited is an archetype for the type of bad relations between coworkers that are all too common. Best friends can quickly become worst enemies during workplace conflicts, and solidarity can vanish in an instant.

These four behavioral domains – resistance, citizenship, the pursuit of meaning, and social aspects of work life – constitute core arenas for attaining and defending dignity at work. They serve as organizing principles for the analysis presented in this book. We will be revisiting them regularly throughout the chapters that follow.

Denials of Dignity

The challenges to workplace dignity also need adequate conceptualization. The attainment of dignity at work can be conceptualized as confronting four principal challenges. These challenges are illustrated in the four settings described previously in this chapter and are listed in the second column of Table 1.1.

First, employees confront the problems of *mismanagement* and *abuse*. Even supervisors who are not inherently ill-mannered, arrogant, or domineering sometimes take unfair advantage of their power and abuse employees. The temptation to exploit power is strong, and the workplace is clearly an arena of widely differentiated power in which supervisors often have unbridled dominion and sometimes act like tyrants. Mismanagement and managerial incompetence can also be chronic problems for workers. The chaos resulting from the lack of leadership at National Wire is deeply implicated in the sense of malaise that pervades this workplace and that undermines the dignity of those who work there.

Second, even under coherent and civil management, *overwork* can rob workers of dignity and meaning. Overwork occurs across a wide range of settings, from assembly lines that run too fast to social service organizations that are understaffed.

Third, incursions on *autonomy* represent a significant challenge to the dignity of workers in many occupations. The surgical interns at Pacific Hospital chafe at any limits on their autonomy and seek to expand their independence and responsibilities at every opportunity. Craft workers in construction and factory settings also defend their autonomy with great vigilance. The struggle for autonomy, however, is not limited to professional and craft workers; to a significant extent the struggle for autonomy is relevant for all workers.

Contradictions of *participation* in new team-based forms of production that solicit heightened employee involvement represent a fourth and final challenge to working with dignity. With the general expansion of responsibility, professionalism, and autonomy in the workplace of the third millennium, the successful negotiation of work teams, quality circles, and "programs-of-the-week" has become a commonplace challenge for increasing numbers of employees. Programs calling for heightened employee involvement have the potential to increase responsibility and dignity at work. But they can also be used manipulatively to pressure workers to work harder and to increase output through intensified self-supervision and peer pressure (Grenier 1988). The story of American Security Bank described earlier in this chapter portrays some of the opportunities and challenges of organizational systems that stress heightened employee involvement.

These four challenges to working with dignity – mismanagement and abuse, overwork, incursions on autonomy, and contradictions of employee involvement – occur both separately and in every possible combination in organizations. We will be revisiting them regularly in the chapters that follow.

Conclusions

The model of workplace dignity developed in this book is one in which management behavior, organizational structure, and technology constitute the structural backdrop. These structural settings pose four challenges for workers – mismanagement and abuse, overwork, incursions on autonomy, and contradictions of participation. Against this backdrop, workers engage in conditionally autonomous performances in the pursuit of dignity. These autonomous practices include resistance, citizenship, the creation of independent meaning systems, and engagement in group relations at work. The pursuit of dignity at work is thus a creative endeavor, but its practice is limited, channeled, and constrained by the surrounding organizational demands and structures. The ultimate well-being of workers and the success of organizations are a result of this complex interaction of structure and agency, of organizations and employees engaged in a simultaneously collaborative and conflictual agenda of production.

The focus of this volume is the practice of dignity – the least analyzed part of this scenario. Organizational structures, the material well-being of workers, and the success or failure of organizations are the focus of countless journal articles and volumes in the social and management sciences. Workers' pursuit of dignity has had a less full hearing.

In Chapter 2 we explore the theoretical foundations for the study of dignity at work. This chapter also notes the unfinished nature of the requisite theoretical work. In Chapter 3 we investigate in-depth ethnographies of organizational life as a valuable source of information and insight for the study of dignity at work. Chapter 3 also outlines a methodology for systematically analyzing organizational ethnographies and defines the major concepts that will frame the analysis.

The remaining chapters of the book investigate the struggle for dignity as informed by the systematic use of ethnographic accounts of organizations as a data source. Chapters 4 through 7 each focus on one of the four major denials of dignity. Chapter 8 highlights the pivotal role of coworkers as both a potential blessing and a potential curse. Each chapter also explores important variations in the pursuit of dignity across race, gender, and nation.

Chapter 9 presents an integrated model of working with dignity, which incorporates both its organizational determinants and some of its key consequences. Finally, in Chapter 10 we return to the broader issues of structure and agency and the implications of our analysis for the nature of work, the effectiveness of organizations, and the attainment of dignity at work in the new millennium.

2

Toward a Theory of Dignity

Dignity is essential for a life well lived, or even for one worth living. But what does dignity at work mean? This chapter provides groundwork for answering this question by considering the work of the some of the founding figures in the social sciences. In addition, we consider the theoretical basis for an analysis of contemporary challenges to working with dignity and behavioral strategies for safeguarding dignity at work. The essential meaning of dignity that emerges includes both inherent human rights, such as protection from abuse, and earned aspects of dignity based on taking valued actions.

The starting point for our discussion of dignity focuses on the ideas of the classic social science theorists. We start with the conceptual insights of Marx, Durkheim, and Weber on themes related to working with dignity and the challenges to achieving this goal.

Alienation, Anomie, and Bureaucratic Rationality

The three founding figures in the social sciences, Karl Marx, Emile Durkheim, and Max Weber, provided groundbreaking ideas on the nature of work and human dignity that set the stage for modern theories of society. Each theorist conceptualized modern industrial society as entailing profound denials of dignity. For Marx, the central challenge to dignity was the control of labor by capitalists and their exploitation of workers, resulting in alienation from meaningful work. For Durkheim, the central challenge to dignity was the breakdown of social norms or rules governing workplace relations due to the drive toward endless expansion generated by modern industry. For Weber, the central challenge to dignity was the imposition of bureaucratic rationality in the world of work and the resulting stifling of human creativity. Each of these ideas captures important aspects of contemporary challenges to working with dignity.

22

Karl Marx on Alienation and Exploitation

According the Marx, the exploitation of workers by capitalists and the resulting alienation from work results in the almost total denial of workers' humanity (Marx 1971). Our species' humanity is realized through meaningful work and the alienation of work under capitalism robs workers of their inherent potential for human growth and development (Bottomore 1963).

The exploitation of workers arises from the fact that capitalists own the means of production (the technology, capital investments, and raw materials) and treat labor as if it were another inanimate factor of production. For a capitalist, labor is to be hired as cheaply as possible, used up, and discarded (Marx 1971). Marx's colleague Friedrich Engels describes the resulting exploitation as seen in the slums of London in the 1840s:

> St. Giles is in the midst of the most populous part of the town, surrounded by broad, splendid avenues in which the gay world of London idles about. . . . The houses are occupied from cellar to garret, filthy within and without, and their appearance is such that no human being could possibly wish to live in them. But this is nothing in comparison with the dwellings in the narrow courts and alleys between the streets, entered by covered passages between the houses, in which the filth and tottering ruin surpass all description. . . . Heaps of garbage and ashes lie in all directions, and the foul liquids emptied before the doors gather in stinking pools. Here live the poorest of the poor, the worst paid workers with thieves and the victims of prostitution indiscriminately huddled together. (Engels 1971:63)

According to Marx the exploitation and misery of workers result directly from the laws of capitalism in which the market system demands that every capitalist buy labor as cheaply as possible in order to produce and sell goods and still turn a profit. If capitalists do not exploit their employees, they will be undercut by other capitalists who do (Marx 1967).

As a result of the control of work by capitalists and the exploitation of workers, work under capitalism becomes an alienating experience. Instead of being a natural expansion of human abilities and interests, work becomes a foreign imposition that is forced on workers in order for them to earn their material subsistence:

> What constitutes the alienation of labour? First, that work is *external* to the worker, that it is not part of his nature; and

> that, consequently, he does not fulfil himself in his work but
> denies himself, has a feeling of misery rather than well-being,
> does not develop freely his mental and physical energies but is
> physically exhausted and mentally debased. The worker,
> therefore, feels himself at home only during his leisure time,
> whereas at work he feels homeless. His work is not voluntary
> but imposed, *forced labour*. It is not satisfaction of a need,
> but only a *means* for satisfying other needs. Its alien character
> is clearly shown by the fact that as soon as there is no
> physical or other compulsion it is avoided like the plague.
> (Marx 1971:127; emphasis in original)

Marx argued that workers are alienated in four aspects under capitalism (Marx 1971). First, they are alienated from the *products* of their labor. They no longer determine what is to be made or how it is to be used. In primitive societies, workers had a direct relationship to the products of their labor. They owned the products and these products became an important part of their material world. In industrial societies, workers no longer own the products they make. Instead these products disappear from the worker's life and are sold to others. Work on these products becomes a *means to an end*; that is, rather than being an end in itself, it is a means to acquire money to buy the necessities of life. Because workers are often denied any meaningful relationship to the products they produce, they come to relate to these products as meaningless objects rather than as extensions of themselves.

Second, workers are alienated from the *process* of work. Someone else controls the pacing, patterns, tools, and techniques of their work. Because workers do not control their moment-to-moment activity, work becomes less meaningful to them. When workers are emotionally separated from their tasks, they become alienated from their identity as human beings. Identity can then be secured only outside the workplace through leisure or family pursuits. Nonalienating work, by contrast, is virtually indistinguishable from leisure. The worker experiences work and hobbies with the same enthusiasm.

In Marx's third aspect of alienation, workers are denied the ability to be creative. Marx believed that the unique, defining characteristic of humans is the ability to be creative. The capacity for self-directed *creative activity* to meet everchanging needs is what distinguishes human beings from animals. If workers cannot express their *species being*, they are reduced to the status of animals or machines. Alienated labor is noncreative and only serves as a means to secure the material conditions of existence. Extreme specialization renders each worker's contribution to the final product obscure and of little consequence. To be self-actualized, human beings have to create freely like artists rather than like bees, which are guided by instincts. Thus, workers, by virtue of their biological nature as human beings, have an inherent drive toward self-actualizing productive experiences.

Fourth, alienated labor is an isolated endeavor, not part of a collectively organized effort to meet a group need. As a result workers under capitalism are alienated from others as well as from themselves. Human beings are social animals and their work always involves others, either directly or indirectly. When labor is alienated, control of these social relations is removed from the worker, who interacts with others on the job only as dictated by a supervisor. Alienated workers do not form an integrated work group engaged in collectively determining the nature and goals of their activity. As a result, workers are isolated from others in the realm of productive activity (Hodson and Sullivan 1995).

In Marx's vision, capitalism robs workers of the creative, purposive activity that defines their nature as human beings by subordinating their productive activity to profit making and thus reducing it to a means to acquire material sustenance. The realization of self-actualizing productive experiences is a key requirement for working with dignity, but it is frequently missing in modern profit-driven economies.

Emile Durkheim on Social Disorganization and Anomie

Writing several decades after Marx, Emile Durkheim also saw industrial society as being exploitative and abusive. He believed that work and economic life were in a chronic state of normlessness (*anomie*) in modern society because of its unrelenting drive toward economic expansion.

Durkheim's view is broadly similar to Marx's in its vision of the causes of these problems: Capitalism's expansionary dynamics create conflicts between workers and owners. The exploitation of workers follows from their lesser power in this relationship. Durkheim, however, believed that these conflicts were not inevitable. Instead, he believed that a new moral order could put limits on the unchecked power of capitalists and give workers their just share of the rewards of industrial society. In Durkheim's vision, the division of labor into finer and finer parts with workers having progressively less power as their tasks are made simpler had outstripped the development of the appropriate moral regulation of economic life. The solution to the problems of industrial society is not then the violent overthrow of capitalism and its replacement by committees of workers. A proletarian revolution would only replace control by one group with control by another group. Rather, the solution is for capitalists and their employees to join together in a shared moral order that orients the behavior of both groups toward common goals. Such a moral code would be based on a *collective conscious* of beliefs and values shared by all members of society (Durkheim 1984).

The absence of a shared moral code guiding the actions of the different classes and occupations in society allows economic exploitation and the harsh physical and emotional abuse of employees as well. Abuse, including capricious fines, beatings, and whippings, were commonplace in the early stages of the industrial revolution. Such abusive practices were commonly reported in factory studies of the times: "We beat only the lesser, up to thirteen or fourteen . . . using a strap" (quoted in Pollard 1965:219).

In primitive society group members were bound together by a moral code based on their common position and interests. Durkheim labeled this sort of cohesion *mechanical solidarity*. By contrast, in modern society, people occupying different positions in the division of labor have different interests. Therefore, in complex modern economies, mechanical solidarity must be replaced by *organic solidarity* in which the different parts performing different roles are nevertheless bound together by common interests. The image is much like that of a biological organism in which the different parts perform different functions, all of which are oriented toward maintaining the life of the whole.

Durkheim identified medieval occupational guilds as an example of a functioning economic system based on organic solidarity. The guilds regulated their members' hours of work, the quantity of goods that could be produced, and the conditions and rights of workers in each trade (Durkheim 1984:13). Durkheim believed that such collective groups, based on strong occupational identities, could protect the interests of individuals from other groups in society who sought to exploit them. In Durkheim's vision, the formation of such occupational groups is essential for achieving a well functioning and moral society based on full participation and equal justice for all.

In Durkheim's vision of a coherent future for industrial society, individual greed and self-interest would be subordinated within collective occupational associations. These associations would aggregate and systematize individual interests and integrate them into a comprehensive value system that protects the interests of all members of society (Durkheim 1984:14). Occupational associations would provide the formal organizational structures which would coordinate the contributions and needs of the various segments in society. In addition, these associations would provide the informal ties, bonds, and associations in the workplace, and in the community, that would regulate and guide the behavior of the individual members of the various occupations. For Durkheim, dignity at work is to be attained through participation in voluntary workplace associations that collectively give direction and meaning to work and that provide safeguards against abuse, exploitation, and overwork.

Max Weber on Bureaucratic Rationality

Max Weber, writing at the dawn of the twentieth century, envisioned the evils of modern society in terms of excessive rationality and bureaucracy, rather than in terms of exploitation, like Marx, or the breakdown or norms, like Durkheim. According to Weber, the essence of modern capitalism is the rational calculation of monetary profit and loss. This formal rational calculation replaces earlier less rational motives, such as those based on allegiance to traditional values or traditional authority. Capitalism is the science of applying formal rationality to economic life.

It is formal economic rationality that displaces shared values and sentiments and that undermines meaning and dignity at work in Weber's vision of modern economic life (Weber 1968). Weber believed that the coercive organization of economic life typical of slave and feudal societies, and of the early stages of capitalism, was not a viable basis for organizing modern society. Formal rationality, as manifest in bureaucratic rules and procedures, however, did provide a workable, though flawed, solution for how to organize a modern industrial economy. Only bureaucratic forms of organization can engage in the long-term planning and integration necessary for a modern economy and society. The significance of bureaucracy, however, is not just its technical efficiency relative to traditional and coercive forms of organizing work. Its significance also lies in its ability to secure the consent of participants by providing a new basis for legitimate power. The legal–rational underpinnings of bureaucracies (formal rules and codes laying out the responsibilities and rights for the different members of the organization) have the ability to secure consent by establishing legitimacy based on the rational allocation of power and rewards.

The features of bureaucracy that constitute its rationality and that make it an efficient system for organizing work include the following (Scott 1998):

- a fixed division of labor among participants with clearly specified jurisdictional areas and responsibilities;
- a hierarchy among offices;
- a set of general rules that guide activity;
- a separation of personal from official property and rights;
- selection of all personnel on the basis of technical qualifications; and
- employment seen as a career by participants.

These characteristics of bureaucracy help make bureaucratic systems technically efficient at accomplishing their stated goals. These principles also displace coercion, favoritism, and nepotism as less efficient foundations for economic life (Perrow 1986). But, according to Weber, these same features also lead to the depersonalizing effects of bureaucracy and to a loss of creativity:

> [The calculability of decision-making] and with it its appropriateness for capitalism . . . [is] the more fully realized the more bureaucracy 'depersonalizes' itself, i.e., the more completely it succeeds in achieving the exclusion of love, hatred, and every purely personal, especially irrational and incalculable, feeling from the execution of official tasks. In the place of the old-type ruler who is moved by sympathy, favor, grace, and gratitude, modern culture requires for its sustaining external apparatus the emotionally detached, and hence rigorously 'professional' expert. (quoted in Bendix 1960:421–422)

As a result of its technical efficiency, the extension of bureaucracy to more and more spheres of economic and political life seemed inevitable to Weber:

> Imagine the consequences of that comprehensive bureaucratization and rationalization which already today we see approaching. Already now . . . in all economic enterprises run on modern lines, rational calculation is manifest at every stage. By it, the performance of each individual worker is mathematically measured, each man becomes a little cog in the machine and, aware of this, his one preoccupation is whether he can become a bigger cog. (quoted in Mayer 1956:126–127)

The only possible escape from the stifling effects of increasing bureaucracy and formal rationality in Weber's view was the advent of new charismatic leaders. Such leaders, by their exceptional heroism or exemplary character, would be able to establish new values and normative patterns that would return a moral component to economic life (Weber 1947). New values and new meanings associated with a charismatic leader could thus transform society and save us from the "iron cage" of bureaucracy. For Weber, dignity at work depends on the ability to transcend the limits of stifling and rigid bureaucracies.

Along with Durkheim, Weber believed that the solution to the problems of modern industrial capitalism lay in the reintroduction of moral values. Weber and Durkheim differ, however, in the proposed source of such values. Durkheim saw them as emerging from occupational groups.

Weber saw them as emerging from charismatic leaders. Both these visions contrast with that of Marx, who saw the solution to the problems of industrial capitalism as the overthrow of capitalists by workers and the imposition of a new class in control – but one resting on a broader base than the capitalist class.

Modern Industrial Society

A century of rapid economic, social, and political transformations has brought many changes to capitalism since the time of Marx, Durkheim, and Weber. The twentieth century witnessed a continuation of many of the trends first identified by the founders of modern social science. But there have been many other changes too, some that were anticipated and others that were not.

One important trend has been the increased rationalization of work. During the early years of the twentieth century, new systems of organizing work were developed in an effort to implement standardized procedures in mass-production industries. The American industrial engineer, Frederick Taylor, developed one such system, which he called "scientific management." Taylor believed that there was "one best way" to do every task. That way can be discovered by first carefully observing how the workers do the task and then devising a more efficient way to do it. For instance, Taylor experimented with different ways of holding cutting tools on metal lathes in order to produce machine parts as efficiently as possible (Hodson and Sullivan 1995).

The following passage summarizes Taylor's principles for organizing work in a "scientific" manner:

> The managers assume . . . the burden of gathering together all of the traditional knowledge which in the past has been possessed by the workmen and then of classifying, tabulating, and reducing this knowledge to rules, laws, and formulae. . . .
>
> All possible brain work should be removed from the shop and centered in the planning or laying-out department. . . .
>
> The work of every workman is fully planned out by the management at least one day in advance, and each man receives in most cases complete written instructions, describing in detail the task which he is to accomplish, as well as the means to be used in doing the work. . . . This task specifies not only what is to be done, but how it is to be done and the exact time allowed for doing it. . . . Scientific management consists very largely in preparing for and carrying out these tasks. (Taylor 1911:39, 63, 98–99)

Taylor was also concerned with the problem of workers who resisted working as fast as possible; he saw this problem as a major impediment to efficiency. Taylor observed that many workers engage in *soldiering*; that is, they intentionally work well below their maximum capacity:

> The greatest part of systematic soldiering . . . is done by the men with the deliberate object of keeping their employers ignorant of how fast work can be done.
>
> So universal is soldiering for this purpose, that hardly a competent workman can be found in a large establishment . . . who does not devote a considerable part of his time to studying just how slowly he can work and still convince his employer that he is going at a good pace (Taylor 1911:32–33).

Taylor's solution was to fire these seasoned workers and hire untrained replacements. The new employees would then be trained to do the work exactly the way Taylor prescribed. These new employees would receive higher wages than they had received for less-skilled work but would be paid less than the skilled workers whom they replaced. In this way everyone would benefit (except, of course, the laid off workers).

The principles of scientific management spread rapidly through industry in the early twentieth century and formed the basis for modern quality control practices, which are based on the establishment of uniform practices under the close control and scrutiny of management (Scott 1998:39). The principles of scientific management were given further embodiment in the automatic assembly line developed by the Ford Motor Company, which would eventually spread around the world. Today the principles of standardized procedures under tight management control are still commonly referred to as "Fordism."

Other changes were less clearly anticipated by the founders of modern social science. For instance, the craft occupations employing highly skilled workers have continued to be an essential component of advanced industrial production systems. Automation and scientific management have tended to deskill and displace semiskilled production workers and unskilled laborers, but skilled workers have proven indispensable to advanced production systems (Thomas 1994). Indeed, the skilled trades have experienced modest growth as the employment demands for maintaining ever greater amounts of complex automated and semiautomated production equipment have increased (Jackson 1984). Today, skilled craft workers are essential for the maintenance and operation of sophisticated (and highly productive) robotics devices and automated production equipment of all kinds. Such highly skilled craft workers are often crosstrained in electronics, pneumatics, and computer programming (Cross 1985).

A second unexpected change has been the rapid growth of professional occupations entailing long training in increasingly specialized and even esoteric fields (Abbott 1988; Wilensky 1964). The professions have expanded in advanced economies to 20 percent or more of the labor force and this growth shows no sign of slowing. If one includes the growing occupational groups classified as semiprofessionals, paraprofessionals, and technicians (such as dental hygienists and laboratory assistants), the share of professionals and closely related occupations in advanced economies exceeds 25 percent of the labor force (Friedson 1994; Hodson and Sullivan 1995). Importantly, these occupations have had significant successes in securing economic privileges and defending their autonomy from the incursions of bureaucracy and scientific management (Leicht and Fennell 1997; Pavalko 1988).

The growth of various forms of worker participation in the late twentieth and early twenty-first centuries provides a final example of an important change occurring in advanced industrial economies that was unanticipated by the founders of modern social science. Durkheim saw the value of, and the necessity for, occupational groups as a safeguard against rising anomie. But he did not anticipate that by the beginning of the twenty-first century one of the most common forms of worker association would be employee involvement in production decisions through formal groups operating within enterprises. Such groups range from quality control circles oriented exclusively toward production decisions in Japanese firms to works councils and codetermination programs in European countries that participate in decisions about benefits, training, and a wide range of enterprise level decisions, including investment decisions (Freeman 1994). Direct worker ownership and partial worker ownership through Employee Stock Ownership Plans (ESOPs) have also expanded in recent decades and provide additional avenues for worker involvement and participation in workplace decisions (Rothschild and Russell 1986).

An American writer on management, Chester Barnard, contributed significantly to the theoretical justification for the formal participation of workers in production decisions within the modern enterprise. In *The Functions of the Executive* (1950) Barnard argues that organizations are essentially cooperative systems that serve to integrate the contributions of their individual participants. He defines a formal organization as "that kind of cooperation among men that is conscious, deliberate, purposeful" (Barnard 1950:4). In order for participants to willingly cooperate and give their fullest efforts they must be induced to do so through various rewards and inducements including material rewards, but also including advancement, prestige, and personal satisfaction and development. In addition, participants must clearly have in mind, and in their hearts, a common purpose. According to Barnard, the core functions of the executive are to establish a coherent system of production, to maintain effective lines of communication, and to encourage "belief in the real existence of a common purpose" (Barnard 1950:87).

During the last half of the twentieth century, the vision of the organization as a cooperative endeavor gave rise to a plethora of forms of employee involvement. Many of these emerging forms of employee involvement were described in the seminal writings of William Ouchi (1981). The range and variety of such forms of worker participation is tremendous. Japanese versions of employee involvement, for instance, tightly circumscribe employee participation to only the most immediate production tasks and do not offer a wider role for Japanese workers to contribute to the direction of their enterprises (Lincoln and Kalleberg 1990). Such forms of employee involvement were nevertheless an essential ingredient in the rapid economic expansion of Japan following the Second World War based on the efficient production of high quality manufactured goods (Cole 1989). European versions of employee involvement, by contrast, are based on elected works councils and legislatively backed codetermination principles and allow a broader range of topics to be considered (Lecher and Rüb 1999).

Most employee involvement programs in the United States start as management initiatives and are motivated by the desire to increase production. Increased production is to be achieved by securing greater effort, and more effective effort from workers by allowing them limited participation in the details of production but not necessarily in decisions that weigh heavily in determining their economic future, such as investment, downsizing or outsourcing (Thompson and Warhurst 1998). Even in the United States, however, the forms of employee involvement are diverse and many include activities that allow employees at least some input in enterprise decisions (Appelbaum and Batt 1994). Even where participation is limited, workers have nevertheless achieved a toehold in decisions previously reserved for management under Fordist systems of production and extreme forms of scientific management (Derber and Schwartz 1983). Such employee involvement programs constitute important new challenges and opportunities for working with dignity (Wilkinson, Godfrey, and Marchington 1997).

Tremendous technological changes have also occurred in the workplace since the time of Marx, Durkheim, and Weber. The development of power-assisted technology has allowed the rapid expansion of automated assembly lines and other forms of automated production systems, such as those used in the chemical industry (Blauner 1964). Assembly-line production gave birth to some of the most stressful and pressured working conditions ever known. Many jobs continue to be machine paced today, although the percentage of employment in such industries has decreased due to job losses following automation. Manufacturing jobs remaining in advanced nations today have a greater percentage of skilled maintenance workers relative to production workers than in the past due to the shifting of many repetitive production tasks from humans to machines (Form 1987). In addition, much routine assembly work has been moved to less-developed countries where labor is cheaper.

Of even greater consequence is the ongoing revolution in production brought about by advances in computer technologies. The widespread changes in production technologies resulting from the use of microprocessors constitute the most significant technological transformation of work since the industrial revolution. Its consequences are magnified because it impacts virtually all forms of work, including services, trade, and telecommunications, not just manufacturing production (Zuboff 1988).

The significance of the computer revolution for the nature of work and the pursuit of dignity at work is unclear. Its greatest effects to date have been an acceleration of automation and increased displacement of semi-skilled workers. Clerical and managerial occupations have also been affected. Expected growth in these fields has not been realized due to increases in clerical and managerial productivity resulting from the increased use of desk-top computers. Some commentators argue that computers will bring about "the end of work" (Rifkin 1994). Although this claim seems exaggerated, one of the major effects of computers on work has indeed been increased downward pressure on job growth for both white-collar and blue-collar workers because of the ability of computers and computer-assisted machines to do work previously done by human beings. Fortunately, at least in the short run, many of these effects have been offset by job growth in the economy as a whole and particularly in service sector jobs. On the other hand, many of these new jobs are poorer paying than the jobs lost to automation (Cappelli et al. 1997). On a worldwide scale, computers appear to be widening the gap in productivity and well-being between nations that are able to computerize their productive facilities and those that are not.

The effects of computers on dignity at work, the central concern of this book, are less clear. There are indications that some work has been rendered less meaningful and rewarding because of the loss of a sensate relationship between workers and their products due to the intervening computerized machinery (Zuboff 1988). An increasing share of workers no longer have direct physical contact with the products they manufacture and only experience them through abstract digital readings on glowing computer screens. The proportion of workers thus affected, however, is difficult to estimate. The ability of workers to adjust to new production technologies and to enjoy a meaningful work experience based on more intellective skills involving cognitive and problem-solving abilities is likewise unknown.

The effect of computers on the nature of work life does not appear to be either overwhelmingly positive or negative. The primary effects appear to be on productivity with resulting consequences for the availability of work. Issues such as overwork, autonomy, and dignity appear less profoundly affected by computer technologies. Even though workers are often significantly more productive following computer automation, they do not typically work fewer hours as a consequence nor does job stress typically decrease. The aspects of work that concern workers on a day-to-day basis appear to be more affected by changes in the social organization of work than by technical changes, even those associated with computerization. Such social aspects of the organization of work include pressures to compete in an increasingly globalized economy, declines in unionization, increases in professional employment, and increasing employee involvement. At the beginning of the twenty-first century, the social organization of the workplace, as realized through competing industrial relations principles, appears to be a dominant force in determining both the meaning of work and the success of organizations (Levine 1995).

Obstacles and Opportunities

A core reality of the contemporary economy is that it includes a tremendous variety of different work settings. These settings present many challenges and opportunities for working with dignity. In this section we develop the theoretical foundations necessary for understanding four key challenges faced by employees as they seek dignity at work in the contemporary economy.

The first two challenges, disorganized and abusive workplaces, and overwork and exploitation, are most likely to occur in situations where management has unilateral control over production. The second two challenges, the defense of autonomy and the new demands of employee involvement, occur where employees have at least a partial say in production decisions. In situations involving bilateral input, new challenges and opportunities arise for working with dignity. We will return to each of these four situations in Chapters 4 through 7 where we examine the lives of the workers as they struggle to meet these challenges.

Mismanagement and Abuse

Social commentators from Marx to Durkheim to contemporary historians have condemned the chaotic and abusive factories of the early industrial revolution. A quote from Marx's seminal work, *Capital*, captures the autocratic nature of workplace relations in early factories:

> In the factory code, the capitalist formulates his autocratic power over his workers like a private legislator, and purely as an emanation of his own will. . . . This code is merely the capitalist caricature of the social regulation of the labour process which becomes necessary in cooperation on a large scale and in the employment in common of instruments of labour, and especially of machinery. The overseer's book of penalties replaces the slave-driver's lash. All punishments naturally resolve themselves into fines and deductions from wages, and the law-giving talent of the factory Lycurgus so arranges matters that a violation of his laws is, if possible, more profitable to him than the keeping of them. (Marx 1967:549–550)

Unfortunately, workplaces characterized by chaos and abuse still exist, even if in lesser frequency, in advanced industrial societies. Contemporary writers in the neo-Marxist tradition have labeled such workplaces "despotic" (Burawoy 1985:88). The description of work at National Wire presented in Chapter 1 represents one such situation. Two related aspects of management behavior define these situations. The first is the failure to provide a coherently organized production system capable of operating without constant chaos and disruption. The second is the arbitrary and abusive use of power (Edwards 1993). In developing nations, such chaotic and abusive workplaces are even more common.

The continuation of chaotic and abusive workplaces in advanced economies indicates a failure by at least some employers to live up to the normative expectations that have developed for employment in the century and a half since the industrial revolution. Contemporary management writers have developed the concept of *organizational citizenship behavior* to describe expectations of positive initiative on the part of workers to facilitate production. Turning this phrase around, we can describe chaotic and abusive workplaces as representing a failure on the part of employers to live up to contemporary expectations for *management citizenship behavior*. The absence of management citizenship behavior constitutes a significant denial of dignity in many workplaces. Contemporary researchers have noted that "it is not the *tasks* workers perform, but *the broader treatment they receive at the hands of management* that [determines the experience of worklife]" (Vallas 1987; emphasis in original). Mismanagement and abuse thus continue to represent fundamental challenges to working with dignity in the contemporary workplace.

Exploitation and Overwork

The concept of exploitation is the central organizing principle in the writings of Marx. Workers are paid less than the value of their labor and forced to give ever greater exertions to increase the margin of profit for capitalists. Exploitation "operates when powerful, connected people command resources from which they draw significantly increased returns by coordinating the efforts of [others] whom they exclude from the full value added by that effort" (Tilly 1998:10).

The development of capitalism entails a continuing effort to intensify the exploitation of workers in order to increase profits. In order to increase profits capitalists try to force workers to work harder and produce more. Under many contemporary versions of capitalist workplace organization, however, work discipline is not necessarily enforced by abuse. Rather, workers consent to overwork and exploitation because they have little recourse. If one wants to survive in an advanced capitalist society, one must generally work for someone else. Opportunities to return to the land to live by hunting and gathering or by farming are almost nonexistent. Opening one's own business is a dream for many, but most dreams of this type are destined to failure (Chinoy 1955). Advertising adds artificial needs to real ones further tying workers to the treadmill of overwork in an effort to get ahead (Schor 1998).

Advanced forms of capitalism in which employees consent to their work because there are no viable options have been labeled "hegemonic" systems by Burawoy (1985:126). The term *hegemony* connotes overwhelming power or influence (Gramsci 1971). Hegemony is achieved by being able to limit options and control ideas and ideologies. Under advanced capitalism, employees do the tasks asked of them, not because of widespread abuse and intimidation, but because they have few (if any) options in a system in which capitalists have overwhelming economic, political, and ideological control. Overwork is widespread and possibly increasing. It is among the most important challenges facing workers today as they struggle to work with dignity.

Autonomy and its Defense

Abuse and overwork are important concepts for understanding the contemporary workplace. But they are not the complete story. Many employees also exercise a significant degree of autonomy in their daily work lives. Skilled craft workers, such as electricians, plumbers, pipe fitters, and carpenters, retain a significant degree of autonomy and control over their work. The rapidly growing professional occupations also exercise significant control over the details of their work. The autonomy of professional and craft employees is based on the reality that extensive training and experience are often necessary in complex production settings to identify and define the work that most urgently needs to be done and the best way to do it.

Managers in professional and craft settings generally do not possess the knowledge needed to make unilateral decisions about work. As a result, professional and craft organizations of work typically include a significant degree of bilateral decision making in which both employees and managers have input. In decisions about the details of a given task, the opinions of the professional or craft worker often are dominant. In decisions involving investments and long-range planning, however, managers generally exercise sole or decisive power because of their control of financial resources.

Additionally, managers are unable to exercise unilateral control in professional and craft settings because the actual work practices that emerge over time often differ from those that are administratively prescribed (Reed 1988:35). Specific work practices emerge as ongoing solutions to problems of production. In many production situations, but especially in settings involving professional or craft work, management may not be fully up-to-date about these emergent practices (Scott 1998).

Professional and craft workers also exercise significant power in broader society through their occupational and professional associations (Abbott 1988; Jackson 1984). While such occupational associations may not be as inclusive or as powerful as Durkheim's vision of "occupational corporations," which he hoped would exert a regulatory force to control the anomic drives of industry, they are nevertheless important participants in contemporary society (Friedson 1994).

Do professional and craft skills and associations protect workers from abuse and exploitation? Not completely. Abuse can still continue in professional and craft settings; however, it is more likely to be contested and short lived. Exploitation is another matter, in part because it is harder to define. Exploitation, defined as extracting more labor value than is paid for (the Marxian definition), may be lessened because of the power of professional and craft employees to bargain for higher wages and a larger share of their contributed value. However, exploitation in terms of sheer overwork may not be lessened. Employers often insist on long hours from professional and craft employees because they prefer to hire as few of these highly paid workers as possible. Professional and craft workers may also willingly work excessive hours because of their desire for higher overtime earnings (for craft workers) or merit raises (for professionals). To the degree that professional and craft employees willingly consent to overwork, they can be seen as collaborators in their own exploitation (Hochschild 1997).

As the ranks of highly skilled professional and craft workers continue to expand, the defense of autonomy and the demand for bilateralism in decision making can be expected to take on ever-increasing roles in the struggle for dignity at work (Power-Waters 1980). Overwork will also in all likelihood continue or even increase, although for highly skilled craft and professional workers, it may be at least partially self-imposed.

The Promise of Participation

Employee involvement is the catchphrase of the new millennium. Employee involvement offers the possibility of new forms of bilateral control of at least some aspects of work. In this sense it extends the power of the craft and professional workers, based on extensive skills and training, to less skilled blue-collar and white-collar employees.

Forms of employee involvement are as complex and varied as workplaces themselves. The most commonly recognized form of employee involvement is organization into work teams that have at least some collective input into how work is to be organized (Hackman 1990). Sometimes teams are restricted by management to discussing only issues directly related to improving productivity. In other situations, wider issues of safety and health, job satisfaction, and work environment are also available for discussion (Appelbaum and Batt 1994).

Formal participation of employees in workplace decisions also occurs via elected representatives. In the United States and the United Kingdom trade unions are the principal mechanism for formal participation and for giving voice to employees' concerns (Ackers, Smith, and Smith 1996; Freeman and Medoff 1984). In many European nations, work councils serve as elected workers' representatives and directly negotiate with management on a range of issues, including choices among new technologies and new investments (Ferner and Hyman 1992). Related forms of participation occur in the United States but are well developed only in the automobile industry and in parts of the telecommunications industry. The United Auto Workers and U.S. automakers, for example, regularly collaborate in joint programs to adapt production practices to new technological challenges and provide needed training programs for workers (Rinehart, Huxley, and Robertson 1997).

Worker ownership, either through direct buyouts or partial ownership through Employee Stock Ownership Plans (ESOPs), represents an important form of worker participation. However, even here the actual nature of participation can vary dramatically. Sometimes employees directly run the company through elected or rotating representatives (Greenberg 1986; Pendleton, Wilson, and Wright 1998). In other situations, where traditional management practices are continued in spite of the nominal change in ownership, employees may have little or no say in company decisions or even in decisions about how their own work is organized (Keef 1998).

Employee involvement is frequently initiated unilaterally by management and in such situations the goals of participation are often restricted to increasing productivity and exclude direct consideration of employees' issues, such as job security, increased satisfaction, or greater meaning in work (Marsh 1992). Such management initiated versions of employee involvement are often simply extended forms of "unobtrusive control" in which management sets the goals (and retains tremendous power through doing so) and then lets workers or work groups decide how best to achieve these goals (Perrow 1986). Unobtrusive control can also become more direct and obtrusive when teams are encouraged to police their own members for adherence to the goals and values of the work group (Barker 1999).

In the United States, in particular, teams and other forms of employee involvement have sometimes been introduced as a stopgap mechanism to avoid unionization or weaken unions (Grenier and Hogler 1991). Such programs may directly interfere with existing grievance mechanisms and undermine worker solidarity and the ability to pursue goals that are in the interests of workers but that are outside management defined goals (Fantasia, Clawson, and Graham 1988). When used manipulatively to undermine autonomous worker goals, employee involvement may heighten management control, increase work intensity, and, ultimately, undermine instead of increase worker dignity (Parker and Slaughter 1994).

The implications of worker participation include many contradictory elements involving both the potential for increased dignity and for increased abuse and exploitation (Rothschild and Ollilainen 1999). The introduction of programs calling for heightened employee involvement does not automatically eliminate conflict from the workplace. Both management abuse and exploitation and worker resistance remain clear possibilities in new and more participatory workplace arrangements (Thompson and Ackroyd 1995).

Within the contradictory elements of worker participation there nevertheless exist opportunities that employees can use to their advantage. For example, in a study of white-collar employees, Smith (1996) finds that workers enjoy additional freedoms allowed by their limited self-management. In addition, they are able to use the language (and skills) of self-management to resist and manipulate difficult clients by enlisting them as "partners in production." The new roles allowed workers in a more participative workplace also have the potential to create new worker expectations of increased democracy in the workplace (Derber and Schwartz 1983). An important implication of the contradictory dynamics of workplace participation is "that employees may not want to forever engage in talk without actually having something to say" (Wolf 1995:12).

Turning Obstacles into Opportunities

The tight control exerted in unilateral systems of management control produces the greatest resistance on the part of workers. Indeed, resistance to overly tight control may be one of the few sociological universals (Foucault 1988; McKinlay and Starkey 1997). Conversely, bilateral systems of control can produce increased citizenship on the part of employees and allow increased dignity (Leicht 1989; Walsh and Tseng 1998). However, abuse and exploitation continue in contemporary forms of workplace organization. The contradictory nature of worker participation schemes that entail bilateral input along with heightened expectations for effort and peer pressure are an important case in point.

The selection among different management systems involving abuse, exploitation, autonomy, or participation is subject to pressures from a variety of sources (Cappelli et al. 1997). These sources include technological changes entailing the necessity for increased worker skills (Thomas 1994), workers' small scale activities of resistance in the local workplace, and workers' demands articulated at the societal and organizational levels through politics and trade union activities (Amenta 1998; Nonet 1969).

Workers' struggles at the organizational and societal levels through trade unions have been tremendously important in improving the quality of work life. These struggles have produced shorter workdays, retirement entitlements, paid vacations days, better health care, increased safety, and numerous other "citizenship rights" in the workplace (Montgomery 1979; Selznick 1992). Antidiscrimination laws, such as the Civil Rights Act of 1965 in the United States, have further increased employees' rights. These extended rights have particularly benefited minorities and women, but they have also benefited all workers by helping to create a normative environment that is less tolerant of management abuse, nepotism, and capricious hiring and promotion practices (Dobbin et al. 1993; Edelman 1990).

Struggles to increase workers' rights at the organizational and societal level have thus had significant positive consequences for the attainment of dignity at work. Smaller scale, more informal actions in defense of working with dignity also place significant pressures on the organization of the work. The mix of resistance and citizenship can be the decisive factor in making a new management system succeed or fail. It is these smaller scale activities and demands for the right to work with dignity that are the special focus of this book.

Working with Dignity

Social science theorists typically study human behavior as it is channeled and constrained by various structural forces. For example, Marx saw workers as exploited by the social relations of capitalism. Durkheim saw people as robbed of normative guidelines for their behavior by rapid and uncontrolled change. Weber saw modern life as imprisoned by formal rationality and bureaucratic structures. Yet each of these theorists also envisioned a role for human agency in the defense of dignity as well. Marx envisioned people rising up to overthrow capitalism and establish communism. Durkheim called for the development of strong occupational communities as a safeguard against anomie. Weber envisioned a future in which charismatic leaders would lead us beyond the iron cage of rationality.

Time has shown each envisioned outcome of human agency in the defense of dignity to be off target to some extent. The ideas of Marx, Durkheim, and Weber about social structure have had much more lasting conceptual value for understanding society than their thoughts about human agency.

Why was this so? One answer is that structures have somewhat predictable consequences in terms of defining, limiting, and guiding human activity. Predicting the outcome of human agency is a more difficult endeavor because of the creative and spontaneous elements involved. Human agency is better understood as a process than as a static pattern or a predictable future. A better strategy for studying agency then is to consider it as a process rather than as a predicted destination.

The processes of human agency *can* be understood. Several social science subfields have made significant progress in utilizing concepts of human agency in their conceptual underpinnings. The study of social movements provides a good example. The concept of mobilization, which has been central to the study of social movements, rests on an understanding of voluntary and creative human agency as a key determinant of social behavior (Lofland 1996). Similarly, the focus of social movements theory on group values and emergent cultural forms highlights the central role of human agency in determining the directions social movements take (Taylor 1999; Zald and Berger 1978). An important goal of this book is to provide a similar foundation for the study of human agency in pursuit of dignity at work.

To understand the active human struggle for dignity at work we highlight four aspects of workplace behavior through which dignity is realized: resistance, citizenship, the creation of alternative meanings systems, and coworker relations. In this section we develop the theoretical foundations necessary for understanding the interconnected roles of these behavioral strategies in the pursuit of working with dignity.

Resistance

Abuse undermines the inherent dignity of workers. Resistance to abuse is thus a foundation for the defense and restoration of dignity. Wherever there is unjust power, resistance inevitably follows (Foucault 1988).

Any individual or small group act intended to mitigate claims by management on employees or to advance employees' claims against management is worker resistance. Worker resistance can include sabotage and theft (Jermier 1988; Taylor and Walton 1971:219; Webb and Palmer 1998), but it also includes less destructive acts that have been referred to more generally as "the withdrawal of cooperation" or as part of the "effort bargain" (Edwards and Scullion 1982:154; Wardell 1992). Specific workplace resistance behaviors include absenteeism and a variety of forms of foot dragging and playing dumb as well as gossip and diverse and subtle forms of noncooperation (Palm 1977; Tucker 1993). Many of the most common forms of workplace resistance involve the violation of rules that workers see as cumbersome or inefficient or that require excessive effort without good cause (Hodson 1995). All of these forms of resistance are attempts to regain dignity in the face of organizations that violate worker's interests, limit their prerogatives, or undermine their autonomy.

Resistance to abusive and constraining relations and unjust authority has been studied in school settings, as well as in workplaces (Giroux 1983; Willis 1977). Students, particularly those of working-class origin, resent unjust authority and this resentment is an explanation for behavior that might otherwise seem capricious, willful, or irrational. Students, like workers, do not want to be abused and will resist. Common forms of resistance in schools include absenteeism, tardiness, and ridiculing teachers behind their backs (MacLeod 1995).

Resistance behaviors are in part a response to the sense of shame and anger brought about by violations of one's dignity. Psychologists have identified shame and its opposite – pride – as two primary emotions (Scheff 1990). Workplaces based on unilateral systems of control are most likely to violate employees' dignity, which results in resistance in an effort to rebalance the scales. Resistance in the workplace can be considered an effort to reestablish justice and equity (Festinger 1957; Homans 1950).

We have defined workplace resistance in terms of individual or small group acts in order to differentiate it from larger scale actions by workers in defense of their interests. This definition, however, should not detract from an awareness that unions and workers' parties have been important actors in pursuit of workers' interests and their dignity at work. Unions and workers' political parties have played a major role in improving working conditions, earnings, and workers' rights throughout the world (Cornfield 1989; Freeman 1994; Kochan, Katz, and Mower 1984). Within organizations, unions have provided an important mechanism for giving voice to employees in negotiations with management (Freeman and Medoff 1984; Wellman 1995). Histories and analyses of the role of unions in the contemporary workplace abound (see in particular Ackers, Smith, and Smith 1996; Freeman and Medoff 1984; Rogers and Streeck 1995; Shostak 1991). What is less developed, however, is our understanding of how repeated, small-scale, informal acts of resistance have also influenced the nature of work in modern society.

Contemporary workplace studies suggest that worker resistance continues even under emerging forms of work organization, including those that are team-based or otherwise include bilateral input from both employees and managers (Edwards 1992a). In some workplaces, heightened demands for "employee flexibility" and intensified effort may have even served to increase worker resistance (Gannage 1995).

Some commentators have suggested that resistance by workers is futile and only serves to perpetuate inequality in the workplace (Burawoy 1985). They argue that informal resistance does nothing to change the underlying exploitative relationship between capital and labor. This position seems unrealistic. Even constrained forms of resistance among slaves have been noted as a significant influence on the nature of slave-holding societies (Genovese 1974). There is much to be negotiated on a daily basis between employees and management. Managers may accept worker resistance and reticence, but not willingly, and they would prefer unquestioning and enthusiastic compliance (Clawson and Fantasia 1983). And even workers who seem quiescent may still resist if the opportunity is right (Scott 1990:70). As E. P. Thompson (1974:399) notes in his discussion of peasant resistance in eighteenth century England, "The same man who touches his forelock to the squire by day – and who goes down to history as an example of deference – may kill his sheep, snare his pheasants or poison his dogs at night."

Citizenship

Taking action that increases the sense of pride in one's accomplishments can also increase feelings of dignity. This component of dignity is the foundation for a sense of "earned dignity" above and beyond the inherent dignity of the human condition (Meyer and Parent 1992:11). A central foundation for the experience of dignity at work is a sense of pride in one's work (Hodson 1998a).

Human beings value themselves and they value their own growth. They want to see themselves as effective players who are *getting somewhere in life* as a result of their own efforts. Hence, they seek activities and relationships that affirm their sense of self-worth and allow them to develop their potential. Activities that create pride and enhance growth and maturation are highly prized. One of the most important sources of pride and personal development for many is work (Marcuse 1991). Work and work roles that support and develop human dignity and capabilities are valued immensely in our society. The conditions under which people earn their livelihood – work roles, workplace relationships, and terms of employment – are of supreme importance to the experience of human dignity and autonomy (Fromm 1966).

The quest for dignity and purpose in life originates at the beginning of the human experience. Historically, men and women have devised ways to move beyond existing limits of self to actualize novel expressions of their own potential. Accounts of these efforts are well represented in the writings of ancient and modern thinkers alike. Included in the thoughts of the great philosophers and scientists is the observation that *the work arena* is of utmost importance in the quest for dignity. Roman philosopher Epictetus, for example, spoke of the importance of comporting oneself with dignity and making progress toward the realization of higher ideals through purposive attention to one's trade, whatever that might be (Lebell 1994).

In his classic book *Man's Search for Meaning*, psychiatrist Viktor Frankl (1963) offers vivid testimony of his own extraordinary will that created self-respect within the confines of a concentration camp. Robbed of his normal, professional work activities, Frankl invented his own "work life" in the concentration camps in which he was held. As a prisoner, Frankl worked to be "worthy" of his own suffering and to advance his claim on inner strength, freedom, and love for the preservation of all. Frankl (1963:79) remarked, "If the man in the concentration camp did not struggle against this [loss of human values] in a last effort to save his self-respect, he lost the feeling of being an individual, a being with a mind, with inner freedom and personal value. He thought of himself then as only a part of an enormous mass of people; his existence descended to the level of animal life." As Frankl so eloquently testifies, the right to produce with pride, purpose, and dignity is a fundamental human need.

Workers are deeply affected and energized by the meaning of their work. Few satisfactions are greater in life than those derived from the self-directed completion of worthwhile tasks (Kohn and Schooler 1983). Work that satisfies a person's need to grow while feeling respectable is meaningful work. And workers have high standards for what constitutes respectable and worthwhile work activity. When particular work tasks or roles don't meet workers' standards, workers often respond proactively by creating more meaningful, helpful, and dignified work experiences for themselves.

Workers are amazingly enterprising and active in the ways in which they transform jobs with insufficient meaning into jobs that are more worthy of their personal stature, time, and effort. The human will to become self-assured and self-expressive is a great catalyst for invention, cooperation, and creative adaptation at the workplace.

Contemporary workplace ethnographies abound with contextually rich accounts of the importance of feelings of pride in one's accomplishments (for example, "Joe possessed pride in his work and boasted of a year's worth of coils without a single rejection" [Seider 1984:26]). Frequent ethnographic references to pride in task completion and the accompanying "proclivity for taking pains" (Veblen 1914:213) suggest that feelings of pride in one's work-related merit is a key determinant of the experience of working with dignity.

Conversely, the lack of ability to take pride in work can be devastating to morale:

> There isn't anyone among us who doesn't resent how the factory is operated so fast and sloppy, because there's no way to respect what we're doing and what we're making.
>
> In fact, most people here like it best when things don't work right and production goes to hell, and I'm right along with them. And that's a crummy way to waste your working time.
> (Turner 1980:61)

In the social psychology literature, pride and associated feelings of self-efficacy have been identified as among the most powerful human motivators (Bandura 1995; Maslow 1970; Rogers 1961; see also Cooley 1922).

Taking pride in work and related "prosocial" behaviors have been widely analyzed in the management literature under the label "organizational citizenship behavior." Worker citizenship behaviors are defined as positive actions on the part of employees to improve productivity and cohesion in the workplace, which are above and beyond organizational requirements (Organ 1988). The implicit model of organizational productivity and effectiveness in studies that highlight worker citizenship is one in which technical factors of production and organizational leadership must be supplemented by worker effort and enthusiasm in order to reach optimal or even competitive levels (Drucker 1993).

Workplaces with bilateral input from both managers and employees can be expected to increase trust, fairness, reciprocity, and justice (Kochan and Osterman 1994). These in turn can be expected to serve as foundations for commitment to the organization, for taking pride in one's work, for giving extra effort to achieve organizational goals, and for the experience of dignity at work. In the realms of dignity and citizenship, there is significant potential for overlap between individual and organizational goals. And it is precisely this overlap that has motivated management to develop diverse programs to facilitate increased employee participation (Littek and Charles 1995).

Autonomous Meaning Systems

Citizenship and resistance are core strategies for building and safeguarding dignity at work. Both citizenship and resistance correspond to the central workplace dynamic defined by relationships between employees and managers and the role of the workplace as a place of economic production. People spend a lot of time at work, however, and the workplace serves many other functions in addition to economic production. Consideration of at least two other aspects of work is needed to adequately understand workers' quest for dignity. These aspects involve the production of autonomous meaning systems and relations among coworkers. Each of these activities have important implications for working with dignity.

Workers often engage in meaningful activities that are outside the central dynamics of power, domination, and production. The worker described in Chapter 1 who every day carefully laid out a makeshift table and ate half her sandwich at morning break was engaged in creating an autonomous area of control and meaning in her life at work. This purposive activity was entirely independent of the central dynamic of production goals and power relations. Nevertheless, it was a significant activity for this worker and was important to her. Related meaningful activities range from posting cartoons on one's locker (or web page), to putting a family picture on one's desk, to joking with coworkers (Collinson 1988).

Such peripheral, meaningful activities are important strategies for holding back the boredom of too many hours spent on the same activity. Even the often inherently interesting tasks of professional employees can become boring when done to excess. The pursuit of independent meanings can thus be expected to be widespread across workplaces.

Max Weber hoped that new charismatic leaders would encompass new values that would save humanity from the formal rationality of bureaucracy. While such leaders do periodically emerge, they generally appear as demagogues or tyrants. We are probably lucky that Weber's vision was not realized in its original form. What has happened instead is that ordinary people, in their daily lives inside bureaucracies, regularly create new and autonomous meaning systems outside formal organizational scripts (Della Fave 1980; Roscigno and Danaher 2001). We investigate these meaning systems further in subsequent chapters as important strategies for working with dignity.

Coworker Relations

Relations with coworkers constitute a final important domain for the realization of dignity at work. Indeed, coworker relations are fundamental for the effective realization of each of the three strategies of dignity discussed so far – resistance, citizenship, and alternative meaning systems. Coworker relations are fundamental to the "social climate" at the workplace, which is often as important for the daily experience of work as are relations with management (Moos 1986). Over time, coworker relations generate stable patterns of rights, obligations, and behavior that constitute a workplace culture. This culture is part of the informal "natural social system" within organizations, which inevitably emerges, even in organizations with formal and rationally defined goals (Scott 1998). Informal work group goals can include oppositional elements that focus on resistance to management practices as well as elements that do not directly oppose management but that still provide a basis for workers to shape a collective identity separate from management (Hodson 1997; Jermier, Knights, and Nord 1995).

Naturally emerging groups at the workplace include friendship cliques, work teams, and interest groups. These groups rest on informal ties, informal structures, and informal control. Informal ties among workers result in regular positive contact and mutual assistance. Informal structures of authority and power permit some individuals to emerge as leaders, influence others, and speak for the group. Informal control pressures group members to follow the emergent group values and norms. Such values and norms can include output restriction, pressure to produce more, or rules specifying with whom one is to be friendly, and whom one should ostracize from the group (Hirszowicz 1982).

One of the most important functions of informal groups at work is to present a united front against the many demands of the workplace

(Pilcher 1972). The foundation of group solidarity is "shared experiences at work" and "the sense of involvement and attachment" that arises from these shared experiences (Goffee 1981:475, 488). Group solidarity at work depends on the willingness of workers to defend each other in the face of challenges, most often from management, but also sometimes from other groups of employees or from customers (Aminzade 1993; Fantasia 1988; Smith 1996). Group solidarity can also help mitigate feelings of alienation that arise from meaningless work (Tausky 1992).

The use of resistance and role distancing to secure "personal space" at work, and the supportive role of informal groups in this effort, is illustrated in the following excerpt from an ethnography of a cigarette factory:

> In leaving the workplace without official permission, the rules
> on 'loitering' in corridors or toilets, on the use of the specified
> toilet, and on smoking, were all broken. Gradually whole
> groups, not always young girls, but also older women,
> emerged as the 'non-conformists' who met each other 'out in
> the back.' The toilets became centres of mild rebellion. They
> came to represent a place of refuge for a smoke and a chat – a
> potential forum for informal communication and organization.
> (Pollert 1981:147)

Supportive coworker relations are essential for the success of even modest agendas of resistance to authority.

Besides being fundamental to the maintenance of solidarity and resistance to authority, coworker relations can also be important for affirming group identities, including gender identities (Pollert 1996). Westwood (1984:94–96) notes how elaborate rituals concerning birthdays, weddings, and births evolved among a largely female work force in a knitting mill. These rituals created solidarity through shared activities and the exchange of small gifts. The rituals were important to the women involved because the rituals displaced time, focus, and resources from the mill work to the workers' own agendas. Worker resistance in this setting focused on symbolic distancing from management agendas and on the creation of alternative, positive, gender-based self-identifications. Similarly, in a study of male factory workers, Collinson (1988) notes how sexual banter among male workers helps to reaffirm masculinity as a parameter of work identity separate from formal job descriptions.

The nature and functioning of informal groups varies widely across workplaces. Work groups can be an important factor in facilitating or in restricting output. They can make life meaningful for workers. But they can also make it intolerable for those who are ostracized or persecuted by the group (Sayles 1958). Sexual harassment can also sometimes become institutionalized as part of the informal work group culture in workplaces with mixed gender work forces (De Coster, Estes, and Mueller 1999; Yount 1991). Thus, it is not uncommon for employees to have "love–hate" relations with the work groups of which they are members (Hackman 1990).

Although informal groups at work are probably not what Durkheim (1984) envisioned as occupational communities sufficient to stand as a bulwark against encroaching anomie, they are, nevertheless, important actors in the modern workplace. They serve important functions for humanizing the workplace and for the pursuit of dignity at work.

Conclusions

Working with dignity is achieved through resistance, citizenship, and the construction of autonomous meaning systems. Informal groups at work are also an important foundation for the successful pursuit of dignity, although informal work groups can also be the source of significant assaults on dignity. The pursuit of dignity takes place within organizational structures that offer a variety of challenges and opportunities. These challenges include patterns of chronic mismanagement and abuse, overwork, threats to autonomy, and participation schemes that offer the promise of bilateral input but do not always deliver on that promise.

We expect resistance strategies to be most widespread in workplaces with unilateral systems of control. Citizenship activities can be expected to be more common in systems that allow at least some elements of bilateral control. However, workers also use resistance, citizenship, and other strategies as the situation demands and several strategies in the defense of dignity may be in operation at any given workplace. In any given setting, employees may resist some elements of management control while practicing citizenship and taking pride in work in other areas.

The challenges to working with dignity and the strategies for achieving it are complex. How then are we to study the quest for dignity at work in order to understand and appreciate it better? The next chapter outlines a strategy for studying the pursuit of dignity across diverse workplaces by systematically analyzing organizational ethnographies.

3

Measuring the Subtle Realms of Work

Working with dignity is a central motivation for workers. The founders of sociology, however, were only secondarily concerned with workers' active struggles to achieve dignity. They focused on the social structures that limit workers' lives and undermine their dignity and well-being. The concepts and theories they developed to understand social structures of exploitation, anomie, and excessive rationality have given direction to sociology for over a century.

But workers are not passive victims of social structures. They are active agents in their own lives. It is through active agency that workers realize dignity at work in the face of the many challenges they confront (Armstrong 1989). The question before us is: "How are we to study the quest for dignity across diverse work settings?" An answer to this question is provided by the systematic analysis of the existing body of ethnographic studies of the workplace.

Contemporary sociological methods reproduce many of the limits of our leading theories. Structures are studied in detail, but agency is routinely slighted. Surveys ask employees about the organization of their workplaces and their attitudes about work, but little is asked about the behaviors through which they adapt to, challenge, and make sense out of the structures they confront. For this reason, workers' views are frequently missing from discussions about what is right or wrong in the contemporary workplace (Freeman and Rogers 1999; Juravich 1985:5).

Employees' voices are given a more sustained hearing in ethnographic accounts of the workplace. Organizational ethnographies are based on researchers observing workers at their places of employment for extended periods or even working directly alongside them. The analysis presented in this book uses such accounts as a source of both quantitative and qualitative data.

Ethnography has been defined as "sustained, explicit, methodical observation and paraphrasing of social situations in relation to their naturally occurring contexts" (Weick 1985:568). Ethnographic accounts are generally rich in detail about both the behaviors being observed and the

50

situations in which these behaviors occur. These detailed observations provide valuable data for new interpretations of existing concepts and for the development of new conceptual insights (Morrill and Fine 1997:425). Organizational ethnographies, in particular, have a long tradition of providing in-depth descriptive accounts of work life across a wide range of settings from factories to white-collar and professional settings (Lee 1999; Smith 2001; Van Maanen 1998).

Organizational ethnographies provide deeper and more nuanced descriptions of organizational life than are typically available in data derived from survey questionnaires. Surveys are inevitably somewhat artificial interactions which separate reports of behaviors and attitudes from the settings in which these behaviors naturally occur. It is these settings that give the behaviors or attitudes their meaning (Edwards 1992b). In addition, surveys often impose the middle-class values of researchers on subjects who are guided down certain lines of questioning. Respondents are often further limited by prescripted options for their answers thus severely restricting their ability to tell their own story in their own words (Singleton and Straits 1999).

Organizational Ethnographies

Early interest in organizational ethnography in the United States began with the famous Hawthorne studies in Chicago during the 1930s (Roethlisberger and Dickson 1939). The findings from experimental methods of studying productivity at the Hawthorne electrical plant created so many anomalies that the researchers decided that direct observation was needed to sort out the complex processes involved (Schwartzman 1993). The key conclusion from these studies was that a rich "informal culture" exists in the workplace and exerts strong influences on productivity.

The Chicago School of Sociology, with its focus on field research, also contributed to the growth of workplace ethnographies. The factory studies of the 1940s and 1950s (Dalton 1959; Hughes 1958; Roy 1954; Walker and Guest 1952) combined the study of informal workplace culture with a focus on organizational characteristics and management behavior. The tradition of factory studies continues today in contemporary ethnographies of machine shops (Burawoy 1979), longshoring (Finlay 1988), and automobile assembly (Graham 1995; Rinehart et al. 1997).

White-collar workplaces became a focus in the 1960s starting with the seminal work of Crozier (1971) on clerical work. Today the study of white-collar organizations has developed its own traditions and interests including a focus on the role of bureaucracy in the workplace. Research on these issues is continued today in contemporary ethnographies of banking (Smith 1990), insurance (Burris 1983), legal offices (Pierce 1995), engineers (Kunda 1992), and direct sales (Biggart 1989). In recent years an increasing number of ethnographies reporting on service work have appeared, including studies of restaurants (Fine 1996; Paules 1991), household service (Cock 1989; Constable 1997; Mendez 1998; Romero 1992) and fast food (Leidner 1993).

The central rationale for organizational ethnographies, both those of factories and those of office and service settings, is that the depth of observation afforded the ethnographer, who spends months or even years in a setting, allows greater insight into circumstances, behaviors, and meanings in a workplace than data based on surveys or company records (Bernard and Ryan 1998). The latter sources are seen as tapping only surface attitudes or organizationally scripted facts (Smith 2001).

Ethnographic studies, by contrast, allow us to observe the emergent subtle life of organizations. Informal normative structures of organizational life and subtle behavioral patterns that may go unnoticed by more casual observers can be observed. Ethnographers have the opportunity to witness actual behaviors in their natural settings, not just second-hand reports and interpretations of behaviors. Perhaps most importantly, we get to see inside the informal groups and relations that constitute a great deal of the real substance of daily life inside formal organizations (Scott 1998:54–55).

Ethnographies, however, have their own limitations. The central limitation of all case study analysis, including that offered by ethnographic accounts, is that it is difficult to distinguish unique characteristics of the case under examination from more generalizable patterns (Ragin and Becker 1992). Researchers have sometimes attempted to more fully mine the methodological potential of organizational ethnographies by systematic comparisons among selected sets of ethnographies (see, for example, Gouldner 1964; Homans 1950; Lipset, Trow, and Coleman 1956). Such efforts, however, have been the exception rather than the rule and have generally been quite limited in scope. As Friedman (1987:293) notes: "A strength of the [workplace] literature is indicted by the case study material it has generated. A weakness of this material is that these observations have rarely been made systematically over a long period of time and with a clear reference to other case studies."

As a result of the limited comparisons that have been made among ethnographies, the insights generated from ethnographies have been used mainly for generating new concepts and hypotheses (Burawoy 1991; Eisenhardt 1989; Feagin, Orum, and Sjoberg 1991; Guba and Lincoln 1994). Ethnographies have been less useful in helping to eliminate outdated ideas (see Ember and Levinson 1991:79; Naroll, Michik, and Naroll 1980:482). The comparisons that are made are based on too few cases to effectively discredit even flawed hypotheses. In principle, other cases could be found that might reverse the conclusions. The successful use of ethnographies as an effective tool for generating rich descriptions, but their limited role in theory testing, is also noted by Ragin (1987:53).

As a consequence of the limited use of systematic comparisons among organizational ethnographies, the depth of observation contained in ethnographies has not been used effectively to select among theories and thus advance our understanding of the workplace. The loss is considerable. There are over one hundred book-length organizational ethnographies published in the English language. Each represents an average of over a year in the field, with at least that much additional time spent in analysis and writing. The accumulated record of organizational ethnographies is thus based on over 200 years of Ph.D.-level observation and interpretation. But this resource has remained *largely unanalyzed* by social scientists studying organizations (Hodson 1999a).

To make full use of the set of existing organizational ethnographies, we must consider and analyze them as a group rather than treat each one separately. In this way we will be able to see patterns and relationships that would be invisible to researchers only considering cases individually. The following section describes the methodological basis for such an analysis.

A New Method and New Insights

Students of the workplace have long identified the archiving and subsequent analysis of organizational ethnographies as a desirable goal (Hammersley 1997; Morrill and Fine 1997:441). The systematic analysis of archives of written records is increasingly used as a method of study across a range of topics in the social sciences. Studies based on archival analysis make effective use of the information contained in large and growing bodies of written accounts. The topics that have been studied using such methods range from strikes (Franzosi 1995; Silver 1995) to popular fiction (Griswold 1992). By using systematic methods of comparison across multiple cases, researchers can introduce the methodological tools of probabilistic (as opposed to deterministic) causality, measurement error, and multiple causation into the interpretation of written accounts (Lieberson 1991).

The systematic analysis of written accounts has the potential to combine the strengths of qualitative and quantitative approaches. The method adds detailed measurement based on in-depth observation to the analytic power of quantitative analysis (Zetka and Walsh 1994:43). The measures developed have potentially high validity because they are based on in-depth observation. Problems associated with the sometimes limited validity and relevance of survey data and government statistics can be directly addressed by this method. Problems associated with the idiosyncratic nature of each case and the subjectivity of observers can be addressed by analyzing multiple cases.

The systematic analysis of cases adds the rigor of hypothesis testing, explicit comparison groups, and controls to the depth of observation provided by qualitative analyses. As Walton argues, case studies "drift without anchor unless they are incorporated into some typology of general processes, made causally explicit within the case, and ultimately referred back to the universe which the case represents" (1992:124). Evaluation of a broader range of cases also increases the variation available for analysis. Because the researcher evaluates a large number of cases, irrelevant variables will be likely to vary randomly rather than becoming a focus of analysis and interpretation because of chance concurrence with the phenomenon of interest (Levinson and Malone 1980).

We turn now to a consideration of two areas that have utilized the systematic analysis of archived documentary accounts.

Two Foundation Projects

Two social science subfields have provided important groundwork for the development of systematic methods of comparison and analysis that can be applied to ethnographic and other documentary accounts. The first of these areas builds on a centralized archive of anthropological studies of primitive societies. Analyses of this archive have focused mainly on structural differences between societies and how these differences influence behavior. The second area exists as a diverse set of studies focusing on social movements and using mainly newspaper accounts of conflict events, such as demonstrations, riots, and strikes. These studies have focused mainly on how collective action emerges and is patterned over time.

Anthropology's Human Relations Area Files. Working over many decades, cultural anthropologists have developed an archive of ethnographic accounts with wide public access called the Human Relations Area Files (HRAF). George Murdock initiated the archive project in 1937 at Yale University. In 1949 it was incorporated as a private nonprofit organization. The archive received early sponsorship from Yale University, the Carnegie Corporation, and several other supporting universities. The National Science Foundation, the Ford Foundation, and the U.S. State Department have provided subsequent funding.

The basic unit of analysis in the archives is whole societies (mainly primitive ones) with nearly 350 societies included in the most comprehensive file. This file contains over 800,000 pages of text based on nearly 7,000 source documents, including books, dissertations, government reports, journal articles, and unpublished work (Levinson 1989:84).

The HRAF is a microfiche-based archive with copies in approximately 300 member libraries. The text pages are precoded and sorted by topics covered. The users of the archives must then code the variables of interest from these pages, but numerous coding projects have been published and are publicly available (Barry and Schlegel 1980). The HRAF has been used as the primary data source for over 750 published articles since it was made publicly available in 1949, including 28 percent published in interdisciplinary journals (Ember and Levinson 1991).

Selected subsets of the data have been made available in recent years on CD-ROM. These subsets are topically focused on selected subjects, such as human sexuality, marriage, family life, childhood, socialization, crime, education, religion, and aging.

Social Movement Event Analysis. Additional foundation for developing a method for systematically analyzing ethnographic studies of organizational life is provided by a series of studies of social movements undertaken by political scientists and sociologists. These projects are largely independent but have inspired a closely intertwined research tradition.

The study of social movements has benefited immensely from the compilation of data from qualitative sources. Indeed, analysis of such data has provided the major empirical background for this field. One reason for the reliance on qualitative sources is that social movement events can be fleeting and social scientists are able to study them mainly through the written records they leave behind. Gamson's (1975) seminal study of social protest used data on fifty-three protest movements taken mainly from professional histories. For each social movement, Gamson coded seventy-four characteristics based on content analysis of movement histories (Gamson 1975:24–25). The variables coded included violence (by or against the group), secrecy, factionalism, hierarchical versus decentralized authority, bureaucracy, alliances, social class of membership, and many other group characteristics.

More recently, social movement researchers have expanded both the types of data used and the range of topics analyzed. The focus, however, has remained on "the occurrence, timing, and sequencing of such events as regime changes, riots, revolutions, protests and the founding of social movement organizations" (Olzak 1989:119). The principal source of information about social movements and social movement events has been newspaper accounts, but official archives, historical accounts, and police records have also been used as data sources. For example, Tilly (1981) reports on an analysis of violent protests using French police records from 1890 to 1935. Shapiro and Markoff (1997) analyze the revolutionary demands of French citizens based on content analysis of a sample of the over 40,000 "Statements of Grievances" sent by local political bodies to the Estates General in the revolutionary year of 1789. Television reports about demonstrations appearing on the nightly news have also provided raw data for the analysis of conflict events (McCarthy, McPhail, and Smith 1996). Newspaper accounts, however, remain the most widely used data source. Newspapers are favored because they are consistently archived, widely accessible, and, among available sources, provide the most inclusive coverage of events (Babb 1996; Cress and Snow 1996; Griffin 1993; Mueller 1997; Silver 1995).

A Workplace Ethnography File

The research strategy for the analysis presented in this book directly builds on these prior projects. We analyze book-length ethnographic accounts of contemporary workplaces in order to establish commonalities and patterns in the quest for dignity at work. The application differs somewhat from the anthropological tradition by focusing on current societies and differs from the social movements tradition by focusing on longer documentary accounts instead of brief newspaper articles and clippings.

The standard tools of content analysis provide a starting point for this method (Weber 1990). Methodological extensions are needed to benefit from the fact that ethnographies provide extended in-depth descriptions of workplaces. These extended accounts provide an opportunity to examine both the structure of workplaces and the behaviors of managers and workers within these workplaces. The nature of the accounts allows for examination of settings and behaviors that would not be accessible in shorter reports. Instead of coding variables based on key words or phrases, we code lengthy episodes that provide in-depth discussions of behaviors. When multiple episodes are available, these are used to substantiate or modify the coding. Examples of these codings are provided later in this chapter and throughout the book.

The quantitative analysis of ethnographic sources should be clearly distinguished from metaanalysis, which is the analysis of effects across studies (Cook 1992). In contrast to metaanalysis, the methods used here utilize ethnographies as *descriptions of settings or events* as if each were a highly detailed research instrument. The analysis strategy treats each ethnographic account as an in-depth description of a different setting or event and then accumulates and codes these descriptions as a data set (Abbott 1992). The commonality between metaanalysis and the quantitative analysis of ethnographies is that each builds on increasingly rich bodies of extant research. Metaanalysis analyzes the findings of quantitative research. The quantitative analysis of ethnographic accounts analyzes the rich descriptions provided by field observation.

The quantitative analysis of ethnographic accounts is also distinct from the analysis of the narrative structure of textual passages. In the analysis of narrative structure, short passages are dissected for their hidden meanings and patterns. These techniques were originally developed in linguistics but have been adapted to the social sciences. Narrative structure analysis has been used in the social sciences to analyze newspaper headlines, reports of violence, and other conflict events (Bond et al. 1997). Application of these techniques in the social sciences has helped spur the systematization of narrative structure coding procedures into computer software programs (Franzosi 2000). Narrative structure analysis is well suited to the study of the types of frequently repeated, narrowly defined behaviors typically reported in brief accounts. It is not as well suited to the lengthy descriptive and discursive accounts provided in organizational ethnographies, which span a wide range of settings, topics, and behaviors. In organizational ethnographies, a wide range of meaningful actions is available to be interpreted and coded. For this purpose, there is no substitute for a skilled and informed coder who can interpret diverse passages for their relevance to the concepts being coded.

The methods and analysis on which this book is based are presented in a manner intended to be accessible to all students of the social sciences, regardless of their statistical skills or backgrounds. The methods utilized are principally quantitative and statistical, but the primary data source is qualitative accounts. The qualitative accounts are also used to illustrate the findings and to give texture and depth to the analysis. Extensive use of these qualitative accounts allows readers to develop their own sense and feel for the strategies through which employees pursue dignity at work across a range of occupations and organizations.

A brief history of the research project producing the data analyzed in the following chapters is presented in Appendix A. The coding instrument is published in Hodson (1999a). A variety of different organizational types, ranging from hospitals, to factories, to restaurants are included in the study. Similarly, the occupations range from maids and laborers to doctors and lawyers. A total of 108 cases were identified and coded for this project. (See Appendix B for a list of the cases included.) These cases represent the existing population of published book-length organizational ethnographies as of the date of the project. The application of systematic techniques of analysis to these cases allows us to examine subtle aspects of organizational life, while at the same time highlighting the significant differences between workplace settings that structure workers' lives and set the terrain for their pursuit of dignity (Tobin 1990).

Limitations of the Analysis

The systematic analysis of the ethnographic record on workplaces faces certain challenges and limitations concerning both the nature of the data and the available cases to be analyzed. Categorization, coding, and quantification can result in the *loss of some of the richness* of the original observations (Levinson and Malone 1980:9). The quantified data used will thus be less precise and less discerning of subtle nuances than the data presented in the individual case studies. This sacrifice in the depth and validity of indicators occurs as part of a tradeoff to achieve increased generalizability and the ability to apply systematic techniques of comparison. To compensate for this loss of detail, we regularly illustrate key findings and patterns with descriptive materials from the primary accounts.

In addition, the set of cases to be analyzed is not a random sample from the population of all workplaces. Inferential statistics are thus inappropriate for generalizing from this population to the broader population of all workplaces. Because the analysis is based on the *population* of published ethnographic case studies of the workplace and because these cases do not constitute a representative sample of all workplaces, reported levels of statistical significance should be interpreted as suggestive only. In interpreting the results, we consider general patterns as well as the statistical significance of coefficients. Generalizations from the analysis must therefore be made with caution. Such generalizations must be defended with additional evidence about the relationships being investigated. Such evidence, for example, might include parallel analysis reaching similar conclusions using other techniques and methods. As with all methods, the systematic analysis of ethnographic accounts is best utilized as part of an ongoing research dialogue involving contributions from a variety of methods.

The coding operations present additional challenges. Consistent and careful coding procedures were implemented and scrupulously followed in order to ensure that the data are reliable (see the discussion in Appendix A; see also Franzosi 1990; Stryker 1996). The trained commitment of ethnographers to rich description also increases the potential reliability and validity of the data. This commitment results in textual accounts containing a wealth of details that lessen the need for inference. Ethnographers try to provide sufficient details to give a full description of the events they are reporting. The commitment of ethnographers to rich description has sometimes been criticized as detracting from theoretical development (Hammersley 1992; but also see Porter 1993). When ethnographies are used as an archived data source, however, rich realistic description becomes one of their greatest assets.

A potentially more challenging problem is the claim of postmodernist theorists that texts have multiple layers of meanings. The author of the text may intend one meaning. Readers, however, based on their own unique positions and experiences, may see other meanings (Derrida 1992). For the current data analysis project, we are acting as readers of ethnographic texts when we code them. We ask of each text a set of questions to which we would like answers. The background for the questions we ask is comprised by a set of social concerns and social science concerns that are widely held in society and in academia involving meaning and dignity at work. Many of these same concerns also motivated the ethnographers whose texts we interview. The readings, nevertheless, are our own and may not always reflect the predispositions, judgements, and conclusions of the original ethnographers.

The analytic strategy we employ does, however, allow an investigation of the role of the ethnographer in producing the data, and, for that matter, of the coder in categorizing it. Along with the primary data, as part of the coding operation, we also recorded the theoretical orientations of the ethnographers along with several other characteristics of the ethnographies, such as their year of completion and the length of time spent in the field. Analysis of these methodological features of the workplace ethnographies is reported in research reports published elsewhere (Hodson 1998b; 1999a). To summarize briefly, few if any significant effects are found. There is little indication that ethnographers deviated significantly from their primary goal of providing rich, realistic descriptions of workplaces and workplace events – ethnographers' theoretical orientations do not appear to have substantially biased their observations about the topics they study.

Strategies for Safeguarding Dignity

Dignity at work is pursued through a variety of strategies. These strategies include resistance, citizenship and pride in work, the development of independent meanings systems, and reliance on social networks and friendships at work. In this section, we illustrate these strategies with descriptive material taken from workplace ethnographies. We focus on resistance and citizenship as the two primary strategies for working with dignity. We will also discuss the creation of independent meaning systems. The social aspects of work are discussed in greater detail in Chapter 8, which is devoted exclusively to coworkers and coworker relations.

Resistance and citizenship represent alternative behavioral strategies in the pursuit of dignity and meaning in work. Citizenship often entails activities that are consistent with the goals of management. And even some resistance behaviors do not directly challenge management authority. But neither resistance nor citizenship is well understood as representing simple "consent" to management definitions and goals. Through selecting the nature and conditions of citizenship, workers influence the workplace and workplace relations. Similarly, production generally continues in the face of resistance, but not always, and not in the same manner or with the same efficiency. Both resistance and citizenship have significant independent elements separate from management definitions. Most fundamentally though, the extent to which workers consent to production is a concern seen through the eyes of management. Dignity is the concern of workers, it is the goal of their behavior, and it is our concern here.

The task before us is to develop operational definitions of resistance, citizenship, and related behaviors that can be reliably measured across diverse settings. We turn first to resistance.

Resistance

Resistance to management can include both passive and active elements (Jermier, Knights, and Nord 1995). Playing dumb, withholding enthusiasm, and avoiding work are well-known examples of passive strategies of resistance. Active strategies include various forms of machine sabotage and social sabotage (such as chronically criticizing supervisors in their absence). Resistance occurs across a wide range of workplaces, but it can be expected to be most common in workplaces where anomic conditions prevail and where management fails to observe normative structures supporting the social and technical relations of production. Such normative structures prescribe that management should respect workers' rights and provide a coherent and functional organization of production. Where management does not support an agreed upon normative order in the workplace, employees also have little reason to abide by the formal norms of production. Resistance is also likely to occur in situations characterized by overwork and exploitation.

Table 3.1. *Resistance Measures, Organizational Ethnographies,*
N = 108

Variables	Codings	Mean[a]	S.D.[b]	N
Resistance	standardized scale[c]	0.00	1.00	105
Effort bargain	(1) extra effort given freely, (2) conditional effort given, (3) reticence practiced widely	1.66	.66	95
Absenteeism	(0) absent, (1) present	73%	.45	64
Withhold enthusiasm	(0) absent, (1) present	71%	.46	80
Work avoidance	(0) absent, (1) present	69%	.47	83
Playing dumb	(0) absent, (1) present	44%	.50	63
Machine sabotage	(0) absent, (1) present	22%	.42	59
Procedure sabotage	(0) absent, (1) present	73%	.45	77
Social sabotage	(0) absent, (1) present	60%	.49	70
Subvert particular manager	(0) absent, (1) present	63%	.49	64
Management conflict				
Conflict with supervisors or managers	(1) never, (2) infrequent, (3) average, (4) frequent, (5) constant	2.85	.90	100
Informal group resistance	(1) absent, (2) infrequent, (3) average, (4) widespread, (5) pervasive	2.17	1.22	89
Strikes	(0) absent, (1) present	27%	.45	94
History of strikes	(1) none, (2) infrequent, (3) frequent	1.80	.83	76
Other resistance variables				
Quits	(0) absent, (1) present	77%	.42	75
Turnover	(1) low, (2) medium, (3) high	2.03	.88	90
Making up games	(0) absent, (1) present	80%	.40	66
Alternative status hierarchies	(1) nonexistent, (2) occasional, (3) clearly articulated	2.10	.84	82
Making out	(1) none, (2) some, (3) half, (4) most, (5) all	2.85	1.33	80
Smooth operator	(1) none, (2) some, (3) half, (4) most, (5) all	2.38	1.23	78
Theft	(0) absent, (1) present	46%	.50	46

[a] The mean is expressed as percent "present" for present/absent variables.
[b] Standard deviation.
[c] See Appendix C for factor analysis results used in the scale construction.

Resistance occurs across at least nine aspects of worker behavior as reported in organizational ethnographies. These nine aspects are listed in Table 3.1. Most of the ethnographies allow the coding of the majority of these resistance behaviors, although many do not discuss one or more. The number of ethnographies that discuss each aspect of resistance is listed in the last column of the table. For use in parts of the analysis, the nine aspects of resistance are standardized, weighted, and averaged into a summary scale based on principal components factor analysis (see Appendix C, Table 1). This scaling technique makes maximum use of the available data.

Effort bargaining is perhaps the most widespread form of resistance. Effort bargaining is realized through withholding full effort, contingent on some desired response from management. An ethnography of long-shoring provides a good example of effort bargaining. In this setting the workers have developed a normative arrangement with supervisors in which they get lengthy breaks but maintain output by having the remaining men on the crew cover for the absent workers:

> 'When you're on, you keep that hook going, you work. In a sense we pay for our time off we do, when you come out of that hold you're wringing wet, because you know you got to put out because if you don't, now you're on the carpet. . . .'
>
> These remarks indicate both the expectation of extraordinary effort from those working on-and-off and the extent to which this deal is an explicit bargain between longshoremen and foremen. Work effort is traded for time off. Foremen use the deal to get the job moving; as one said to me, 'I tell them: "You've had your hours off, now it's time to go to work." ' (Finlay 1988:106)

This example illustrates giving extraordinary effort but giving it only conditionally.

Employees also engage in a wide variety of more individualistic behaviors to improve their situation at work. One of the most common of these is simply not showing up for work. High levels of absenteeism are illustrated in an ethnography of an underground mining operation. Management had recently initiated procedures that mandated greater overtime and stiffer penalties for absences. The employees responded to the new demands with even higher levels of absenteeism:

> Management had decreed that those who were absent without permission, or a 'good excuse,' would be laid off for the same number of days that they had taken. Far from inhibiting absenteeism, this rule actually encouraged it in the mine, for the miners took the regulation as a direct challenge. When several miners had been penalized in the specified way, others would deliberately take off without excuses. The result was that the number of absentees in any team was greater than

usual, and the team would be unable to function. (Gouldner 1964:151)

Withholding enthusiasm is also a common response to work that denies dignity. An ethnographer reports the following conversations with employees in an automobile factory. The discussions evoke a clear sense of withheld enthusiasm:

> These features of work . . . which alienate the worker from his labor and from himself lead to deprivations which are not easily verbalized. Yet they do show themselves in various ways: in the sad comment, 'The only reason a man works is to make a living'; in the occasional overflow of resentment, 'Sometimes you feel like jamming things up in the machine and saying good-bye to it'; in the cynical observation, 'The things I like best about my job are quitting time, pay day, days off, and vacations'; . . . and in the resigned answer to questions about their work, 'A job's a job.' (Chinoy 1955:85)

An ethnographer reporting on work in a steel fabrication mill finds a similar lack of enthusiasm. A worker's comment reveals a reservoir of withheld enthusiasm: "They'd be surprised if they would figure out in a turn how much pipe did not get made for them because the men just didn't have the incentive to put out" (Walker 1957:165).

Procedure sabotage implies more conscious intent than simply declining to give full effort. Procedure sabotage is often used as part of a strategy to get work completed in a way that does not exhaust the worker or require excessive or unnecessary effort. An ethnographer in a paper products mill describes how employees violate procedures to reduce their workload:

> Operators are aware that many of the [paper] cones that they reject would actually be perfectly acceptable to the customer. Almost all operators in the department therefore engage in a practice of separating out the cones that are substandard but still usable. They hide these around, and they wait for an inspector to pass by and approve a case before they pull these out of hiding and pack them. (Kusterer 1978:58)

Social sabotage against management is slightly less common than procedure sabotage but it was nevertheless observed in well over half of the workplaces studied (see Table 3.1). An example of social sabotage is provided by an ethnography of a cigarette manufacturing plant in Great Britain. During summer the employees are provided with a lemonade break in the afternoon. On a particularly stifling summer afternoon the lemonade is delayed. A personnel manager makes the mistake of walking into the production room at this moment, where he is met with a barrage of 'Where's our lemonade?' A senior worker continues the assault:

> *Ivy*: Where are going for your holidays this year, Mr. Dowling?
>
> *Mr. Dowling*: I'm not going anywhere. I can't afford it. I bought the wife a car and I've spent our money. Honestly.
>
> *Ivy*: Have you? Ah! What a shame. Can't you sell some of your shares then?
>
> *Mr. Dowling*: No, can't do that.
>
> *Ivy*: Come on, just a few.
>
> This produced laughter all round, the manager and his attempt at being 'just one of the workers' exposed to ridicule, and at the same time exploited for a laugh. (Pollert 1981:152–153)

Through ridiculing the personnel manager, the workers vent their frustrations of the moment and also undermine the status and authority of management personnel more generally.

The following episode, which takes place in an automobile assembly plant, reveals an ongoing conflict between a union shop steward and a supervisor. It provides an example of the sort of episodes that we coded as evidencing resistance through subverting a particular manager. The history of the episode dates back several years and involves various "unwritten agreements" between the shop steward and the supervisor, which the supervisor subsequently violates under pressure from upper management. The conflict between the steward and the supervisor eventually becomes personalized:

> Eventually, [Jack Jones, the shop steward] filled in a procedure report calling the supervisor a 'perpetual liar.'. . . The supervisor went to law, but he wasn't allowed to push it too far. Higher management persuaded him that the case was better dropped and Jack Jones escaped his chance to testify in the dock. (Beynon 1975:144)

In addition to the nine resistance behaviors, additional indicators of direct conflict between employees and managers are also available in the ethnographies. These include worker conflict with managers or supervisors, informal group resistance, strikes, and a history of strikes at the company.

A largely female, racially-mixed work force in a British garment factory provides an example of informal group resistance to management. Following the delivery of a new baby garment to be sewn, the workers spontaneously resist because of the unacceptably low piece rate attached to the work:

> 'Every time the minutes are given they get worse, they want more from us every time. Well it won't work. I can't do that target. . . .' Some sat defiantly with arms folded while others talked together in small groups. The unit had disintegrated. . . . Gillian [the supervisor] was looking distraught and said: 'I hate this minutes thing; it's the worst part of my job. I feel sick, I've got a headache. . . .' Lisa, the assistant supervisor, was also looking very worried as the fury from the women grew. (Westwood 1984:51)

Such conflicts are not restricted to blue-collar factory work. As Morrill (1995) notes in *The Executive Way*, even managers engage in systematic individual and group conflict with superiors and coworkers. Such conflicts can include acts of vengeance, public insulting, secret complaining, backbiting, interpersonal sabotage, and, in extreme cases, even violence (Morrill 1995:73; see also Jackall 1988).

Employees also distance themselves from their work in ways that do not necessarily involve direct resistance or conflict. These distancing mechanisms include quitting, making up games, creating alternative status hierarchies, making out, being a smooth operator, and theft. Again, the meaning of these behaviors is best illustrated by examples from the ethnographies.

Making up games is a common activity among workers who are bored or otherwise disaffected with their work. A worker in a coil winding shop is alienated from his job, and from much of society as well: "He hated the company and 'all the rich people'" (Seider 1984:31). A weekly gambling pool among the employees seems to be the only thing about his job that gives him any pleasure:

> Only on payday, and then for only a short while, did Charlie's behavior change. He looked forward to the Winding Room's weekly check pool. Whoever had the best poker hand based on the nine single identifying digits on his check won the pot. It wasn't much. We each put in only a dollar. But Charlie's enthusiasm to play and his curiosity about the winning hand suggested it meant more to him – maybe an impossible dream of winning a really big prize, and leaving ACME behind forever. (Seider 1984:31)

Games at work can also be highly informal and spontaneous. "Playing around" on the job is an important way to distance oneself from the formal definitions of the job and to transform one's regimented work life into something more personal and satisfying. Playing around on the job also typically involves coworkers and can be an important way to build group bonds. An ethnographer notes the aggressive play typical of concrete workers:

> Many enjoy physical horseplay. At one sewer plant project, one favorite pastime was ripping the clothes of one of the concrete finishers. Pete's clothing inevitably had some tear or hole. The men always teased him about his tattered work clothing. A number of times, one of the foremen and Pete would engage in a clothes-tearing fight. Each man would try to get his finger into a hole in the other man's shirt or pants and then pull. Away would come a shirt or pants leg, revealing bare limbs that would set off peals of laughter from the other men. (Applebaum 1981:33)

Another strategy for creating greater meaning and dignity in one's job involves the creation of alternative status hierarchies – often ones that invert the status ranking between employees and managers (Creighton and Hodson 1997). In this way, employees elevate their status and symbolically redress insults and slights that may have accumulated over the years. An example of an inverted status hierarchy can be seen at National Wire, one of the cases discussed in Chapter 1. At National Wire, the supervisor frequently proposes changes that the employees perceive as being not well thought out. One afternoon he decides a heating gun used in production needs to be suspended from the ceiling by a spring in order to make it more accessible. The production workers, as well as the maintenance worker assigned to install the gun, all suspect that it is a foolhardy plan:

> We had a good time on the floor while I worked on this set-up, because the women were as skeptical as I was. They kidded me, but mostly we kidded about Carroll [the foreman]. 'He'd hang anything from the ceiling if you'd let him,' said Linda. . . . 'I'd like to hang him from the ceiling,' said Carol, who watched all this from her sewing machine. (Juravich 1985:101)

The enthusiasm of each social class for identifying the failings of other classes and for rearranging the status hierarchy so that they come out on top is developed at greater length in Lamont (2000).

Workers also engage in a variety of strategies to simplify tasks in order to make their lives at work less burdensome. The centerpiece of these strategies is the effort to organize work so that it can be completed in an efficient and timely fashion without heroic effort. The colloquial expression *making out* is often used to describe ways of organizing one's job to get the work done without being exhausted at the end of the day. Making out depends on workers organizing their tasks so that they have fewer hassles and maybe even some slack time. An example from a piston ring factory illustrates this strategy:

> To the degree I was able to organize the job into routines and stick to them, the likelihood of doing a good job was increased. Fixing routines not only gave me a sense of some control over the job, it allowed me also to organize my time so that as I became more efficient I could reserve some free time. In the event of disruptions that free time gave me the capacity to absorb the disruption without throwing off my entire schedule. In the event of a trouble-free workday, I had time to talk to other workers or to hide. (Pfeffer 1979:57)

The term *smooth operator* is used to describe employees who manage to get extra rewards through carefully calculated actions. An example of a smooth operator is provided in an ethnography of Pullman Car porters. A porter carefully formulates his answer to a passenger's question to increase his odds of getting a good tip:

> I had Mrs. Will Rogers, practically on her deathbed. I had to lift her from one bed to another, accompanied by a nurse in

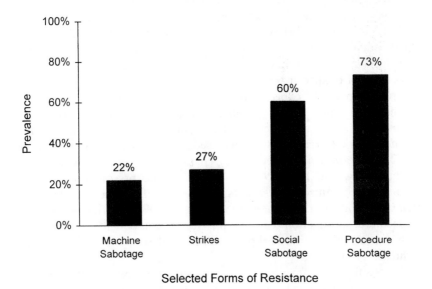

Figure 3.1. Resistance as strategy.

the room, and I had to pick her up out of this bed and put her over on this bed, and vice versa, as long as we could keep her comfortable. So on one occasion, while I was doing that thing, she asked me, 'Porter, how much do you think I weight?' She didn't weigh but a feather. I said, 'You weigh 135 pounds.' So she said, 'Thank you!' And when she got off, I got 135 skins! Beautiful! (Santino 1989:72)

The prevalences of some common resistance behaviors across the ethnographies are displayed in Figure 3.1. Machine sabotage is least frequent, being evidenced in only 22 percent of the workplaces studied. Strikes are slightly more common. But neither strikes nor machine sabotage are as common as social sabotage and procedure sabotage, which occur in between half and three-quarters of the workplaces studied.

Citizenship

Instead of resisting management workers sometimes engage in cooperative behaviors in which they voluntarily give extra effort to ensure that production takes place efficiently. Such citizenship behaviors are widespread in workplaces and are an important contributor to feelings of earned dignity at work. Workers feel increased dignity because they actively help achieve organizational goals or otherwise help to improve the environment of the workplace. When practicing citizenship, workers treat the organization as an "association of cooperative efforts" (Barnard 1950:4). Citizenship behaviors are often informal and subtle, but just like resistance behaviors, they are cumulative and they strongly influence the efficiency of the workplace, the quality of work life, and the daily experience of dignity at work (Organ 1988:16).

Citizenship can be expected to be especially prevalent in normatively organized workplaces where a sense of organizational fairness serves as a foundation for commitment to the organization and for taking pride in one's work (Organ 1988). Increased effort, cooperation, and peer training have been identified as key characteristics of such workplaces (Farh, Earley, and Lin 1997). Additional indicators of citizenship in normatively organized workplaces include use of insider knowledge to facilitate production and loyalty. Taking pride in work and helping to facilitate production can be important components of working with dignity where the workplace allows and supports such activities (Schnake 1991).

Citizenship can be measured across seven core aspects in the descriptions typically provided by workplace ethnographies. These seven aspects are presented in Table 3.2. For use in parts of the analysis, the seven

Table 3.2. *Worker Citizenship Measures, Organizational
Ethnographies, N = 108*

Variables	Codings	Mean[a]	S.D.[b]	N
Citizenship	standardized scale[c]	0.00	1.00	108
Cooperation	(1) absent, (2) mixed, (3) widespread	2.39	.60	101
Commitment to organizational goals	(0) absent, (1) present	55%	.50	93
Pride in work	(1) rare, (2) average, (3) a great deal	2.20	.75	100
Extra effort	(0) absent, (1) present	77%	.42	93
Extra time	(0) absent, (1) present	74%	.44	92
Peer training	(1) none, (2) very little, (3) average, (4) more than average, (5) extensive	3.09	1.12	87
Other citizenship variables				
Insider knowledge	(1) none, (2) very little, (3) average, (4) more than average, (5) extensive	3.87	.81	92
Good soldier	(1) none, (2) some, (3) half, (4) most, (5) all	3.09	1.35	87
Loyalty to particular manager	(0) absent, (1) present	57%	.50	83

[a] The mean is expressed as percent "present" for present/absent variables.
[b] Standard deviation.
[c] See Appendix C for factor analysis results used in the scale construction.

citizenship variables are standardized, weighted, and averaged into a summary scale based on principal components factor analysis in a fashion identical to that used for resistance (see Appendix C, Table 2).

One of the core elements of citizenship at work is taking pride in one's work. Pride is the emotional "consequence of a successful evaluation of a specific action" or "joy over an action ... well done" (Lewis 1993:570). Pride both motivates workers and provides a lens through which they experience their work (Biggart 1989; LeMasters 1975). Pride in work is thus central to our understanding of workplace citizenship.

Pride in work is exemplified in an ethnography of ironworkers. The worker responsible for maintaining the large crane used to lift the steel girders evidences great pride in his daily chores:

> Most oilers are nearly invisible, fueling and lubricating their rigs before the day begins for the rest of us, vanishing to God knows where during the bulk of the day, reappearing at 4:00

to preside over putting the rig to bed. Beane, however, was not of that stripe. He fussed over the crane like a stage mother, constantly wiping away puddles of oil or grease, touching up scratches with fresh paint, agonizing loudly whenever a load banged into the stick. (Cherry 1974:166)

Peer training is another important component of worker citizenship. In some workplaces, informal training of coworkers is important not just for productivity, but for safety as well:

I learned a lot just by listening, you know to those old war stories. . . . One of the things that I learned was to search a room with a straight stream about three feet off the floor to look for a window; to bust the window first and then open the wide fog, because if you open that wide fog you're going to get your ass burnt right there at the door; no two ways about it. (McCarl 1985:141)

Many workplaces rely on such peer socialization as a key mechanism for skills training. In such workplaces peer training also becomes a central building block of coworker relations.

Another aspect of citizenship is being willing to give full effort in spite of obstacles and difficulties. This behavior is sometimes called being a "good soldier" or "soldiering on." An example of being a good soldier is reported in an ethnography of deep-sea fishing:

I hed a boil come up under my right eye. That got so bad that ow Woggy Blowers, the mate, lanced it one day when we were in the wheelhouse. 'I'll cure that for yuh, boy,' he say. 'Look out o' the winder.' So I did. He got his shut-knife out o' his pocket an' he just slit across my cheek. Well, the pus flew everywhere! But that eased the pain. Two days later my eye wuz black an' blue. I could only sleep on one side. We got called out that night t' haul an' I slept on. The crew left me down there. Next thing I knew, the ow skipper wuz a-shakin' me all ways. 'Aren't yuh gorn t' do no bloody work t'night?' I swore at him, but I went up on deck an' stuck the rest o' the trip out. When we got in, I hetta go up the hospital with it. (Butcher 1980:54–56)

In spite of his initial, and perhaps well considered reluctance, the seaman continued to work, to soldier on.

The use of insider knowledge to facilitate production occurs across a wide range of workplaces and is an important supporting aspect of citizenship. The distribution of the use of insider knowledge to facilitate

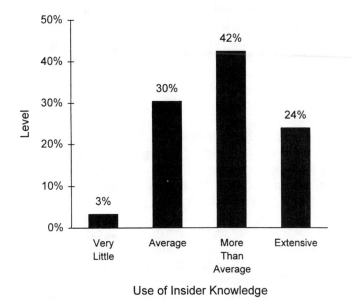

Figure 3.2. Citizenship as application of knowledge.

production is displayed in Figure 3.2. An example of the use of insider knowledge in support of production is reported in an ethnography of commercial inland fishing:

> The nets . . . need to be custom-made by individual fishermen
> with the necessary skill. . . . Net design and construction . . .
> demand a vast knowledge of the interdependent variables of
> water, weather, lake geography, fish behavior, fishing
> technique, and the capabilities of net material. . . . While some
> fishermen may scheme out their trap, gill, or seine net patterns
> on graph paper, the actual construction of nets – particularly
> of a 1,500-pound, 100-foot-long trap-net structure containing
> a series of complicated tapers of different angles made by
> counting 'so many meshes over, so many meshes down' – is
> done largely by memory and by hand in the net yard or shed.
> (Lloyd and Mullen 1990:61, 63)

We expect professional and craft workers to evidence especially high levels of insider knowledge. Highly skilled professional and craft work is based on long training and on work practices that include significant autonomy from managerial oversight.

Resistance and citizenship occur in all organizations but in different mixes according to the nature of the workplace. The central chapters of this book examine patterns of resistance and citizenship across workplaces differentiated by the challenges they present to working with dignity. We expect workplaces typified by a great deal of resistance to have lower-than-average levels of worker citizenship. But resistance and citizenship are not just opposite poles of a single continuum. Workers may be enthused about being as productive as possible and exhibit a great deal of citizenship. Simultaneously, however, they may resist some management agendas or aspects of the organization of work. Conversely, workers may be alienated from their work but be relatively steadfast in their behaviors. In this situation, they may exhibit neither high levels of resistance nor high levels of citizenship.

The statistical correlation between the resistance and citizenship scales is −.413. Thus, resistance and citizenship are negatively correlated, but they are not polar opposites. They share only about 17 percent common variance (the square of their correlation). In other words, 83 percent of the phenomena the two scales are measuring is unique to one or the other scale and is not shared in common. As we review the causes of resistance and citizenship in following chapters, it will be useful to remember that they are measuring distinct phenomena. We will learn more about these two phenomena and their relationship in upcoming chapters as we examine their patterns across different workplace settings.

Autonomous Meaning Systems

Meaning in work and coworker relations are also key contributors to working with dignity. Meaning at work is achieved in part through resistance against mismanagement and abuse and through taking pride in one's work. Resistance and citizenship are thus central to the attainment of meaning at work. Meaning at work, however, can also be attained in ways that are largely independent of the dynamics of resistance and citizenship, which revolve centrally around production issues. Meaning at work is achieved in some circumstances through activities that are entirely independent of production dynamics. The worker at National Wire, for example, who spread a table and ate half her lunch sandwich every day at break contributed to meaning in her work through these simple rituals.

In a different context, construction workers often come to identify with the rigors and physical demands of their work. Their ability to meet these demands contributes to a strong sense of meaning and identity:

> Physical strength and stamina . . . play a large part in
> determining construction workers' self-respect. . . . Much
> construction work involves hard physical labor under trying

conditions. Construction men must develop the stamina to persevere through very adverse conditions – extreme cold; arm-weary shoveling; leg-weary sloshing through mud; the chilling effect of high winds; the backstraining pushing and lifting of heavy weights. Men who must do this work are proud of their physical capabilities. (Applebaum 1981:32–33)

Workers at Electronics Components Limited (also discussed in Chapter 1) found meaning at work in a different way. At Electronics Components Limited, a meaningful experience of work life was achieved in part through generosity among coworkers and the sharing of treats and small gifts (Cavendish 1982:67).

Meaning at work can be attained through the construction of individual and social identities that allow feelings of pride and self-respect, even where these feelings are grounded in aspects of work life that are tangential to production. In both the construction and the factory work examples just discussed, workers' work-related identities also take on gender-related aspects and gained depth in so doing. The construction workers' sense of masculinity is strengthened by their physical prowess and toughness at work. And the female assembly workers confirm important family-based roles through their focus at work on birthdays, weddings, showers, and other personal celebrations. Integrating work roles with roles from life outside work can often increase a sense of meaning at work.

The experience of creativity on the job can also contribute to meaning and dignity at work. In a study of a chemical plant, an ethnographer notes the pride and satisfaction that came from keeping the plant working. "Keeping [the plant] 'on line' in the early days, however, had been an extremely difficult task. . . . The plant itself was initially a fairly redoubtable enemy" (Harris 1987:47). Increased meaning at work is experienced through creative activity, self-respect, and identity, as well as indirectly through resistance and citizenship activities.

Coworker relations are also important for meaning and dignity at work, as is shown in several of the examples presented. Coworker relations are complex and include positive aspects entailing solidarity, support, and mutual defense, as well as negative aspects entailing conflict, infighting, and gossip. The complex world of coworker relations will be the special focus of Chapter 8.

Denials of Dignity

In addition to developing appropriate concepts and measures for the strategies that workers use in their quest for dignity, we also need to develop appropriate measures of the challenges workers face. We have identified four significant challenges to the attainment of dignity at work: mismanagement and abuse, overwork, incursions on autonomy, and contradictions of emerging systems of employee involvement. In this section we operationalize these challenges in a manner that can be evaluated across ethnographic accounts of the workplace.

Direct Supervision, Mismanagement, and Abuse

The most widespread mismanagement and abuse can be expected in workplaces that rely on direct personal supervision. Such systems of control are unmediated by technical or bureaucratic considerations or by institutionalized protections for workers' rights. Where direct personal control is used to organize the workplace, organizational norms prohibiting abuse of employees will be relatively weak and workers will be vulnerable to abuse based on the personal sentiments of managers and supervisors as these vary from day to day. In brief, direct personal control can lead to despotic relations and the abuse of power (Edwards 1992a). In such settings the struggles of workers will be mainly focused on defense against abuse and mismanagement. Workers and managers can be expected to be in a running battle over norms that delineate the power of management and that defend the rights of workers.

The majority of the workplaces studied by organizational ethnographers utilize direct personal supervision to a significant degree (see Table 3.3). An example of direct personal control is provided by an ethnography of a British garment factory. "The supervisors had a major role in organising the technical division of labour on their units. It was they who set the work onto the units and they who judged how many different tasks were necessary and in what proportion to the number of workers" (Westwood 1984:18–19).

Table 3.3. *Direct Supervision and Resisting Mismanagement and Abuse*

Organizational Settings	Number of Ethnographies	Challenge to Dignity
Direct personal supervision	65	Resisting mismanagement and abuse
Indirect supervision	39	
Missing cases	4	

Gender can sometimes be a facilitating factor in allowing the continuation of direct personal control and abusive management behavior (Cockburn 1991). A study of factory workers in the burgeoning economy of South China notes that it is socially acceptable for the male supervisors to criticize the young female workers in a harsh and abusive manner. And, equally importantly, it is not socially acceptable for the young women to talk back (Lee 1998).

Direct supervision paves the way for mismanagement and abuse, but not all direct supervision is inherently abusive. Nor are mismanagement and abuse restricted to settings organized on the basis of direct supervisory control (Swerdlow 1998). In Chapter 4, where we examine these issues in greater detail, we will also develop more direct measures of mismanagement and abuse to supplement direct supervisory control.

Overwork

Understaffing and excessive pressure to increase output frequently characterize assembly-line work and other factory settings. Assembly work is strenuous, tiring, and even exhausting (Roberts 1994). The overwork and exploitative nature of such settings have been notorious since the time of Karl Marx. Table 3.4 displays the distribution of the workplace ethnographies across production settings involving assembly work. Bench assembly refers to assembly work that is done at a stationary table and then put to the side to be picked up and moved to the next work station by the box, stack, or cart full. This type of assembly work is contrasted with that in which work is brought to the worker via a continuously moving assembly line. A significant number of the workplace ethnographies describe both bench-assembly work and assembly-line work.

In recent decades, much assembly work has moved offshore from industrialized nations. Conditions in offshore factories are often

Table 3.4. *Production Technology and Excessive Work Demands*

Organizational Settings	Number of Ethnographies	Challenge to Dignity
Assembly line	25	Negotiating excessive work demands
Bench assembly	16	
Nonassembly work	67	

reminiscent of conditions in the early industrial revolution. A great deal of assembly-line work continues to take place in industrially advanced nations, particularly in the food processing industries, such as meat and poultry packing and canning (Fink 1998; Griffith 1993).

Professional and Craft Autonomy

Autonomous work practices and their defense can be expected to be particularly common in professional and craft settings where mastery of work is achieved only through long training and substantial experience. In such workplaces, employees' skills and knowledge are essential if production is to proceed at all. As a result, professional and craft settings typically include at least limited systems of bilateral input into workplace decisions. Professional and craft organizations lessen the need for close supervision of work based on management imposed coordination, inspection, and evaluation because professional and craft workers are the front-line inspectors of much of their own work (Granovetter 1985). The workers carry out significant parts of what are otherwise management duties as part of their normal daily activities. Systems of work organization entailing bilateral control in professional and craft settings thus allow greater autonomy for employees and rely on greater employee initiative. High levels of effort, however, are typically expected in return as part of the bargain with management (Friedson 1994).

The distribution of workplace ethnographies across professional and craft settings is displayed in Table 3.5. These workplaces are contrasted with workplaces that utilize either bureaucratic control or purely personal control. Ethnographies of contemporary craft settings include studies of firefighters (Chetkovich 1997), machinists (Thomas 1994), and construction employees (Eisenberg 1998). Ethnographies of contemporary professional settings include studies of engineers (Fruin 1997;

Table 3.5. *Management Control and the Defense of Autonomy*

Organizational Settings	Number of Ethnographies	Challenge to Dignity
Professional	10	Defending autonomous work practices
Craft	21	
Bureaucratic	48	
Supervisory fiat	29	

Kunda 1992), medical doctors (Bosk 1992; Hunter 1991; Zussman 1992), and research scientists (Pierce 1995; Rabinow 1996; Traweek 1988; Vaughan 1996).

The nature of work life in bureaucratic settings is generally much more rigid and scripted by organizational rules than in craft and professional settings (Baron, Jennings, and Dobbin 1988; Bridges and Villemez 1994). This rigidity is illustrated in the following description provided by a worker in a bureaucratically organized insurance company:

> I'm in a framework, a corporate framework, where I have to abide by their rules and regulations for everything, which gets to me because of all the bureaucratic junk that I have to go through to complete something. I know there's a faster way to do something, but I have to follow their ways, which is frustrating sometimes. (Burris 1983:157)

In bureaucracies, in contrast to professional and craft settings, the organization of work and of workers' lives and behaviors is closely controlled by bureaucratic rules. At Walt Disney World, for example, even guidelines on personal appearance are rigid and exacting. These guidelines include requirements such as "fingernails should not extend more than one-fourth inch beyond the fingertips" (Leidner 1993:9). We expect resistance to be increased and citizenship reduced in closely controlled bureaucratic settings and in settings with unilateral supervisory fiat. Professional and craft settings should exhibit the opposite pattern. Settings without professional or craft autonomy and without bureaucratic rules are classified as organized on the basis of supervisory fiat. Such settings are based on unmediated direct personal control.

Employee Involvement

The forms of employee involvement are diverse and a wide range of settings that incorporate employee involvement have been described in organizational ethnographies. The various forms of employee participation include worker-owned cooperatives, union–management partnerships, formal consultation, and self-managing teams. The distribution of workplace ethnographies across these forms of participation is presented in Table 3.6. The majority of the workplaces described include at least some form of employee involvement.

An illustration of participation in a *worker-owned cooperative* is provided by an ethnography of a plywood plant:

> Central to life in the cooperatives is the sense that the worker–shareholders are in charge, that they run the enterprise, are responsible for what goes on in it, and have the

Table 3.6. *Organizational Participation and the Pursuit of Meaningful Involvement*

Organizational Settings	Number of Ethnographies	Challenge to Dignity
Cooperatives and ESOPs[1]	15	Pursuing meaningful
Union–management partnerships	16	involvement while avoiding
Formal consultation	20	management manipulation
Self-managing teams	25	
No participation	32	

[1] Employee Stock Ownership Plans.

> opportunity, within certain boundaries, to make of their environment what they will.
>
> "If it comes down to it, the stockholders have absolute rule down there. In fact it has happened in this mill before. . . . If things get too bad, the stockholders can just say, 'Wait a minute . . . we are going to change this.' And if they have enough of them, they can do it, if enough guys get together." (Greenberg 1986:36–37)

Worker ownership, however, does not guarantee cooperative relations. An ethnography of a cooperatively owned feminist birth control clinic notes how initially egalitarian relations based on consensus and rotation of duties eventually turned sour. Over time mistrust became pervasive. Eventually, the chief administrator gave negative evaluations to two of the founding members who subsequently resigned (Simonds 1996:224). Employee participation and employee involvement thus provide significant opportunities for improved workplace relations, but even worker ownership is no guarantee that these opportunities will be realized (Russell 1993). Workplaces with Employee Stock Ownership Plans (ESOPs) entailing substantial voting rights for employees are also included in this category.

Union–management partnerships build on explicit collectively negotiated agreements between unions and management to jointly sponsor programs involving workers. In the United States, such programs have been particularly common in the automobile and telecommunications industries (Womack, Jones, and Roos 1990). The core focus of these programs has been on improved worker training to meet the challenges of automation and global competition (Milkman 1997:160).

Formal consultation involves regular meetings between management and employees, or employees' representatives, at which various work-related issues are discussed. Formal consultation can occur in either union or nonunion settings. Management generally controls the topics available for discussion. These topics can include both production issues and personnel issues but generally exclude pay and benefits, which are either negotiated in union environments or determined by management fiat in nonunion environments.

Formal consultation at a whiskey distillery is described in an ethnography from Great Britain:

> Joint consultation meetings with all the stewards took place
> ... about every six weeks, chaired by the plant mangers. . . .
> The meetings were organized by management who also set the
> agenda. . . . Notice of meetings could be very short, as little as
> a couple of hours. The meetings took the form of a quick
> summary of the order position. . . . This was followed by new
> points tabled by the manager or the stewards. There was no
> formal [mandate], except that pay negotiations were not
> discussed, although in practice discussion often spilled over
> into issues about bonus payments. (Cressey 1985:21–22)

Similar forms of formal consultation also occur in other settings, including police work (Martin 1980) and banking (Smith 1990).

Employee involvement based on a significant degree of self-management by *production teams* has become increasingly common in industrially advanced economies. The growth of teams reflects many forces, including changes in management theory about how best to organize production, increased skill demands associated with sophisticated technologies, and worker demands for increased voice at the workplace. As with the other forms of worker participation, the nature and meaning of team production can vary widely across settings.

Mutual aid and cooperative relations in a team setting are evidenced in the following example from an ethnography of an automobile assembly plant:

> How the team organizes itself is up to its members. . . . The
> only contract the workers have with management is to deliver
> a certain number of finished doors, or installed brake systems,
> or interiors, every day. If a team fills its buffer zones, the
> members feel free to stop for coffee or a cigarette. . . .
> Improved contact with fellow workers sometimes led one
> person spontaneously to help another. . . . Many people were
> interested in learning new tasks from each other.
> (Gyllenhammar 1977:65, 89–90)

In other workplaces, however, teams have been associated with work intensification (Parker and Slaughter 1994:24; Rinehart, Huxley, and Robertson 1997), peer monitoring of team members (Barker 1999), and antiunion campaigns (Grenier 1988:47,132). In later chapters we explore the diverse varieties and consequences of employee involvement and team production in greater depth.

Conclusions

In this chapter we have described some of the resistance and citizenship behaviors that give substance to the pursuit of dignity at work. We have also identified some of the variations in work settings that set the backdrop for workers' quest for dignity. In the chapters that follow we examine the struggle for dignity across a wide range of workplaces. Issues of mismanagement and abuse, overwork, autonomy, and participation play a leading role in organizing these discussions. And the often subtle but very real workplace behaviors of resistance, citizenship, and the pursuit of independent meaning systems comprise much of the substance for these discussions – these are the tools that workers use in their struggle to find meaning, satisfaction, and dignity in work.

As we will see, the nature of management control and the organization of work in different settings provide openings and incentives for different forms of resistance and citizenship. In turn, resistance and citizenship become limiting factors in the further development of systems of workplace organization. Every existing organization of work has strengths, as well as weaknesses and internal contradictions. Workers' struggles and their quest for dignity are often decisive factors in highlighting these contradictions and forcing the development of new, more humane ways of organizing work.

Part II

The Practice of Dignity

4

Deflecting Abuse and Mismanagement

The first thing a worker typically asks about a new job is: "What is the boss like?" A good boss can make a difficult job bearable and a bad one can make otherwise good work a nightmare. In small firms, the organization and flow of work is often determined entirely by the whims of the owner or manager. Even in larger firms, supervisors have a great deal of latitude in staffing and assignments and these decisions can have a tremendous influence on the quality of work life. Supervisors also evaluate employees' performances and set the tone for a supportive or hostile atmosphere. Direct supervisors thus have tremendous power over workers. Their management styles can evoke either loyalty and extra effort from workers or resentment and resistance. The first hurdle in the quest for dignity at work is thus the possibility of mismanagement and abuse.

In this chapter we examine the influence of direct personal supervision on resistance and citizenship. We also develop and analyze the effects of more direct measures of mismanagement and abuse. We find that mismanagement and abuse have a central role in generating resistance and undermining citizenship in the workplace.

A History of Mismanagement and Abuse

Both Karl Marx and Emile Durkheim saw the power of owners and managers as the key to understanding the dire working conditions of the early industrial revolution. Marx believed these conditions arose from capitalists' exploitation of workers and that the solution to these problems depended on workers overthrowing capitalism. Durkheim theorized that poor working conditions arose from the unmediated drive toward competition and endless expansion. For Durkheim, the solution lay in the emergence of a new normative order to control the organization of work life. This new normative order would arise from bargaining between owners and employees, who would be organized into occupational communities.

83

Employees are often treated abusively by supervisors, either physically or psychologically, and workplaces are frequently run in a chaotic fashion. An important goal of employees in such settings is to deflect, negate, or "get even" with management for abuse and chaos in their daily work lives. Systems of work organization in which employees are directly and personally supervised in the details of their work involve the greatest likelihood of abuse and the fewest guarantees of coherent organization (Edwards 1979). Direct personal control is more prone to abuse and chaos than more institutionally mediated forms of control involving either bureaucracy or bilaterally negotiated norms (Freeman and Rogers 1999). Management abuse provokes some of the fiercest forms of resistance from employees. Abuse, however, is not restricted to workplace systems relying on direct supervisory control, and the deflection of abuse is a widespread agenda for employees across a variety of settings.

Managers who abuse employees and fail to provide a coherent organization of production not only undermine the dignity of their employees, but they also fail in their obligations to the organization as a whole. Abuse, chaos, and the resulting worker resistance are the antithesis of organizational efficiency. Managers and supervisors can also be the objects of abuse by those higher in the authority hierarchy. The sting of abuse is no less severe for managers and the consequences for the organization are no less destructive. Indeed, abusive behavior and poor leadership starting in upper management can be reproduced and passed down the chain of command until everyone in the organization is negatively affected (Morrill 1995; Watson 1994).

Abuse comes in many forms but always involves some aspect of status degradation. A worker caricatures the abusive managers at an electronics factory in the following manner:

> Tweedledum, Tweedledee and the other managers seemed like cardboard characters, and we thought them rude and bad mannered. Even if they stopped right by you or took the [product] out of your hand, they acted as if you weren't there. If they went through the heavy rubberised swing doors into the main assembly in front of you, they let them swing back on you, which no worker would ever do. . . . They had so little respect for the workers that they couldn't even admit we existed. . . . When they came to wish the supervisors and chargehands 'Merry Christmas' they made a feeble attempt to include us in the greetings, although they never even acknowledged our existence at any other time. They stood at

the top of the line and repeated 'Merry Christmas' down the line, as if to thin air, not addressing anyone in particular. (Cavendish 1982:97)

Employees respond to abuse and chaos in the workplace in diverse and creative ways. Strategies for deflecting abuse include relatively direct approaches, such as restricting effort or directly confronting supervisors. The deflection of abuse, however, can also be achieved indirectly through expressive mechanisms, such as venting, which create a momentary sense of empowerment and self-efficacy. In abusive and chaotic situations, dignity is thus defended at least in part through direct or indirect conflict and resistance. Perhaps the most common type of resistance is a simple "withdrawal of cooperation."

Withholding cooperation as a strategy of resistance to abuse is well illustrated by an example from a study of the relationship between masters and indentured servants:

> Lifelong indentured servants most characteristically expressed discontent about their relationship with their master by performing their work carelessly and inefficiently. They could intentionally or unconsciously feign illness, ignorance, or incompetence, driving their masters to distraction. . . . This method of passive resistance, provided it was not expressed as open defiance, was nearly unbeatable. (Edward B. Harper, as cited in Scott 1985:33)

A particularly compelling example of resistance to abuse is seen in the life of Frederick Douglass, author of one of the most famous American slave autobiographies. Douglass was hired out in 1834 to Edward Covey, who had a "reputation for being able to break resistant slaves." Covey abused Douglass for six months until Douglass finally resisted:

> A protracted fight between Covey and Douglass followed. . . . Finally, after two hours, Covey 'gave up the contest,' related Douglass. 'Letting me go, he said – puffing and blowing at a great rate – "now you scoundrel, go to your work, I would not have whipped you half so much as I have had you not resisted." The fact was, *he had not whipped me at all.*' The effect of the struggle on both sides was remarkable. 'During the whole six months that I lived with Covey, after this transaction, he never laid on me the weight of his finger in anger,' Douglass recollected. ' . . . I was a changed being after that fight, I was a *nothing* before; I WAS A MAN NOW.' (Kolchin 1978:466)

Abuse, unfortunately, has not vanished from the contemporary work-place, even if abuse often occurs in more subtle forms now. The follow-ing episode from the British Merchant Marine provides an example of both abuse and incompetence on the part of management and of resis-tance as a means of deflecting abuse:

> Towards the end of one long stretch of tank-cleaning, I was down in a tank with another seaman. It was late and we were tired. We were running out of buckets and had only two left .... Before starting the outermost compartments we called our foreman, but the answer came back that all the buckets were out, and they had no permission to take any more from the store; we must manage with the two we had.
>
> Certainly we could manage, but it meant that every time we had scraped up two buckets of sludge we would have to creep the whole way from the outer compartments to the central compartment so that these could be heaved up, instead of being able to pass all the sludge from one compartment to the centre in one go. The job would take twice as long. We would be paid overtime, but extra pay means nothing to men who only want to lie down on the deck and go to sleep. We had been in the tanks for a week and *this was too much....* For a moment we looked at each other without saying anything. Then the other seaman grabbed the bucket alongside him and flung it with all his might against a bulkhead and smashed it to smithereens. I did the same. (Ramsay 1966:56–57)

This act of resistance served to vent the frustrations of the workers involved. It may also have helped to redefine the effort bargain between these workers and their foreman in relation to future work assignments.

The exaggerated status hierarchy typical of relations between officers and crew in the merchant marine generates a chronic pattern of abuse and resistance:

> It was not unusual for members of the catering staff (who were subjected to a stream of 'do this, do that, do this, do that' orders from obnoxious second stewards) to feel so fed up they would heave a whole pile of dirty dishes through an open porthole instead of washing them. Stewards who do personal laundry are quite capable of 'making a mistake' and burning through a shirt with the iron. When sailors are loading stores and accidentally let a sling load crash on the wharf below, their reaction is usually one of suppressed glee rather than

sorrow. Deck crews who are driven too hard can quite calmly paint over oil and water and take a malicious delight in doing so. (Ramsay 1966:63)

Anger and frustration are clearly involved in these incidents, but such acts of resistance can also work to boost workers' sense of empowerment and self-efficacy. Revenge can be sweet. Acts of resistance can be highly significant for employees who have few opportunities for the exercise of creative or autonomous activity within the confines of their jobs. Acts of resistance can thus be a foundation for whatever experiences of self-efficacy workers are able to attain in abusive and chaotic workplaces.

We expect resistance to be especially common, and citizenship to be suppressed in situations involving abuse and chaos. Management has already established belligerence and chaos as the prevailing standards and employees have little ability or motivation to redefine the situation. As a result, abuse, chaos, and resistance can become part of a stable pattern of relations that is intrinsic to such systems (Bensman and Gerver 1963:595; Willis 1977).

In the sections that follow we examine patterns of abuse, mismanagement, and resistance as evidenced in organizational ethnographies reporting on a wide range of workplaces. We first examine resistance and citizenship as responses to direct supervision. Next, we develop and examine the effects of more direct measures of mismanagement and abuse.

Direct Personal Supervision

Most organizational ethnographers report significant elements of direct supervisory control. Many workplaces, however, are also characterized by bureaucratic rules, by professional or craft standards, or by self-organizing teams. These alternative systems of work organization will be considered in later chapters.

Table 4.1 reports levels of resistance and citizenship across workplaces relying on direct and indirect forms of supervision. Indirect forms of supervision include all other forms of work organization that do not rely centrally on direct personal control (for example, bureaucratic rules or craft or professional standards). The last column of Table 4.1 reports tests of statistical significance for the contrasts between direct and indirect supervision. Resistance is more common under direct supervision. Citizenship, in contrast, is more common under indirect supervision. The summary resistance and citizenship scales, as well as the majority of the

Table 4.1. *Working under Direct Supervision*

Variables	Direct Supervision	Indirect Supervision	Significance[a]
Resistance scale	**.14**	**−.31**	**.025**
Effort bargaining	1.80	1.40	.004
Absenteeism	.81	.59	.061
Quits	.80	.72	.442
Conflict with supervisors or managers	2.92	2.68	.226
Machine sabotage	.25	.17	.500
Procedure sabotage	.73	.71	.891
Social sabotage	.70	.42	.024
Strikes	.35	.01	.002
Citizenship scale	**−.26**	**.59**	**.000**
Cooperation	2.25	2.64	.001
Pride in work	1.98	2.55	.000
Commitment	.43	.79	.001
Meaningful work	1.63	2.29	.000
Creativity	2.00	3.11	.000
Job satisfaction	2.62	3.34	.001
Ethnographies (N)	65	39	

[a] Two-tailed t-test.

more specific indicators of resistance and citizenship, support this general pattern. The contrasts are even larger for citizenship than for resistance suggesting that direct supervision depresses self-initiated citizenship activities even more strongly than it generates resistance. Meaning in work and creativity are also much more common in workplaces that are not based on direct personal supervision.

A good example of conflict over capricious supervisory practices is provided by an ethnography of an automobile assembly plant in Great Britain:

> In the early years at Halewood the day to day life of the plant was virtually one endless battle over control. . . . The overwhelming majority of the problems . . . were related either to speed-up or 'the blue-eye system', the favouritism practised by foremen in allocating the work and overtime or in moving men from one section to another. (Beynon 1975:145)

An ethnography of an apparel factory illustrates increased effort bargaining in response to intensified supervision. During a period of expansion and reorganization, the owner increases direct supervision, bypass-ing older craft organizations of work. Skilled workers eventually came to terms with the new arrangements, but only after substantial informal resistance and bargaining involving the establishment of acceptable stan-dards of effort:

> [The owner] designed an open plant in which all work areas were clearly visible, and he encouraged his supervisors to be out on the floor to motivate the workers by their presence. . . .
> One of the tailors told me how he [challenged the new system]: 'At first the supervisors tried to push me, but I am an independent type and too old to be scolded. Now I work in a way that does not attract attention. I work slowly, but the inspectors never return a jacket that I have sewn. This way I demand and get good treatment.' (Savage and Lombard 1986:161–162)

Social sabotage is also more common under systems that rely on direct personal supervision. A worker at an electrical components factory in Great Britain has made a significant sideline of criticizing management. The goal of such social sabotage is both to undermine the object of attack and to elevate the attacker:

> Reuben had a sharp eye for the shortcomings of management and supervisors . . . he took a delight in watching the stupidities of those who were supposed to be more intelligent than he. I have rarely met a more shrewd and hard-hitting critic of authority than Reuben. (Lupton 1963:120–121)

Social sabotage has a long history in the workplace. At the start of the twentieth century, the Wobblies in the United States used social sabotage as an explicit pressure tactic. The tactic, known as "open mouth sabo-tage," was to "divulge to competitors trade secrets . . . and to inform patrons, customers, clients and the general public when owner–mangers compromised quality or abused workers" (Jermier 1988:108). Similarly, contemporary students of the workplace report that gossip is one of the most widespread strategies of resistance in response to disliked managers and supervisors (Tucker 1993).

Strikes are also noticeably more common in workplaces utilizing direct personal supervision. Wildcat strikes by workers are almost always sparked by a particular managerial action. At an open pit mine in Aus-tralia, pressures to work under unsafe conditions sparked a week-long strike:

> A truck driver was suspended at Goonyella by the mechanical superintendent for refusing to drive a truck whose [tires] the

> driver considered 'ripped' and therefore unsafe. The whole
> Goonyella manual workforce went on strike for a week to
> demand the man's reinstatement. (Williams 1981:52)

Strikes represent the workers' "collective voice" over working conditions
(Freeman and Medoff 1984; Godard 1992). It is particularly revealing
that this voice is needed more frequently under conditions of direct personal supervision.

Citizenship behaviors are less common under direct supervision than
under indirect supervision. These contrasts are even larger and more consistently significant than are those involving resistance behaviors. It
appears that one of the most significant consequences of direct supervision is to rob employees of their desire to take independent initiative in
support of production (Drucker 1993). Cooperation, pride, commitment, creativity, meaningful work, and satisfaction are all markedly
lower under direct personal supervision. An example of reduced citizenship is provided by Alvin Gouldner's classic study contrasting underground gypsum miners with the more closely supervised workers in the
associated above-ground gypsum board factory:

> On the surface, though, even when an emergency occurred
> many workers showed but little motivation. . . . There was a
> break-down at the wet-end today. . . . The younger men *relax*
> and *make jokes*. They lean across the board machine and *talk
> with each other* in clusters. The foremen, though, work hard.
> One of the younger men *jokingly* pushes the button that lets
> loose a sharp whistle against the flat blast of the emergency
> buzzer. A foreman hustles down from the mixer. He asks,
> 'Who done it?' . . . The above observations reveal . . . that
> energetic and cooperative work efforts on the surface were not
> even brought about by an emergency situation. (Gouldner
> 1964:140)

In contrast, workers in an automated chemical plant, who are not
directly supervised, reveal substantial levels of creativity, initiative, and
pride in their work:

> Control room work was vital for the efficient running of the
> plant and the safety of the shift. . . . Despite all the automatic
> monitoring devices, there was still much scope for individual
> decisions about the settings of the controls. The plants were
> not uninfluenced by the natural environment. Because they
> used an enormous intake of air, fluctuations in external
> temperatures and atmospheric pressures required adjustment
> to the controls. Supervisors had an ultimate responsibility for

plant productivity, but the men on Plant X had won a
considerable degree of freedom to work in the control room
without being continually checked. . . . Efficiency depended to
a considerable extent on the ordinary man. (Harris 1987:117)

The absence of direct supervision in this plant and the substantial autonomy of the workers allowed them to take initiative to ensure the productivity and the safety of the plant's operations – responsibilities they
gladly undertook.

The patterns reported in Table 4.1 strongly suggest that employees
resist direct personal supervision and are less cooperative in workplaces
utilizing such forms of control. It is also possible to develop more direct
measures of mismanagement and abuse based on the descriptions provided in organizational ethnographies. These measures will allow us to
examine how employees respond to specific types of mismanagement
and abuse.

Workplace Norms against Mismanagement and Abuse

Direct personal supervision threatens dignity at work because it encourages capricious management and violations of workers' rights. Personal
control is thus a breeding ground for mismanagement and abuse. While
management often gives verbal support to respecting employees' rights,
there is a major "disconnect" between verbal claims and actual behavior in many workplaces (Pfeffer 1998). Mismanagement has also been
identified as a major cause of lack of competitiveness in industry. Mismanagement can include inappropriate choices of technology, inadequate
attention to quality control, and nepotism and cronyism (LeRoy 1987:4).
Mismanagement and abuse violate important norms of production that
have emerged in industrially advanced societies.

The workplace is governed by norms of production just as society is
governed by norms of behavior. "A norm . . . is a rule or a standard that
governs our conduct in the social situations in which we participate. It
is a societal expectation. It is a standard *to which we are expected to
conform*" (Bierstedt 1963:222). The failure of management to live up to
emergent norms of production represents a core challenge to the attainment of dignity for workers.

A general formulation of the importance of an agreed upon normative order in the workplace can be developed by noting the importance
of legitimacy for the effective use of power. Etzioni (1961) argues that
compliance will be more prevalent and more enthusiastic when the

exercise of power is seen as legitimate. Legitimate power rests on adherence to an agreed upon normative order (Marshall 1958; Selznick 1992). Mueller et al. (1994) present research supporting the importance of legitimacy for employee attachment and commitment.

A central element in the normative organization of work is the establishment of trust between employees and managers. Ouchi's seminal writings (1981) on the Japanese system of production highlight trust based on job security and lifetime employment. The focus on lifetime employment has remained part of the conceptual discussion of the Japanese system but the more general idea of trust has played a less central role and it is this idea that may be the more important concept. "The first lesson of Theory Z is trust. Trust and productivity go hand in hand" (Ouchi 1981:5). Trust can only be maintained when the behavior of both parties is guided by an agreed upon normative order (Edwards 1993).

Workplace Norms

Early writings in industrial sociology included a strong focus on the norms governing employment. Dunlop (1958) stressed that enterprises need to develop and adhere to norms concerning recruitment and promotions, compensation, training, work practices, and grievances. Barbash (1984) adds to this list the provision of fringe benefits, such as vacation time and health care. All of these norms are important for establishing trust and legitimacy.

One of the most central workplace norms is for management to refrain from abusive practices (Adler and Borys 1996). The provision of grievance procedures, especially independent union sponsored procedures, has been one of the most important mechanisms in the contemporary workplace for ensuring that abusive practices are limited and that redress is available when violations occur (Eaton, Gordon, and Keefe 1992). The continuation of abuse in the contemporary workplace provides an opening for unions to revitalize themselves through recruiting new membership. The success of recent unionization efforts among service workers has been significantly fueled by the recognized ability of unions to provide mechanisms to limit managerial abuse (Shostak 1991).

Additional important workplace norms include job security and the absence of capricious layoffs (Kochan, Katz, and McKersie 1994). Job security has increasingly become an established worker right in many workplaces. The right to job security recognizes employees as significant stakeholders in the corporation (Pfeffer 1998). Ongoing training has also come to be an increasingly common workplace norm as a result of rapid technological change in recent decades. Organizational values promoting job security and internal training and promotion of employees have been identified as a central part of the matrix of organizational norms that define the Japanese system of production (Marsh 1992).

In addition to norms concerning the rights of employees, managers are also expected to comply with norms concerning the organization of production. Barnard (1950) identifies the maintenance of communication, the organization of production, and the establishment of goals (leadership) as among the most essential tasks that management must achieve. An important component in establishing a workable system of production is the procurement and maintenance of effective tools and technologies (Dunlop 1958). Accomplishing these tasks is essential in order for production to occur effectively.

Norms defining appropriate management behavior in the workplace can thus be seen as representing two distinct but related realms. On one hand, workplace norms involve the *treatment of employees with dignity and respect* and the recognition of their material needs. Additional workplace norms specify the responsibilities of management for *maintaining a working system of production* that allows employees to fulfill the requirements of their jobs. The failure of management to live up to these norms results in workplaces characterized by abuse and chaos (Hodson 1999b; Meyer and Zucker 1989).

Norms for management thus involve two distinct realms: (1) respect for employees and their rights, and (2) ensuring the technical viability of production (Barnard 1950; Batstone 1984; Drucker 1993). These realms parallel the social and technical aspects of work as first conceptualized by Roethlisberger and Dickson (1939). *Management citizenship behavior* in the workplace thus involves abiding by norms concerning the treatment of employees and providing a workable technical system of production. Such management citizenship behavior has been observed to be an important prerequisite for worker citizenship (Hodson 1999b).

Abuse

Six aspects of abusive management practices that infringe on the dignity of workers can be identified across organizational ethnographies. The behaviors include direct physical and verbal abuse, inappropriate firings, absence of job security, frequent layoffs, reductions in hours, and an absence of on-the-job training. These behaviors, their codings, means, and standard deviations are displayed in Table 4.2. These six variables are also factor analyzed and the results are used to construct a standardized management abuse scale. The factor analysis results are reported in Appendix C, Table 3. The factor analysis indicates that the six characteristics are closely related and form a single scale with high internal reliability.

Table 4.2. *Management Abuse Measures*

Variables	Codings	Mean[a]	S.D.[b]	N
Management abuse	standardized scale[c]	0.00	1.00	108
Abuse	(1) never, (2) rarely, (3) sometimes, (4) frequently, (5) constantly	2.46	1.13	85
Firings	(0) absent, (1) present	70%	.46	80
Job security	(1) high, (2) average, (3) minimal, (4) none	1.97	.95	101
Layoffs	(1) never, (2) seldom, (3) sometimes, (4) frequent	2.21	1.20	78
Reduced hours	(0) absent, (1) present	49%	.50	85
On-the-job training	(1) extensive, (2) more than average, (3) average, (4) very little, (5) none	2.74	1.34	101

[a] The mean is expressed as percent "present" for present/absent variables.
[b] Standard deviation.
[c] See Appendix C for factor analysis results used in the scale construction.

Abusive management behaviors are closely linked to direct personal supervision. The score on the standardized abuse scale for workplaces utilizing direct personal supervision is .20, versus −.39 for workplaces utilizing indirect forms of control (F-test, p = .002).

Direct physical or verbal abuse is the most recognizable component of abusive management behavior and, unfortunately, occurs across a wide range of workplaces. Inappropriate firings are also reported in 70 percent of the ethnographies. Job security is essential for employees who depend on their jobs for their livelihood and job security has been identified as a key foundation for a normative organization of work. Conversely, frequent layoffs are a particularly destabilizing experience. Reduced hours are also an important concern in the modern economy as many employees struggle to secure full-time employment in an economy increasingly typified by part-time work, temporary work, and other forms of marginal employment (Henson 1996; Hodson 2000; Tilly 1996). Significant on-the-job training is also increasingly essential in the modern high-technology economy characterized by continuous learning. The failure to provide regular on-the-job training can constitute a significant lapse in the normative order of the workplace of the third millennium (Ferman, Hoyman, and Cutcher-Gershenfeld 1990).

Widespread abusive behavior toward employees is evidenced in an ethnography of a steel mill. For example, aggravated by a minor complaint from a worker, a supervisor "flew into a rage, and shouted, 'Get back on your job. You don't know what-in-hell you're talking about. I've been watching you, and you've been sitting on your [expletive] all morning'" (Spencer 1977:171). Another worker was given a rapidly sequenced series of disciplinary suspensions based on manufactured charges as a prelude to firing him for union activity (112–113).

Abusive relations are also reported in an ethnography of a Japanese apparel factory with a primarily female work force and managerial staff:

> There used to be a lot of malicious teasing. I cried a lot. . . . It
> was a supervisor – a woman – who was the mean one. . . . She
> yelled at us for brushing against the clothes that were hanging
> up in the changing room. . . . And if you were sewing labels on
> garments and you asked for some more, she would take a
> bunch and throw them at you, so they'd fall all over the place,
> and then you'd have to pick them up. It takes time to pick
> them up, and then you'd have to rush like crazy to catch up
> to your quota. I cried a lot. (Roberts 1994:61)

More subtle, yet still highly destructive management abuse, also occurs in many workplaces. Often these behaviors involve treating workers as objects rather than as human beings or simply being chronically disrespectful. An example of aggressive and disrespectful management behavior is reported in a study of white-collar office work:

> I'll walk into the room in the morning and the first thing she
> says is something like 'I don't want you to assume
> responsibility for letting people know this, this, or this,' or
> 'Who gave you the authority to work overtime last night,
> again?' No preface, no 'Good morning Alec.' It will be the
> first thing I hear. (Gwartney-Gibbs and Lach 1991:622)

Abuse, however, is not always subtle. Employees are also sometimes physical abused by their employers. Repeated examples of both verbal and physical abuse are reported in a study of Filipina domestic employees in Hong Kong. Workers frequently report being yelled at and being called extremely offensive and racist names. In addition, reports of beatings are not uncommon. One employer became angry with a domestic worker for putting her own clothes in the washing machine:

> Ms. Lu threw Margie's clothes in the garbage, then hit her on
> the head with her fist many times. In September, Ms. Lu's son
> hurt himself playing outside. Although Margie informed her at
> once, Ms. Lu 'got very angry and hit me again thrice on the
> head. Since then every time she is angry with me she hits me.'
> (Constable 1997:147)

The humiliation of domestic workers is often compounded by the fact that the children of their employers, who on the basis of age should be deferential, are also frequently abusive. "Children are very impolite because they are the same as their parents. Their parents show them how to treat the Filipinas. . . . So if the parents growl then the children will growl too" (Constable 1997:106).

As this example shows, abuse can thus build on social and cultural differences between workers and managers and exploit these as justifications for abuse. Sexual harassment provides one of the most widespread examples of exploiting the social characteristics of workers as a justification for abuse (Brant and Too 1994). An ethnography of a largely female work force in a British apparel factory illustrates some of the problems of a sexualized workplace culture:

> Not only were they subjected to the discipline of work and of factory rules, on top of this, as women, they were exposed to constant sexist patronisation. . . . 'Hey gorgeous,' 'Do us a favour, love,' 'Come here sexy' – all are familiar addresses for most women. Supervision was sexually oppressive, the manner usually cajoling, laced with intimate innuendo, and provocative jokes, hands placed on girls shoulders as they worked, imposition mixed with flattery. (Pollert 1981:142–143)

The subordinate status of young female employees can also be used as a basis for extending workplace control through family connections (Adkins 1995). A study of an electronics factory in an industrial compound in South China illustrates the utilization of family roles in workplace discipline:

> Deng Su-ying, a nineteen-year-old woman from Jiangxi, was subjected to the 'parental' supervision of her uncle and aunts, both working at Liton. . . . Su-ying said that because her parents had entrusted her to her uncle, he and his wife kept very close tabs on her: 'In the dorm, my aunt, my cousins, and I live in the same room. My aunt's bunk is just below mine. Every time I go out, she asks where and with whom I am going.' (Lee 1998:124)

Unjust firings can quickly certify a workplace as abusive and hostile. A study of a Japanese-based automobile plant in the United States reports the use of firings to eliminate employees who complain about injuries (Graham 1995). Similarly, an ethnographer reports that workers active in organizing a union at a pharmaceutical plant were fired for trivial rule violations (Grenier 1988:102).

Sometimes the legal conditions of employment can be used to force employees to stay on a job and endure abusive conditions. To immigrate to Hong Kong, Filipina domestic workers must sign a two-year contract with a particular employer. The law also requires that they must leave the country within two weeks of being terminated by their employer. And if they quit their employer, they are not allowed to sign another contract. These legal restrictions have been cited as a major reason why Filipina maids endure abusive working conditions. Leaving a job necessitates both leaving the country and returning home to likely unemployment (Constable 1997:150).

Mismanagement

The second potential normative failure of management is pervasive mismanagement. Four facets of management incompetence can be identified across organizational ethnographies. These four aspects of mismanagement concern the organization of production, leadership, communication, and repair. Variables measuring these aspects of mismanagement, their codings, means, and standard deviations are presented in Table 4.3. These four variables are factor analyzed and the results are used to construct a standardized mismanagement scale in a manner identical to that used for management abuse. The factor analysis results are reported in Appendix C, Table 4. The factor analysis indicates that the four characteristics are closely related and form a single scale with high internal reliability.

Table 4.3. *Mismanagement Measures*

Variables	Codings	Mean	S.D.[a]	N
Mismanagement	standardized scale[b]	0.00	1.00	108
Organization of production	(1) exceptional, (2) good, (3) adequate, (4) marginal, (5) catastrophic	2.87	1.03	99
Leadership	(1) exceptional, (2) good, (3) adequate, (4) marginal, (5) catastrophic	2.83	.92	103
Communication	(1) good, (2) average, (3) poor	2.13	.80	101
Repair	(1) good, (2) average, (3) poor	1.78	.73	78

[a] Standard deviation.
[b] See Appendix C for factor analysis results used in the scale construction.

As with abusive management behaviors, mismanagement is closely linked to direct personal supervision. The score on the standardized mismanagement scale for workplaces that rely on direct personal supervision is .23, versus −.34 for workplaces based on indirect forms of supervision (F-test, p = .004).

Failure to provide an effective organization of production is the most fundamental act of mismanagement. Ineffective organizations of production can involve the purchase of faulty components, failure to schedule activities in a coherent fashion, or any number of other failures. Leadership implies setting standards for excellence and identifying effective ways to achieve these standards. Good communication is important for keeping employees informed about goals, procedures, and expectations. Finally, having equipment in good repair is essential for effective production, and for the safety of workers.

An example of mismanagement is provided by an ethnography of a bank. In this setting, chronic ineffectiveness has become an assumed way of life:

> There is this paralysis at the middle levels of the organization. If you want anything done, you have to go to the top. You can't get anything from the middle because they're all scared stiff. . . . I was an officer [for four years]. I finally had to drop it because it really got to my health. It was always being caught in the middle and not being able to do a good job. That's why bankers drink a lot. They don't like their job, and they use alcohol to relax. (Jackall 1978:140)

The secretarial staff confirms this evaluation of the bank management as incompetent: "I get really annoyed with people sometimes. Like T., the assistant manager, had customers at his desk yesterday; and I must have spent one-half hour at his desk trying to find out what I had to type for these people's accounts, and *he didn't know the answer*. That type of thing really gripes me. . . . They should just fire him" (Jackall 1978:146; emphasis in original).

Repeated reports of bad leadership also emerge from an ethnography of clerical work:

> 'Mostly, they are old fogies who have been here for twenty or twenty-five years. They made it by virtue of seniority and are not very competent. Mine would do best to retire to the country.'
>
> 'Mr. X is not a real manager. He does his work, but he does not have a manager's temperament. All in all, we are badly managed, badly compensated, badly encouraged.'

'. . . What an employee hates most is to be criticized in front of everyone; that's not the way to do things.' (Crozier 1964:117)

An example of *good* leadership and communication is provided by an ethnography of a plant producing home tableware. The ethnographer describes the manager's activities in the following terms:

> In the plant [the manager] discussed production problems and passed the time of day with groups of workers. He appeared alert and attentive and obviously enjoyed conversation with everyone, especially the older heads of factory families. Talking with people and listening to them was what he did best. (Savage and Lombard 1986:59)

Mismanagement and abuse are present in many workplaces, especially those characterized by direct personal supervision, and are experienced by workers as significant challenges to their dignity and well-being. How then do employees respond to mismanagement and abuse and, conversely, to good management citizenship?

Responses to Abuse

We have seen that employees frequently resist direct personal supervision. But how do they respond more directly to mismanagement and abuse, which we have identified as the underlying problems arising from direct personal supervision? Figure 4.1 displays resistance and citizenship activities by levels of management abuse. The figure shows a strong gradient for citizenship and resistance from low abuse (1st quintile) to high abuse (5th quintile). As abuse increases, resistance increases and citizenship declines. The gradients for both citizenship and resistance are highly statistically significant (F-test for linearity, $p < .001$).

An example of worker solidarity in resistance to abusive conditions is provided by an ethnography of agricultural workers at a sugar cane plantation. Small-scale confrontations between workers and supervisors over reduced wages and deteriorating conditions occurred over several days eventually escalating into a series of work stoppages and refusals to plant. These actions became precursors for larger scale actions in which workers organized in mass at the hacienda and directly confronted the owner of the plantation with their demands (Rutten 1982:151–155).

A similar but more quickly developing series of events occurred at an apparel factory when workers were accused of missewing garments. The episode started with the following confrontation:

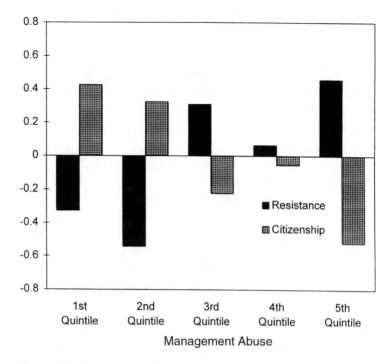

Figure 4.1. Management abuse, worker resistance, and citizenship.

> If you continue to treat us like animals you will find your
> work in this factory becoming very difficult. We are not
> animals to be treated without any respect. We are human
> beings. I have been a tailor with Narayan Bros. for over seven
> years and have never during this time sewn short trousers like
> that pair we are talking about now. (Kapferer 1972:243)

As the dispute progressed, other tailors gathered around and began
chanting derogatory names at the offending supervisor who quickly
exited the line to avoid a confrontation. Such forms of informal resistance can be highly effective in combatting abuse if workers have the
courage to carry them out, and if they are backed by their coworkers.

Abusive management behavior can have significant sting to provoke
the possibility of sabotage from workers as a response. An example
occurs when a new and stricter supervisor is assigned to an automobile
assembly line to increase output:

> With a tight grip on the whip, the new bossman started riding
> the crew. No music. . . . No working up the line. No leaving

the department. No doubling-up. No this, no that. No questions asked.

No way. After three nights of this imported bullyism, the boys had had their fill. Frames began sliding down the line minus parts. Rivets became cross-eyed. Guns mysteriously broke down. The repairmen began shipping the majority of the defects, unable to keep up with the repair load. (Hamper 1991:206)

Workers are also sometimes assertive in resisting sexual harassment and other forms of abuse based on their social characteristics. One way to cope with sexual harassment is to respond in kind. This creates an atmosphere of sexual banter in which everyone is victimized. This solution may not be optimal, but at least it makes the abuse a two-way exchange. An ethnographer at a British apparel factory reports: "On a day-to-day basis the women produced a steady stream of taunts and jibes on the sexual prowess (or lack of it) of the men. None of this, however, altered the unequal relations between the men and the women" (Westwood 1984:23).

Unwanted physical contact can sometimes provoke a physical response. A study of shipyard workers reports an example of direct retaliation by a female worker. "This fellow came up and took hold of my ankle and without even thinking I just brought that hammer right down on his hard hat and knocked his glasses off and broke them. That's the only time anybody ever tried anything" (Kesselman 1990:61). Alternatively, employees can simply request that the abuse or harassment stop. An ethnography of police work reports an episode in which a sergeant puts his arm around a new recruit. She responds by saying: "If you want to put your hands on me, put me under arrest; otherwise, keep your hands off" (Martin 1980:149).

Resistance to abuse can also involve symbolically turning the tables on the abuser by inverting the status hierarchy so that the abuser is declared the fool. Paralegals working in law firms practice this strategy in dealing with arrogant and abusive lawyers. They get together in "gripe sessions" when the lawyers are not around and denigrate them as "egotistical jerks, petty tyrants, 'drones,' 'dweebs,' and workaholics with no social skills" (Pierce 1995:162). In addition, they commonly refer to them as "helpless whiny babies" thus reversing the asymmetrical power relation between attorneys and paralegals. The use of gossip as a means for inverting the status hierarchy between corporate secretaries and their bosses is also noted by Sotirin and Gottfried (1999).

Management expectations that employees work under unsafe conditions can be important in igniting resistance. An ethnographer describing a commercial construction project reports an episode in which a supervisor stands up to the job superintendent to protect his work crew from unsafe conditions. In this instance, safety concerns have pitted employees and their immediate supervisor against higher management:

> The bricklayer foreman said that he was not going to permit the removal of any of the braces that were holding the timbers and boards. . . . He said the braces would have to be built into the manhole and burned out after the manhole was completed. The braces were hydraulic shoring braces that were rented from an equipment supplier and cost a good deal of money. The assistant superintendent taunted the bricklayer for showing fear over working in the hole without braces. All of the other men in the room jumped on the assistant super for being willing to jeopardize the lives of the men over a matter of money. No one questioned the courage of the bricklayer foreman. Rather, he was seen as exercising good judgment in protecting the welfare of the men working for him. (Applebaum 1981:87)

Unions have played a leading role in helping workers resist abuse (Juravich and Bronfenbrenner 1999). Along with higher wages and better benefits, protection from arbitrary management actions has been a central concern for trade unions. Unions protect workers from abuse through providing grievance procedures and through acting as ombudsmen for employees. An ethnography of a steel mill reports on how the union successfully contested the unfair firing of a worker just prior to his retirement:

> When the doctor examined Bill Fenderson, a mill operator who blacked out while on the job, he diagnosed it as 'due to high blood pressure,' and ruled Fenderson unfit for any work in the plant. . . . Whereupon, the company terminated Fenderson.
>   Fenderson had fourteen years in the plant, and under the union contract in force at that time, it was necessary to work fifteen years to qualify for a company pension due to disability. He was short one year. If Fenderson were let go he would have got nothing from the plant – no pension, no insurance, no severance pay, and only the slimmest chance for a job in some other plant. . . .
>   When Fenderson's local union grievanceman produced the letter from the family physician stating that Fenderson was

being treated by him for the flu, and that his past medical history showed *low* blood pressure, Dr. Small and the company hastily retreated, and Fenderson was restored to his job. (Spencer 1977:186–188)

Unions have been a central force in challenging management abuse. They have played a crucial role in limiting some of the worst forms of abuse and in contesting management by fiat (Ackers, Smith, and Smith 1996; Wellman 1995).

One of the continuing challenges to dignity and well-being for workers in contemporary society is to find full-time, nonmarginal employment. Various forms of contingent, marginal, and part-time employment have become prevalent across many industrialized nations (Freeman 1994). In workplace ethnographies, the issue of reduced or restricted hours is often highlighted as an important problem facing workers. Reduced hours are reported in almost half of the workplace ethnographies analyzed. The consequences of reduced hours for resistance and citizenship are reported in Table 4.4.

Table 4.4. *Working under Reduced Hours*

Variables	Full-time	Reduced Hours	Significance[a]
Resistance scale	−.43	.24	.002
Effort bargaining	1.51	1.85	.025
Absenteeism	.56	.85	.021
Quits	.76	.73	.777
Conflict with supervisors or managers	2.54	3.26	.000
Machine sabotage	.17	.24	.547
Procedure sabotage	.60	.81	.059
Social sabotage	.41	.75	.005
Strikes	.12	.47	.000
Citizenship scale	.00	−.20	.366
Cooperation	2.35	2.25	.456
Pride in work	2.26	2.11	.412
Commitment	.56	.39	.133
Meaningful work	2.00	1.79	.254
Creativity	2.56	2.31	.348
Job satisfaction	2.98	2.79	.457
Ethnographies (N)	43	42	

[a] Two-tailed t-test.

Reduced hours appear to have relatively few consequences for citizenship. That is, employees with either full-time or part-time work are equally likely to engage in citizenship behaviors, such as taking pride in work and being committed to organizational goals. Reduced hours, however, generate significant resistance on the part of workers, including greater absenteeism, conflict with supervisors, social sabotage, and strikes.

An example of absenteeism in response to anticipated seasonal layoffs is provided by an ethnography of a pickle factory:

> At dinner break, the veterans group makes its first reprisal. We are at Oxie's, a bar about three minutes' walk from the factory. . . .
> 'What happens if we just don't go back on time? They can dock us, but I bet they wouldn't fire us all.'
> 'Couldn't even start the line,' Alfred says. 'We got the briner, the capper, and the pasteurizer all right here. Right?'
> Carl then points out that he is assigned as backup to all three machines. We think about it for a moment. Then Johnson T. turns and yells, 'Hey, at the bar – send us another pitcher.'
> It is the best beer I will drink all year. (Turner 1980:57–58)

These workers are making a rational calculation of their commitment to the job based on the commitment of their employer to them. Employers utilizing contingent employment strategies put themselves at risk of such calculations.

Heightened conflict with management following a period of reduced hours is also evidenced in an ethnography of a British truck manufacturing company. The company experiences several waves of declining market share across a period of years. The early waves are of limited duration and are offset by shortened workweeks and voluntary retirements. However, the company eventually enters a period of more sustained decline. In response, management downsizes employment, reduces wages, and intensifies work. The expectation that things will quickly "return to normal" is soon lost to layoffs, chronic shift reductions and limitations on hours. "[Workers] just don't want to work for Liftco any longer. . . . The feeling of loyalty goes nowhere in the company. People used to like working for Liftco but now they feel there is no future" (Cressey 1985:63). The ethnographer summarizes the experiences of the period as follows: "What was a smoothly operating system that combined a form of direct democracy with consultation and bargaining and had the support of the mass of the work-force ended in disarray. . . . Sectional disputes were heightened, the morale of the work-force hit rock

bottom and delegates saw no future in either the company or its con-
sultative system" (Cressey 1985:63).

Social sabotage is also a common response to shortened working
hours. Social sabotage occurs in 75 percent of the ethnographies that
report reduced hours. A union splinter group among dockworkers in
New York City engaged in social sabotage against the employers *and* the
union through an underground newsletter in response to an agreement
calling for reduced working time. According to the official paper of the
International Longshoremen's Association: "Since the very first issue [the
newsletter's] only interest has been to stir dissension, to manufacture
grievances, to attack the ILA leadership" (DiFazio 1985:47).

Responses to Mismanagement

Workers respond negatively to incompetence as well as to abuse.
Worker's responses to mismanagement are summarized in Figure 4.2.
Resistance and citizenship are strongly correlated with mismanagement.

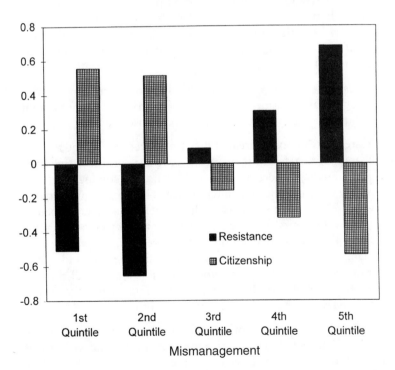

Figure 4.2. Mismanagement, worker resistance, and citizenship.

Resistance increases and citizenship declines as organizations move from effective management (1st quintile) to mismanagement (5th quintile). These trends are even more pronounced than those for abuse (F-test for linearity, $p < .001$).

Incompetent management can be a profoundly demoralizing experience for workers – one that strongly undermines citizenship and encourages resistance. Even workers whose tasks may be somewhat alienating generally manage to take some pleasure from daily accomplishments. Management bumbling, however, can severely undermine even limited meaning and dignity in work: "These small satisfactions were upset when machines broke down or when Carroll disrupted production with one of his schemes. Those were the hardest days for all of us. Without the pleasure of watching our completed work pile up, the day became exactly what it was: routine, long, and boring" (Juravich 1985:132).

In response to a pattern of inept actions by a series of poorly trained supervisors, the workers and shop stewards at a British automobile plant mobilize to undercut the power of new management recruits:

> There are lots of things you can do to make it bad for them. The lads would do half the job, and play around with them. I'd set him up for cases and destroy him in the office. Every time I was in the office I'd say something about him. That's what we *had* to do. We *had* to destroy the foremen. (Beynon 1975:132)

Worker resistance, however, can easily provoke repression by management. For instance, prior to the start of a strike at an automobile assembly plant, management turns out in mass to intimidate workers:

> Yesterday the bosses treated us with contempt. Today, a change of tactics: it's their presence. And what presence! The entire factory echoes with their shouts, their coming and going, their meddlesome interference. They come out of the walls. There were so many of them, then, lying low in their glass-walled lairs! Blue coats, white coats, grey coats, even the three-piece suits, arriving on various pretexts. Everything gives them an opportunity for nagging the workers: this soldering's no good! this spraying's no good! this join's no good! this retouching's no good! . . . They're harassing us as we work, and they stay there to intimidate us. (Linhart 1981:89)

Management responses to worker resistance can range from harassment to outright firings. How effective are repressive management reactions to the withdrawal of effort by workers? The available evidence suggests that the effectiveness of repression is highly variable (Hollinger and Clark 1983:117). In the face of repression it is easy for workers to temporarily discontinue resistance, increase the subterfuge involved, or substitute less observable forms of resistance. Workers' diverse strategies for withholding effort are so adaptable that they are difficult to contain, let alone eradicate.

Because of the possibility of repression, however, resistance is often concealed by duplicitous conformity. Dissimulation is an important cover for many forms of resistance (Scott 1990). An ethnographer reporting on work in a slaughterhouse notes how even symbolic resistance is often cloaked by duplicity:

> A foreman [would] talk to a worker in a non-work related, seemingly friendly conversation. The worker would be smiling and conversing congenially, yet the moment the foreman turned to walk away, the worker would make an obscene gesture (usually involving the middle finger) behind the foreman's back, so that all other workers could clearly see. (Thompson, William 1983:222)

Similarly, Molstad (1988:357) reports on brewery workers' strategies of impression management: "When I'm working for [my current supervisor], I always spend about ten minutes working right under his nose. Then I disappear for the rest of the hour. After my break I go back and do the same thing again. It always works; he thinks I'm busier than hell."

Without the practice of duplicity, many acts of resistance would be perceived and challenged by management. And even where resistance is not entirely concealed, some minimum use of duplicity is still necessary to provide management with a graceful way of ignoring the breach when this is the jointly preferred outcome.

As an initial step in recognizing and confronting mismanagement, workers must first symbolically reject the definition of the situation provided by those in power. Such definitions attribute greater competence, and even infallibility to those in power. Thompson (1978) argues that "every class struggle is at the same time a struggle over values." Only after the existing value system has been rejected, or at least impugned, can resistance emerge. "The refusal to accept the definition of the situation as seen from above and the refusal to condone their own social and ritual marginalization, while not sufficient, are surely necessary for any further resistance" (Scott 1985:240). Once rejection of the dominant definition of the situation occurs, new meanings can evolve and new patterns of behavior become possible (Taylor and Walton 1971:220). Efforts to delegitimate incompetent management behaviors are thus a first crucial step in resisting mismanagement.

Delegitimating incompetent management behaviors almost always involves the construction of an alternative value system in which employees and their values are given greater recognition and weight (Lamont 2000). Gender-based orientations and concerns can sometimes provide a basis for alternative meanings systems. Male employees thus sometimes seek to invert the status hierarchy of the workplace through a focus on masculinity. Masculinity can be demonstrated through aggressive joking and pranks and through claims of sexual prowess and escapades. As Collinson (1988:186) reports: "The uncompromising banter of the shop-floor, which was permeated by uninhibited swearing, mutual ridicule, displays of sexuality and 'pranks,' was contrasted, exaggerated and elevated above the middle class politeness, cleanliness and more restrained demeanour of the offices." A young worker makes explicit use of this alternative meaning system to invert the status system of the factory: "Fellas on the shop-floor are genuine. They're the salt of the earth, but they're all . . . nancy boys in th' offices" (Collinson 1988:186). Such evaluations, heavily colored with moral tones, are essential for establishing shared values and norms for group behavior that are independent of management agendas.

Similarly, Westwood (1984:103–104) notes a strong orientation toward issues of sexuality and dating among young factory women in her study of a British apparel plant. Dating and marriage are central topics of conversation among the women. By focusing on these topics, they divert attention away from the factory hierarchy onto their own concerns. Engagements and weddings become central events carrying greater weight and importance than the production issues identified as crucial by management. Such alternative meaning systems are particularly important where management is seen as incompetent or acts in an abusive manner to undermine the dignity of workers.

The failure to provide an effective organization of production is perhaps the defining characteristic of mismanagement. Table 4.5 reports a range of resistance and citizenship behaviors evaluated across levels of managerial competence. Resistance and citizenship are strongly differentiated by levels of management competence and the linear gradients are statistically significant for most variables. The patterning of resistance and citizenship across the dimension of how well production is organized is among the strongest and most consistent reported in this chapter.

The patterns of resistance and citizenship across the organization of production reiterate many of the points already illustrated through quoted materials. The statistical results indicate greater effort bargaining, quits, and machine, procedure, and social sabotage under marginal or incompetent management. Conversely, greater cooperation, commit-

Table 4.5. *Working under Incompetent Management*

Variables	Exceptional	Good	Adequate	Marginal	Incompetent	Significance[a]
			Organization of Production			
Resistance scale	−.96	−.47	.24	.35	1.01	.000
Effort bargaining	1.25	1.48	1.76	1.67	2.50	.004
Absenteeism	.50	.70	.78	.85	1.00	.063
Quits	.67	.55	.91	.95	.75	.010
Conflict with supervisors or managers	2.36	2.81	2.67	3.10	3.12	.062
Machine sabotage	.17	.10	.18	.42	.67	.016
Procedure sabotage	.17	.59	.77	.95	1.00	.000
Social sabotage	.17	.33	.73	.76	1.00	.000
Strikes	.00	.42	.23	.21	.00	.462
Citizenship scale	.47	.43	−.12	−.26	−.99	.000
Cooperation	2.75	2.61	2.31	2.27	1.50	.000
Pride in work	2.38	2.55	2.03	1.96	1.25	.000
Commitment	.63	.77	.52	.40	.00	.002
Meaningful work	1.88	2.04	1.86	1.71	1.25	.081
Creativity	2.25	2.54	2.43	2.44	2.00	.789
Job satisfaction	3.13	3.34	2.93	2.39	1.50	.000
Ethnographies (N)	8	31	30	26	4	

[a] F-test for linearity.

ment, pride in work, and job satisfaction are reported in workplaces with a good or exceptional organization of production.

Chaotic and mismanaged workplaces undercut workers' pride and erect barriers to quality work. The consequences of poorly organized workplaces can also spill over to coworker relations, further undermining organizational effectiveness. An example is provided by an ethnography of an insurance company where mismanagement and favoritism have made employees suspicious of each other and wary of everyone:

> Frequent complaints were competitiveness, lack of cooperation, favoritism, and politicking. Laurie, for instance, finds the friendliness in her department a 'false kind of friendliness,' with underlying competitiveness; Ruth says that 'the natives are restless . . . and disgruntled' in her area due to favoritism and competitiveness; Herman says that the long-term coworker relationships tend to become intense and claustrophobic. (Burris 1983:232–233)

Conversely, an effective organization of production, including appropriate technology and equipment, can be a foundation for pride and satisfaction in work. An ethnography of a British fishing fleet provides evidence of the pleasure that workers take in being able to use the best procedures and equipment:

> You used t' carry two lots o' bobbins, big ones an' small ones, an yuh bridles used t' be more or less the same. They'd be long ones an' short ones. Yeah, you'd hev the long ones f' cod an' rooker an' the swimmin' fish, an' you'd hev the short ones f' the soles an' plaice. You used t' swap bridles just like yuh did ground-ropes. That wuz one o' the good things about trawlin' – you could change yuh gear t' suit yuh fishin'.
> (Butcher 1980:83)

Social Group Differences

In this chapter, we have focused on the consequence of direct personal supervision, mismanagement, and abuse. But what of potential differences between social groups in how they respond to the workplace? How might these differences influence resistance and citizenship? One of the benefits of analyzing organizational ethnographies is the range of workplaces studied. This range allows us to examine not only a variety of management styles, but also a variety of different labor force compositions.

Table 4.6 displays some of the key factors discussed in this chapter across social groups defined by union membership, gender, race, time period, and nation. All contrasts that are statistically significant at or above the .10 level are highlighted in the table.

There are fewer significant differences across social groups than when resistance and citizenship are evaluated across levels of mismanagement and abuse. Resistance and citizenship thus appear to be more a consequence of management behavior (or misbehavior) than of social differences between groups at work. There are, nevertheless, some significant differences between social groups.

The pattern of management abuse appears to be undifferentiated by unionization, gender or racial composition of the work force, time period, or nation. Unjust firings, however, appear to occur more frequently in workplaces with higher minority representation which gives credence to claims of discriminatory treatment (Feagin 1991; Williams 1987). Layoffs, by contrast, are only differentiated between union and nonunion environments. The finding that layoffs occur more frequently

Table 4.6. *Abuse, Mismanagement, Worker Resistance, and Citizenship across Social Groups*

Variables	N	Abuse Scale	Firings	Layoffs	Organization of Production[a]	Resistance	Citizenship
Union	69	.02	.71	**2.47**	2.78	.08	−.10
Nonunion	33	.00	.68	**1.74**	3.00	−.15	.20
Significance[b]		*.759*	*.804*	*.011*	*.346*	*.297*	*.154*
Exclusively male (100%)	36	−.13	.57	3.03	**2.50**	−.25	.15
Some female	17	.22	.80	3.47	**3.12**	−.08	.21
Gender mixed (25%–75%)	30	−.18	.74	3.38	**2.93**	.17	−.19
Mostly female	19	.07	.73	3.28	**3.29**	.09	−.05
Significance[c]		*.748*	*.241*	*.160*	*.011*	*.113*	*.222*
Majority group (100%)	14	.15	**.50**	2.42	2.67	−.40	**.28**
Some minority	24	.07	**.78**	2.38	2.95	.00	**.47**
Ethnically mixed (25%–75%)	16	−.12	**.91**	2.20	2.93	.38	**−.42**
Mostly minority	8	.81	**.86**	1.60	2.71	.05	**−.14**
Significance[c]		*.383*	*.072*	*.241*	*.845*	*.102*	*.036*
Pre-1975	46	.05	.67	2.21	3.16	.08	−.10
1975 and after	62	−.04	.73	2.20	3.11	−.06	.08
Significance[b]		*.641*	*.562*	*.965*	*.811*	*.465*	*.355*
United Kingdom	31	−.08	.67	2.40	2.89	**.34**	**−.35**
United States	57	.12	.69	2.28	2.91	**−.13**	**.18**
Significance[b]		*.367*	*.867*	*.708*	*.945*	*.043*	*.020*

Note: All contrasts that are significant at p ≤ .10 are in bold type.
[a] Organization of production is coded so that high numbers represent poor organization (see Table 4.3).
[b] *t*-test for contrast between two groups.
[c] F-test for linearity.

in union settings is consistent with the widely recognized strategy of management use of temporary layoffs in union settings and wage reductions in nonunion settings (Edwards 1995). This pattern has emerged, at least in part, because wages are more resistant to downward pressure in union settings than in nonunion settings (Freeman 1994).

The coherency of the organization of production is differentiated only by gender, with women tending to work in more disorganized settings. This difference is consistent with the employment of women in part as an auxiliary labor force used in marginal settings (Hakim 1996; Reskin and Padavic 1994). Note, however, that abuse, resistance, and citizenship are undifferentiated by the gender composition of the work force (see also Hodson 1989; Loscocco 1990). It thus appears that men and women are equally likely to experience abuse at the workplace, although the specifics of the abuse may differ. Similarly, men and women are equally likely to engage in resistance or citizenship behaviors, although, again, the specifics of the forms of resistance or citizenship may differ between the sexes (Crompton and Harris 1998; Lee-Treweek 1997).

Work forces with a significant proportion of minority employees are not more likely to engage in resistance behaviors. However, minority work forces are less likely to exhibit citizenship behaviors. This reluctance to be good citizens in the workplace may be a direct outgrowth of the heavy reliance on firing and on other forms of discriminatory management behavior regarding minority work forces.

The only social characteristic that consistently differentiates workers' resistance and citizenship behaviors is nation. Workers in the United Kingdom exhibit more resistance and less citizenship than workers in the United States. The comparison is consistent with observations based on international survey data. Cheng and Kalleberg (1996), for example, note that American employers report higher levels of performance than do British employers (see also Edwards 1995). The ethnographic data suggest that this contrast is based on both higher levels of citizenship in the United States and on lower levels of resistance.

A worker in a British apparel factory evidences the sort of soldiering that appears to be more typical in the United Kingdom than in the United States:

> Sometimes I think I could throw all this work out of the window. Sometimes it gets on top of you. . . . I just feel I want to pack it all in. I want to get miles away. I just can't go on any more. . . . I feel I would like to go to the doctor and be able to have a few days off. (Pollert 1981:119–120)

A contrasting example from the United States is provided by an ethnography of an inland fishery:

> There is a note of pride in Lewis Keller's voice when he says that Lay Brothers was the biggest fishery in the world at that time. He clearly gives credit to John Lay's drive to succeed for this accomplishment, and as a worker he feels a sense of sharing in it. (Lloyd and Mullen 1990:103)

The more clearly differentiated class boundaries in the United Kingdom are likely contributors to the pattern of greater resistance and less citizenship in the United Kingdom than in the United States. Such differences have long been noted by researchers as components of "American exceptionalism" leading to lower levels of class awareness and labor organizing in the United States (Form 1973; Wright 1997).

Perhaps one of the most notable findings from Table 4.6 is actually the absence of a finding. None of the aspects of organizational life or worker behavior are differentiated across time – no time trends are observed for abuse, mismanagement, resistance, or citizenship. To evaluate time trends, we use two time periods differentiated by the end of the post-Second World War economic boom in the mid-1970s and the beginning of a period of increased world competition and accelerated organizational restructuring. These same findings are repeated, however, in analyses using a linear time trend.

In summary, we observe relatively few differences between social groups in the nature of the challenges they face to dignity at work, or in the nature of their quest for dignity. The differences that are observed, such as the greater employment of female workers in marginal settings, are consistent with prior knowledge about the workplace. And even these differences appear muted relative to the strong patterning of resistance and citizenship by mismanagement and abuse.

Conclusions

Mismanagement and abuse appear to be principal causes of worker resistance. They are also deeply implicated in the undermining of worker citizenship. Across a wide range of workplaces, employees are interested in taking pride in their work and gaining meaning from it. Mismanagement and abuse, however, rob them of this opportunity in many employment settings. Few employees can take pride in their work or will give extra effort when faced with abuse or under circumstances in which those in control have made it impossible to work effectively. The role of management in providing a minimally effective organization of production seems especially important in reducing resistance and encouraging citizenship.

There appear to be no secular trends in the occurrence of abuse, mismanagement, citizenship, or resistance (see also Barley and Kunda 1992). This finding supports neither wholly optimistic nor wholly pessimistic projections about the future of work. Worker resistance and the absence of worker citizenship in abusive and poorly managed workplaces may act as limiting factors on the spread of such workplaces. But worker resistance has not eliminated such workplaces. Worker resistance and limited citizenship behaviors, however, may be more directly implicated in the erosion of purely personal forms of supervision and their replacement by hybrid forms that include technical, bureaucratic, and bilateral forms of control. We turn to the quest for dignity and the nature of worker resistance and citizenship in such workplaces in upcoming chapters.

It does not appear likely that mismanagement and abuse will be eliminated at any time in the near future. The continued prevalence of mismanagement and abuse in the workplace in the early years of the third millennium poses one of the most significant challenges to creating a humane workplace in which all employees can find dignity and meaning in work.

5

Avoiding Overwork

Many people come home from work physically and emotionally exhausted. For those who are lucky enough to avoid abusive bosses and chaotic work settings, overwork can still be a serious obstacle in the quest for dignity at work. Although workdays have shortened appreciably since the sixteen-hour days of the early industrial revolution, overwork continues to be a problem for many. An easy way for companies to increase their competitiveness, and their profits, is to demand longer hours and greater effort from their employees. Greater effort and longer hours are frequently offered as solutions to heightened global competitiveness, but at great cost in terms of human exhaustion and misery.

Assembly work, in which the division of labor is pushed to extreme levels, is the locus of some of the most concerted efforts to intensify work to the limits of human endurance. In this chapter we examine the nature of assembly work and the experiences of those who do assembly work. We also examine the responses of employees to the challenges of assembly work. In this and subsequent chapters we also examine the problems of overwork for nonassembly workers as well.

Assembly work can be organized either around a moving conveyor line or around stationary workbenches. On an assembly line, the work is brought by a continuously moving conveyor line directly to the worker, who stands in a single position and completes one or more tasks on each item as it passes. Assembly-line work is typical of automobile manufacture, food processing, and many other types of manufacturing work. In bench assembly, workers perform a specific task on a product or component and then pile these products or components up in boxes, trays, or racks to be taken away when filled. Bench assembly is typical of apparel manufacturing and many types of electronics assembly.

The world of assembly work is largely invisible to the typical consumer of manufactured goods. In urban areas, assembly work often occurs in large, often featureless buildings in isolated industrial areas that are far removed from the daily rounds of most people. Much assembly work

115

also occurs in rural areas and in less industrialized nations where labor costs are low.

An important type of assembly work common in both industrialized and less industrialized nations is food processing. Hogs, cattle, and chickens, for example, are all processed using assembly-line methods. Similarly, shell fish, seafood, and canned foods of all kinds are processed by workers who either work at moving conveyor lines or who work at stationary benches doing highly repetitive cutting, cleaning, handling, and packing work (Griffith 1993).

Highly repetitive assembly work has not been eliminated by the technological revolution brought about by microprocessors (Garson 1988). One reason is that the application of microprocessor technology has proceeded much more rapidly in the handling of information than in the handling of physical objects. The reasons for this are basically economic. A $2,000 personal computer can be an effective tool for increasing the productivity of a white-collar worker. Industrial robots, however, cost $100,000 to buy and potentially another $100,000 annually in maintenance and operating costs. In relation to the high costs of industrial robots, low-wage assembly workers remain economically competitive in many applications. Unfortunately, the pace of assembly work may be further intensified by competition from robots and by the pace set by robots in handling selected aspects of assembly (Thomas 1994).

Assembly work is typically organized according to the principles of scientific management first developed by Frederick Taylor (1911) and later applied to the automobile assembly line by Henry Ford (Womack, Jones, and Roos 1990). Scientific management involves the simplification of work to its most basic components. Workers are then hired to perform these simplified actions in a repetitive, highly scripted, and time-pressured fashion. These principles see some of their most rigorous applications in assembly work. Scientific management, however, is not a perfect system. One of the factors limiting the spread of scientific management is that much work retains at least some element of indeterminacy because of variability in equipment and components (Stinchcombe 1959). Breakdowns are not uncommon but deskilled and alienated workers may lack the skills or the motivations to prevent or resolve problems in production.

In spite of the limits of scientific management resulting from continuing variability in products and components, extreme rationalization pervades many sectors of employment leading to increased routinization and stress at work. The rash of repetitive strain injuries, such as carpal tunnel syndrome, that have followed the spread of personal computers into offices suggests that, even with new computer-assisted technologies, repetitive work activities continue to define many jobs.

Overwork can occur through excessive hours as well as through intensification of work. Many assembly workers find that they cannot earn enough to live on without working frequent overtime. Workers involved in the "miracle of industrialization" in South China, for example, frequently work excessive hours to make ends meet. Employees in one factory submitted a lengthy portfolio of letters describing problems of overwork and exploitation to the Labor Management Bureau responsible for protecting employees' rights. "The low wage rate is exploitation. ... You repress the hourly rate and force workers to make a living by doing overtime shifts. ... A worker can earn [a living] only if she does 200 hours of overtime [per month]. This is outright exploitation, pushing workers to work like a machine" (Lee 1998:60).

Excessive hours are often expected of workers in more industrially advanced nations as well. Companies consider it easier and cheaper to require overtime of existing employees than to undertake the effort and expense of hiring and training new workers. Low wages help ensure that workers will want and need extra hours. And even where the sting of necessity is more distant, consumer-oriented societies are still successful in motivating extra hours spent on the job in exchange for satisfying wants that are at least in part created through advertising. Recent increases in consumer debt further constrain many workers to work long hours in what is experienced by many as a twenty-first century equivalent to debt bondage (Schor 1998).

The latest surge of rationalization and intensification of work in the global economy has been produced by the spread of Japanese work practices, both through Japanese transplant operations and through international and transnational companies mimicking Japanese practices (Elger and Smith 1998). Japanese production practices entail many diverse elements but at the core is the idea of *kaizen* or "continuous improvement." *Kaizen* implies a continuous effort to increase efficiency. One of the chief ways to increase efficiency is to work harder. A fundamental corollary of *kaizen* is thus the concept of "full utilization" of working time. Unneeded movements are eliminated and time away from immediately productive activities is reduced to a minimum. An important consequence of *kaizen* has been an intensification of work under Japanese production techniques (Dohse, Jurgens, and Malsch 1985).

An additional component of the success of the Japanese system of production has been the rigorous application of the principles of scientific management implemented through the work group rather than through an industrial engineer. As part of *kaizen* procedures, workers are trained to do time studies on each other and to brainstorm on how to lessen the time needed to complete each task. Employees are told that "they are the source of the knowledge needed to run the plant." This gives support and recognition to their contributions, but as part of the bargain they are also expected to intensify their work efforts (Graham 1995:105).

Through the application of *kaizen* and the related concepts of full utilization and production teams, Japanese manufacturers strive to achieve continuous increases in productivity. As a consequence, in a typical U.S. automobile plant, assembly-line employees apply approximately forty to fifty seconds out of every minute to direct production tasks, while in Japanese automobile plants direct production activities occupy close to sixty seconds per minute (Fucini and Fucini 1990:37). These differentials also show up in terms of the total labor hours needed to assemble a car. The average time per assembled vehicle in U.S. plants is 25.1 hours; in Japanese transplants in the United States it is 21.2 hours; and in plants in Japan it is 16.8 hours (Womack, Jones, and Roos 1990:92). Work intensification in Japanese plants has contributed to lower costs for Japanese cars than similar quality cars built in other industrially advanced nations. Through the related principle of "zero-defects" Japanese companies have also sought continuous improvement in product quality. As a result of these cost and quality differentials, Japanese firms have been able to expand their share of the world automobile market (Perrucci 1994; Womack, Jones, and Roos 1990). But these successes have been obtained at the expense of an intensification of work under Japanese production systems and a corresponding increase in overwork, exhaustion, and repeated stress injuries (Graham 1995:143).

How do workers respond to excessive and repetitive work that leaves them exhausted at the end of the day? The development of the assembly line at Ford Motors quickly led to the birth of the United Auto Workers as workers organized to seek alleviation from the cruelest rigors of the assembly line through collective action (Brecher 1972). But for the many employees who do not have the benefit of a union, and even for many of those who do, the most common reaction may be a grinding acceptance of their working conditions as an inescapable fate. In many assembly jobs, workers are expected to turn off their minds when they enter the factory gate. Such workers must seek life satisfaction through their off-hours activities instead, although even these pursuits may be dampened by limited energy left over after a long day of continuous effort (Chinoy 1955; Lee 1998). In this chapter we explore the nature of contemporary assembly work and workers' responses to assembly work in the quest for dignity at work.

Assembly Work

Assembly work involves a steady and often demanding pace in which workers must repeat a limited and repetitive range of activities. The characteristics of assembly work as reported in organizational ethnographies are summarized in Table 5.1. The table differentiates between assembly-line jobs and stationary bench assembly and contrasts these with nonassembly jobs.

The contrasts in working conditions between assembly and nonassembly work could hardly be starker. Freedom of movement is restricted. The pace of work is much more steady, grinding, and difficult. The comfort of the work area is reduced. Skill and autonomy are restricted and creativity and meaning are reduced. For each aspect, assembly-line work is the most restrictive organization of work with bench assembly generally being intermediate between assembly-line work and nonassembly work.

The packaging warehouse of a chemical factory provides an example of routinized handling and packing work organized on an assembly-line basis:

> The work in the warehouse was . . . completely routine and unskilled. Men filled, sewed and palleted sacks of the product on moving conveyor belts. They controlled the pace of their work but only within the limits set by the belt, and they could not vary the way or order in which the tasks were performed.

Table 5.1. *Assembly Work*

Variables	Assembly Line	Bench Assembly	Nonassembly Work	Significance[a]
Freedom of movement	1.33	1.87	2.33	.000
Difficult pace	2.92	2.40	2.57	.063
Steady pace	.83	.75	.24	.000
Comfort of work area	1.43	1.93	1.90	.044
Skill	1.36	1.87	2.22	.000
Autonomy	1.84	2.50	3.25	.000
Creativity	1.64	2.00	2.81	.000
Meaningful work	1.50	1.62	2.07	.006
Ethnographies (N)	25	16	67	

[a] F-test.

> It was a typical conveyor belt situation with stereotyped
> motions to be performed. (Wedderburn and Crompton
> 1972:81–82)

The employees have no liberty to move from the line or to deviate from
the pace set by the conveyor. Being in a state of continuous activation
can be extremely tiring, both physically and emotionally, leaving workers
drained at the end of the day. It is much easier on the human body and
the human psyche to work at an irregular pace where periods of activity, even intense activity, are interspersed with periods of rest. The
unceasing pressure of the assembly line allows no relaxation from the
demands of the job (Molstad 1986).

An early study of automobile assembly work by Chinoy (1955) notes
how workers seek to avoid work on the assembly line in preference for
maintenance work or other support activities. "They sought to avoid
jobs in which 'you can't take a smoke when you want to,' or 'you can't
go to the toilet when you have to but have to wait for the relief man.'
. . . A frequent complaint was that the fatigue after a day on the line or
at a machine is so great that one has little energy left for other things
one wishes to do" (Chinoy 1955:70).

The principles of rationalized assembly work are much the same
whether an automobile is being assembled on an automated line or a beef
cow is being disassembled on one. Indeed, Ford's inspiration for the automobile assembly line came initially from the moving chains and hooks
used in slaughterhouses. Upton Sinclair's *The Jungle*, which tells the story
of life in the Chicago packing houses of the early twentieth century,
remains one of the most compelling accounts of assembly-line work.

In a contemporary slaughterhouse, which butchers cattle at a rate of
over 180 an hour, workers are constantly pressured by worries about
"getting in a hole." The carcasses go by at a rate of one every twenty
seconds and the workers constantly worry about falling behind and
not being able to catch up. A constant hurried pace defines the daily
experience of work for the men and women on this slaughter line
(Thompson, William 1983:220).

The experiences of another worker in a different slaughterhouse in a
different state highlight the exhausting nature of the work:

> I had never done the monotonous, repetitive motions that I
> did [at the slaughterhouse]. . . . With commuting, the job
> consumed nearly twelve hours of my day – sometimes more –
> and I would reach home stiff with the cold and totally
> exhausted every evening. . . . I dozed whenever I tried to read
> or watch television. I even dozed off one evening when [my

husband] and I were trying to visit with friends. (Fink 1998:37)

A study of a small manufacturing establishment in Taiwan similarly notes the long hours and physically demanding nature of assembly work. Employees in this factory are expected to work no fewer than twenty-eight days a month. They work from nine to eleven and a half hours a day and they are given only a half-hour off for lunch, which is prepared by the owner's wife. When the observer asks a worker how she can work so hard, she replies, "After a while, you get used to it" (Hsiung 1996:115).

For those who can adjust to the pace of assembly work, new challenges emerge. One of these is to avoid injuries and to stay healthy enough to keep up the pace. Another challenge is to find relief from the grinding nature of the work. Assembly-line workers frequently engage in the practice of "working ahead" so that they can take a short break. This practice allows them to take pride and pleasure in momentarily being ahead and to have a few seconds rest as the moving line catches back up. Working ahead also gives workers some sense of control over their activities. Most importantly, however, is the fact that working in short energetic bursts followed by slower periods gives some relief from the grindingly steady pace of the assembly line.

An ethnography of work on a Japanese automobile assemble line reports on how the small pleasures associated with working ahead help workers get through the day and experience some meaning in their work:

> Those of us who remain have to find some pleasure somehow. Shimoyama, for instance, works ahead and then comes to help me. He takes over my position, puts the six bolts into the lock, and tightens them all at once with a nut runner – which takes some skill. When he succeeds he yells excitedly. I do too, whenever I can manage it. Completing the task in two or three seconds, hearing the bolts slide in with a nice click, gives me real pleasure. Even in this kind of detailed, boring work, you need some sort of satisfaction, or you can't go on.
> (Kamata 1982:88–89)

Assembly workers suffer from a lack of autonomy on the job, as well as from overwork. Autonomy involves making choices about the methods or techniques to use, the order in which to do tasks, or the criteria used to evaluate when something has been well done (Breaugh and Becker 1987). These aspects of autonomy have been largely removed from assembly work. Autonomy is even lower for assembly-line workers than for bench assembly workers (see Table 5.1). The lack of autonomy in assembly work has long been noted as leading to lower job satisfaction for assembly workers than for other employees, even employees in the same plant who are doing more skilled and varied maintenance work (Goldthorpe et al. 1968:17). A worker in a brewery reports on the emotional consequences of assembly-line work for his internal mental life: "My hot, noisy brewery allowed me no freedom; I stood tired and listless inspecting bottle after bottle. . . . I preferred to stay in my fantasies, which were less painful than the real world" (Molstad 1986:227).

Assembly work allows significantly less latitude for creativity and meaning than other types of employment. In a classic study of a semi-automated steel mill, a researcher notes how automation has altered the nature of production work. Now that the work is automated, the workers have fewer functions, but they are still tied to one spot and there are high demands for constant alertness:

> The men called it *watching*, and many felt it to be the greatest difference between the old jobs and the new ones. . . . The worker must clearly be on guard to intervene quickly if and when the automatics fail. . . . 'I have to *watch* my two strippers and make sure bar and pipe get kicked into the right trough for the stripper. I have to *watch* the conveyor down to the reheat furnace to make sure we don't pile up or let a pipe hit the bumper. . . . I also *watch* the inserter.' (Walker 1957:32)

The exercise of creativity is essential for working with dignity but creativity has a very limited role in assembly work. A worker in a food processing plant reports little meaning or satisfaction from the job outside of the paycheck:

> It's the kind of job that you can do and not think about. Money's the most important thing here. I wouldn't be in this job if I didn't need the money would I? I'll work hard and get as much in as I can. I offer my body and they pay me for it. I want nothing more to do with them than that. (Nichols and Beynon 1977:74)

Employees in assembly jobs often express frustration at the limiting nature of their work with its stifling repetitiveness and lack of creativity. An ethnography of plywood factories reports the following complaints:

> 'The work? It's boring, I mean, that's the first thing that pops into anybody's mind that works there. That's the worst fight down there is fighting not to get bored. . . .'

'You're doing something that's basically unpleasant. . . .
Most jobs are monotony and repetition. It can drive you
nuts. . . .'
      'I go through times when I get so depressed. But like I say,
it's the only god damn thing I'm programmed for right now.
It's too late for me to go back to school at 45 years old. It's
just that I was stupid when I was young.' (Greenberg
1986:82)

Even supervisors on assembly lines report a fragmented experience of
work based on the demands of the assembly line as the organizing principle of their worklife. A classic ethnography of assembly-line work
reports that the supervisors' interactions are typically brief, lasting less
than a minute. Conversations are often cut short because of the compelling need to attend to some emergency on the line. "Discontinuity and
interruption, these characteristics of the foreman's contacts with others,
may be traced to the compelling demand to keep the line moving and to
take immediate care of any source of difficulty which might cause a stop-
page" (Walker, Guest, and Turner 1956:88).

Yet no work is without its pleasures and we should not overlook meaningful elements of assembly work just because on average it has less
autonomy and more pressure than other types of work. Even seemingly
unskilled work often requires substantial "working knowledge" of the
machinery used, of potential variability in materials, and of the roles of
other workers (Kusterer 1978:178). The mastery of the working knowledge required by a job can be a source of pride and pleasure, even for
those whose work is otherwise repetitive.

Simply meeting the demands of assembly work can also be a source
of pride and pleasure in work. A worker doing highly repetitive inspection work in an apparel factory experiences her job as difficult but
reports great pride in meeting the challenge: "Any work is hard. But I
like whatever is given to me. If it's inspection, I work with a target, trying
not to let anyone else beat me. I like work – any kind of work" (Roberts
1994:88).

Bench assembly contrasts favorably with assembly-line work in terms
of the pace, skill, autonomy, creativity, and meaningfulness of the work
(see Table 5.1). Relative to assembly-line work, bench assembly and
related forms of stationary equipment operation more often involve
significant responsibilities for understanding the limitations of the
equipment and even for light repair and ongoing maintenance. In
assembly-line work these responsibilities are almost always handled by
skilled maintenance workers, leaving the production workers with even
fewer responsibilities and less variety.

An ethnographer reporting on a paper products factory describes how in their daily activities machine operators use working knowledge of repair to distinguish between minor adjustment problems and problems demanding more significant retooling. "[M]achine parts work out of position – chipper knives are particularly prone to do this – and have to be put back where they belong. . . . Operators use the weights from their balancing scale [to tap the chipper knives back into position]. . . . Mechanics expect good operators to use the technique judiciously, that is, to know under what circumstances it is appropriate and under what circumstances a more basic repair is called for" (Kusterer 1978:52–53).

The ability of operators in this paper products plant to keep their machines running also requires judgement about appropriate levels of cleanliness and how cleanliness can influence machine operation:

> Production [requires] that certain critical working parts of the machine be kept free of built-up ink, glue, or paper scraps. If the operator allows these materials to build up, sooner or later the machine will either jam or start to produce defective products. When the machine is running smoothly and everything is going well, this puts the operator in a dilemma. Her basic feeling is that she has a good thing going and she does not want to stop and possibly mess it up. Yet the trouble-making build-up is inexorable. When the machine is running well, it is asking for trouble to stop it – the glue and ink begin to dry and thicken, the stop and start might throw the print out of register. But not stopping and not cleaning the machine is asking for trouble too. (Kusterer 1978:53)

Such decisions provide an opportunity to use judgement and related human abilities that frequently go unused on the assembly line. By exercising these abilities in their daily tasks, production workers achieve a sense of dignity in their work.

Monotony, Exit, and Resistance

What then are the behavioral responses of assembly workers to the monotonous conditions they face in their daily work lives? Is assembly work a breeding ground for resistance and sabotage as it is often portrayed? Ethnographic descriptions of assembly work provide a range of answers to this question. These patterns are displayed in Table 5.2. An examination of the table does not suggest a one-to-one correspondence between assembly work and resistance and sabotage. Rather, assembly workers appear to be selective in the nature of their resistance to

Table 5.2. *Monotony, Exit, and Resistance on the Assembly Line*

Variables	Assembly Line	Bench Assembly	Nonassembly Work	Significance[a]
Resistance scale	.12	.30	−.12	.253
Absenteeism	.85	1.00	.58	.007
Quits	.89	1.00	.67	.019
Effort bargaining	1.90	1.85	1.54	.052
Informal group resistance	2.95	2.25	1.86	.001
Strikes	.48	.43	.14	.002
Theft	.17	1.00	.41	.007
Machine sabotage	.33	.33	.14	.231
Procedure sabotage	.75	.67	.73	.873
Social sabotage	.63	.77	.54	.330
Making out	2.61	3.00	2.94	.590
Making up games	.69	1.00	.79	.135
Ethnographies (N)	25	16	67	

[a] F-test.

monotonous work. Assembly workers quit their jobs and are absent more often than nonassembly employees. They are also more likely to engage in strikes and other collective actions intended to change the conditions of their employment. Sabotage and more individualistic strategies of resistance, such as procedure sabotage, making out, or making up games, however, appear to be equally common in assembly and nonassembly work.

The summary resistance scale shows higher levels of resistance among assembly workers, but this contrast is not statistically significant. Part of the reason for the subdued nature of this contrast may be that the constraints presented by the limited job autonomy and physical movement of assembly workers also act to limit their ability to engage in resistance (Simpson 1999). Employees in more autonomous and skilled positions may simply have greater opportunities to resist management agendas.

One response to the monotony of assembly work is not to show up regularly or to quit the job altogether (see Figure 5.1). As Walker and Guest note in their classic study of assembly-line work, "men with highly repetitive jobs, conveyor paced, and so forth, were far more likely to take time off from work than those whose jobs did not contain such job characteristics" (Walker and Guest 1952:120). A contemporary study of an apparel factory in Japan notes that approximately 30 percent of the work

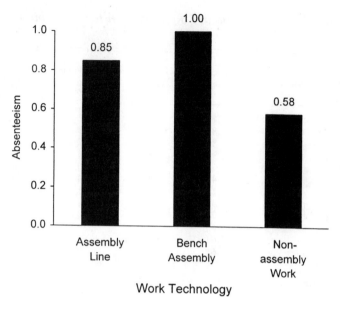

Figure 5.1. Absenteeism and assembly work.

force quits each year (Roberts 1994:56). Assembly workers vote with their feet. By contrast, absenteeism is usually quite low in craft work. An ethnography of skilled construction work notes the virtual absence of turnover. "Absenteeism, turnover, and grievances are almost nonexistent among construction workers. . . . I was aware of five cases where men were fired because of chronic absenteeism. They were all new to construction. On my present road project, it is rare for anyone to be absent" (Applebaum 1981:92).

Another common response to the demands of assembly work is to seek redress in terms of higher pay or improved working conditions through collective action. Both informal group resistance and strikes are markedly higher among assembly workers than among nonassembly workers. Informal group resistance, for instance, is reported as widespread or pervasive in more than 40 percent of the ethnographies of assembly-line work but in only 12 percent of the ethnographies of nonassembly work.

Informal group resistance generally involves conflicts between small groups of workers and their immediate supervisor. Informal group resistance, however, can easily spill over to larger scale actions. A famous ethnography of a British automobile assembly plant, *Working for Ford*, reports how several hundred employees in the Paint, Trim, and Final

Assembly Department walked off the job following the posting of changes in the system of unemployment benefits. A union shop steward describes how the wildcat strike developed:

> It was just after the dinner break. One of the lads on the section said 'the trim lads are walking out.' Well all the lads stopped work then. . . . A number of the lads on my section were really pissed off about it. We all were in fact. The section next to us stopped work and a lot of lads started walking past. Some of them were running and shouting. . . . They were past talking. They just wanted to get outside the gate. I thought, 'If that's what you want you go ahead and do it.' . . . I've seen nothing like it in my life. We had no warning or nothing. They just went outside the gate. Hundreds of them just walking off the job; just like that. (Beynon 1975:169–170)

The spontaneity of these actions and the rapidity of their spread suggest a deep underlying reservoir of resentment among these assembly workers.

This same assembly plant also had a long history of more formal strikes dating from the period when it was first unionized. The stories of these strikes are told to newcomers as part of the plant lore and are recounted by activists, particularly at times of crisis. "The fact that [these stories] were told so often indicates the significance of this period. . . . In handling the present, men call upon the past for guidance. The lessons of the past are learned and handed on as stories" (Beynon 1975:74–75). Strike lore can play a crucial role in building positive self-identities for workers who in their daily work lives have limited power to alter their circumstances.

Worker resistance under assembly work is often directed at regulating the amount of work that is required. Workers want work that is sufficient but not excessive. The intensity and duration of work is thus a key area of conflict between employees and managers. A focus on regulating the amount and intensity of work is most likely to emerge under systems of work organization involving control by technology or by scientific management rather than control by individual supervisors. Under direct supervision, as we saw in Chapter 4, the foremost concern of employees is with problems of mismanagement and abuse. By contrast, under scientific management, work is organized according to minutely detailed procedures. Alternatively, under technical control, the physical layout and organization of the workplace determine the arrangement and pace of work. Scientific management and technical control are designed to extract the maximum possible effort from workers. These defining characteristics of assembly work also become the defining characteristics of employee resistance to assembly work.

Worker resistance oriented toward regulating the amount and intensity of work is largely instrumental in nature. Such activities are sometimes called "effort bargaining" or "making out" (Edwards 1991). For instance, it has long been noted that workers under piece-rate systems typically produce just enough more than the base rate to make a small bonus but resist producing beyond this level in order to avoid having the base rate increased (Burawoy 1979). The efforts of workers to control the pace of work and the associated rewards were an important topic of investigation in early ethnographic studies of factory life. "The objective of the operators was good piece-work prices, and that end justified any old means that would work. One cardinal principle of operator job-timing was that cutting tools be run at lower speeds and 'feeds' than the maximums possible on subsequent production" (Roy 1954:257). Effort bargaining under technical systems of work organization, such as those typical of assembly work, thus tends to have highly specific targets, such as a piece rate or a work rule that a worker finds particularly restrictive, taxing, or unnecessary.

A contemporary example of effort bargaining is provided by an ethnography of small manufacturing shops in Taiwan. The ethnographer describes a group of female employees whose jobs entail painting designs on drinking glasses before the glasses are glazed and fired. The women are engaged in a constant battle over the piece rate for the work. In one episode reported by the ethnographer, the owner stresses the importance of taking extra care with the work and the workers offer their rebuttal:

> 'In principle, you shouldn't rush. Don't let the dye get outside of the lines. The flowers should look natural. They should be painted nicely,' Mr. Lai said.
>
> 'In principle? How dare you business guys talk about principle? Your conscience has long been eaten up by the dog. How can you talk about principles?' (Hsiung 1996:136–137)

The motivation for this running battle is to ensure the workers' earnings while keeping expectations for effort at reasonable levels. But the women also admit to the ethnographer their broader reasons. "We [wrangle over piece rates] a lot. It's just a way to make sure that they won't think we are living at their mercy" (Hsiung 1996:136). The negotiation of expectations about levels of effort is thus an important part of daily work life for these employees.

A sense of empowerment, and the maintenance of a shared community among workers, can also be achieved through petty theft and pilferage as forms of resistance. A study of workplace theft suggests that, besides financial gain, revenge against management and thrill seeking are among the most common motivations (Terris and Jones 1982). Shorting one's oppressors can be a great source of pleasure. Often stories of pilferage are told and retold for the pleasure of their symbolism. For example, after detailing the range of small articles that "quietly disappear" from a knitting mill, an ethnographer reports one episode that has been almost mythologized by workers. In this episode, a group of textile workers bundle cloths from racks at night and throw them out into a waiting van below. The employees are eventually caught. "But everyone enjoys the story" (Westwood 1984:99).

Petty theft is thus a common response to felt grievances. Thefts of small items occur at most workplaces and are an important mechanism through which a sense of equity and justice can be reestablished. Indeed, these activities are not typically identified by their practitioners as theft (Mars 1982). Rather, they are seen as part of the fringe benefits offered by the job or as symbolic compensation for inadequate salary or excessive work demands (Hollinger and Clark 1983). Theft appears to be substantially more common under bench assembly than under assembly-line operations (see Table 5.2). The reasons for this differential may lie less in the motivations for theft than in the limited range of opportunities available to assembly-line workers who typically have few occasions to leave their work stations.

In spite of being more likely to quit their jobs and to resist through both informal and formal means, assembly workers are not more likely to engage in sabotage or other more individual strategies of resistance. The contrasts presented in Table 5.2 do not show consistently higher levels in assembly work than in nonassembly work for these more individual forms of resistance.

Procedure sabotage is an especially common form of resistance across both assembly and nonassembly work. An example of procedure sabotage in an assembly-line setting is provided by an ethnography of a slaughterhouse:

> It was a fairly common practice for workers who were covered with beef blood to come over to the tub of swirling water designed to clean the tongues, and as soon as the inspector looked away, wash their hands, arms, and knives in the tub. This procedure was strictly forbidden by the rules. If witnessed by a foreman or inspector, the tub had to be emptied, cleaned, and refilled, and all the tongues in the tub at the time had to be put in the 'inedible' tub. (Thompson, William 1983:231)

The ethnographer also notes that the workers seemed to delight in successfully pulling off this violation of procedures.

Procedure sabotage is also common in bench assembly work. An ethnography of a paper products factory provides an example of how employees routinely violate procedures. Their motivation in this instance is to complete the work without wasting too much time with faulty materials:

> Paper that is too waxy is too sticky and too thick. Both
> characteristics can increase the likelihood that the paper will
> jam the machine. . . . The operators' principal strategy to deal
> with waxy paper is to try to get the material handlers on their
> side to agree that this particular roll of paper is so waxy that
> it physically cannot be run at all. . . . The material handler will
> use his knife to 'cut down' the roll, removing the outer inches
> of paper in hopes that the inner parts of the roll will be less
> waxy. If the inner layers are not any better, the material
> handler may keep cutting right down to the core. . . . Since it
> is only very rarely the case that the paper is literally so waxy
> that it cannot be run on the machine, management defines this
> 'cutting down' operation as unnecessary paper waste.
> (Kusterer 1978:48)

Ethnographic reports of procedure sabotage suggest that such practices are common across workplaces and are not restricted to assembly work. An ethnography of police work, for example, reports a chronic pattern of procedure sabotage. Many of the evasions require no elaborate or formal cover. "Many jobs turn out to be unfounded, crank calls. . . . The officer can simply refrain from telling the dispatcher the call is unfounded, taking the time he would use for the assignment for his own purposes" (Rubinstein 1973:117).

Making out by organizing work to maximize benefits relative to efforts is also common across workplaces. An example of making out in a service setting is provided by an ethnography of waitressing. Waitresses strive to boost their tips by providing special services and being friendly. As one waitress put it, "I'll sell you the world if you're in my station" (Paules 1991:27). Waitresses also control the flow of customers, and thus of tips, by bypassing the hostess and chaperoning customers directly to their own sections. They also avoid tasks that are time consuming and produce little tip income. For instance, it is not uncommon for a waitress to tell a customer that the milkshake machine is broken because she prefers activities that generate a higher income relative to such time consuming activities as making milkshakes. All of these strategies maximize income and avoid unnecessary work, which the waitresses define as work that does not directly produce tip income. Strategically, these activities are identical to those used by assembly workers operating under piece rates to make out at the end of the day.

Employees in assembly jobs may have greater motivations to engage in procedure sabotage, making out, and other forms of withholding effort than employees in nonassembly work because of the greater physical pressures of the work and the stress of continuous activity. However, they do not appear to engage in these forms of resistance with greater frequency than do other workers. The reason for this may lie in the constrained physical mobility of assembly workers and the manner in which this limits opportunities for resistance. The argument here is similar to one made in the literature on social movements and protest activities. The birth of a social movement requires that a group has a strongly felt set of grievances. But grievances are not sufficient for the success of a social movement. The group also has to have the resources or capacities to transform their grievances into action and to demand redress (Aminzade 1984:451).

The strict application of scientific management and technical control to assembly work can thus be seen as successful, both in getting the work out and in limiting at least some forms of resistance. But this "success" is achieved at considerable cost in terms of the human dignity of those who labor under these most rationalized and pressured forms of work. The success may also be a Pyrrhic victory for management. As we have seen, assembly work results in increased rates of informal group resistance and formal strikes. In addition, as we will see in the next section, assembly work is also associated with reduced worker citizenship. Production systems have become increasingly complex over time and have come to require ever greater worker initiative. With these changes it is increasingly apparent that the "successes" of scientific management come at a great cost in terms of lost potential for implementing newer and more productive organizations of work based on increased employee involvement, initiative, and citizenship.

Lost Opportunities for Citizenship

The overwork and physical stress associated with assembly work can erode enthusiasm and citizenship on the part of employees. Scientific management and technical control may be efficient in getting the work out in a formal sense but much is lost in the process. Not only is the dignity of workers eroded through excessive work, but opportunities to increase output or improve product quality, which regularly occur in production, will be left largely undeveloped by overworked and exploited workers. Rigid forms of production devised to increase the profitability of enterprises through work intensification may thus be counterproductive in the long run.

The ongoing drive toward exploitation embodied in capitalism was clearly anticipated in the writings of Karl Marx. Marx saw the full development of capitalism as desirable because capitalism's productivity would lay the foundation for a revolutionary transformation toward a society with a more equal distribution of accumulated wealth. It was Max Weber though who first identified the possibility that the logic of capitalism might itself be limited by being rational only in a formal sense while being substantively irrational. The undercutting of human initiative under the formal rationality of assembly work provides a compelling case in point.

Research in the social sciences has convincingly demonstrated that organizations of work that deny workers the opportunity to participate in daily decisions about work and that fail to respect their dignity as human beings generate less effort on the part of employees (Drucker 1993). Conversely, work organizations that provide for participation and recognition elicit greater effort (Pfeffer 1998; Walsh and Tseng 1998). The pattern of reduced effort and citizenship under assembly work is clearly evidenced in Table 5.3. The standardized citizenship scale is negative for both assembly-line work and bench assembly work and positive for nonassembly work. The various components of citizenship reinforce this general pattern. Cooperation, effort, pride, peer training,

Table 5.3. *Reduced Citizenship in Assembly Work*

Variables	Assembly Line	Bench Assembly	Nonassembly Work	Significance[a]
Citizenship scale	−.39	−.24	.20	.024
Cooperation	2.24	2.19	2.48	.092
Extra effort	.64	.57	.88	.009
Pride in work	1.77	2.13	2.37	.004
Job satisfaction	2.30	2.71	3.14	.004
Good soldier	2.59	2.57	3.45	.011
Peer training	2.67	2.75	3.33	.033
Insider knowledge	3.44	3.54	4.07	.004
Ethnographies (N)	25	16	67	

[a] F-test.

and the use of insider knowledge to facilitate production are all higher under nonassembly work than under assembly work.

An ethnography of an automobile assembly plant in France provides an example of the loss of pride and enthusiasm in work for assembly-line workers:

> Everyone here is a case. Everyone has his story. Everyone chews over his tactics and in his own way tries to find a way out. How can I find a direction in this semi-penitentiary, indefinitely provisional universe: who can imagine that he can 'make a career' as a semiskilled worker? Who doesn't both resent deeply his presence here and see the wretchedness of his small-time bits of work as a kind of decline or accident? People dispense with scheming, they dream of going back to their own country and opening a little business. (Linhart 1981:60)

Work in this setting provides little intrinsic satisfaction. Instead, workers dream of a life elsewhere, in which they can find meaning and dignity in work.

As a consequence of lost pride and enthusiasm in work, fewer assembly workers than nonassembly workers are willing to give extra effort to ensure that production occurs successfully. Figure 5.2 illustrates the

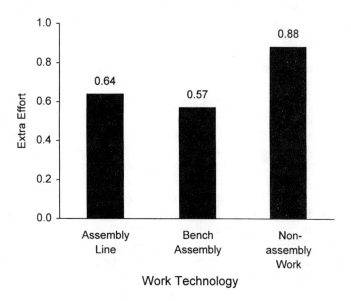

Figure 5.2. Extra effort and assembly work.

prevalence of extra effort as observed across assembly and nonassembly settings. Bench assembly work appears to generate even less extra effort than assembly-line work. One reason for this may be that automation has eliminated some of the most tedious and enervating assembly-line jobs. Only when work is organized into a continuous coordinated process, as on an assembly line, can it begin to be automated (Blauner 1964). In contrast, most work at stationary benches is unassisted by any sort of automated process and tedious repetition defines much of the work experience.

A classic ethnography of a steel mill undergoing automation provides some clues concerning the potential for modestly greater cooperation and effort under more automated assembly-line conditions. The basis for this potential lies in improved machinery and equipment, which makes the work easier and more efficient. A production worker in the steel mill explains his appreciation of automation in the following way. "We're in the swing of things. We have the mill tuned better" (Walker 1957:90). The workers on the automated assembly line enjoyed "the new rhythm that had come into their working day" (Walker 1957:91). Assembly-line work, because of increasing automation may thus encourage worker citizenship and extra effort to a somewhat greater extent than more repetitive bench assembly work. But it is also important to remember that both bench assembly and assembly-line work evidence significantly lower levels of worker citizenship and effort than nonassembly work.

Social Group Differences

In our investigation of overwork we have sought to understand the relationships between assembly versus nonassembly jobs and worker resistance and citizenship. It is also important, however, to consider differences between social groups in the patterns of overwork and resistance to overwork. Several possible differences between social groups in overwork, resistance, and citizenship are evaluated in Table 5.4.

The first panel of the table shows differences between union and nonunion enterprises. Several aspects of overwork and resistance vary between union and nonunion establishments. A steady pace of work and a relatively high level of absenteeism characterize unionized workplaces. These characteristics are typical of the sorts of establishments that are hospitable to unionization. Employees in such settings frequently join unions in order to seek redress for chronic problems concerning the conditions of employment. Unions give these employees a voice in workplace issues. Union establishments are also characterized by higher levels

Table 5.4. *Work Experiences, Resistance, and Citizenship across Social Groups*

Variables	N	Steady Pace	Absenteeism	Skill	Pride	Meaningful Work	Informal Group Resistance	Strikes
Union	69	.55	.82	1.93	2.17	1.88	**2.51**	.42
Nonunion	33	**.19**	**.56**	2.13	2.29	1.94	**1.69**	**.00**
Significance[a]		*.001*	*.028*	*.208*	*.491*	*.743*	*.003*	*.000*
Exclusively male (100%)	36	.31	.67	2.03	**2.42**	2.03	2.44	.26
Some female	17	.53	.60	2.37	**2.24**	2.07	1.69	.27
Gender mixed (25%–75%)	30	.60	.88	1.80	**2.07**	**1.74**	2.61	.35
Mostly female	19	.39	.80	1.79	**1.94**	**1.59**	1.44	.06
Significance[b]		*.207*	*.165*	*.087*	*.016*	*.032*	*.075*	*.345*
Majority group (100%)	14	.46	.63	1.57	2.29	1.93	2.36	.08
Some minority	24	.40	.70	2.21	2.40	2.00	1.94	.16
Ethnically mixed (25%–75%)	16	.50	.91	2.00	1.88	1.73	2.08	.29
Mostly minority	8	.38	.80	1.50	2.00	1.50	2.67	.33
Significance[b]		*.930*	*.238*	*.984*	*.118*	*.189*	*.741*	*.127*
Pre-1975	46	.53	**.86**	1.91	2.11	1.75	2.34	.36
1975 and after	62	.40	**.63**	2.00	2.27	1.96	2.00	.18
Significance[a]		*.170*	*.036*	*.549*	*.311*	*.197*	*.188*	*.061*
United Kingdom	31	.37	**.89**	1.79	**1.96**	1.87	2.22	**.40**
United States	57	.39	**.63**	2.09	**2.34**	1.96	2.14	**.15**
Significance[a]		*.846*	*.047*	*.083*	*.035*	*.653*	*.813*	*.017*

Note: All contrasts that are significant at p ≤ .10 are in bold type.
[a] *t*-test for contrast between two groups.
[b] F-test for linearity.

of informal group resistance and by strikes. These mechanisms serve as bargaining tools with management over the conditions of employment. They are important mechanisms through which workers struggle to create a workplace that respects their dignity (Wellman 1995).

Unions are extremely important for protecting employees from the worst excesses of overwork and exploitation. Without unions, many employees would be reluctant to protest their conditions individually. Unions have thus had an important long-term influence as pressure groups working toward improved conditions and greater dignity for all workers (Cornfield 1991; Kochan, Katz, and McKersie 1994).

Unions continue to provide a mechanism through which employees can express their voice in the contemporary workplace (Edwards 1995; Hirschman 1970; Langford 1996). "Voice means discussing with an employer conditions that ought to be changed, rather than quitting a job. In modern industrial economies, and particularly in large enterprises, a trade union is the vehicle for collective voice – that is, for providing workers as a group with a means of communicating with management" (Freeman and Medoff 1984:8). Unions provide a collective voice in two ways: 1) they aggregate preferences on issues of common interest to workers and present these to management, and 2) they provide grievance machinery so that individual complaints can be heard. Freeman and Medoff (1984:10) argue that "by taking account of all workers and by appropriately considering the sum of preferences for work conditions that are common to all workers," collective voice increases the efficiency of the workplace.

The principal mechanism through which unions express the will of their members is through contract negotiations. Strikes, however, provide the ultimate backup for the voice of workers if collective bargaining fails. Strikes have thus been, and in all likelihood will continue to be, a significant part of the union arsenal of bargaining tactics (Brecher 1972; Franzosi 1995).

Unions and strikes have also been an important mechanism for extending the benefits of industrial society and the protection of modern normative workplace standards to minorities, women, and new entrants to the workplace (Shostak 1991). Even in nations in which unions are relatively weak, unions play an important role in standardizing conditions of employment thus helping to reduce exploitation and unequal treatment (Roberts 1994).

The ethnography of the Paint, Trim, and Final Assembly Department in a British automobile assembly plant discussed earlier in this chapter reports both a strong pattern of informal group resistance and a history of organized strikes (Beynon 1975). The workers walked out in a wildcat strike – an important form of informal group resistance – during the period of the ethnography. In addition, the plant had a long history of organized strikes, the lore of which was passed down to new entrants to the labor force as part of their education about strategies for defending dignity at work. This pattern of collective resistance relying on both formal and informal means is typical of union establishments.

The ethnographies also show significant differences in the meaningfulness of work between predominantly male and predominantly female workplaces. Workplaces that employ a primarily female work force evidence less pride and meaning in work. Less meaning and pride in work in establishments with a primarily female work force is consistent with the employment of many female employees in more marginal workplaces with fewer rewards and fewer reasons for taking pride in work (England 1992; Sotirin and Gottfried 1999).

An example of limited pride and meaning in work is provided by an ethnography of clerical workers subcontracted through a temporary help agency, a traditionally female occupation and employment situation:

> In the case of the large, complex organisation such as the one where I now found myself, the division of labour is such that filing becomes a total occupation, and time-and-motion experts have rigidly excluded the possibility of personalising the system. . . . The degree of consensus regarding the unsatisfying nature of the work in hand is particularly interesting when one considers that these temps were highly diversified in terms of social background, domestic circumstances and previous work experience. (McNally 1979:163–164)

This example evidences the spread of scientific management principles well outside factory settings and into the sorts of lower-level, white-collar work staffed primarily by women. In either white-collar or blue-collar settings, the consequences of scientific management in terms of reduced pride and meaning are similar. And it is women who hold many of these routinized positions, both in factories and in office settings.

A contrasting example from the world of railroad engineers, a largely male occupation, evidences the pride and meaning that workers experience based on high levels of skill and autonomy:

> The learning experienced by enginemen may be classified into at least four broad areas. The first is manual operative skills coupled with technical knowledge. . . .
>
> The second area is codified knowledge of rules and guidelines for operating procedures. It comes from intensive study, practical application, and constant interpretation and restudy of various written sources. . . .
>
> The third area is on-the-job judgment, apart from the skills noted in the previous two areas. This area cannot be readily taught and cannot always be easily learned. . . .
>
> The fourth area is learning the railroaders' code of etiquette. Here a rail internalizes the mores or values governing interpersonal relations within the railroad social system. . . .
>
> A good rail excels in all four areas. (Gamst 1980:42–44)

Railroad engineers have a strong occupational identity and experience great pride in their work. Fewer ethnographies of the work of women evidence such high levels of pride, identity, and meaning in work.

Workplace ethnographies set in the United Kingdom evidence greater absenteeism and less pride in work than ethnographies set in the United States. British ethnographies also more frequently report organizational histories of strikes. These contrasts are consistent with the view of British industrial relations as relatively conflictual (Edwards 1992a; Thompson and Ackroyd 1995).

Few time trends in workplace relations are evidenced in the ethnographies. Absenteeism appears to decline modestly after the mid-1970s. Steadily paced work, typical of assembly jobs, also appears to be slightly less common in more recent decades, although this contrast is not statistically significant. These findings are consistent with research literature that reports an absence of clear temporal trends in the nature of work (Form 1987).

None of the aspects of overwork, resistance, or citizenship evaluated in Table 5.4 are differentiated by the racial composition of the work force. This finding is somewhat surprising given the employment disparities suffered by minority employees (Dill 1994; Tuch and Martin 1991). The absence of significant differences in overwork, resistance, and citizenship between minority and majority work forces may result from the relatively small number of organizational ethnographies dealing with predominantly minority work forces. There may simply be too few ethnographies of predominantly minority work forces to reliably establish such patterns.

Conclusions

Overwork and exploitation associated with the extreme rationalization of production in assembly work lead to some of the most alienating working conditions in modern economies. These conditions represent significant challenges to the goal of working with dignity. Workers experience reduced freedom of movement, a steady and grindingly hard pace, and have less skill, autonomy, creativity, and meaning in their work. In turn, these alienating conditions lead to resistance against work and against management on the part of employees. In particular, workers are likely to quit and have higher rates of absenteeism. Assembly workers also resist through informal group actions, unionization, and strikes.

Assembly work, however, does not produce the highest levels of *all* forms of resistance. Procedure sabotage, social sabotage, making out, and making up games are no more common in assembly work than in nonassembly work. Assembly workers may have the motiva[tion to] engage in these individual forms of resistance but their ability to eng[age] in them is significantly limited by the constraints they experience. T[he] inability of assembly worker to move freely around the shop or factory floor is a particularly important constraint in this regard. Thus, the opportunity to resist appears to be as significant as the motivation to resist.

In Chapter 4 we described the consequences of mismanagement and abuse for worker resistance and citizenship. Comparing the consequences of mismanagement and abuse with those of overwork, it appears that mismanagement and abuse have even farther reaching consequences than overwork. Mismanagement and abuse spark almost every form of resistance from employees. In contrast, the effects of assembly work are largely limited to either exiting the workplace or engaging in collective forms of resistance.

An important consequence of assembly work that has received less attention in the academic literature is its strong suppression of citizenship behaviors. Almost every form of worker citizenship discussed in the ethnographies is significantly reduced in assembly work. This reduction in voluntary positive initiative on the part of employees may be the greatest failing of the rationalization of assembly work. Owners and managers may have succeeded in getting a steady pace of strenuous effort from assembly workers, but effective production often requires more than grudging adherence to requirements. In the modern economy with its increasingly sophisticated production systems, effective production often requires significant initiative on the part of employees. Opportunities for worker initiative are regularly squandered in highly rationalized forms of assembly work. The undermining of worker initiative and citizenship by the overrationalization of work is an important limiting factor in the viability of this form of work organization.

Worker initiative is increasingly required for successful operations across an increasing range of production settings. In the next chapter we explore traditional craft work and the expanding sphere of professional work as settings that require extensive worker initiative. In these settings employee autonomy and initiative are essential for organizational success. The defense of autonomy and the right to take independent initiative are centrally important to working with dignity for professional and craft employees. In subsequent chapters we also explore encouragement of worker initiative throughout the economy through programs stressing employee involvement.

g Autonomy

A third challenge facing modern workers as they struggle to work with dignity is the possibility of incursions on their autonomy. Autonomy is particularly important for professional and craft workers whose jobs depend on the daily exercise of autonomy in relation to tools, techniques, and work priorities. A professional or craft worker can often be the only person on site with the requisite skills and knowledge to make appropriate decisions about production – decisions that sometimes have life and death consequences. For these and other reasons, the defense of autonomy is of utmost importance to professional and craft workers.

The skills of professional and craft employees are essential for effective functioning in many organizations because these workers possess important skills that are required to solve ongoing problems in production. As a result of their unique skills, they are typically allowed a significant degree of independence at work. Professional and craft workers thus have greater input into decisions about how work is to proceed than workers in settings organized around direct supervisory control or around bureaucratic rules. The fact that their skills are essential to the organization, however, also makes them a problem for managers who may resent being dependent on them. Managers thus frequently seek to limit the autonomy of professional and craft employees in order to gain control of work and to organize it according to their own agendas. Managers attempt to control the work of professional and craft workers through bureaucratic rules or through direct supervision. The resulting tensions often result in running battles between managers, on the one hand, and professional and craft employees, on the other.

The independence of professional and craft workers also faces challenges arising from the increasing size of organizations and from the decline of local enterprise ownership. Both these changes lead to increasing layers of bureaucracy that undercut professional and craft autonomy. Large size, ownership by sprawling conglomerates, and increasing bureaucracy limit input by professional and craft workers because decisions are increasingly made at remote locations. Professional and craft workers defend their autonomy and dignity through control of insider knowledge, taking pride in their work, and insisting on quality work, regardless of pressures toward volume production or cost-cutting.

Professional and Craft Autonomy

Many types of work, whether the work involves the construction of a building or the removal of a tumor, require substantial judgement, interpretation, and selection among alternative options. Under professional and craft organizations of work, many moment-to-moment decisions about work are made and implemented by those directly involved in production. Management enters such systems primarily as a procurer of additional work and as a "purchaser" of completed goods or services. When management attempts to take a more active role in production through the imposition of bureaucratic rules or through direct supervision, workers generally perceive it as an interloper or even a parasite. Reporting on underground miners' opinions of supervisors, Gouldner (1964:108) notes: "[M]iners looked upon [supervisors] in much the manner that the stars of a show look upon the stagehands."

The power and status of skilled craft workers is based on their "functional autonomy" – their control of the necessary skills to ensure that production proceeds correctly and efficiently (Friedman 1977; Montgomery 1987:13–16; Stark 1980:99). Professional employees similarly believe that their work proceeds most efficiently if operational control is left to those actually involved in the work and to professionally determined standards (Abbott 1988; Kelly 1980). As in the case of craft workers, management is generally seen as an unwelcome interloper.

What exactly do we mean by *autonomy in determining work practices*? Autonomy includes the right and the responsibility to make choices about the methods and techniques used for a given task. It also includes input into the sequencing, scheduling, and prioritizing of work activities. Finally, autonomy includes independently determining when a task is satisfactorily completed (Breaugh and Becker 1987). The bilateral role of professional and craft workers in workplace decisions means that they are engaged in an ongoing process of negotiation with management about how best to prioritize, organize, and complete work (Abbott 1988; Steiger and Form 1991).

Autonomy in determining work practices and possession of the skills on which autonomy is based result in professional and craft workers having greater power in relation to management than do other workers. Their power allows them to negotiate better wages and conditions. As a result of exercising autonomy in their daily work lives, they are also likely to experience greater self-efficacy, job satisfaction, and meaning in work than other workers (Bandura 1995; Kohn and Schooler 1983).

Craft Autonomy

Craft workers constitute about 10 percent of the labor force in advanced industrial economies. This figure has been relatively stable over the last century, even in the face of significant automation of industrial processes. Automation tends to displace semi-skilled production workers and unskilled laborers. Some skilled workers may also be displaced, but the demand for skilled craft workers continues and is even growing in some sectors as a result of the continuing need for workers capable of maintaining complex equipment in both manufacturing and service industries.

Many craft workers are employed as precision production operators. These occupations are primarily located in factories and range from tool and die makers to power plant operators. Other craft workers are employed as mechanics and repairers, including vehicle and equipment mechanics, telephone line installers and repairers, heating, air conditioning, and refrigeration mechanics, and heavy equipment mechanics. A third group of craft workers are employed in the construction trades as carpenters, electricians, and plumbers (Hodson and Sullivan 1995).

Craft workers combine a broad knowledge of tools, materials, and processes with manual skills acquired through long training and experience. The expertise required for craft work is thus based on a combination of formal training, often acquired in joint union-management sponsored apprenticeship programs, and experience on the job. The knowledge learned in the formal programs is sharpened and refined over time through first-hand experience (Rothman 1998:114).

A defining characteristic of craft workers is intense pride in their work. Long experience coupled with substantial technical training produce a level of expertise that workers experience as a source of great pride. The personal identities of craft workers thus tend to be firmly grounded in their occupational skills and activities (Haydu 1988).

Professional Autonomy

Professional occupations are learned through substantial periods of formal training. In contrast to the relative stability of craft occupations, the professions grew five-fold over the last century from only 4 percent of the labor force to close to 20 percent and are expected to rise above the 20 percent mark in the early twenty-first century. If associated technical occupations, such as dental and medical technicians, are included, the percentage of professional and related occupations already approaches a quarter of the labor force. The rise of the professions, coupled with the decline of agricultural work, is the most dramatic transformation of the labor force during the last hundred years (Hodson and Sullivan 1995:286). While not all workers in modern society are involved in jobs requiring the application of substantial formal knowledge, the professions as a group are the single largest occupational category in industrially advanced economies. The professions hold an important role in modern economies both because of their numbers and because of the importance of their contributions to the effective operation of advanced production systems.

Professional occupations are characterized by: (1) control of a large body of abstract, formal knowledge, (2) substantial autonomy, (3) authority over clients and over subordinate occupational groups, and (4) a claim of altruism as a guiding principle for professional behavior (Hodson and Sullivan 1995). While each of these characteristics is not equally important for all professions, they do set a standard against which much professional behavior is evaluated. We expect a professional to be in possession of substantial useful knowledge that is not readily available to the broader public. Similarly, we expect that they will use that knowledge to the benefit of their clients, putting their clients' interests above their own when necessary. We are sometimes disappointed in these expectations because professionals do not always live up to these standards. But our very disappointment indicates that the public has high expectations for professional behavior.

Along with the growth of the professions has come a proliferation and diversification in professional occupations. The largest professions, in rank order, are teaching, health related professions (such as doctors, dentists, and nurses), engineers, writers and entertainers, computer scientists, social workers, and lawyers (Hodson and Sullivan 1995). Professional occupations are frequently studied by ethnographers with recent contributions including studies of doctors (Hunter 1991; Porter 1993; Simonds 1996), lawyers (Granfield 1992), research scientists (Koskinen 1999; Rabinow 1996), social workers (Miller 1991), engineers (Kelly 1990; Meiksins and Smith 1993), and technicians (Barley and Orr 1997).

The organizational settings in which professionals work have also changed over time. No longer does the typical professional work in a private or group practice in medicine or law. Instead, doctors, lawyers, and other professionals are employed in large nonprofit organizations, government agencies, research institutes, universities, foundations, and large for-profit corporations of all kinds (Leicht and Fennell 1997).

Based on control of the knowledge base in a field, professionals are often granted substantial power over occupational training and licensing in that field. They often use this power to restrict membership in the profession through limiting enrollments in professional schools and through restrictive licensing practices. These practices tend to drive up the wages of professional employees. Professionals also engage in turf wars with other professions involving legal battles to determine who has the right to certain types of work. Thus, lawyers promote laws that prevent nonlawyers from dispensing legal advice and doctors lobby legislators to restrict the practice of medicine to only those with medical degrees from accredited colleges and with licenses from the American Medical Association.

Professionals also argue that they are the only ones qualified to supervise other professionals in their field. Nonprofessionals, including managers, who do not possess the relevant technical knowledge, are considered insufficiently informed to supervise professional work. Professionals are thus often granted a large degree of self-supervision in their work. When they *are* supervised by others, the supervision is generally by committees of professionals working in the same field. Although these realities have changed somewhat with greater employment of professionals in large organizations, professionals still seek to protect their right to substantial input into workplace decisions through defending the principles of autonomy and self-supervision.

As part of their bargain with society, professionals often work long hours, well beyond a forty-hour week. Indeed, excessive hours have long been associated with professional work. These long hours reflect the effort needed to stay current with developments in the knowledge base that supports the professionals' claim to expertise. Long hours also help to substantiate the professional worker's claim to altruism – to self-sacrifice for the benefit of clients – and to high earnings.

Since the 1970s the annual hours worked by full-time workers in the United States has increased by 140 hours – an average of three and a half weeks (Schor 1992). Much of this increase in hours has been among professional workers. Many contemporary professional workers appear to be developing a pattern of "self-exploitation" in which self-supervision results in greater work effort than even close management supervision. Workplace ethnographers have even noted an increasing tendency for some workers, especially professional employees, to freely choose additional time at work over leisure or family activities (Hochschild 1997).

The professions and the skilled crafts have much in common as occupations. Both are based on high levels of skill involving both formal training and substantial hands-on experience. And both take tremendous pride in their work and rigorously defend their autonomy. Professional and craft workers differ in that professional employees have somewhat greater power in society than craft workers and generally receive greater rewards for their efforts. In addition, many professional employees appear to have few reservations about wholesale abandonment to work, even in preference to leisure and family activities. Workaholism, which is centered in the ranks of professional and managerial employees, has become a significant problem in modern societies. For professional workers, workaholism may represent one of the greatest challenges to working with dignity.

Bureaucracy and Supervisory Fiat

The principal alternatives to professional and craft autonomy are organizations of work based either on bureaucratic rules or on the personal authority of managers and supervisors. These two organizations of work form the backdrop for evaluating the consequences of professional and craft autonomy for working with dignity. In Chapter 4 we examined the consequences of direct personal supervision in the workplace and noted its potential implications for heightened mismanagement and abuse. The organization of work according to bureaucratic rules is the most central manifestation of the rationalization of social life first analyzed by Max Weber. Direct supervisory control by management and control through bureaucratic rules present alternative logics of control to professional and craft autonomy. In this chapter we directly contrast the consequences of these different logics of control for dignity at work.

We identify professional and craft workplaces using standard census definitions of professional and craft occupations. Bureaucratic organizations are defined as noncraft and nonprofessional workplaces organized around bureaucratic rules. Workplaces based on supervisory fiat involve direct personal control in the absence of either craft or professional autonomy *and* in the absence of an organization of work based predominantly on bureaucratic rules.

It is important to realize, however, that the various forms of control are deeply intertwined and any given workplace may evidence a variety of forms of control. Workplaces based on professional or craft control may thus also evidence elements of bureaucratic or supervisory control. Indeed, many of the central dynamics in professional and craft workplaces involve the struggle between worker autonomy, on the one hand, and bureaucratic control or supervisory fiat, on the other (Perrolle 1986; Scott 1998).

Work practices in many professional fields, for example, are deeply enmeshed in bureaucratic rules. Engineering, in particular, has been discussed as an example of a "bureaucratic profession" based on the intermingling of professional and bureaucratic rationalities (Vaughan 1996:204). Engineers focus on technical efficiency as the organizing principle in their work, but "cost is itself a criterion of technical efficiency" (Zussman 1985:121). An overlap between professional criteria and administrative logics that stress cost is thus built into the professional orientation of engineers.

Even in organizations that rely heavily on professional or craft organizations of work, the greatest power is still often held by the owners of the organization and their hired managers and supervisors. Through control of the purse strings, these organizational actors have the power to expand or downsize the organization, end its existence, or shut it down in one location and reopen it elsewhere. We should be aware that organizational behavior ultimately reflects the goals and relative power of the various actors in the organization and that managers and owners are the most powerful of these actors because of their control of organizational finances. As Perrow (1986:15) notes "organizations are tools designed to perform work for their masters." Professional and craft autonomy is thus always contingent on decisions by managers to employ a given professional or craft specialty in the first place.

The Experience of Professional and Craft Work

Professional and craft work involve high levels of skill and considerable freedom and autonomy in determining the content of work. These characteristics of professional and craft work are contrasted with conditions under bureaucratic rule and under supervisory fiat in Table 6.1. Greater skill, meaning, and creativity in work are clearly evidenced in professional and craft settings.

Ethnographies of professional and craft workplaces report some direct supervision as indicted in the first line of Table 6.1. Direct supervision, however, plays a much less significant role in professional and craft workplaces than in nonprofessional and noncraft workplaces. Direct supervision is much more frequently combined with bureaucratic control than it is with professional or craft control.

An example of bureaucratic control in combination with direct personal supervision is provided by an ethnography of a British garment factory. In this setting, work is organized according to administrative rules and the workers have little or no input into production decisions. In essence, the worker's role is administratively reduced to that of a machine:

Table 6.1. *Autonomy in Professional and Craft Settings*

Variables	Professional	Craft	Bureaucratic	Supervisory Fiat	Significance[a]
Direct supervision	.30	.35	.70	.82	.001
Management abuse	−.77	.00	.05	.18	.071
Skill	2.90	2.25	1.80	1.69	.000
Autonomy	4.00	3.80	2.43	2.31	.000
Freedom of movement	2.56	2.44	1.78	1.96	.007
Creativity	3.60	3.11	2.17	1.93	.000
Meaningful work	2.44	2.71	1.58	1.70	.000
Pace	2.89	2.26	2.64	2.79	.065
Job ladder steps	4.56	3.31	3.98	2.04	.008
Size (ln)	5.56	6.40	6.80	4.48	.000
Local ownership	.60	.32	.16	.42	.018
Ethnographies (N)	10	21	48	29	

[a] F-test.

> Production was marked in a work-book with the code from the ticket the worker received with each new bundle of work. The book, which was marked with the woman's name, contained her production record and it was checked by the supervisor with the help of a calculator. . . . A woman might sew side-seams all day, every day, week in and week out. . . . The individual worker had no control over what she would do. (Westwood 1984:19–20)

This example also highlights the low levels of creativity and meaning in work typical of systems based on bureaucratic rules and supervisory control.

Management abuse is also clearly differentiated across the various systems of work organization. Professional workplaces evidence the greatest respect for employees and the least abuse. Workplaces based on managerial fiat, in contrast, evidence the greatest likelihood of abuse and direct personal assaults on the dignity of employees. Abuse under conditions of direct supervision in combination with bureaucratic rules is illustrated in an ethnography of a French automobile factory:

> Fear is part of the works, it's a vital cog in the system. . . . Inside the works you're in an accepted police state, on the brink of lawbreaking if you're found a few yards from your

work station or in a corridor without a paper duly signed by a superior, in trouble for a defect in production, liable to be fired on the spot if there's a scuffle, punishable for being a few seconds late or for an impatient remark to a charge hand, and endless other things which hang over your head. (Linhart 1981:64)

Workplaces based on supervisory fiat or bureaucratic rules also make the least use of workers' skills. Skill levels among professional and craft workers, in contrast, are much higher. In professional and craft settings, workers are expected to possess and utilize high levels of skills – skills that differentiate their job performance from that of someone without the relevant skills. The expectation of skilled job performance is clearly manifest in the following quote from a senior resident at a medical school hospital:

The intern who calls you up and says X has a fever does not inspire your trust; but the intern who calls and says X has a urinary tract infection is altogether different. He reports the symptoms, gives you his diagnosis, and tells you what he plans to do. I don't need housestaff to tell me my patients have fevers – any secretary can do that. . . . The subordinate who requires further questioning has by this fact alone led [to questions about] his competence and trustworthiness. (Bosk 1979:97)

The sophisticated integration of technical, diagnostic, and interpretative skills as a requirement for successful performance of professional work has also been noted for engineers (Zussman 1985:59) and technical workers (Orr 1996:113).

Autonomy is also sharply differentiated between professional and craft workplaces, on the one hand, and workplaces utilizing bureaucratic rules or supervisory fiat on the other. Similarly, freedom of movement, creativity in work, and meaning in work are also much more prevalent under professional and craft organizations of work. Meaningful experiences of work are modestly higher in craft work than even in professional work. An example of high levels of meaning in craft work is provided by a quote from a female ironworker: "Working the steel and seeing a building rise from the ground is right up there with giving birth. To know that your quality of work ensures the safety of so many people in a high-rise gives a feeling of satisfaction unlike any other" (Eisenberg 1998:1).

The opportunity to exercise creativity at work is an important component of working with dignity. The level of creativity experienced on

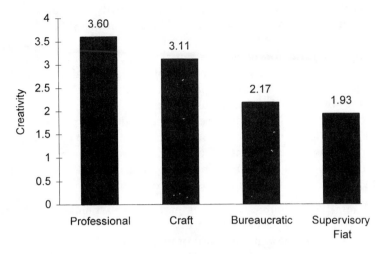

Figure 6.1. Creativity in professional and craft work.

the job across different settings is displayed in Figure 6.1. The pattern for creativity at work parallels many of the other distinctions between professional and craft settings and other workplaces. Professional workplaces allow the greatest creativity, followed by craft and bureaucratic settings. Human creativity is more stifled under supervisory fiat than under any other form of work organization.

Creativity is especially important in professional work. Studies of the successful Japanese expansion into the world electronics and automobile markets give much of the credit to the creativity of well-trained Japanese engineers who have been able to use their intellectual capital to fuel the "Japanese miracle" (Fruin 1997; Lillrank and Kano 1989). Similarly, research scientists applying their creative energies to unlocking the secrets of DNA have fueled the spectacular growth of the biotechnology industry in the United States and Europe (Rabinow 1996). The growth of the space industry in the United States is also a story told in the, sometimes imperfect, language of scientific creativity (Vaughan 1996). In the words of an engineer in the computer industry: "I work with extremely bright and capable people who move quickly, both intellectually and conceptually" (Rogers and Larsen 1984:139).

Even outside the glamour professions associated with growth industries, creativity is required in the daily work lives of professionals across a wide range of settings. In police work, for example, new officers must show their peers not only that they have the courage to do the job, but also that they have the intelligence and creativity needed to respond to each new situation in an effective manner (Martin 1980:8).

We have seen that professional and craft work are similar in many ways. They are not, however, identical in all aspects. The area of work life that most strongly differentiates professional and craft work is the pace of work. Professional employees, along with workers under bureaucratic and supervisory control, work at a faster pace than do craft workers. Professional employees experience the most pressured work life of any group. Craft workers, in contrast, are able to control their pace of work and to keep it at a more humane level. Examples of extremely stressed working conditions in a professional occupation are provided by quotes from a classic ethnography of lawyers:

> 'If you look at the young partners, you'll find that they got there by hard, hard work....'
> 'We have a great deal of night work. A slow guy can produce a hell of a lot of work if he doesn't go home. Once I worked twenty-four hours straight and then I worked six more hours just to see if I could do it. I've heard of people who've had breakdowns after six months of steady work.' (Smigel 1969:102–103)

Similar experiences of excessively hard work and long hours are also noted for nurses and other health-care professionals (Foner 1994). For many professionals, the problem of long hours and hard work is compounded by having too many competing job responsibilities and obligations that arrive unannounced, uncoordinated, and all in need of immediate attention.

Research scientists and engineers involved in time-pressured projects oriented toward bringing out new products prior to competitors also sometimes experience excessively long hours and demanding work:

> We set the pace ourselves. If the wheel were running at 100 percent, we would spin it up to 120 every morning. Nothing's happening unless you're a little frantic. I've often seen design groups induce this frantic feeling themselves in order to get their juices flowing. There's nothing like a little fear and urgency to force creativity. (Rogers and Larsen 1984:138)

Part of the "problem" of hard work among professionals is that many professionals simply like their work and are willing and even eager to put in long hours.

From the standpoint of the employer the "problem" of excessive work among professionals looks a lot like a solution. From the standpoint of the worker, it is more of a mixed blessing and may come at the expense of family life and leisure activities that would lead to a more diverse and balanced life experience (Hochschild 1997). In Japan, overwork among professionals and managers has been noted as a cause of early death from heart attack and related illnesses. Early death from overwork has been given a name in Japan – *Karoshi* – and has been identified as a significant national health concern (*Karoshi* 1990).

The number of steps in the career ladder of interconnected positions typical of different organizations of work is also displayed in Table 6.1. Professional settings have the longest and most elaborate career ladders followed by bureaucratic settings, which also organize work into finely graded and ranked positions. Craft settings also have significant career ladders. Organizations based solely on supervisory fiat have almost nonexistent job ladders comprised by only about two steps.

The significance of mobility ladders of interconnected and ranked positions has often been noted in studies of professional occupations. These ladders serve as motivators for young professionals as they strive to move up in their profession. They also serve as mechanisms for the socialization of novice professionals to the world views of the profession. The long period of socialization involved in moving up through ranked positions serves to inculcate medical interns, for example, in a world view less critical of doctors and more sympathetic to their interests:

> Advanced students are less vocal in their questioning and criticisms of the medical profession. They attribute many of their earlier concerns to naivete and argue for a more sympathetic view of doctors and the profession. . . . The students' shift from an idealistic perspective is accompanied by a change in the way they view and treat patients. Their priorities change as they learn how to negotiate their way through the program successfully, and they adopt the profession's rationales for treating patients as objects. (Haas and Shaffir 1987:98)

A final significant distinction between professional and craft settings and other workplaces concerns the size of the employing organization and its ownership pattern. The largest organizations utilize bureaucratic rules, although craft organizations of work are also found in large enterprises. Smaller organizations rely more often on professional organizations of work and especially on supervisory fiat. Work settings are also differentiated by ownership patterns. The majority of professionals work in organizations that are locally owned. Enterprises that are locally owned are much less likely to utilize bureaucratic rules. We will return to patterns of organizational size and ownership later in the chapter as additional potential challenges to working with dignity for many employees.

In summary, professional and craft work have a great deal in common. Both types of work are based on high levels of skill and job autonomy. Meaning and creativity in work are also high in both professional and craft settings. The most notable difference between professional and craft occupations lies in the pace of work. Craft workers have been able to negotiate and maintain a reasonable pace of work. Professional employees, in contrast, often seem to work at or beyond full capacity. In many situations this extremely high level of effort is at least in part voluntary and reflects the rewarding nature of professional work. In other cases, excessive effort reflects the expectations of bosses and peers. And all too often it may come at the expense of personal development and self-realization in other areas of life.

Citizenship in Professional and Craft Work

Professional and craft workers typically exhibit extremely high levels of citizenship in their work. Indeed, the level of citizenship in professional settings is nearly one full standard deviation above the mean (see Table 6.2). This high level of citizenship contrasts sharply with below average levels of citizenship in bureaucratic settings and in work settings that rely on supervisory fiat. This pattern is repeated both for the summary citizenship scale and for the detailed components of citizenship.

Table 6.2. *Pride and Citizenship in Professional and Craft Work*

Variables	Professional	Craft	Bureaucratic	Supervisory Fiat	Significance[a]
Citizenship scale	.88	.47	−.30	−.14	.000
Pride in work	2.78	2.83	1.91	2.07	.000
Commitment to organizational goals	1.00	.68	.38	.52	.002
Cooperation	2.80	2.55	2.28	2.29	.036
Job satisfaction	3.70	3.50	2.49	2.86	.000
Insider knowledge	4.80	4.13	3.82	3.46	.000
Peer training	3.67	4.12	2.63	2.85	.000
Good soldier	4.11	3.13	2.76	3.20	.054
Ethnographies (N)	10	21	48	29	

[a] F-test.

Pride in work is pervasive in both professional and craft settings. An ethnography describing the development of the polymerase chain reaction (PCR), which profoundly transformed the human potential to identify and reproduce segments of genetic code, reports on the extreme pride which the chemists and biologists engaged in the project felt in their work. The development of PCR has made possible not only cloning but a vast array of genetic interventions in the areas of medicine, agriculture, biology, and related fields. A young biochemist recalls:

> Probably I worked harder in that time in my life than I ever had in terms of hours. I was very interested in the job. It was really fun to learn how to synthesize DNA. . . . It was the heyday of biotechnology. There were all kind of bold ideas floating around all the time . . . and there was absolutely no constraint on the imagination. . . . The company was really fun. . . . [We] were right in the middle of something that was a red-hot kind of an area. (Rabinow 1996:90)

Pride in craft work is, if anything, even higher than pride in professional settings. An ethnography of concrete finishing provides an example of craft-based pride in doing quality work. Following the pouring of the floor for a sewage treatment plant, a rainstorm scars the surface but the workers won't have their work ruined:

> About four o'clock, it began to rain – a hard, pounding, saturating rain. With a downward rush, a blanket of rain picked a million points in the freshly troweled concrete. . . .
> The next morning the slab looked diseased. But thousands of pounds of flash patch cement were purchased and the slab was troweled as smooth as polished wax. When we walked on it, our legs were reflected on the shining surface. . . . Later, the floor was coated with a black asphalt waterproofing. Finally, it was under water as sewage passed through the equalization tank. . . . [The workers] knew it would eventually be covered but the specifications called for a smoothly troweled surface and that's what [they] insisted on. (Applebaum 1981:11, 16)

Craft pride rests on applying knowledge and skill to physical tasks. Skilled construction workers, for example, show great pride in overcoming the physical challenges of their work:

> [Pride in the work results in part from] winning out over the elements and showing persistence in the face of adversity. Construction work is often hard and dirty, requiring one to work in foul weather (freezing or boiling), breathing dust, and

> being soaked to the skin by rain or snow. A construction
> man's hands are usually swollen and scarred, with a high
> incidence of broken or missing fingers. Construction workers
> enjoy the challenge of difficult tasks and the satisfaction that
> comes from doing a difficult job well. (Applebaum 1981:109)

Craft workers generally see their jobs as representing "honest work" and
as "making an honest living" (LeMasters 1975:24). They sometimes contrast their work with what they see as the vaguely less honest living to
be made by "shuffling papers" (Lamont 2000).

Enthusiasm and even joy in work are common themes in studies of
craft workers. Enthusiasm for daily work tasks is reported in a classic
ethnography of underground gypsum mining:

> I observe Chuck as he is working and he presents a pretty
> demonstration of a capable prop man. He works *briskly*,
> setting up three or four props in succession, hammering in the
> wedges with *powerful* drives. He then *grabs* his bar and tests
> the roof at several places, pulling down some pieces of loose
> rock. Next he checks the entire area *quickly* by walking
> around it and looking for bad spots. The shuttle-buggy comes
> up with some more props and Chuck yells at him, 'You're my
> buddy!' (Gouldner 1964:139–140; emphasis in original)

The pride and satisfaction of professional and craft workers can be
contrasted with the more alienated experiences of employees whose daily
tasks are organized around bureaucratic rules. An ethnography of a
piston ring factory reports on the absence of pride and satisfaction in
this bureaucratically organized work as evidenced by the orientation of
a long-term employee:

> He had learned to expect nothing from his job but money. He
> treated the company the way the company treated him, coldly
> and with calculation. . . . When, after more than two decades
> on the job, he received his annual merit report, he just signed
> and ignored it. 'They're always the same,' he said. They said
> he needed to improve and take better care of the equipment.
> But, 'how,' he asked rhetorically, 'can you take better care of
> 40-year-old equipment?' He didn't appreciate being treated
> like a child by the company, but he didn't fight back or
> complain much any more. He just hung in there, doing his
> job. (Pfeffer 1979:78–79)

The use of insider knowledge to facilitate production and the prevalence of peer training also vary sharply between professional and craft

work and other settings. Professional work evidences the highest levels of insider knowledge. Insider knowledge is job relevant knowledge that can be acquired only through long on-the-job experience. Craft work evidences the highest level of peer training. Insider knowledge and peer training are not absent in bureaucratic settings or under direct personal supervision, but they operate at significantly reduced levels.

Figure 6.2 displays levels of insider knowledge and peer training across work settings. The acquisition of insider knowledge in professional settings takes place through ongoing occupational socialization. Professional employees do not resist learning this new knowledge; indeed, they demand it, knowing that their competence depends on it. An ethnography of a teaching hospital illustrates the eagerness of novice professionals to acquire insider knowledge. Beginning interns often complain that the learning process is moving too slowly and that they are not getting enough opportunity to learn and to exercise judgment:

> In the dinner line this evening, Brian, an intern, [complains] to Josh, a second-year resident, about doing a breast biopsy with Ernest, Baker's chief resident. Brian said, 'I lost my biopsy to Ernest today.' Josh asked, 'What do you mean? Didn't he let you do it?' Brian answered, 'Yeah, he let me do it. But he's real intrusive to work with. He couldn't keep his hands out of my operative field. If that ever happens again, I'll refuse to

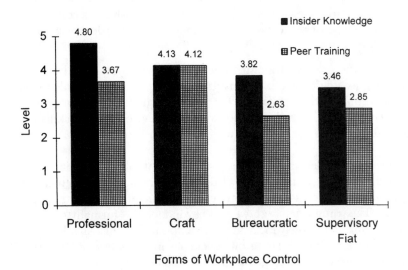

Figure 6.2. Insider knowledge and peer training in professional and craft work.

scrub with him again.' The threat is idle, but the complaint is real. (Bosk 1979:42)

The importance of insider knowledge reaches its zenith in professional work, but peer training is highest in craft settings. Here, even more than in professional settings, on-the-job training is crucial to successful job performance. An ethnography of underground gypsum miners illustrates the importance of peer training in a craft setting:

> Typically, prop men learned their techniques in some informal apprenticeship, by working closely with and watching a regular prop man; they cling to and pass on the particular methods they have learned. (Gouldner 1964:122)

An ethnography of firefighters further illustrates the crucial role of peer training in craft occupations:

> The techniques required to execute a job are based on experience and association with other workers. For example, for one man to properly raise a ground ladder, he must learn to use the leverage of the ladder to swing it into place. The mastery of this technique is necessary for the successful accomplishment of this task. . . .
>
> Fire fighters are members of a unique culture, one which radically shapes their perception of themselves and the outside world. With each other they share a bond of experience and camaraderie based on a proven ability to push their collective envelope of protection to its ultimate limit in order to save a life or put out a fire. (McCarl 1985:28,181)

The importance of peer training in acquiring craft knowledge has long been noted as a defining characteristic of craft work across a wide range of occupational settings (Cherry 1974; Chetkovich 1997). Insider knowledge, peer training, and the maintenance and development of skills are crucial foundations for working with dignity in professional and craft settings.

The role of insider knowledge is less important but still significant in bureaucratic settings. Insider knowledge in bureaucracies often includes knowing how to successfully negotiate the bureaucratic rules of the organization. This knowledge is above and beyond what is formally required to do the job and is largely local and unique to each setting. An additional aspect of insider knowledge in bureaucracies involves learning the personal procedures that often grow up alongside bureaucratic procedures:

> The secretarial job thus rested on a *personal set of procedures and understandings* carved out by secretary and boss. . . . The

corporation provided only the merest skeleton for the relationship; its substance depended on the unique qualities and agreements of the two people involved. Unlike other bureaucratic relations, which certainly included *some* component of special understandings generated by the unique personalities of those who interact, the secretary/boss relation was defined *largely* by the special relationship developed by two particular individuals. (Kanter 1977:80–81; emphasis in original)

While insider knowledge is important for successfully navigating bureaucracies, it does not reach the same level of importance as in professional and craft settings where insider knowledge is an essential part of the core working knowledge needed to accomplish work tasks correctly and efficiently.

In summary, professional and craft workers evidence great pride and citizenship in their work. These high levels of pride and citizenship are particularly striking in relation to the much lower levels of pride and citizenship in bureaucratic settings and in settings organized on the basis of supervisory fiat. Insider knowledge and peer training are at the heart of work in both professional and craft settings, with insider knowledge being most central in professional settings and peer training being most central in craft settings. This difference reflects the greater weight of formal training in professional settings and the greater weight of on-the-job experience in craft settings.

Resistance in Professional and Craft Work

In contrast to their similarity in terms of pride and citizenship, professional and craft employees are quite distinct in their patterns of resistance to infringements on their autonomy. Professional employees exhibit relatively little overall resistance. Table 6.3 shows that professional workers exhibit the least resistance of any of the groups considered. Craft workers are involved in resistance activities at a level more typical of workers in settings organized around bureaucratic rules or supervisory fiat. The contrasts involved are not large but the pattern is reinforced by similar patterns for other more specific resistance variables. The patterns for subverting particular managers and for conflict with supervisors and managers, for example, reinforce the general pattern of resistance activities. Craft workers show the highest levels of resistance to managerial authority and professionals evidence the least resistance.

The pattern for subverting particular managers highlights the contrast between strong craft resistance and the virtual absence of professional

Table 6.3. *Resistance and Conflict in Professional and Craft Work*

Variables	Professional	Craft	Bureaucratic	Supervisory Fiat	Significance[a]
Resistance scale	−.55	−.02	.22	−.06	.127
Subvert particular manager	.33	1.00	.62	.55	.030
Conflict with supervisors or managers	2.30	3.29	2.89	2.70	.031
Withhold enthusiasm	.50	.57	.86	.64	.053
Turnover	1.57	1.67	2.32	1.93	.024
Work avoidance	.67	.71	.76	.57	.490
Playing dumb	.44	.33	.46	.47	.915
Alternative status hierarchies	1.78	2.31	2.11	2.09	.556
Smooth operator	3.22	1.69	2.65	2.05	.007
Ethnographies (N)	10	21	48	29	

[a] F-test.

resistance. Ongoing tensions between a group of craft workers and their supervisor are described in an ethnography of construction work. The workers experience management largely as a source of interference:

> At the sewage treatment plant, there were several occasions when the men placed a thousand yards of concrete in a single day. No one from management told them to do it. . . . Pete expressed the pride and satisfaction that comes from extraordinary accomplishment, and said: 'If they'd leave us alone, we can take care of the work and make money for the company. We did a thousand yards today. But I've done better. As long as Carmen [the employer] leaves Earl [the superintendent] alone we can turn out the work.' (Applebaum 1981:63)

Conflictual stances in relation to management are routinely reported in ethnographies of craft work. Recall the quote from Gouldner's (1964) classic study of underground gypsum miners reported at the beginning of this chapter in which managers are referred to as "mere stagehands." Professional employees, conversely, evidence the least conflict with management, and also the lowest turnover. These two characteristics of professional work are not unrelated. Once someone has made the educational investment to become a professional worker, with all its attendant status, pay, and privileges, they are unlikely to jeopardize their career by overt conflict with management. Professional conflicts with management are thus likely to be subdued and behind the back or displaced to other actors in the workplace, such as other professionals or subordinates (Abbott 1988; Pavalko 1988).

This relatively constrained orientation is part of what makes professionals such valued employees from the standpoint of management. As a result of their general nonresistance to administrative logics, professionals are often treated as "trusted employees" and given significant supervisory responsibilities over subordinates (Whalley 1991; Zussman 1985). Adherence to management definitions, in combination with the lack of a culture of resistance and a willingness to work long hours, makes professionals ideal employees from the standpoint of management.

From the standpoint of other employees, however, professionals' support for management orientations may make them relatively indistinguishable from management (Whalley 1991). The administrative authority vested in professionals by management may appear to be their defining characteristic to other employees more than any claim of greater knowledge based on professional expertise. This may be especially true for supporting technical employees who may possess some of the same skills and knowledge as the professionals to whom they report.

Professional and craft workers are also differentiated in terms of creating alternative status hierarchies at work. Craft workers exhibit the greatest prevalence of this type of symbolic independence from management and professional workers exhibit the lowest level. Sometimes the alternative status hierarchies created by craft workers involve a heightened focus on seniority. Senior workers may be considered almost a separate caste above novice workers with rigid codes for who may address whom and on what subjects (Gamst 1980:71; Gouldner 1964:75). Alternative status hierarchies among craft workers can also involve physical prowess or racial or gender identities (McCarl 1985:95). While these alternative status hierarchies are not necessarily oppositional to management, they do carve out areas of evaluation and status that are independent of management and over which the craft workers have collective control. The existence of these independent spheres of evaluation reinforces the independence of the craft worker from management evaluations and management concerns.

In contrast to the importance of alternative status hierarchies among craft workers, professional employees exhibit the highest prevalence of smooth operators – employees who manipulate situations to their advantage in terms of promotions and rewards. One important aspect of being a smooth operator involves impression management. Student doctors, for example, learn impression management early in their careers: "What you want to be able to do is to speak correctly using the right language and forcefully. . . . If you are able to talk that way it usually means you know your business" (Haas and Shaffir 1987:69). Displaying the symbols of professionalism in speech and dress thus becomes equally important as actually possessing the correct knowledge and being able to take correct actions. Student doctors also learn to display their new knowledge in a circumspect manner. They should appear bright and informed but never appear to know more than teachers or senior residents: "If you happen to believe something . . . you try to defend yourself but in a very diplomatic manner, all the time being careful not to step on anybody's toes" (Haas and Shaffir 1987:75). The role of impression management in smoothing career paths for professional employees has also been noted for lawyers (Smigel 1969), police officers (Martin 1980), and research scientists (Koskinen 1999).

It would be inappropriate, however, to characterize professional employees as never resisting administrative logics. Professionals simply resist less often than do other workers. In addition, their forms of resistance are likely to be more subdued and subtle. For example, an ethnographer reports on the behaviors and attitudes of engineers working in a high technology firm in the midst of a somewhat heavy-handed implementation of a new organizational culture stressing high worker commitment. He observes that engineers' forms of resistance rarely involve direct confrontation but do involve significant symbolic distancing from the new and more intrusive organizational cultural (Kunda 1992).

Professionals do sometimes directly challenge administrative behavior through "whistle-blowing" when they feel that administrative behavior is immoral or illegal (Rothschild and Miethe 1999; Vaughan 1983). Such actions often receive substantial publicity and can result in considerable losses for the organization in terms of financial expense and public embarrassment. The rarity of whistle-blowing, however, may be partly explained by professional employees' reluctance to jeopardize their own careers by directly challenging management (Glazer and Glazer 1989; Weinstein 1979).

Partly as a consequence of professional workers' reluctance to "make waves" for their employers, much conflict involving professionals is turned inward toward competition with peers and with other professions. One of the chief imperatives of a profession is to carve out a niche area in which it holds exclusive power based on control of the knowledge base defining the area. Such areas are aggressively defended by professional organizations against incursions by other professions through licensing and other restrictive practices (Abbott 1988).

Professionals do sometimes engage in activities resembling effort bargaining or even in theft to increase their rewards and earnings. But these activities are generally targeted toward weaker groups, such as customers or clients, rather than toward employers. For example, medical doctors can abbreviate patient visits or prescribe unnecessary surgeries and treatments and file fraudulent medical insurance claims. Similarly, lawyers can pad their bills or fabricate complications for clients that necessitate additional fees (Green 1997). Professional conflict can also be directed toward colleagues and coworkers. Professionals are often fiercely competitive (Pierce 1995), and as we will see in Chapter 8, group solidarity and supportive relations among professional workers are significantly lower than among other groups of workers, especially craft workers.

Organizational Size and Outside Ownership

In this chapter we have contrasted professional and craft organizations of work with bureaucracy and with supervisory fiat as principal challenges to autonomous and bilateral work practices. The rationalization of work life, however, is a complex phenomenon that is not well represented by a single indicator of bureaucracy. In this section we consider organizational size and outside ownership as additional indicators of the rationalization of work life with potential implications for working with dignity. Both organizational size and outside ownership have been identified as significant challenges to meaning and fulfillment in work (Kimberly 1976; Ritzer 1993).

The consequences of organizational size for working with dignity are displayed in Table 6.4. Many aspects of resistance increase with organizational size. The contrasts involved are not large, but the pattern is consistent across types of resistance. In each case, organizations with less than 100 employees generate the least resistance and organizations with more than 1,000 employees generate the greatest resistance.

The negative effects of organizational size on the experience of work have been evidenced in many of the ethnographies already quoted. For example, the mass walkout in the Ford assembly plant in Great Britain described in Chapter 5 reflected in part the alienating consequences of both large organizational size and outside ownership (Beynon 1975).

An example of the conflict engendering consequences of organizational size in a white-collar setting is provided by an ethnography of the offices of a large corporation employing 50,000 people of whom 3,000 work at the headquarters office alone. In this setting the extreme division of labor is reflected in the finely graded ranks of employees leading to heightened tensions between the ranks. "One of the striking things about secretaries, then, was that their presence made nearly everyone in

Table 6.4. *Employment Size and Alienation*

Variables	Less than 100	100 to 1,000	More than 1,000	Significance[a]
Resistance scale	−.18	−.01	.11	.272
Conflict with supervisors or managers	2.61	2.78	3.10	.038
Withhold enthusiasm	.65	.59	.88	.071
Machine sabotage	.00	.30	.27	.059
Alternative status hierarchies	1.87	2.14	2.35	.049
Strikes	.15	.27	.39	.043
Citizenship scale	.13	.00	−.06	.451
Insider knowledge	3.52	4.11	4.04	.015
Productivity	2.07	2.40	2.66	.001
Ethnographies (N)	30	36	33	

[a] F-test for linearity.

the exempt ranks a 'boss,' generating a shared managerial orientation among exempt personnel and further drawing the caste lines between exempt and nonexempt groups" (Kanter 1977:71). The heightening of conflict and the emergence of alternative status hierarchies as organizational size increases is a common experience for employees in large organizations.

Citizenship, in contrast, declines with the increasing size of organizations. Although the pattern for the overall citizenship scale is not statistically significant, it is reinforced by being the inverse of the pattern for resistance.

Some characteristics of work life often associated with citizenship, however, appear to increase with organizational size. The use of insider knowledge and productivity, for example, both increase with organizational size. Insider knowledge can be especially important in large bureaucracies because of the intricate rules and procedures that must be followed. Mastering these procedures often represents a second layer of knowledge necessary for successful job performance above and beyond the skills required for the actual job tasks. An example of the use of insider knowledge in a large bureaucracy is provided by an ethnography of a commercial bank. In this setting a new manager encourages workers to develop plans for how to do their work more efficiently. As a result of the changes made the number of settlement errors is greatly reduced and employee morale rises sharply. The workers are now able to "do

Table 6.5. *Citizenship and Resistance in Locally Owned Enterprises*

Variables	Local Ownership	Outside Ownership	Significance[a]
Resistance scale	−.39	.15	.015
Management incompetence	−.44	.21	.003
Absenteeism	.50	.80	.024
Withhold enthusiasm	.52	.78	.025
Conflict with supervisors or managers	2.36	3.10	.000
Work avoidance	.54	.76	.037
Social sabotage	.38	.69	.017
Strikes	.11	.36	.019
Informal group resistance	1.57	2.56	.000
Citizenship scale	.46	−.12	.006
Pride in work	2.40	2.10	.072
Commitment to organizational goals	.84	.48	.002
Cooperation	2.62	2.30	.014
Ethnographies (N)	30	68	

[a] Two-tailed *t*-test.

their work more efficiently, with less tensions and problems, and leave an hour earlier in the day. 'This is much better; the day doesn't seem so hectic and disorganized. . . . I go home in the afternoon, I don't feel like collapsing like I used to'" (Kusterer 1978:172). This example clearly illustrates the reservoir of insider knowledge existing in large organizations that all too often goes unutilized.

Outside ownership of organizations appears to have even stronger negative consequences for the nature of work than organizational size. Table 6.5 compares several aspects of resistance and citizenship between locally owned and externally owned enterprises. The contrasts consistently show working in locally owned enterprises to be associated with greater citizenship and fewer resistance behaviors.

An ethnography of a French automobile plant that is part of a large international conglomerate reveals with painful clarity the lack of enthusiasm for work in settings characterized by outside ownership. "Everyone carries out his order as slowly as possible and toward midday the spectacle of these shadows wandering in silence along the dark racks, apparently prey to an incurable lethargy, has something of unreality about it" (Linhart 1981:108).

Figure 6.3 displays graphically the higher levels of social sabotage and work avoidance in enterprises owned by outside entities. The lack of

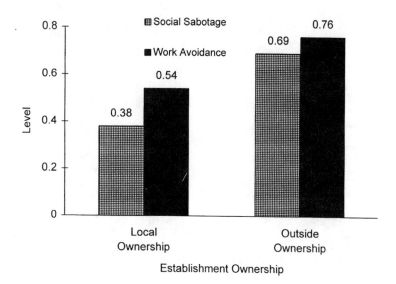

Figure 6.3. Work avoidance and social sabotage under outside ownership.

commitment by external owners to their employees is often recognized by workers and reciprocated. An ethnography of an automobile assembly plant in the United States reports on the alienation of workers from the company and on their negative views of management: "During a period of slow work on the assembly line, a group of workers spend their time in criticizing [management]" (Hamper 1991:125). The workers also mock supervisors behind their backs with derogatory nicknames and make up jokes and stories involving their demise.

In sharp contrast, a strong commitment to work is evidenced in an ethnography of a textile mill that has recently been bought by the employees. The workers in this plant often stay late to finish the day's work. In essence, this work is unpaid overtime:

> Pat, Brenda and Sue were good machinists and would often
> stay back to finish off their own work and that which had
> been left unfinished by the women on the part-time shift.
> Nancy, Edna and Natalia could not machine. They organized
> the work – counting, packing, checking and assessing the
> work that had been done. These six women all spoke of
> Fakenham Enterprises as their own factory. (Wajcman
> 1983:87)

Small size and local ownership have significant positive consequences for meaning and dignity in work. The increasing size of organizations and their continuing merger into larger and larger entities may thus exert a downward force on citizenship and encourage greater distancing from work and greater resistance.

It is possible that these negative consequences of large size and outside ownership may even extend to the professions, which otherwise exhibit strong patterns of citizenship and only limited resistance. Recall from Table 6.1 that professional settings are characterized by a relatively high likelihood of local ownership. This reality, however, is in the process of rapid change. Professional workers are increasingly employed in large organizations that are often parts of national or even multinational corporations. The medical profession provides a case in point. Recent decades have witnessed the transformation of medical care from an organizational structure based on private or group practice to one based on large hospitals and health maintenance organizations. In the United States the funds provided by Medicare and Medicaid have encouraged the construction of new for-profit hospitals and the financial restructuring of not-for-profit community hospitals to for-profit status (Cassell 1991). Subsequent mergers and reorganizations have created multi-hospital systems and large sprawling health care organizations (Fennell and Alexander 1993).

The new organization of health care in large multisite enterprises has resulted in doctors relinquishing significant autonomy and authority over medical decisions to administrators located in distant cities. Administrators now use profit-based criteria to make decisions about the selection of which tests and which procedures will be reimbursed. These decisions may conflict with a doctor's judgement about what is appropriate in any given case. Through the control of which tests will be paid for, administrators exert what is often the decisive influence on decisions that were previously the exclusive domain of the doctor. The reorganization of health care into large for-profit, multisite enterprises has thus eroded the autonomy and authority of doctors over decisions that in the past they made on the basis of professional judgement. These organizational incursions on autonomy constitute significant challenges to working with dignity for medical doctors and for the professions more generally (Bosk 1992; Zussman 1992). Whether or not professionals will respond to these challenges with increased resistance remains to be seen.

Social Group Differences

In seeking to understand the defense of autonomy at work, we have contrasted professional and craft settings with bureaucratic settings and with settings characterized by supervisory fiat. It is also important, however,

Table 6.6. *Autonomy, Resistance, and Citizenship across Social Groups*

Variables	N	Withhold Enthusiasm	Alternative Status Hierarchies	Autonomy	Cooperation	Creativity	Job Satisfaction	Good Soldiers
Union	69	.77	**2.27**	2.76	2.35	2.36	2.89	2.89
Nonunion	33	.56	**1.65**	2.97	2.42	2.56	2.97	3.41
Significance[a]		*.055*	*.002*	*.451*	*.553*	*.428*	*.729*	*.106*
Male majority (100%)	36	.68	2.10	**3.06**	2.46	**2.55**	3.03	3.07
Some female	17	.57	2.31	**3.41**	2.41	**2.76**	3.25	2.93
Gender mixed (25%–75%)	30	.86	2.14	**2.40**	2.29	**2.24**	2.46	3.19
Mostly female	19	.64	1.71	**2.37**	2.44	**1.95**	3.00	3.07
Significance[b]		*.563*	*.273*	*.007*	*.596*	*.044*	*.283*	*.830*
Majority group (100%)	14	.58	2.10	2.57	**2.69**	2.00	2.79	3.67
Some minority	24	.77	2.11	3.10	**2.65**	2.83	3.00	2.88
Ethnically mixed (25%–75%)	16	.85	2.09	2.69	**2.06**	2.33	2.67	2.93
Mostly minority	8	.60	2.67	2.50	**2.29**	1.86	2.50	2.83
Significance[b]		*.489*	*.304*	*.756*	*.005*	*.784*	*.447*	*.156*
pre-1975	46	.76	2.15	2.57	2.28	2.21	2.82	**2.71**
1975 and after	62	.67	2.05	2.98	2.47	2.56	2.95	**3.34**
Significance[a]		*.424*	*.567*	*.089*	*.123*	*.134*	*.552*	*.032*
United Kingdom	31	.86	1.85	2.62	2.22	2.38	2.64	3.32
United States	57	.65	2.14	2.96	2.44	2.51	3.13	2.96
Significance[a]		*.071*	*.190*	*.230*	*.117*	*.639*	*.063*	*.303*

Note: All contrasts that are significant at $p \leq .10$ are in bold type.
[a] *t*-test for contrast between two groups.
[b] F-test for linearity.

to consider differences across social groups in the patterns of autonomy and the defense of autonomy.

Table 6.6 evaluates several aspects of autonomy and the defense of autonomy across social groups. This table shows relatively few differences between social groups in relation to the defense of autonomy. In general, different groups appear to respond similarly to challenges to job autonomy. Nevertheless, several specific contrasts do emerge that are worth considering. Union environments are the only identifiable locus that distinctly encourages alternative status hierarchies. In Chapter 5 we described a unionized automobile assembly factory in which strike stories were passed down as factory lore to new recruits (Beynon 1975). Such strike stories and the union environment in general help create a cultural setting supportive of alternative workplace identities independent of those offered by management (Edwards 1992a; Fantasia 1988;

Ferner and Hyman 1992). Other groups differences, such as those based on gender, race, country, or time period appear largely unrelated to the emergence of independent identities.

Autonomy and creativity, however, are differentiated by the gender composition of the work force. Women appear to work disproportionately in environments that are characterized by relatively low levels of autonomy and creativity in work (see also England 1992). Many of the professional and craft environments in which employees have relatively high levels of autonomy involve occupations that have traditionally been dominated by men. The historic channeling of women into occupations with low autonomy and creativity constitutes a significant challenge to working with dignity for the women involved.

The racial composition of work forces is significantly related to the level of cooperation with management. The role of racial tension in undermining cooperation in a mixed-race work force is evident in the following exchange between minority pickers and their Anglo foreman:

> 'You know you've got it, you're loaded. You make a fortune off poor people.' 'How do you know? I've got a big family to take care of.' And Red replied, 'For what you make a week, you could take care of ten big families. We're poor and we've got nothing. You're rich and you've got everything.' (Friedland 1971:55)

The ethnographer describes how the workers later became agitated about picking cherries from tall trees because of the wind and the danger of falling from precarious ladders: "They complained how much they hated cherry picking and started slowing down. Several people were beating the trees with sticks, trying to knock cherries down rather than pick them. This was done quite violently, as if they hated the trees and were trying to kill them" (Friedland 1971:78).

Racial tensions can also play a role in undermining cooperation in service occupations. In a study of domestic workers, an ethnographer notes how covert racial tensions can fuel informal resistance:

> I remember one Sunday morning, this woman told me to scrub her kitchen floor on my hands and knees. I got mad at her. . . . So I got a whole lot of ammonia and . . . just poured it over the floor. And then half wiped it up. . . . That floor looked bad for two or three days. I wouldn't wash it 'cause I told her I'd already scrubbed it. . . . She had wanted me to get on my knees and scrub it. And I wasn't *thinking* about getting on my knees and scrubbing it. And, after that, I could just mop it up and it would look nice. No, my knees weren't made for walking all over the floor. (Rollins 1985:142–143)

Temporal changes in autonomy, creativity, cooperation, and related aspects of work are evidenced in the ethnographic data in only a relatively muted fashion. Although few individual trends are statistically significant, the overall pattern does suggest some modest increase in autonomy, creativity, and workplace cooperation over time. No significant contrasts distinguish the United States from the United Kingdom. In general, social groups appear to respond similarly to challenges to autonomy on the job. Many aspects of the human quest for dignity at work thus appear to be relatively universal across status groups, time, and place.

Conclusions

Professional and craft work are similar in that each relies on substantial training and experience. Significant autonomy on the job is required for the successful utilization of that training and experience. As a result of their skills and autonomy, both craft workers and professional workers take great pride in their work and display high levels of citizenship across a variety of dimensions that contribute to the overall efficiency of production and the success of organizations.

Craft workers and professional workers differ, however, in important ways. Craft workers resist management and management directives on a regular basis. Indeed, in terms of conflict with management, subversion of particular managers and creation of alternative status hierarchies, craft workers offer more resistance to management directives than workers in any other situation. It appears that craft workers use the power provided by their unique skills to redefine the workplace on their own terms and to resist subordination to management demands and agendas. Professionals, in contrast, exhibit *less resistance* than any other category of worker. The contrast in resistance behaviors between professional and craft employees is particularly surprising in light of other similarities between these groups.

The fact that professionals work extremely hard and with a minimum of resistance helps explain why they are so often looked upon favorably by management. Hard work in the absence of a culture of resistance, however, may also help explain why so many professional employees report working excessively long hours (Schor 1992). Full effort in the absence of significant resistance encourages management to chronically exploit professional workers through understaffing and work overloads. Through practicing high levels of citizenship and abstaining from resistance to management definitions, professional workers may have invited various types of "lean production" strategies into white-collar settings.

Understaffing and overwork in professional settings can lead to an intensification of work analogous to the drive toward "full utilization" of working time in factory settings. If professional workers continue to be "trusted employees" who rarely if ever resist management directives, the future for professionals may well be characterized by continuing overwork and excessive hours (Hochschild 1997).

The growth of a large and highly educated group of professional workers in advanced industrial economies has sparked discussions in the social sciences of the professions as a "new class" situated between managers and workers (Creighton and Hodson 1997; Whalley and Barley 1997). It is argued that professionals are more liberal in their political views than managers because of their greater education. However, they are also strongly differentiated from the working class by their education, status, and income (Wuthnow and Shrum 1983).

What do the current findings, based on an appraisal of the ethnographic evidence about professional's work lives suggest about the class position of professionals? Based on workplace behaviors, it is difficult to see professionals as clearly differentiated from managers. Professionals are reluctant to risk their hard won privileges through resistance to management agendas, and they appear willing to work long hours without reservation. To the extent that an independent stance in the workplace is necessary for the emergence of a distinct class position, professionals do not qualify. In the workplace, professionals appear to be well characterized as "trusted employees" operating at the request of and in the interests of management (see also Burris 1993).

The professions, however, are also in a period of rapid change. The professions are expected to continue to expand as a proportion of the labor force with the more poorly paid technical and semiprofessional occupations providing the bulk of the employment growth (Hodson and Sullivan 1995). In addition, professionals are increasingly employed in large for-profit corporations that are often parts of even larger corporate or financial entities. Professionals have also come under increasing risk of layoffs as their employment has expanded. Instead of a privileged and protected elite, professionals are now the modal occupational category in many high-technology and research-oriented enterprises. As a result, layoffs and unemployment have become increasingly common experiences for professional workers, especially in the volatile high-technology industries (Rogers and Larsen 1984).

Will the expansion of professional employment and the possible dilution of professional privilege affect the willingness of professionals to work long hours without contesting administrative agendas? Will continuing changes in the organizational locus of professional work radicalize professionals? Will professionals be able to establish an independent agenda in the workplace distinct from management and administrative agendas? The answers to these questions are yet in the process of emerging and provide important topics of research for social scientists. The answers to these questions are also important for professional employees in their quest for dignity at work.

The spread of professional training and orientations to more and more workers provides a solution for management to some of the contradictions entailed in employing craft workers, who are highly skilled but who have their own agenda and their own independent culture and identity. The expansion of professional orientations in technical fields represents a possible erosion of craft employment. The continued expansion of the professions, however, may significantly change the orientation of at least some professional employees. As a result, some professionals may develop their own independent agendas in the workplace separate from those of management and possibly more similar to those of craft workers. In addition, although the professions are important in advanced industrial economies, not all members of the labor force are, or will ever be, professional workers.

The challenge for management is to try to extend the unquestioning work effort typical of professional workers to more and more sectors of the work force. In addition, management hopes to remain firmly in charge of setting the agenda and determining the logic of production, as they have successfully done with professional workers. Management's latest efforts to achieve these goals rely on expanding the involvement of all employees through various team and participative arrangements. The challenge for employees is to find new ways to protect and expand their own autonomy and well-being in defense of working with dignity within the new more participative workplace of the future. We turn to team production, employee involvement, and the quest for dignity in participative settings in the next chapter.

7

Negotiating Employee Involvement

Employees are increasingly being asked to take a more active role in work-related decisions across a wide range of organizational settings. The movement toward increased employee involvement results from the demands of increasingly complex production systems that require greater employee involvement and initiative in order to operate efficiently. Increased worker initiative in developing strategies to meet production goals is expected from factories (Starkey and McKinlay 1994) to offices (Heckscher and Donnellon 1994) to service settings (Mueller et al. 1994; Smith 1996). The fourth challenge to working with dignity facing employees today is the challenge of translating productivity gains resulting from employee involvement into similar gains for employee dignity. Employee involvement has the potential to extend the sort of bilateral involvement with management previously reserved for skilled professional and craft workers to a wider range of employees. But increased employee involvement has also been associated with downsizing and work intensification and therefore has many contradictory elements – not all of which have positive implications for working with dignity.

The demand for increased employee involvement has attracted considerable attention both in the academic literature and in the business world (Drucker 1993; Pfeffer 1998). The prevalence and diversity of employee participation have been highlighted by Appelbaum and Batt (1994), Osterman (1994), Smith (1997), and Vallas (1999). Employee participation will not be introduced comprehensively all at once since different types of work in complex societies vary greatly in their requirements and organization. In many work settings, however, increasingly complex social and technical systems demand not just new skills but also greater worker initiative grounded on new values, attitudes, and motivations. Frenkel et al. (1995) call such systems "info-normative" in recognition of their integration of "technical, bureaucratic, and normative" components. The future of work life is likely to be colored much more by heightened employee involvement than by technological

171

displacement or by a catastrophic "end to work" as some have predicted (Rifkin 1994).

Although success rates vary dramatically across different versions of employee involvement, the general consensus is that productivity is, on average, increased by heightened worker participation (Doucouliagos 1995; Whyte, Hammer, and Meek 1983). It also appears that workers in participatory settings, again on average, experience greater autonomy and pride in their work than workers in nonparticipatory settings (Hodson 1996; Tausky and Chelte 1991). The spread of organizational structures entailing increased employee participation thus seems inevitable given ever increasing technological and organizational complexity (Appelbaum and Batt 1994).

Will participative systems of production solve management's problems of controlling and motivating workers and simultaneously bring an end to the alienation of work? Such far reaching positive expectations seem exaggerated at this point. However, productivity is often modestly increased in participative settings (Eaton 1994) and workers are generally positive about participation (Hill 1991; Freeman and Rogers 1999; Spector 1986).

The analysis presented in this chapter suggests that current versions of employee participation and involvement are unlikely on their own to bring about an end to alienation at work. Too often calls by management for increased participation are coupled with programs of work intensification and reduced job security under the guise of "increased flexibility." Significant changes in management orientations that are not yet on the horizon will need to be made before the promise of participation for increased dignity at work can be fully realized.

The Varieties of Participation

Workers are being increasingly asked to take part in various forms of employee involvement, such as quality circles, quality of work life programs, joint union–management programs, and various forms of employee ownership (Reich 1992; Rothschild and Russell 1986). Although there is great diversity among these programs, all try to involve employees more actively in increasing productivity and improving product quality. Employee participation builds on the idea of "responsible autonomy" (Friedman 1977) by attempting to meld the interests of workers and their employing organizations. Participation schemes concede to workers a greater role in decision making concerning the details of production in exchange for workers committing themselves to the goal of increased productivity (Dohse, Jurgens, and Malsch 1985).

Because they rely on heightened employee involvement in the process of production, however, these programs can also create openings for expanded worker voice concerning other aspects of work life as well – aspects of work life with possibly significant consequences for working with dignity.

In the participative workplace, instead of detailed plans for increasing productivity being drawn up by management, planning is increasingly delegated to the work group (Walton and Hackman 1986). Workers and work groups are expected to develop detailed plans and procedures to increase productivity. Central to these plans and procedures are new behavioral norms for workers that prescribe their attitudes and behaviors at work (Endo 1994). Thus, instead of management prescribing standards for performance, workers are being asked to develop these standards. The goals to be achieved, however, are still typically set by management and focus on increased productivity and improved product quality.

The heightened role of employees in determining production standards is often characterized as representing a new way to organize work. Instead of work being organized by bureaucratic rules or supervisory fiat, work is increasingly organized on a normative basis by work groups (Barley and Kunda 1992). These work group norms emerge through the process of workers developing detailed procedures to meet goals set by management for productivity and quality. In this new organization of work, management still sets the goals as specified in classic management theory (Barnard 1950), but workers are asked to devise the detailed plans for achieving these goals.

Although teams and employee participation are sometimes introduced as an alternative to unions, the greatest successes of employee participation programs have actually occurred in unionized settings (Appelbaum and Batt 1994; Leicht 1989). Union settings typically employ more skilled workers who have greater commitment to their jobs (Rogers and Streeck 1995). The power base provided by unions also allows at least some protection against manipulative uses of employee participation, protections that may be necessary for the benefits of heightened employee participation to be fully realized (Keller 1995).

The Underside of Employee Involvement

A complicating factor in understanding the role of employee participation in the contemporary economy is that many of the forms of participation have been introduced simultaneously with an intensified utilization of unbridled market forces in the organization of work (Wolf 1995). The underlying rationale for employee involvement programs put forward by management is almost always the "stick" of job loss rather than the "carrot" of greater meaning and dignity in work. Workers are thus asked to participate in the context of heightened job insecurity and reduced corporate commitment to workers.

Many participation schemes are perceived accurately by employees as part of a manipulative drive to raise productivity while offering employees only harder work and greater insecurity. Simultaneously, workers are asked to increase their commitment to the job, to give greater intellectual and physical effort at work, and to increase their level of compliance with management demands (Ray 1986). Most forms of employee involvement do not constitute "real industrial democracy wherein workers and managers share profits, ownership, and high-level governance of firms" (Lincoln and Kalleberg 1990; see also Rothschild and Ollilainen 1999).

When calls for increased participation emerge as part of a package that combines layoffs with calls for increased effort, workers tend to be rightfully suspicious about the range of goals that will be given a full hearing. Even more ominously, employee involvement programs have often been associated with management drives to resist unions and unionization (Grenier 1988). The primary goal of some management-initiated employee involvement programs is to undermine an existing union or prevent the certification of an emerging one (Fantasia, Clawson, and Graham 1988). A more typical goal is to elicit more input and greater effort from workers to compensate for a downsizing of the work force (Parker and Slaughter 1994; Smith 1990). Even where work groups and employee involvement are not blatantly used to undercut workers' rights to independent collective representation, employees and their representatives are still sometimes suspicious that management organized employee involvement is an attempt to gain control of workers' detailed knowledge of the production process without any compensating exchange from the management side (Parker and Slaughter 1994; Thomas 1988:174).

In the United States and the United Kingdom, suspicions about employee participation programs have been particularly high because these programs have come into being simultaneously with employment cutbacks, reduced staffing, increased overtime, and thinly concealed threats about job security (Parker and Slaughter 1994). Increasing numbers of people are working under the implicit or explicit threat of losing their jobs to lower-paid labor overseas, to lower-wage regions inside industrially advanced nations, or to technological displacement (Harrison 1994).

Workers are also wary of the possible use of employee involvement to increase competition among coworkers, particularly in the absence of an organized base of worker power, such as that provided by an independent trade union (Dohse, Jurgens, and Malsch 1985:138). The self-disciplining nature of work groups can be manipulated by management to encourage employees to monitor each other and, potentially, to report the results to management (Parker and Slaughter 1994). Under team organizations of production, increased employee involvement can ironically mean greater autonomy from direct managerial supervision but, simultaneously, greater peer pressure. Management is less visibly present at the point of production, but the work group can be extremely effective at exacting high levels of effort from its members. If workers resist their team's demands, they risk being made to feel unworthy as a team member. Criticism and ostracism by one's peers are powerful forms of social control. Team-based organizations of work can thus provide the basis for an even tighter control of work life than management systems based on bureaucratic rules or supervisory fiat (Barker 1999).

Peer surveillance of coworker behavior in team settings is not just a hypothetical possibility. Peer surveillance is an explicit component of Total Quality Management (TQM) systems, which are increasingly popular in workplaces of all kinds (Hill 1991). In workplaces employing TQM, employees are routinely expected to fill out reports evaluating the performance of other team members (Grenier 1988:47). Such team-based surveillance can even include time studies of other team members to make sure that their performance meets established standards (Graham 1995:105). In this way, responsibilities previously held by management are shifted to the work group. Unfortunately, the tasks may not be redefined in the process to become more humane or more supportive of working with dignity. As a result, work intensification, increased injury rates, and unkind acts towards team members have all been reported in team settings (Graham 1995:143).

Greater surveillance by team members also comes at a time of heightened electronic, and even chemical surveillance of workers. Such surveillance includes video cameras aimed at work stations, monitoring of employee e-mail, and even mandatory drug testing (Marx 1999). In combination, greater team surveillance and greater electronic surveillance have significant potential to undermine the autonomy and dignity of employees across a wide range of settings.

In summary, rather than employee involvement representing greater autonomy for workers, it may represent even closer control, but control now exerted through team members rather than though management. In combination with other aspects of modern production systems, such as just-in-time delivery and sophisticated management information and surveillance systems, teams have the potential to become a core component of an increasingly tight net of control and supervision of work life. In modern production systems, instead of management showing up periodically as supervisor, management may become even more omnipresent in the form of peer supervision and electronic monitoring (Delbridge 1998; Sewell and Wilkinson 1992).

Four Forms of Participation

The forms of employee involvement in the new participatory workplace are quite diverse and vary widely both between and within countries (Cole 1989). The varieties of employee involvement include formal consultation, joint union–management initiatives, work teams, and various versions of employee ownership based on stock shares and sometimes wholesale buyouts by workers. The differences between these varieties of participation can have significant consequences for the meaning of participation and for its implications for working with dignity.

National variations include American Human Relations approaches, Swedish and British Socio-Technical approaches, Japanese Lean Production, Italian Flexible Specialization, and German Quality Production (Appelbaum and Batt 1994). The diversity of these forms of participation suggests the need for a model that is not unidimensional but that instead captures some of the diversity manifest in contemporary participation schemes. For the purposes of this book, I group the various systems of employee involvement into four major categories: team-based systems, formal consultation, joint union–management programs, and full or partial worker ownership.

Team-based systems. Team systems of production based on significant degrees of self-management by work groups have become increasingly important in contemporary organizations. Team-based production systems, however, have a long history in the workplace. Miners, seafarers, and other skilled trades have long relied on teams to coordinate work in situations involving complex tasks (Jackson 1984).

The increased importance of teams in the modern workplace reflects many forces, including increased skill demands associated with sophisticated technologies, new management theories about how best to organize production, and worker demands for increased voice at the workplace. As with all forms of employee participation, the nature and meaning of team production can vary widely across settings (Ortiz 1998).

Japanese companies and their affiliates around the world have led the way toward increased utilization of team-based production systems. Under Japanese team production systems, employees are expected to be ever vigilant for opportunities to work more effectively by identifying and eliminating underutilization of time and resources.

An important underpinning of Japanese quality control circles and other initiatives to improve productivity and increase quality has been the tying of the worker to the company through lifetime employment and through finely graded systems of seniority-based pay (Dore 1973). The tying of the employee and the firm together in a life-long partnership encourages workers to use their skills to improve productivity and thus ensure the firm's future. This shared interest also makes the costs of leaving the firm very high for the employee in terms of lost seniority and earnings (Besser 1996; Thomas 1988).

Lillrank and Kano (1989) note that Japanese workers are not necessarily enthusiastic about involvement in team-based production. Rather, they see participation in quality control circles and related team activities as a requirement for the economic success of their enterprise. Japanese workers participate in problem-solving activities with honesty and candor, but not generally with great enthusiasm or a sense of personal gratification.

In many workplaces Japanese-style teams have been associated with work intensification (Endo 1994), increased pressures for production (Parker and Slaughter 1994:24; Rinehart et al. 1997:27,78), employee monitoring of peers (Roberson 1998:78), and antiunion campaigns (Grenier 1988:47,132). In a discussion of participation programs in Japanese industry, Dohse, Jurgens, and Malsch (1985:128) argue that: "Toyotism is, therefore, not an alternative to Taylorism but rather a solution to its classic problem of the resistance of the workers to placing their knowledge of production in the service of rationalization." It is also mistaken to assume that managers and supervisors disappear in team production settings. Under Japanese team-based systems, front-line supervisors continue to play an active role in controlling and evaluating workers. In many ways, workers are more tightly controlled in team settings than in traditional supervisory settings. The power of the supervisor is not removed; rather, it is extended through allocating additional supervisory functions to the team as a whole (Rinehart et al. 1997:86).

Formal consultation. Formal consultation involves regular meetings between management and employees, or employees' representatives, in which various aspects of work are discussed. Formal consultation can occur in either union on nonunion settings. Formal consultation occurs in settings ranging from manufacturing (Cressey 1985) to police work (Martin 1980) to banking (Smith 1990). Management generally sets the topics for discussion. These topics can include both production related issues and personnel issues but generally exclude pay and benefits, which are either negotiated in union environments or determined unilaterally by management in nonunion environments. The issues discussed may even include long-range planning and the acquisition of new technologies. The range of issues discussed by such committees varies tremendously across settings. At a minimum, almost all such committees concern themselves with issues of safety and health in the workplace. At the other end of the continuum, committees debate issues concerning new investments, layoffs, hiring, and outsourcing of employment (Rogers and Streeck 1995).

Formal consultation has been an important mechanism for improving communication between workers and management and can be an important building block in establishing greater trust in the workplace. The importance and prevalence of systems of formal consultation has spread along with the increased complexity of production systems and the need to involve employees and to solicit their input to achieve maximum productivity and product quality.

Formal consultation has sometimes been criticized for providing routine access by management to employees' opinions without a substantive change in the power relations of the workplace (Rogers and Streeck 1995). Thus, management learns of workers' concerns, but only takes account of these to the extent that it is consistent with management agendas. Shared power and true bilateral negotiation are frequently missing from such systems. Nevertheless, formal consultation does provide a mechanism for employees' voices to be expressed and to have an influence on management behavior.

Joint union–management programs. Joint union–management programs are based on explicit collectively negotiated agreements between union and management to jointly sponsor programs based on employee involvement. In the United Kingdom such programs are relatively commonplace across a wide range of industries (Marks et al. 1998). In the United States such programs are concentrated in the automobile and telecommunications industries (Cooke 1990). Other well-established programs exist in steel, construction, and the public sector. The key focus of many of these programs is on improved worker training to meet the challenges of automation and global competition (Milkman 1997:160).

In joint union–management programs, the issues to be discussed are not necessarily restricted to management-defined agendas. Workers in the automobile industry have successfully bargained for various forms of accelerated training under joint union–management programs and voice a great deal of satisfaction with these programs (Ferman et al. 1990). In these programs, workers receive additional training as part of an exchange for their greater involvement in the workplace and increased contributions to productivity. The programs often involve supplemental training both on and off company time.

Increased communication and direct consultation with workers are also hallmarks of joint union–management programs. A joint program at an American car manufacturer includes the following principles:

- establish effective lines of communication among all employees;
- encourage participation of all employees who wish to become involved;
- strive for expeditious resolution of mutual problems;
- treat all employees with dignity and respect; and
- recognize the contributions of each individual (Milkman 1997:161).

Note that these principles include a focus on employees and their rights and contributions rather than focusing solely on production related issues as is typical of Japanese-style team production systems.

Workers in joint union–management programs are also increasingly allowed to go on purchasing and sales trips previously reserved for management and sales personnel. Workers provide valuable hands-on information in negotiations to secure the best components and new technologies. They also work directly with customers to learn how to improve quality and meet customer needs. The new knowledge and flexibility that such programs generate provide workers with opportunities to develop better relationships with their coworkers and with workers up and down the production chain. The opportunities provided by joint programs encourage employees to construct their organizational roles more actively. This generates new roles and new ideas that are often missing when work roles are unilaterally prescribed by management. In general, workers have been very enthusiastic about joint union–management programs and about participating in decision-making processes historically reserved for management (Milkman 1997; Pfeffer 1998).

The bilateral nature of joint initiatives provides a legitimacy to these programs that is sometimes missing when programs are initiated unilaterally by management. This legitimacy has been identified as a significant foundation for the success of joint union–management programs in stimulating productivity and improving working conditions. The initiatives emerging from joint union–management programs are often more complementary with the public purpose than unilateral management initiatives because they include a focus on the preservation of employment and on the quality of employment as well as on increased productivity (Ferman et al. 1990:187).

Worker ownership. Employee ownership of firms represents a final type of participatory arrangement with possible significant consequences for working with dignity. In situations where employees own the enterprise, they have ultimate rights over its activities and the disposition of its assets. Such ownership rights can be expressed directly through participatory democracy or indirectly through elected delegates (Lindenfeld and Rothschild-Witt 1982). Employee participation provides important opportunities for improved work-life experiences, but even worker ownership is no guarantee that these opportunities will be realized.

Employee ownership generally results in improved productivity and improved employee satisfaction (Pendleton et al. 1998). A core underlying reason for these improvements is that worker-owned enterprises are simply more concerned with the well-being of their employees than organizations owned by outside shareholders (Tucker 1999). They are able to solicit high levels of worker involvement and participation because of the genuine overlap between the goals of the enterprise and those of the employees (Bradley, Estrin, and Taylor 1990). Improved communication, teamwork, and participation under employee ownership are important underpinnings for the relative success of worker-owned enterprises. Work ownership has also been shown to increase employees' political efficacy and involvement in community organizations, as well as their participation in the workplace (Elden 1981).

Worker-owner enterprises, however, still often face precarious circumstances because of factors outside their control. Worker ownership often occurs as a result of an employee buyout of a plant engineered as a last attempt to save the plant and the jobs it represents. In such situations, market forces may already be working against the enterprise. The market niche it serves may be shrinking or its production technology and equipment may be outdated. Employee buyouts, in particular, often face a precarious future because of the circumstances of their birth (Keef 1998).

Worker ownership can be complete or partial. Complete employee ownership occurs when the employees directly own the company through holding all the shares in the company either collectively or individually. Partial ownership occurs through Employee Stock Ownership Plans (ESOPs) in which workers own shares in the company, either as part of a retirement plan or as part of a buyout. But other groups or individuals may also own shares, including shares that constitute the controlling interest in the company. Tax laws, which provide a variety of tax credits and deductions to companies with ESOPs, have encouraged their spread (Russell 1993). Through ESOPs, workers have a voice as partial owners in the company, but they may be one among many voices. The consequences of ESOPs for productivity and improved work lives have generally been more limited than those of full employee ownership. Even where the employees are the sole owners, however, their prerogatives may still be constrained by legal barriers to the exercise of their options imposed by banks or other lenders (Russell and Rus 1991).

What then is the nature of work life, resistance, citizenship, and worker dignity in these new participative settings that are proclaimed by many as harbingers of the future? Participatory organizations in the workplace provide many opportunities for an increased role for employees' voices in the workplace. But increased participation can also be part of a package of changes that include threats to workers' jobs, to their independent self-organization in labor unions, and to their autonomy and dignity. Workers, however, are not naive, and narrowly self-serving management agendas are often quite transparent. Calls for increased employee involvement in meeting company goals with no concern for employees' concerns or even with negative implications for employees' rights are often met with caution and even suspicion on the part of employees (Jackall 1978:142).

Sexton (1981:178) reports divided responses to calls for increased participation. Workers' orientation toward participation is often, "What's in it for me?" When the answer is increased opportunities to expand their training and increase transferable skills, considerable enthusiasm may be evoked. When the answer is that it is necessary to save their jobs, employees often response with grudging acceptance. When the answer is that they must work harder to make up for layoffs and staff cutbacks, but their jobs are still in jeopardy anyway, workers may have significant reservations about giving increased effort through employee involvement schemes. In the following sections we explore both working conditions under various participative plans and the nature of workers' responses to these plans.

Work Life under Employee Involvement

Indicators of the quality of work life across the different versions of employee participation are evaluated in Table 7.1. What is most immediately noticeable is the strong contrast between all of the forms of participation and the absence of employee participation. Employee involvement, whatever its form, results in more meaningful, creative, and positive work-life experiences. These differences are large, consistent, and statistically significant.

An example of high levels of motivation and initiative in a classic team production setting is provided by an ethnography of underground gypsum mining:

Table 7.1. *Employee Involvement and Working Conditions*

Variables	None	Teams	Formal Consultation	Joint Programs	Coop/ ESOP	Significance[a]
Skill	1.53	2.13	2.50	2.00	1.93	.000
Autonomy	2.13	3.12	3.61	2.56	3.00	.000
Freedom of movement	1.57	2.40	2.36	2.06	1.93	.002
Difficult pace	2.76	2.44	2.69	2.75	2.50	.480
Creativity	1.93	2.75	3.00	2.19	2.40	.014
Meaningful work	1.59	2.14	2.14	1.71	1.93	.065
Job ladder coverage	2.93	4.26	4.27	3.20	5.00	.000
Direct supervision	.90	.48	.47	.68	.40	.001
Management abuse	.54	−.31	−.27	.21	−.49	.001
Mismanagement	.52	−.15	−.24	.03	−.57	.003
Size (ln)	5.46	5.22	7.02	6.40	6.00	.104
Local ownership	.25	.41	.28	.20	.40	.571
Ethnographies (N)	32	25	20	16	15	

[a] F-test.

> Mining supervisors never complained about their workers' willingness to work. On the contrary, they typically volunteered expressions of confidence in the miners' motivation. As one of the mining foremen said: 'I think they (the miners) should be given the chance to show initiative. Here in the mine we give the man a job to do and he does it without being watched. . . . The men have to do a job themselves. They're not controlled.' (Gouldner 1964:141)

Gouldner's ethnography of mine workers also illustrates high levels of autonomy in a team-based production system:

> If a miner wished something done, he usually went *directly* to the man who could do it. After searching around and finding him, the miner would discuss the matter and get his consent. . . . Also noteworthy was the fact that when help was requested, the miner requesting it did not need to claim *delegated* authority: that is, he did not usually say, 'Old Bull asked you to help me.' (Gouldner 1964:109)

A more contemporary example from a Volvo automobile assembly plant also illustrates the high levels of group autonomy afforded employees in team-based production systems and the positive responses of

Figure 7.1. Skill and autonomy in participatory workplaces.

workers to this heightened autonomy. A survey at the plant shows that: "Nine out of ten workers want to take responsibility for the quality of the product, and feel that they are partly able to do so" (Gyllenhammar 1977:71).

Levels of autonomy and skill across forms of participation are displayed graphically in Figure 7.1. The highest levels of skill and autonomy are found in production settings that involve formal consultation with workers. An example is provided in an ethnography of an automated steel mill. In this setting, the skills of the workers are essential to production. As a result, supervisors regularly consult with employees concerning the details of production:

> In the steel mill the nature of the process, the physical layout of operations, and the high degree of worker skills made for a closer relationship between the men and upper supervision. Supervisors above the foreman level often consulted with individual men, especially the key workers, on production

problems, since the judgment of the individual worker was important. (Walker and Guest 1952:94)

Production systems based on employee involvement are generally char-acterized by a lessening of direct supervisory oversight of work. This pattern is clearly evidenced in Table 7.1. An example of reduced man-agement oversight in a team setting is provided by an ethnography of deep-sea fishing in which the workers independently devise their own division of labor and their own system of job rotation:

> There'd be six blokes haulin' altogether: one haulin' the back and one haulin' the net-rope, and then there'd be four down in the hold. . . . You swapped over. You didn't stay in the same place all the while. Oh no. See, if a bloke started by haulin' the net-rope, he'd haul his spell on there and then he'd come down and stow the net-rope. . . . The cast-off was on the capstan and the cook was coilin' the ropes all the while. He used t' coil 'em right round. There was a knack in that. Ol' Alec Seamons, you could roll a marble on his ropes. When they were new they took some doin'. (Butcher 1979:72)

This quote also illustrates the pride that workers in team settings take in being part of a team effort that accomplishes difficult tasks through shared skills and effort.

Workers in participative settings also evidence greater creativity in their work than is evidenced by workers outside such settings. Workers involved in team production and formal consultation evidence the highest levels of creativity. The case study discussed in Chapter 1 of employee involvement in a bank undergoing reorganization, for example, reported high levels of creativity among both workers and branch managers as they strove to devise collective and team-based strategies to avoid downsizing (Smith 1990).

The prevalence of mobility ladders within the organization is also strongly differentiated across forms of participation. Settings without any form of employee participation have by far the most limited job ladder coverage providing access to upward mobility within the organi-zation. In contrast, worker cooperatives and organizations with ESOPs evidence the widest access to career-oriented job ladders. An example is provided by a employee-owned garbage collection cooperative in which workers have the opportunity to run for the board of directors that over-sees the entire company: "So what we have now is a democratic form where a guy can come in and run for the Board of Directors. . . . We've now got three new guys signed up to run for the Board this year. One's a mechanic" (Perry 1978:43–44).

Some of the most significant differences between settings with and without worker participation involve management abuse and incompetence. Workplaces without any form of employee participation have higher levels of both mismanagement and abuse than more participatory workplaces. The case study of work in a wiring harness factory reported in Chapter 1, for example, evidenced high levels of mismanagement and abuse in a setting that was notable for its absence of any form of formal *or* informal worker participation (Juravich 1985). It appears that one of the most significant contributions of worker participation is to develop and enforce normative constraints on management so that competence is encouraged and abuse is disallowed. In participative settings management appears to be more likely to live up to its duty to provide a coherent, workable, and respectful organization of production.

Levels of mismanagement and abuse, as these vary across forms of employee participation, are displayed graphically in Figure 7.2. The

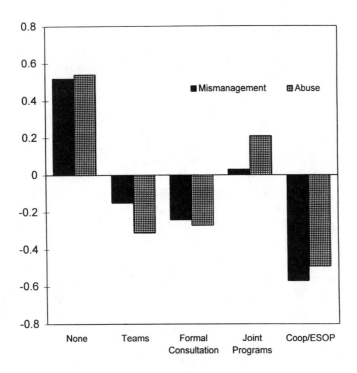

Figure 7.2. Mismanagement and abuse in participatory workplaces.

strong contrast between workplaces with and without employee participation is clear in this figure. The highest levels of management competence and respect for workers are evidenced in settings with substantial
worker participation. A good example of management competence and
respect is provided by an ethnography of life on a Norwegian freighter
in which work is explicitly organized according to the principles of industrial democracy: "[A worker reports,] I like it that the captain doesn't
put anyone down. He's keeping the whole trip together, but he doesn't
bark or growl at anyone. He seems to be drawing everyone's ideas out"
(Schrank 1983:39).

One of the few characteristics of work that is not differentiated
between workplaces with and without employee participation is the pace
of work. The pace of work shows no clear pattern in relation to worker
participation. Ethnographers describing Japanese production systems,
however, typically report a very demanding pace of work and argue that
this is a characteristic of Japanese production systems. For example, an
ethnography of an automobile assembly plant in Japan reports:

> Now the work is nearly three times tougher than when I came
> here six or seven years ago. . . . Until a couple of years ago we
> still had enough workers, and the line used to stop ten
> minutes before finishing time. . . . They keep speeding up the
> line. The faster the line gets, the harder we work to catch up.
> . . . But when we finally get used to the speed, then they make
> it even faster. Right now it's a minute and fourteen seconds
> per unit, but I bet they'll speed it up. The new guys can't
> handle it any more. . . . Personally, I enjoy physical labor. I
> like to work with my hands. But here, it's just too fast. I guess
> I can put up with the hard pace, but the trouble is I never
> know when I can go home. When I come home all I do is
> take a bath, have something to eat, and go to bed. I don't
> have more than an hour to talk with my wife. (Kamata
> 1982:144–145)

Although such observations of a pressured pace of work are relatively
common in the ethnographic literature on Japanese factories, such a
contrast is not evidenced when systematically comparing the full
range of team production systems to other forms of production. Many
workplaces demand a rapid pace of work and, on average, team-based
production systems do not appear to be significantly different from
other settings in this regard. However, there have been relatively few
in-depth studies of Japanese-style team production and the findings
reported here do not represent the final word on the pace of work in
such settings.

Employee Involvement and Resistance

We have seen that worker participation is associated with a wide range of improved working conditions, including increased skills and greater autonomy, creativity, and meaning in work. The particular form of participation seems to matter less for improved working conditions than merely the fact of participation, in any form, versus nonparticipation. Given the relatively positive characteristics of work life in participatory settings, how do workers respond to employee involvement in terms of resistance and citizenship on the job? In other words, how does employee involvement influence the defense of dignity on the job?

Patterns of resistance across forms of employee involvement are presented in Table 7.2. The patterns are not particularly strong as shown in the muted levels of statistical significance. The absence of strong patterns of resistance suggests that increased employee involvement has not brought about an end to worker resistance.

Certain patterns in resistance behaviors, however, do emerge. As in the case of working conditions, the principal contrast is not between different forms of participation, but between participation and nonparticipation. For five of the nine measures of resistance, the highest levels occur

Table 7.2. *Resistance under Employee Involvement*

Variables	None	Teams	Formal Consultation	Joint Programs	Coop/ ESOP	Significance[a]
Resistance scale	.29	–.32	.09	.15	–.35	.117
Effort bargaining	1.96	1.61	1.36	1.62	1.50	.039
Withhold enthusiasm	.82	.62	.71	.83	.55	.361
Conflict with supervisors or managers	3.05	2.54	3.24	2.81	2.50	.047
Informal group resistance	2.50	1.90	2.08	2.31	1.87	.398
Strikes	.33	.10	.21	.43	.21	.181
Turnover	2.31	1.85	1.53	2.07	2.29	.047
Alternative status hierarchies	2.30	2.09	2.08	2.08	1.75	.493
Making out	3.00	3.40	2.82	2.43	1.89	.039
Ethnographies (N)	32	25	20	16	15	

[a] F-test.

in workplaces without any form of employee involvement. These aspects of resistance include the summary resistance scale, effort bargaining, informal group resistance, turnover, and the creation and maintenance of alternative status hierarchies. It appears that workers are most likely to engage in resistance behaviors when they are denied participation in the workplace.

Conversely, the lowest levels of resistance are observed in cooperative workplaces based on employee ownership, even if this ownership is only partial, as in the case of ESOPs. Six of the nine measures of resistance reach their lowest levels in cooperative workplaces. These measures include the summary resistance scale, withholding enthusiasm, conflict with supervisors, informal group resistance, the maintenance of alternative status hierarchies, and making out by maximizing individual gains relative to effort.

Joint union–management plans have been a hallmark of the automobile industry in the United Kingdom and the United States (Womack, Jones, and Roos 1990). Joint programs have emerged in an environment of increasing competition, declining sales, and resulting overcapacity. Joint initiatives have often been preferred to Japanese-style team concepts because of the importance of securing union support for new programs. The goal of the programs is still to increase productivity and product quality in order to meet increased global competition, but union and management bilaterally negotiate the strategies for increasing productivity instead of management unilaterally imposing them.

The responses of workers to these joint programs, and to programs of formal consultation, are generally very favorable. Although resistance is not eliminated to the extent that it is under worker ownership, it is nevertheless much reduced from its level in workplaces without any form of participation. Overall resistance levels under joint programs and formal consultation are similar to their levels under team production systems. In addition, the lowest levels of effort bargaining and turnover are evidenced in production systems that include formal consultation.

Team systems of production register the lowest level of strikes but are otherwise not distinguished from other forms of participation. The low level of strikes under team systems supports the argument of many researchers that teams systems are sometimes developed by management for the express purpose of avoiding unionization (Grenier 1988).

Researchers have frequently argued that team systems of production displace worker loyalty from coworkers to management and to the organization. Indeed, some researchers argue that this displacement is a significant part of the corporate rationale for introducing team systems of production. In this vision, a core goal of management-initiated teams is to shift the loyalty of the worker away from the work group and toward management and the organization. The values and motivations of employees thus come under more direct management control because management defines the team's goals. This shift in loyalties is further reinforced through changes in corporate "culture" that emphasize loyalty to the organization and explicit rewards for group performance (Casey 1995; Delbridge 1998).

A systematic comparison of the case study data on team systems of production, however, indicates no such shifting of loyalties. The creation and maintenance of alternative status hierarchies is not differentiated between forms of participation or even between participation and nonparticipation.

It appears that team systems of production are not necessarily successful in shifting loyalties toward management, even though team systems sometimes include such an agenda as an implicit or explicit goal. Researchers have noted the limited success of team systems of production in overcoming the historic rift between management and workers across a variety of settings (May 1999). For example, a study of workers in Canadian pulp and paper companies in the process of implementing greater employee involvement suggests that the workers continue to "perceive the organization as made up of opposed parts with workers on one side and owners on the other" (Glenday 1995:496). Similarly, a study of British workers suggests that employees retain a "them versus us" orientation even in the face of new industrial relations systems stressing greater involvement (Kelly and Kelly 1991). In the United States, a study of a Mazda automobile assembly plant located in the industrial heartland of Michigan reports that one of the principal motivations behind the successful unionization drive in the plant was the desire of the workers to maintain identities and loyalties that were independent from management (Fucini and Fucini 1990:211). In summary, based on a systematic comparison of the case study evidence, there is little indication that team-based production systems have been successful in shifting workers' loyalties away from their coworkers and toward management.

Employee Involvement and Citizenship

We have seen that workers' resistance to management is modestly reduced under arrangements that encourage employee involvement. The least resistance occurs in workplaces with the most fully developed forms of industrial democracy based on full or partial employee ownership. More limited forms of employee involvement also result in lessened worker resistance, but the reduction is more modest.

Table 7.3. *Citizenship under Employee Involvement*

Variables	None	Teams	Formal Consultation	Joint Programs	Coop/ESOP	Significance[a]
Citizenship scale	−.47	.34	−.06	.12	.40	.011
Cooperation	2.11	2.52	2.29	2.50	2.67	.018
Commitment to organizational goals	.31	.64	.78	.53	.58	.028
Pride in work	1.81	2.44	2.67	2.13	2.21	.001
Extra effort	.60	.92	.71	.81	.91	.063
Peer training	2.76	3.25	3.00	3.50	3.09	.330
Insider knowledge	3.32	3.96	4.50	4.00	4.00	.000
Job satisfaction	2.40	3.21	3.19	2.88	3.07	.038
Productivity	2.25	2.32	2.44	2.53	2.60	.483
Ethnographies (N)	32	25	20	16	15	

[a] F-test.

Citizenship, in contrast, is influenced by employee involvement in a stronger and more widespread fashion. Table 7.3 indicates that workplaces with employee involvement evidence much higher levels of worker citizenship than workplaces without participation. The contrasts across forms of participation are significant for each dimension of citizenship and form a consistent pattern. The lowest level for each aspect of citizenship considered occurs in workplaces without any form of employee involvement. These dimensions of citizenship include cooperation, commitment, pride in work, extra effort, and use of insider knowledge to facilitate production. The lowest levels of job satisfaction and productivity also occur in workplaces without any form of employee involvement.

The type of participation that elicits the greatest citizenship varies with the dimension of citizenship considered, but employee ownership again stands out as eliciting especially favorable responses from workers. The summary scale of citizenship, cooperation, and productivity are all highest in enterprises with worker ownership.

An ethnography of an employee-owned plywood mill provides an example of the positive consequences of participation for cooperation and productivity:

> It's altogether different here [than in my former job]. It took
> me a little while to get used to this because where I worked
> over there . . . you did your job and you didn't go out and do

> something else. Here you get in and do anything to help. Everybody pitches in and helps. The people stick together, that's the reason we've gone so far and production is so high, cuz everybody works together. (Greenberg 1986:38)

Similarly, an ethnography of a garbage collection cooperative reports that workers take "the greatest pride in both the service they provide and their business ownership" (Perry 1978:13). Spontaneous cooperation between workers and between work crews is common as the owner–employees strive both to do their work well and to create a humane working environment for themselves:

> Cooperation between crews was common. Indeed, one time when Ernie had to quit early because he hurt his back, a nearby crew took over a few blocks of collection so that Freddie and his men would get through sooner. . . . They pitched in with energy and cheer to help him out. (Perry 1978:96–97)

The workers identify strongly with the company and experience the pride and commitment that comes with a sense of ownership and long-term commitment. As one worker reports, "I've been raised in the company. . . . I loved it from – when I was old enough to count money, I collected garbage bills" (Perry 1978:119).

Levels of cooperation across forms of participation are displayed graphically in Figure 7.3. This figure again highlights the contrast between the lowest levels of cooperation in settings with no worker participation and higher levels of cooperation under any of the forms of employee involvement. For example, high levels of cooperation and peer support are reported in a study of a Swedish automobile assembly plant in which "employees were involved from the first planning stages and their contributions were important in the eventual success of the factory" (Gyllenhammar 1977:106). Workers in this factory are organized into works councils, which provide a venue for both formal consultation and the initiation of joint union–management programs.

Other aspects of worker citizenship are also seen at high levels under the various forms of employee involvement. Pride, job satisfaction, and the use of insider knowledge to advance production reach their highest levels under team systems or formal consultation. The lowest levels of both pride and insider knowledge are evidenced in situations without any form of participation. The case study of employee involvement in a bank that is reported in Chapter 1 provides many examples of significant levels of pride in work and of the use of insider knowledge in support of production (Smith 1990).

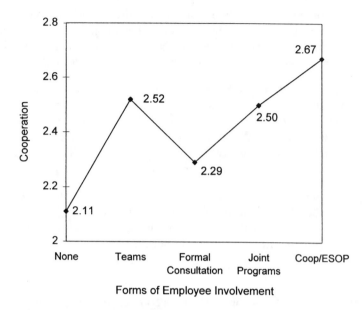

Figure 7.3. Cooperation in participatory workplaces.

Team-based production setting and settings utilizing formal consultation evidence the highest levels of job satisfaction. Results reported in Table 7.2 also indicated that strikes are least common in team settings. The infrequent occurrence of strikes in team settings may reflect relatively good working conditions and satisfied workers, but it can also reflect a lack of unions and a lack of worker power to engage in strikes. It is also noteworthy that the highest levels of effort are evident in team-based production settings. This complex and somewhat contradictory picture of team-based production systems has often been noted in the literature on emerging forms of employee involvement.

An ethnography of a pharmaceutical factory in the United States that utilizes a system of employee participation that includes both teams and formal consultation reports on the contradictory nature of work in participatory settings. Employee benefits at the factory are the best in the area and include excellent health insurance coverage and maternity benefits, which are especially appealing to the mostly female work force. In addition, the clean-room working conditions lend "a dignity to the monotonous manufacturing process" (Grenier 1988:31). However, extremely high levels of effort are expected and the participation program is used to divide the workers against each other and undermine an ongoing unionization drive:

> People are willing to put up with a great deal for this type of
> work. They will defend it by attacking fellow workers and by
> justifying outrageous abuses of power by management. . . .
> One male worker, a strong union activist, knew why the union
> had a rough time organizing at Ethicon. He knew why
> workers fluctuated, to the very end, between voting for or
> against the union. He knew why management was able to
> convince the workers that a vote for the union was a vote
> against the company and that the company, not the union,
> was the true friend of the workers. 'Working at Ethicon,' he
> said, 'is the best and the worst you can imagine.' (Grenier
> 1988:32)

In this setting job satisfaction is high, but so are job pressures, and
employees are caught in the crossfire between a management committed
to remaining nonunion and a substantial core of workers committed to
a forming a union.

Team-based production systems have often been noted for embodying
such contradictory elements and for the often stressful nature of the
working environment (Roberson 1998). The contradictory nature of
modern team-based production is deeply connected to the conditions
of its birth. Team-based systems appeal to employees because of the
increased participation allowed, but teams have frequently been introduced as a mechanism for heightening productivity (Fucini and Fucini
1990:175). In such settings, the team organization of work often includes
significant aspects of "management by stress" as supervisors push teams
to increase productivity and improve quality, often under implicit or
explicit threats of layoffs or plant closures (Parker and Slaughter
1994:24).

Social Group Differences

In order to explore the consequences of employee participation, we have
examined patterns of resistance and citizenship across various forms of
employee involvement. It is also important, however, to consider the
possibility of differences across social groups in the prevalence of, and
responses to, heightened employee involvement.

Table 7.4 evaluates several aspects of work life of particular concern
in this chapter across social groups based on unionization, race, gender,
time period, and nation. Access to workplace participation is not clearly
differentiated across these different social settings. None of the contrasts

Table 7.4. *Employee Involvement, Resistance, and Citizenship across Social Groups*

Variables	N	Participation[a]	Commitment	Peer Training	Insider Knowledge	Job Ladder Coverage	Mismanagement	Conflict with Management
Union	69	71%	.48	2.17	3.84	3.79	-.03	2.98
Nonunion	33	76%	.67	2.29	3.90	4.20	.04	2.67
Significance[b]		.620	.114	.333	.775	.312	.719	.105
Exclusively male (100%)	36	78%	.42	3.21	3.94	**4.26**	**-.35**	2.74
Some female	17	71%	.69	3.47	4.00	**3.88**	.20	2.82
Gender mixed (25%–75%)	30	63%	.59	2.72	3.71	**3.33**	.05	2.93
Mostly female	19	68%	.67	2.91	3.75	**3.39**	**.42**	2.78
Significance[c]		.294	.126	.132	.279	**.040**	**.008**	.653
Majority group (100%)	14	57%	.71	3.50	3.64	3.09	-.33	2.58
Some minority	24	80%	.73	3.07	4.27	4.55	-.03	2.80
Ethnically mixed (25%–75%)	16	69%	.37	3.00	3.71	3.53	.11	3.07
Mostly minority	8	12%	**.17**	3.86	3.50	2.50	.15	2.93
Significance[c]		.073	**.005**	.833	.397	.371	.241	.254
Pre-1975	46	67%	.49	3.08	3.89	3.70	.03	2.87
1975 and after	62	73%	.59	3.10	3.85	3.90	-.02	2.83
Significance[b]		.563	.335	.924	.831	.578	.769	.842
United Kingdom	31	77%	.44	2.95	3.92	4.11	.00	2.93
United States	57	70%	.57	3.22	3.98	3.98	.05	2.88
Significance[b]		.472	.291	.385	.752	.763	.824	.822

Note: All contrasts that are significant at p ≤ .10 are in bold type.

[a] Participation is coded as percent of ethnographies indicting any form of worker participation.

[b] *t*-test for contrast between two groups.

[c] *F*-test for linearity.

across social groups is statistically significant. Several of the contrasts, however, are in expected directions. For example, participation appears to have increased over time. In addition, minority employees appear to have less access to participatory workplaces. The limited access of minority workers to workplace participation programs may be at least partially responsible for the lower level of commitment in workplaces with primarily minority work forces, which is also evidenced in Table 7.4.

In general, the contrasts across social groups for the remaining work characteristics are also quite modest. Social differences appear to be considerably less important as determinants of resistance, citizenship, and related work life experiences than the nature of worker participation (or the lack of participation).

The only notable exception to this general pattern involves the work of women. Female employees appear to have less access to job ladders for upward mobility and are more likely to suffer from mismanagement. The limited mobility opportunities of female workers have long been noted and are much discussed in the workplace literature (England 1992; Kanter 1977). The finding that women have a greater likelihood of working under mismanagement, however, has not been widely reported in the research literature. This oversight may be due in part to the failure by social scientists to adequately conceptualize, measure, and study mismanagement in the workplace (see Hodson 1999c). An example of the corrosive effects of mismanagement on worker morale in a setting employing a largely female work force is provided by an ethnography of a British electronics assembly factory. Following an episode in which the foreman causes a recently hired worker to get fired by failing to train her in the job requirements, the workers start talking and "in ones and twos we agreed that you couldn't trust [the supervisor], that he was two-faced" (Cavendish 1982:82).

The systematic examination of ethnographic accounts of the workplace strongly suggests that mismanagement is more prevalent in establishments with predominantly female work forces. The reasons for this association may lie at least in part in the relatively low wages typical of such workplaces and in the more casual approach by management to the supervision of female employees as a low-wage labor force. Another component may lie in reduced respect for female employees by both male and female supervisors.

Conclusions

Increased employee involvement is associated with significant improvements in the quality of work life across a wide range of organizational settings. Employee involvement is associated with increased skills and autonomy, reduced mismanagement and abuse, and greater pride and citizenship at work. These positive transformations of the workplace create new opportunities for rewarding work lives for an increasing proportion of the labor force.

The differences between various types of participation, while sometimes notable, appear to be much less significant than the simple contrast between participation and lack of participation. Employee ownership, either full ownership or partial ownership through ESOPs, and the resulting increase in workplace democracy appears as a positive outlier among the various forms of participation on some dimensions. Even this pattern, however, is not consistent across all aspects of resistance or citizenship. Based on the analysis presented here it is difficult to certify one form of participation over another in terms of its consequences for working with dignity. All appear to be potentially positive contributors to an improved workplace environment and to improved opportunities for working with dignity (Derber and Schwartz 1983; Klein 1991).

The effects of employee involvement appear to be more pronounced in terms of improved citizenship than in terms of reduced resistance. While participation does decrease resistance behaviors, the patterns are less dramatic than those involving citizenship (see also Fernie and Metcalf 1995; Tsui et al. 1997).

Do new forms of worker participation signal an end to the kinds of alienation from work that have been so prevalent since the start of the industrial revolution? In the last two chapters we have discussed two forms of work organization that involve at least limited bilateral negotiation of workplace norms – professional and craft organizations of work and participatory organizations of work. Both of these forms of bilateral negotiation of workplace norms and standards appear to contribute to a more humane workplace and to increase opportunities for dignity at work.

We should not be too quick, however, to proclaim an end to alienation from work. Not all workers are involved in professional or craft work or in participatory arrangements at work. In addition, we have seen that professional and participatory arrangements are often associated with increased workloads and demands for extra effort on the part of employees. In such settings, externally imposed exploitation may be replaced by workers' self-exploitation in exchange for higher wages and greater autonomy or in response to peer pressure.

It is noteworthy that resistance is less influenced by increased participation than is citizenship. Workers appear to be aware that much remains to be achieved in the struggle for dignity at work. Worker resistance has not been eliminated in the participatory workplace and workers' independent voices still need to be heard. Many forms of employee involvement only provide opportunities for workers' input on issues that are consistent with management goals. Issues of interest to workers that are inconsistent with management agendas are commonly defined as outside the range of acceptable topics for discussion (Wolf 1995). Given the continuing reality of only selected topics being available for consideration in employee participation programs, independent avenues of worker voice will continue to be important in the workplace (Clawson and Fantasia 1983). Such avenues include those provided by trade unions and by individual and collective forms of resistance. It is also worth noting that the greatest reductions in resistance and the greatest increases in citizenship are observed in workplaces based on full or partial worker ownership. Such workplaces incorporate the greatest opportunities for discussion of a full range of topics of interest to workers and do not abridge these to match management-defined organizational goals.

In workplaces with strongly circumscribed forms of employee participation, workers are likely to continue to resist management agendas in an effort to make their voices heard (Gannage 1995; Thompson and Ackroyd 1995; Webb and Palmer 1998). Relevant strategies can include "resistance through distance" as workers decline to become more than minimally involved in participation programs (Collinson 1994:28; Kunda 1992). Continuing resistance strategies are also likely to rely on the maintenance of independent identities separate from management prescribed ones. Such identities can rest on class, gender, or professional distinctions that allow workers to construct and maintain a group identity separate from, and partly in opposition to, management (Ezzamel and Willmott 1998; Rinehart, Huxley, and Robertson 1997).

A significant part of the responsibility for improving participation programs and making them more meaningful to workers rests directly on managers. Researchers have long identified management commitment as crucial to the success of programs of workplace transformation, including those based on employee participation (Delbridge 1998; Lorenz 1992). Without sustained management commitment to broad-based worker participation, the road to achieving increased employee involvement and commitment will be slower and bumpier (Chelte et al. 1989). To the extent that management maintains an orientation based on achieving flexibility at the expense of reduced security, dignity, and well-being for workers, continuing conflicts between employees and managers over the meaning and nature of employee involvement can be expected to continue (Smith 1997; Vallas and Beck 1996).

In participatory systems, management also runs a heightened risk of being defined as inefficient or inept – as restricting the development of productive capacity (Wajcman 1983). Worker concerns and worker resistance in participatory settings thus have a tendency to spread from shop floor production concerns to issues that have traditionally been discussed by management behind closed doors (Derber and Schwartz 1983). Under participatory forms of production the work group takes on an increased role in organizing production and negotiating and enforcing work standards. In theory, workers' goals in such settings converge with organizational goals. When employees are encouraged to identify with the fate of the company, however, they implicitly gain the right to be concerned with broader company policies. These new rights can generate increased concern with managerial choices and management competence.

Participative programs in the workplace create many possibilities for heightened worker power that have yet to be fully realized. These empowering aspects of employee involvement create potential contradictions for managers and capitalists. From the management viewpoint, the broadly empowering nature of employee involvement can reduce its value and usefulness and may, in fact, represent limiting factors on the spread of employee involvement programs.

Worker participation, however, is here to stay and will in all likelihood be extended to include more and more workers. The dynamics leading to increased employee involvement include increased levels of worker education, more complex production technologies, and resulting heightened demands for involvement and teamwork. In addition, increased employee involvement and increased teamwork are themselves sources of new skills and abilities for workers. These new abilities include interpersonal skills, cross-training in new specialties, and heightened cognitive skills acquired in the process of learning and using new and more complex technologies (Smith 1996). These new skills are an additional source of potentially heightened worker power in the participatory workplace.

Depending on the nature of the involvement that is solicited, workers' responses can range from enthusiasm for new training and new duties, to grudging acceptance, and even to cynicism and active resistance. Much is yet to be revealed about the new participatory workplace and about the responses it will evoke from employees. New forms of employee involvement potentially expand the realm of worker power and autonomy. But can the range of topics to be discussed truly be expanded under participative programs to include broader organizational goals and strategies that deeply influence workers' well-being? What proportion of the labor force will be involved in such programs? Will attempts to substitute direct participation for union representation undermine employee rights that have taken decades to win? The crucial agenda for workers as they increasingly confront programs of employee involvement is to bend such programs to achieve the goal of increased worker dignity as well as heightened productivity.

8

Coworkers – For Better or Worse

Coworkers represent a fifth challenge to working with dignity, but they also represent an important resource. Coworkers help provide meaning in work through the sharing of work life experiences and through friendships. Coworkers can also provide a basis for group solidarity and mutual support in the face of denials of dignity at work. Some minimum amount of support from coworkers is essential for the successful defense of dignity in almost any situation – from the smallest encounter with a supervisor to large scale and lengthy strikes. Coworkers, however, can also make daily life at work a nightmare through gossip, cliques, interference, scapegoating, and ostracism. The greatest ally in the defense of dignity can sometimes become its greatest enemy – significant abuse at work can come from coworkers as well as from employers.

The importance of coworkers will only increase in post-bureaucratic workplaces because of increased pressure toward employee involvement. Indeed, greater employee involvement is often associated with increased conflict among coworkers as problems and stresses are transferred from worker–management relations to relations among coworkers (Delbridge 1998). Maneuvering, brown nosing, and backstabbing among workers can increase. The challenge for workers is to take advantage of the opportunities offered by heightened involvement to improve their working situation while maintaining solidarity with their coworkers and avoiding intensified competition (Hodson et al. 1993). Increasing racial and gender diversity in the workplace, which may result in additional stresses on coworker relations, also heightens the significance of coworker relations (Jackson and Ruderman 1995).

The Social Context of Work Life

Coworker relations have both instrumental and affective underpinnings. Some minimum of support from coworkers is instrumental, even essential, for defending dignity at work. Widespread management abuse can evoke high levels of group solidarity in defense of dignity (Fantasia 1988; Linhart 1981:35). The work of railroad porters, who suffered both racial and class-based degradation, illustrates the importance of coworker solidarity in defending dignity at work:

> Porters ... had to hustle and force themselves to swallow a thousand and one indignities a day and worse. . . . [In response, porters] aided each other – for example, covering a fellow porter's car while the man stole a few hours' sleep, warning each other if somebody learned that a spotter was on board, and teaching new porters the tricks of the trade. (Santino 1989:70)

These supportive group activities were essential for survival on the job. Supportive relations with coworkers also had an affective aspect – they helped affirm porters' positive self images in an environment that was frequently hostile and abusive (see also Halle 1984:171).

Group solidarity is not restricted to male workers. Westwood (1984: 90) describes how elaborate rituals concerning birthdays and weddings evolved among a largely female work force in a knitting mill. These rituals create solidarity through shared activities and the exchange of gifts. The rituals are important to the women involved because they displace time, focus, and resources from the mill work to their own agendas. Group activities in this setting focus on symbolic distancing from management and on the creation of alternative, positive self-identifications (see also Pollert 1981:129).

An important avenue for reclaiming self-esteem in an abusive environment is to develop strong group ties (Ezzamel and Willmott 1998; Roy 1958). Identity and status can then be achieved through group activities and through affirming group values. Halle (1984:181) notes how workers in a chemical factory develop their own alternative value structures, which elevate generosity and wit as character traits. Many of their group activities, both on and off the job, involve realizing these values through gift giving, mutual aid, and joking and teasing. Similarly, an ethnographer working as a participant observer in an electronics factory reports being overwhelmed by the generosity of the poorly paid women with whom she works:

> [After returning from a two-week sick leave without pay,] I was talking to Anna when she stuffed a £10 note in my trouser pocket so quickly I wasn't even really sure what it was. She was giving it to me because I would be short, having lost two weeks' wages. . . . I was quite overwhelmed by her generosity; the gift was completely genuine and she really

> didn't want the money back. The whole attitude toward
> money and seeing that others had got enough was so different
> from my previous job where although we earned much more,
> people remembered who owed whom a cup of coffee. All the
> women were very generous, sharing out sweets and crisps and
> whatever they bought for themselves. (Cavendish 1982:67)

Coworker relations at work include both affective and instrumental functions, each of which may have supportive and conflictual facets. The affective aspects involve sentiments of affiliation and belonging on the one hand and, potentially, ostracism and rejection on the other. Positive instrumental coworker relations involve providing assistance in work-related aspects of the job and the maintenance of solidarity against abuse or excessive demands from management. On the other hand, coworkers can also interfere with one's work and create roadblocks to completing a job effectively and on time. Often such roadblocks involve passive and well-cloaked noncompliance with work-related requests from others rather than active interference, which can provoke strong sanctions from management.

Because of the complexity of social relations at work and the simultaneous positive and negative aspects of these relations, workers often have a love–hate relationship with their work groups (Hackman 1990; Kolb and Bartunek 1992; Sayles 1958). Conflict among coworkers is not fleeting, extraordinary, or episodic but is often a pervasive and regular feature of work life. Just as conflict between management and employees is a pervasive reality of organizational life, so too is conflict among employees:

> The picture of the giant corporation as a peaceful cooperative
> of its participants is more than highly improbable, it is
> extraordinarily fraudulent. . . . The modern corporation is
> socially a theatre of all the conflicts that might be expected
> when hundreds and thousands of highly charged,
> exceptionally self-motivated, and more than normally, self-
> serving people work closely together. (Galbraith 1986:21)

Coworkers can simultaneously be a blessing and a curse. Yet studies of coworker relations have held at best a secondary place in the analysis of the workplace, lagging far behind the study of sociotechnical relations, labor process control, organizational structures, and individual attributes and attitudes. As a result of our relative inattention to work groups and coworker relations, our knowledge of vertical relations of authority and power at the workplace and individual attitudes about work far outweighs our knowledge of lateral relations among coworkers. Yet social relations constitute an important part of the "social climate" at work (Moos 1986:14) in which workers experience meaning, identity, and dignity (Gabarro 1987:174).

It is widely acknowledged that supportive coworker relations and team performance are increasingly important for the successful functioning of the contemporary workplace. Coworker relations thus take on an increasingly central role, not just in determining the experience and meaning of work but also as key determinants of organizational efficiency and productivity.

Coworkers and the Meaning of Work

Studies that take the role of coworker interactions as a central focus have only recently begun to appear in the published literature (see, for example, Smith 1996). Many important questions remain unanswered, and even unasked, about the role of work groups in the contemporary workplace. What is the role of groups in the informal training of workers? What is their role in enforcing minimum (as well as maximum) levels of output? What kinds of internal conflicts do groups generate, and how do these conflicts influence the group's performance of work tasks? How do groups ensure cohesion? In this chapter we provide preliminary answers to some of these questions and suggest some new directions for workplace studies as they grapple with the changing nature of coworker relations in the workplace.

Ethnographic observations suggest at least four major functions of coworker relations: (1) socialization to occupational norms, (2) solidarity and mutual defense, (3) resistance to authority and role distancing, and (4) the affirmation of occupational, class, and gender identities at work.

Work groups are a key mechanism through which new employees are trained on work tasks and the key mechanism through which regular feedback about work performance is provided. Training for production tasks and monitoring for standards is much more often left to coworkers than is imagined in the management literature, which often depicts an idealized version of workplace training. Simultaneous with the instruction workers receive from their peers in job-related skills, however, they also receive instruction in how to set limits on the expectations that management sets for them. Deviations from prescribed methods and standards that cost other workers extra effort or risk are quickly sanctioned by the work group. Deviations that come at no expense to other workers may not be sanctioned, unless they result in perceived inequalities of effort relative to rewards.

In a classic ethnographic study of occupational socialization, Haas (1972) demonstrates how kidding and ridicule are crucial aspects of the initiation process for apprentice ironworkers. Teasing and ridicule serve as tests to determine if apprentice workers will be willing to accept ongoing on-the-job training from the journeymen. Senior workers reason that apprentices who are unwilling or unable to respond with good natured repartee to personal barbs may also be unwilling to accept directions concerning work tasks. Such apprentices are considered a hazard to themselves and to others in the dangerous world of high steel and are quickly ostracized. In this craft setting, coworkers constitute an important screen through which workers must pass to become a member of the occupation.

Joking relationships and their role in establishing and affirming core group values of friendship and generosity are also a central focus in Halle's (1984) ethnography of a chemical plant. These values are important for the workers in the plant as they strive to humanize their environments against the forces of technology and bureaucracy and as they work to maintain the solidarity necessary for collective protection of their hard won privileges as relatively well-paid blue-collar workers.

In the process of developing and defending group norms, work groups strive to maximize two goals: control of work tasks and fairness. Workers are quite assertive in demanding at least some control over the pace and content of their work. Workers are also extremely sensitive to any hint of inequalities in rewards or in effort between themselves and their coworkers and are quick to anger over such inequalities.

Group solidarity and mutual defense, the second function of work groups, are based on the willingness of workers to defend each other in the face of challenges. These challenges generally come from management, but they also sometimes come from other groups of workers or from customers (Fantasia 1988; Jermier, Knights, and Nord 1994; Smith 1996). The foundation of solidarity is "shared experiences at work" and "the sense of involvement and attachment" that arises from these shared experiences (Goffee 1981:475, 488). Worker solidarity can be galvanized around oppositional elements that focus on resistance to management practices, but solidarity can also focus on more mundane aspects of work life that do not directly oppose management but that still provide a basis for workers to shape a collective identity separate from management (Jermier, Knights, and Nord 1995; Kelly and Kelly 1991).

A third function of work groups is to support role distancing in order to secure "personal space" at work. This function was illustrated in an example discussed previously concerning workers in a cigarette factory who loitered in the toilet for a smoke and a chat. This activity came to represent a mild form of rebellion against management authority and also provided an opportunity for the emergence of social friendships among the workers (Pollert 1981:147).

A fourth function of coworker relations is to provide a forum for affirming group identities, including class and gender identities (Wharton and Baron 1987). For example, sexual banter among male factory workers can help to reaffirm masculinity as a work identity above and beyond formal job descriptions (Collinson and Hearn 1996). The importance of coworker relations for defining group identities is not limited to blue-collar settings. Kunda (1992:154) reports on how engineers use strategies of role distancing and mild ridicule to deal with demands for heightened allegiance and loyalty under new "participatory" management systems.

Because of their many functions, work groups have a tremendous amount of power to determine whether or not work will proceed smoothly and whether or not dignity can be attained and successfully defended at work. This power involves organizing and defining work tasks, training workers, and enforcing occupational norms. Researchers have long been aware that the most effective work groups are those that have clearly agreed upon norms of behavior (Hackman 1990). Group relations are also crucial for overcoming social isolation at work – a key contributor to the experience of alienation. Work groups and coworker relations are of central importance for work and work life across a variety of settings.

In this chapter we focus on two aspects of coworker relations. First, coworker relations can provide, or fail to provide, a foundation for solidarity and collective resistance to management. Solidarity is an important foundation for collective action and for trade unionism as well as for more informal forms of struggle over workplace issues (Fantasia 1988; Molstad 1988). Second, coworker relations can be conflictual or harmonious, leading to feelings of alienation and distress, or affinity and comfort. The ethnographic evidence suggests that solidarity, on the one hand, and coworker conflict, on the other, are crucially important for job satisfaction, meaning in work, worker well-being, productivity, and dignity at work.

In our attempt to understand the nature and role of solidarity and conflict in the workplace, we will revisit the various structural challenges to working with dignity considered in previous chapters and examine patterns of solidarity and coworker conflict across these situations.

Solidarity and Infighting

Solidarity is a necessity if workers are to defend themselves against management abuses. Solidarity and positive coworker relations can also mitigate feelings of alienation that arise from meaningless work that is fragmented and separated from broader purposes in life. Solidarity and coworker relations are crucial underpinnings in the struggle for dignity at work. In this section we develop operational definitions of both solidarity and coworker conflict that we then use to examine the patterns, causes, and consequences of coworker relations on the job.

Solidarity

Work group solidarity rests on a foundation of mutual protection, friendships, shared meanings, and shared norms. Work groups use social pressure to sanction both those who exceed production quotas and those who hamper their attainment – both overproduction and underproduction can be threats to workers' collective well-being (DiFazio 1985).

Adherence to group norms intended to regulate the intensity of work is not always automatically forthcoming. The enforcement of group solidarity often relies on such tactics as gossip, character assassination, and shunning. One way to pressure coworkers is through the use of belittling nicknames:

> A quiver full of epithets awaited the deviant: 'hog,' 'hogger-in,' 'leader,' 'rooter,' 'chaser,' 'rusher,' 'runner,' 'swift,' 'boss's pet' to mention some politer versions. And when a whole factory gained a reputation for feverish work, disdainful craftsmen would describe its occupants . . . 'as comprised half of farmers, and the other half, with few exceptions of horse thieves.' (Montgomery 1979:13)

Solidarity can entail seemingly contradictory elements (Fantasia 1988: 5). A high solidarity work group may vigorously defend its members against management sanctions while, because of pride in their work, also strictly enforcing norms of productivity or safety that may be looked on favorably by management. Thus, worker solidarity should not be reduced to the presence of a "strong stance against management." Solidarity can also be used to enforce high standards and a commitment to quality work (Sabel 1982).

Workplace ethnographies describe four major behavioral facets of solidarity: mutual defense, cohesion, group leadership, and the enforcement of a group normative structure. Table 8.1 describes measures of these four aspects of solidarity. Appendix C, Table 5 reports the factor analysis results used for constructing weights for computing the summary solidarity scale based on these four facets.

Mutual defense is the willingness of workers to put themselves at risk to defend fellow employees. Mutual defense is the aspect of worker

Table 8.1. *Worker Solidarity Measures*

Variables	Codings	Mean	S.D.[a]	N
Worker solidarity	standardized scale[b]	.00	1.00	97
Mutual defense	(1) little or none, (2) average, (3) strong	2.20	.86	87
Cohesion	(1) absent, (2) infrequent, (3) average, (4) widespread, (5) pervasive	3.47	1.11	89
Group leadership	(1) little or none, (2) average, (3) strong	1.93	.85	71
Group discipline enforced by workers	(1) never, (2) occasionally, (3) frequently, (4) principally	2.41	1.13	79

[a] Standard deviation.
[b] See Appendix C for factor analysis results used in the scale construction.

solidarity most frequently identified by students of the labor process. Eugene Debs, the famous American socialist, extolled working-class mutuality as a "Christ-like virtue" (Montgomery 1979:22). Strong group solidarity and mutual defense are evidenced in an ethnography of an underground mine. The ethnographer reports the following episode in which a lead worker and his men gather at the head of a mineshaft to search for coworkers trapped by fire:

> Suddenly Jimmie Isom picks up a mask from the jeep. 'Put one on me, Dan,' Jimmie says. Dan stares at his friend, with the deep-etched lines from his heart attack. Dan usually works Jimmie on the outside crew these days, afraid of working him inside. Now Jimmie is volunteering to go into the smoke. Dan doesn't know how to turn him down. (Vecsey 1974:190)

Cohesion is the extent to which workers seek each other out for social contact. Cohesion is a fundamental precondition for solidarity. In a noncohesive group, workers are relatively indifferent to each other (Hurlbert 1991). In cohesive groups, friendship networks provide an essential mechanism for the development and implementation of collective strategies (Gouldner 1964).

An ethnography of construction work provides a clear example of group cohesion:

> On one feed we had during the sewer plant project, the men used concrete blocks and an oxyacetylene torch to make a stove. Several men brought in their favorite dishes and during lunch time, instead of the usual sandwiches, we all had a hot,

> gourmet meal. Another time, the men organized a 'wild
> meat' feed, which featured only meat from animals that had
> been hunted. The meal was accompanied by hunting stories
> full of frustration, comic situations, and triumphs. This
> activity – the kidding and horseplay, the storytelling and feeds
> – contributes to group cohesion and produces in the men
> feelings of fellowship and affinity. (Applebaum 1981:34)

An example of group cohesion in direct sales work is provided by an ethnography of Tupperware distributors. For these workers, regular company meetings are important occasions for sharing information on how new products are selling and which sales techniques are most effective. These meetings are also important for developing social cohesion: "Meetings become an important social occasion as well as a business function for many. . . . One Tupperware dealer, for example, said, 'Rally is every Monday morning. I wouldn't miss it. I'd kill to go to Rally'" (Biggart 1989:152).

Leadership is the third component of solidarity. Without leadership, solidarity will tend to be episodic and noncumulative. The emergence of group leadership provides a more durable basis for collective action (Fantasia 1988:109). Strong leadership does not typically emerge until a group needs to take some collective action, such as defending a member against management or sanctioning a member for violating group norms. Leadership reflects a relatively high level of preexisting solidarity.

The *enforcement of group discipline* is the final aspect of solidarity. The enforcement of work norms by groups has been widely recognized since Roy's (1954) early research on output restriction. Across diverse settings, researchers have recorded repeated instances of workers informally pressuring other workers to restrict production. But this is only one side of the enforcement of group norms. Work group norms can also involve cultural practices like generosity (Halle 1984), quality standards (Littler and Salaman 1984) and safety standards (Harris 1987). Positive goals are as likely to be enforced by work groups as restrictive goals. Sloppy work and poor standards irritate and demoralize workers (Juravich 1985); pride in doing even relatively simple tasks well motivates workers to demand at least a minimum of cooperation from coworkers (Zander and Armstrong 1972).

An example of the enforcement of restrictive group norms by coworkers is reported in an ethnography of a defense industry subcontractor. "Many of the winders did poke fun at Danny Watt in a mean-spirited way. Much of it concerned Watt's 'boy scout' image and his righteous religious pose. But the real focus of their taunts was his rapid work pace" (Seider 1984:44).

Group discipline can also emerge in the process of socializing new workers to appropriate job performance as the following example from an ethnography of ironworkers illustrates:

> He did everything wrong, of course. . . . He was forever on the wrong side of the pieces, and it still amazes me that he wasn't knocked over the side. . . . Jiggs continually screamed at him to be careful. Several times I pulled and held pieces away from him and told him I wasn't going to let him have his end unless he stopped bouncing around. (Cherry 1974:186)

Solidarity at work thus serves a wide range of instrumental and affective functions. Group solidarity is essential for making the workplace a more humane setting in which workers can lead their lives in relative safety and security.

Coworker Conflict

Conflict within work groups has many sources. Actions oriented toward defending autonomy need not be directed only at management. Workers' efforts at engineering more viable circumstances for themselves can also be directed against other employees and groups of employees.

One important source of conflict in the workplace is when a worker avoids work by shifting it to others. Any slacking of effort will be perceived negatively by other employees if they are inconvenienced or if their own work is made harder as a result. Perceived unfairness in rewards is an additional source of intragroup conflict. A distribution of rewards that is perceived as unfair is likely to generate a good deal of verbal undercutting of anyone whom the group perceives as receiving more than their just share. Workers are highly sensitive to the slightest nuances of perceived favoritism.

Much competitiveness in the workplace is played out in the realm of gossip and slander – undermining people behind their backs by undercutting their credibility. Sometimes competitiveness evidences itself more directly in rudeness or in intentional interference. Rudeness generally involves avoidance or ostracism; open hostility or interference between coworkers is less common because of strong norms in most workplaces against open conflict.

The structural conditions that appear to give rise most often to intragroup conflict are those found in abusive and disorganized organizations. In such situations, cohesive work group relations are undermined and the emergence and enforcement of shared group norms is replaced with conflict and competition. Such settings are typified by an absence or weakening of norms that prescribe appropriate behavior. Work life in

Table 8.2. *Coworker Conflict Measures*

Variables	Codings	Mean[a]	S.D.[b]	N
Coworker conflict	standardized scale[c]	.00	1.00	101
Within group conflict	(1) nonexistent, (2) occasional, (3) frequent	1.95	.55	85
Within group gossip	(0) absent, (1) present	85%	.36	65
Within group interference	(0) absent, (1) present	48%	.50	60
Between group conflict	(1) nonexistent, (2) occasional, (3) frequent	2.05	.63	80
Between group gossip	(0) absent, (1) present	76%	.43	55
Between group interference	(0) absent, (1) present	48%	.50	56

[a] The mean is expressed as percent "present" for present/absent variables.
[b] Standard deviation.
[c] See Appendix C for factor analysis results used in the scale construction.

such workplaces can be highly anomic. Because of the centrality of norms prohibiting open conflict, however, intragroup conflict is largely realized through gossip and backbiting, even in the most anomic workplaces.

Workplace ethnographies allow us to identify six aspects of coworker conflict. Coworker conflict can involve generalized conflict, gossip or interference, either within or between work groups. Table 8.2 describes measures of these six aspects of coworker conflict. Appendix C, Table 6 reports the factor analysis results used for constructing weights for computing the summary coworker conflict scale based on these six facets of coworker conflict.

Gossip is the most commonly used mechanism that work groups use to enforce standards for appropriate behavior and levels of effort by members of the group. In settings with high task interdependence, reduced effort by one person can cause more work for others. In settings where tasks are more independent, poor workers are condemned, not because they cause others extra effort, but because they are getting paid the same but are putting in less effort. In either setting, even the suspicion of reduced effort can make a worker a target for gossip and ridicule.

Gossip is pervasive at the workplace because it serves so many functions. These functions include providing an outlet for boredom and stress, social control and boundary maintenance, bragging and self-glorification, disseminating information, and reinforcing norms. Gossip is most pervasive in settings where there is a high degree of competition among workers and in settings with a lack of organizational leadership or with strong organizational ambiguities. Gossip becomes a particularly important means of disseminating information in situations of sustained ambiguity (Kanter 1977:97). The importance of infighting and cliques in the social order of the factory has been known for some time (see Homans 1950) but its role and implications have not been rigorously developed in the workplace literature.

Gossip and character assassination are front line tactics in interpersonal conflicts at the workplace. Character assassination is popular because it inflicts harm with minimal risk to the attacker. Directly antagonizing coworkers or disrupting their work runs the risk of being called to task by other workers or by management for intentionally disrupting production. An ethnography of bank employees describes a social world of invidious comparison and backbiting that contributes significantly to reduced job satisfaction and to feelings of alienation:

> Individuals try to fashion . . . personal identifications by
> criticizing others, thus indirectly asserting their own individual
> worth and even superiority. . . . Each individual knows that she
> herself may become an object of criticism. This creates an
> enervating apprehensiveness of others' judgements. (Jackall
> 1978:121–122)

A records clerk at the bank, when asked if she is staying for a holiday party, expresses a widely felt anxiety: "I stay because if I don't, they'll talk about me" (Jackall: 121). Another worker reports: "Everyone is two-faced, and you have to watch out for yourself" (122). A third reports: "They're a bunch of phoneys. . . . They are snotty. I feel awful if I'm around any of them" (121). Although gossip is a common tactic in intragroup conflict, in the long run it can result in a prolonging and even intensification of conflict as insults are levied, grudges accumulated, and competing cliques strengthened.

In addition to invidious comparisons, character assassination, and gossip, a common tactic in infighting is to intentionally shift work to another person. Outright interference with others' work is less common, but it is not unknown. An ethnography of a steel plant illustrates active interference between workers in a setting characterized by a pervasive pattern of mismanagement. In this highly charged and competitive setting, millwrights are secretive with their knowledge and are unwilling to share it with new apprentices:

> Steve was beginning to boil over, and one morning when the
> millwright was thumbing over a blue print, holding it
> purposely out of Steve's view, as though it were personal and
> confidential, he popped off, 'Look here . . . I'm gonna' learn

everything there is to know about this [expletive] millwright job, no matter what you think.' (Spencer 1977:64)

Conflict at work can also occur *between* different work groups as well as within groups. An example of ongoing conflict between work groups is provided by an ethnography of a medical school hospital:

> Between the house officer group and the private doctors there is a fundamental and constantly arising conflict of interests. . . . It is in the private physician's interest (in matters of finance, personal convenience and legal self-protection) to admit and keep all of his sick patients in the hospital and to administer a cautious and complete battery of diagnostic tests and treatments. On the other hand, the interests of the residents and interns are best served by admitting only a select portion of these patients (those with interesting diseases), by learning and practicing challenging diagnostic procedures on these patients, and by getting them released from the hospital as soon as possible after the diagnosis is made. (Millman 1976:61–62)

As with most workplace conflicts, tensions between work groups are often played out in the realm of invidious comparisons and gossip. A pattern of chronic gossip between work groups is evidenced in an ethnography of temporary clerical workers:

> Not only were individual temps the butt of contemptuous and often bitchy remarks made by the permanents, but the whole group of us were sometimes subject to generalised insults and cool behavior. Temps were often discussed by the permanent staff. This usually happened when all the temps had left at 4.30 p.m. (McNally 1979:169)

Active interference between work groups is relatively uncommon. But groups do sometimes interfere with other groups' work either through carelessness or intentional negligence. An ethnography of construction work reports on one crew of pile drivers who were seen as careless and neglectful in their work:

> They were the wild bunch. They did crazy things, engaged in horseplay, and were always fighting with each other, both verbally and physically. One time they toppled a crane onto a small steel building on the job site. They thought it was hilarious, seeing men scatter in all directions as the crane slowly started to tip and then came crashing down on the empty building. (Applebaum 1981:96–97)

This crew managed to earn a bad reputation among other workers. They were held in poor regard because they were sloppy, took their time, and delayed other crews.

As we have seen, coworkers can provide essential support to each other and can contribute to a meaningful work life. But they can also represent some of the worst roadblocks to a humane and liveable experience at work. In the following sections we investigate the organizational settings that generate the best and the worst in coworker relations.

Coworker Relations under Bad Management

How do coworkers relate to each other under conditions of disorganized and abusive management? Most readers will recognize such situations as painfully unpleasant, and sometimes even untenable. Worse, as we shall see, management abuse and disorganization do not necessarily stimulate worker solidarity and mutual aid as a protective shield. Rather, management abuse can produce increased conflict and infighting among coworkers. Management abuse and disorganization can generate a culture of disrespect and chaos that permeates the workplace.

Table 8.3 displays patterns of solidarity and coworker conflict across levels of management abuse. Solidarity and mutual defense are greatest

Table 8.3. *Coworker Relations under Abusive Management*

Variables	Abusive Management					
	1st Quintile	2nd Quintile	3rd Quintile	4th Quintile	5th Quintile	Significance[a]
Solidarity	.48	.35	−.62	−.32	.23	.069
Mutual defense	2.58	2.41	1.85	1.95	2.41	.046
Alternative status hierarchies	1.71	1.95	2.11	2.19	2.62	.004
Coworker conflict	−.29	−.34	.24	.35	.06	.035
Within group interference	.40	.25	.57	.70	.60	.055
Sexual harassment	.45	.23	.50	.36	.80	.103
Brown nosing	1.56	1.77	1.60	1.92	2.25	.048
Ethnographies (N)	22	21	21	22	22	

[a] F-test for linearity.

at the extremes of the management abuse scale and lowest in more average workplaces. This pattern suggests that worker solidarity is not solely a reaction against management abuse. Rather, group solidarity also occurs in well organized and managed workplaces in which workers have the opportunity to work together effectively and in the process to develop bonds of affiliation, mutual respect, and support.

Workers use solidarity and mutual defense across a range of workplace settings and for a wide range of purposes. An example of the use of solidarity to defend against overaggressive supervisors is provided by an ethnography of a chemical plant:

> If [crew chiefs] push the interests of management too hard, the workers will find ways of taking revenge. One chief, for instance, tried to exert more authority than the men in his crew thought appropriate. To retaliate they used to creep up behind him in the control room and bang pieces of corrugated iron. His nerves soon deteriorated, and to escape he bid into a low-paying job sweeping up in the yard. His fate was an object lesson to other chiefs not to antagonize their crews. (Halle 1984:153)

A similar episode of workers relying on solidarity to support informal negotiations with management about working conditions is reported in an ethnography of police work. The ethnographer describes how the men in the platoon responded to the return of a disliked sergeant as a temporary replacement for their vacationing regular sergeant. After the replacement sergeant went over several rules the men considered petty, one man walked up to the podium and:

> . . . took a long drag from a cigarette he had left burning in an ashtray, staring directly at the sergeant. As he entered the line, the others turned to him and smiled their approval. That was just the beginning. . . . [During an equipment inspection, as the sergeant] passed down the line, each man turned toward him silently, grinning broadly, while the men ahead openly talked to each other. At no time did anyone write down any of his instructions since they had no intention of doing any work for him. (Rubinstein 1973:57)

An ethnography of a British apparel factory similarly reports widespread mutual defense among coworkers. Examples of solidarity and mutual support range from participation in industry-wide marches, to demands for three-day work weeks instead of layoffs in order to distribute available work, to the practice of pranks against supervisors:

> Pranks were not uncommon and were enjoyed by everyone
> because they relieved the monotony of the working day.
> [A group of women] set the buzzer off and emptied the
> department ten minutes before the end of the day. . . .
> Everyone who was asked about it [the next day] shook their
> heads wisely, at once 'agreeing' with management's view that
> this was a very serious matter, while keeping quiet about the
> identity of the buzzer-pusher. (Westwood 1984:91)

Coworker conflict, in contrast to solidarity, clearly increases with management abuse. Conflict, within group interference, sexual harassment, and brown nosing are all higher under abusive management. Rather than organizing themselves collectively against abusive management, it appears that cultures of disrespect and disorganization initiated by management disrupt the entire workplace, including relations between coworkers.

Sexual harassment, for instance, is most common in situations with the highest levels of management abuse. The escalation of sexual harassment in abusive workplaces highlights the role of management cultures of disrespect and chaos as key contributors to negative relations among coworkers (Paludi 1991).

Alternative status hierarchies and brown nosing are also most likely under situations characterized by management abuse and disrespect (see Figure 8.1). Thus, both withdrawal from management definitions and obsequious adherence to management definitions are typical of organizations based on abuse and disrespect. Neither condition is conducive to organizational effectiveness or to working with dignity.

An ethnography of a bank provides an example of how an abusive and alienating management staff generates a morass of status games and infighting. The negative social atmosphere in the bank results in personal antagonisms between employees, both within and between work groups:

> A boarding clerk comments [. . .]: 'The way things have gone, it's made people turn against one another. On one side, you get hassled by [the supervisor]. And then, on the other, people talk about you. Everybody is two-faced, and you have to watch out for yourself.' [A young worker reports further:] 'There is a division between us and [another group of workers]. . . . They go around with their noses in the air. . . . [They're] *female, very female.* Like when a male walks in the office, they're like a bunch of high school girls. They're always giggling. . . . There's one who drives me crazy the way she walks. She is shaped like a seahorse and the way she walks is

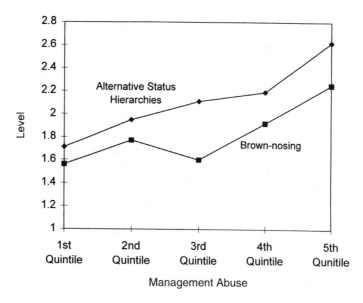

Figure 8.1. Worker responses to management abuse.

like she's saying, "I'm beautiful." ' (Jackall 1978:121–122; emphasis in original)

Brown nosing is being ingratiating toward one's supervisors and expecting favors or privileges in return. Reports of brown nosing are always in the third person: brown nosing is something *other* people do. Brown nosing is a tainted behavior because it violates workplace norms of solidarity with other workers and opposition to management. The attribution of brown nosing to others is not an everyday occurrence in the workplace. What is more commonly condemned is management favoritism. The blame is placed on management for treating workers differently rather than on workers for seeking to brown nose management. The social construction of such behaviors as favoritism maintains the image of solidarity against an unjust and manipulative management. The implicit consensus seems to be that everyone tries to get ahead. The greater offense is in management inappropriately rewarding ingratiating behavior.

In the bank setting just described, favoritism, nepotism, and cronyism are experienced as widespread problems. Few things are more aggravating to workers than favoritism and its variants: "She's a friend of [the assistant operations officer]. That means she's getting a raise. That's not *fair*" (Jackall 1978:127; emphasis in original).

Table 8.4. *Coworker Relations under Mismanagement*

	Mismanagement					
Variables	1st Quintile	2nd Quintile	3rd Quintile	4th Quintile	5th Quintile	Significance[a]
Solidarity	.33	.36	−.03	−.31	−.27	.010
Cohesion	4.15	3.76	3.26	3.00	3.35	.007
Group discipline enforced by workers	2.83	2.89	2.22	2.13	1.93	.005
Coworker conflict	−.54	−.13	−.04	.11	.52	.001
Within group interference	.11	.41	.46	.55	.90	.001
Between group gossip	.44	.71	.86	1.00	.83	.027
Between group interference	.20	.43	.31	.89	.70	.003
Sexual harassment	.40	.40	.23	.46	.89	.048
Ethnographies (N)	20	22	22	21	23	

[a] F-test for linearity.

Abusive and unjust management is destructive to good relations among coworkers. Mismanagement can be even more destructive. Mismanagement results from lack of clarity about organizational objectives, poor communication of these goals, confused criteria for evaluation, and a lack of coherence and integration among goals (LeRoy 1987; Levinson 1959).

Table 8.4 reports the prevalence of worker solidarity and infighting evaluated across levels of mismanagement. Even more aspects of solidarity and infighting are influenced by mismanagement than by management abuse. In addition, the contrasts are more pronounced. Solidarity is consistently undermined by mismanagement and infighting is increased. These patterns again suggest that solidarity is not just a reaction against bad management: Solidarity among coworkers is higher under conditions of competent management than under mismanagement. Disorganized workplaces and the resulting anomic conditions are highly destructive of coworker relations and these destructive aspects of mismanagement appear to override any consequences of mismanagement for heightening worker solidarity and mutual defense.

An ethnography of a poorly managed tractor factory in Eastern Europe, for example, reports pervasive patterns of competitiveness, gossip, and interference:

> The only concern one worker has for the others is jealous suspicion. Are the others a few fillers ahead? Is their hourly rate going up more quickly? Are they getting more of the best 'good' jobs that are going? Such rivalry is equally fierce over all matters in which the head foreman's decision is final: holidays, overtime, bonuses, awards. (Haraszti 1978:90)

Conversely, an ethnography of direct sales reports high levels of cohesion and mutual support in a setting characterized by competent and effective management:

> Everybody wants everybody else to succeed. It's not like competition that you get in some jobs where I don't want you to know what I know because if you do, then you can take my job. I want to share with you what made me successful, so you can be successful too. . . . In this business we encourage people to go ahead of us. . . . If they want to make eight times more money than I made, that's great. (Biggart 1989:90)

Sexual harassment follows a similar pattern in relation to mismanagement as in relation to managerial abuse. Sexual harassment is somewhat equally distributed across levels of mismanagement except for the highest level where it increases dramatically. An organizational culture of disrespect based on high levels of management abuse and incompetence appears to severely limit cooperation, solidarity, and civility among workers. In such conditions, sexual harassment becomes a chronic accompaniment to broader patterns of infighting and conflict (see also Collinson 1988; Welsh and Nierobisz 1997; Yount 1991).

The two summary scales measuring solidarity and coworker conflict are displayed graphically across levels of mismanagement in Figure 8.2. The figure highlights increased coworker conflict and decreased solidarity under mismanagement. Social relations in organizations appear to constitute a cohesive whole in which managerial competence, positive relations between workers and managers, and positive and supportive relations among coworkers all rise or fall together. In this matrix of social relations, managerial competence and a culture of respect for workers appear to play decisive roles in setting the tone for positive relations among coworkers.

An ethnography of life aboard a Norwegian freighter, which we discussed in a previous chapter as an example of managerial competence

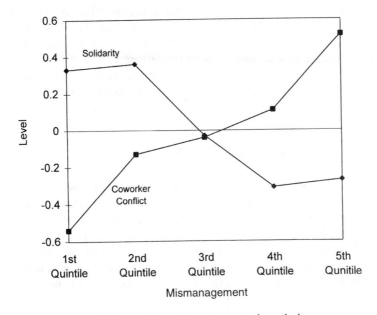

Figure 8.2. Coworker relations in mismanaged workplaces.

and respect, also provides many examples of positive and supportive relations among the crew members:

> [There was a] high degree of cooperation and cohesion among the crew. The drills and the meeting seemed to demonstrate the mutual concern of the Norwegian sailors and a real feeling of community. Each member of the crew knew his job when it came to protecting the others. . . . Everyone was involved. (Schrank 1983:39)

A culture of respect associated with managerial competence and respect for workers' rights thus encourages positive relations among coworkers and creates a positive atmosphere for the entire matrix of social relations in the workplace.

The finding that heightened coworker solidarity is often associated with good management relations contrasts sharply with theoretical propositions that describe workplace solidarity as being hardened in the fires of conflict with management (see Fantasia 1988). Solidarity does not appear to be as much hardened in the fires of conflict as formed in the process of identifying with a job and deciding that it is worth defending. Norms of solidarity, therefore, do not appear to be solely oppositional in origin or content (see Tannenbaum and Kahn 1958).

We now turn to other possible structural determinants of positive and negative coworker relations. These determinants include assembly versus nonassembly work, professional and craft autonomy, and worker participation. Several significant and interesting contrasts emerge in these analyses. But none of them rival the pervasiveness and magnitude of managerial respect and competence as determinants of positive coworker relations.

Coworkers in Assembly Jobs

Much is known about the pressures and stresses of assembly work. In Chapter 5 we provided ethnographic evidence indicating that these characterizations of the harsh conditions of assembly work are indeed accurate. The question before us now, however, is not about assembly work itself, but about relations among coworkers in assembly jobs. One might reasonably expect that assembly workers would have high levels of solidarity and group support in response to the demands of their jobs.

The results presented in Table 8.5 suggest, however, that solidarity and coworker relations are roughly similar across assembly and nonassembly work. Few of the facets of solidarity or coworker relations are differentiated by assembly work. Managerial competence and respect appear to be much more significant determinants of social relations among coworkers than the technical organization of work tasks.

The only aspect of solidarity that is differentiated by assembly work is group discipline. Group discipline is highest under bench assembly

Table 8.5. *Coworker Relations and Assembly Work*

Variables	Assembly Line	Bench Assembly	Nonassembly Work	Significance[a]
Solidarity	−.14	.21	−.05	.585
Group discipline enforced by workers	1.83	2.73	2.54	.042
Social friendships	.68	1.00	.82	.066
Coworker conflict	−.03	.23	−.04	.636
Between group gossip	1.00	.88	.68	.074
Ethnographies (N)	25	16	67	

[a] F-test.

where workers have a direct interest in controlling those who would work too fast and who may open the door to demands for more intense effort. The second highest level of group discipline is in nonassembly work, where such threats may also be very real, even if less specific in nature than in settings explicitly organized around piece rates. Group insistence that coworkers carry their fair share of the work load may also be relatively common in nonassembly work, where undone work is frequently shifted to someone else's desk until it is completed. Group discipline is lowest under assembly-line conditions, where the pace of work is rigidly controlled by the technology and where workers have little opportunity to deviate from the pace set by the line.

An example of strong group pressure to restrict output to what the work group sees as a reasonable level is provided by an ethnography of a tableware pottery plant organized around bench assembly:

> Anyone in the position of polisher who behaved inappropriately posed a threat to the whole group. . . . Mateo was caught between conflicting desires to impress [the supervisors] with his productive capacity on the one hand and to conform to the group's values . . . on the other. The group, not without sympathy, sensed Mateo's dilemma, but there were larger issues at stake. . . . [Mateo] worked rapidly, took no time out for relief, and ran up a high score. His neighbors made jokes about him and threw pieces of scrap in his direction. They used his nickname, which was an unflattering one. (Savage and Lombard 1986:125)

The only other feature of coworker relations that differentiates assembly work is the prevalence of friendships. As with group discipline, friendships are most prevalent in bench assembly and least common in assembly-line work. Friendships are at an intermediate level in nonassembly work.

Extensive friendships in an apparel factory organized around independent bench work are evidenced in the following account:

> Friendships were an essential and vital part of life on the shop floor; they made work tolerable and at times even fun. Friends were the major antidote to the pressures of work: 'Well, we don't like the work that much, but we don't like to move around either. You get friends here who keep you going, so you say, "It's not so bad, really."' [Another worker reports] 'I like working here. People say factories are terrible, but they aren't, you know. If you've never been in one they seem bad, but working here you see all your mates and you get good money.' (Westwood 1984:90)

In bench assembly settings, workers have shared interests because of their common position as production workers and frequently have at least some opportunity to interact. These features of bench assembly work result in the emergence of friendships and other forms of group support.

Assembly-line work, in contrast, tends to isolate workers because of the noise of the production line, the distance between workers, and the common practice of rotating workers. As an ethnographer in a food processing factory reports: "Introductions come slowly because everyone's relationships to the place and to each other are temporary and casual. . . . So most conversations occur without an exchange of names" (Turner 1980:19).

In many workplaces, however, friendships are quite common. Friendships provide important social support and help to bring dignity to work life. Even in highly dispersed work, such as personal household service, workers rely on friendships to give meaning and dignity to their lives: "All the workers . . . said they were friendly with other servants in the neighborhood or area. . . . The majority spent their time together talking and 'moaning about our difficulties'. The cost of living and 'our employers' appear to be the favorite topics of conversation" (Cock 1989:46).

Social support is important for all workers. Patterns of social support are only modestly differentiated by the technical organization of work. Many of the differences that do emerge appear to result from the ability of workers to interact and converse with each other on a regular basis.

Job Autonomy and Workplace Relations

We have seen that job autonomy based on professional training and craft skills is a core determinant of positive work experiences. But does autonomy also operate to improve the social climate among coworkers and to limit conflict and infighting?

Table 8.6 shows the patterns of solidarity and coworker conflict across professional and craft settings and contrasts these with workplaces organized around bureaucratic rules or supervisory fiat. Craft workers exhibit the highest levels of group solidarity across all dimensions reported, including mutual defense, group discipline, group boundaries, and friendships. Professional workers show a similar, although much more subdued pattern. Bureaucratic settings exhibit the least solidarity. Craft work also produces the highest levels of conflict among coworkers. It appears that the job autonomy of craft workers, and to a lesser extent of professional workers, provides a supportive milieu for robust group relations of both a supportive and conflictual nature. Workplaces that

Table 8.6. *Coworker Relations under Various Forms of Workplace Control*

Variables	Professional	Craft	Bureaucratic	Supervisory Fiat	Significance[a]
Solidarity	−.08	.65	−.34	.16	.003
Mutual defense	2.43	2.80	1.93	2.22	.006
Group leadership	1.71	2.38	1.67	2.10	.046
Group discipline enforced by workers	2.11	3.38	2.03	2.55	.001
Group boundaries	3.70	4.00	2.95	3.56	.012
Friendships on the job	.88	1.00	.69	.85	.049
Friendships off the job	.71	1.00	.66	.83	.061
Coworker conflict	.01	.23	−.01	−.15	.664
Ethnographies (N)	10	21	48	29	

[a] F-test.

allow a great deal of job autonomy also appear to support a robust pattern of both positive and negative interpersonal interactions.

High levels of friendship and social cohesion in a craft setting are evidenced in an ethnography of underground mining: "Over the years, the men build up friendships with each other that are not equaled in many marriages or families.... Men call each other 'buddy'... with an open affection" (Vecsey 1974:124). An ethnography of firefighters similarly reports strong friendships and camaraderie in a craft setting:

> It's hard to describe the closeness that you felt with the guys in the fire house. I don't think my wife has ever really understood it. I just used to love to come to work – especially on those long Saturdays when we'd have a big roast or a ham or something and sit around and talk or play cards.... Firemen then were a great bunch and a rough bunch.... They played hard and rough. But when the bells hit, nobody would do any more good for you than a fireman. It's a group of men with a unique brotherhood feeling – they'll never let you down. (McCarl 1985:97)

Craft settings also support the highest levels of mutual defense against the demands of management: "The miners [all] stick together to beat the Company. They always help each other. They always cover up for each other" (Gouldner 1964:126). Social relations and personal contacts among craft workers also constitute important informal networks, networks that are crucial for securing work in markets that are often highly seasonal: "The most frequent and surest way to get into construction is to know someone in the industry. . . . Father–son and brother combinations are still prevalent in the industry. The personal basis of recruitment reinforces and supports the personalized nature of the work process" (Applebaum 1981:125). Such contacts, of course, also provide the basis for exclusionary practices against groups not well represented in the current work force.

In contrast to the situation in craft work, bureaucratic settings encourage the greatest anonymity, impersonality, and distance in social relations. A clerical worker in a large insurance company reports the following sentiments: "I feel a little different. I mean, they're good people, and they could probably be my friends, but I don't think that we share the same interests" (Burris 1983:157).

In summary, solidarity reaches its highest levels under craft organizations of production. More moderate levels are evidenced in professional settings and the lowest levels of solidarity are evidenced in bureaucratic settings. An example of significant but circumscribed mutual defense in a professional setting is provided by an ethnography of medical doctors: "Although doctors may have differences and rivalries among themselves with regard to defining, blaming and acting on mistakes, all doctors will join hands and close ranks against patients and the public" (Millman 1976:93).

Craft work, and to a lesser extent professional work, provide relatively robust interactional settings in which workers experience significant solidarity and mutual support. Interestingly, these are also the same settings that are likely to have the greatest coworker conflict and infighting. It should not be surprising that sustained social interactions have both supportive and conflictual elements. These aspects of work life are not polar opposites. Rather, they are both reflections of organizations of work that rely on regular, sustained interactions among workers to facilitate production. In interactionally intense settings, both supportive and conflictual relations can be expected to proliferate. The key opposing contrast is thus not between coworker solidarity and coworker conflict, but between robust interactional settings and more socially constrained settings, such as those organized around bureaucratic principles. The latter settings produce more constrained and anomic interactions and a paucity of both positive and negative social relations.

It is also important to recognize, however, that the contrasts involving professional and craft work are more partial and subdued than those involving the damage that can be done to the social fabric in a workplace by managerially based cultures of disorganization and disrespect.

Such managerial cultures of disrespect are the crucial determinant of conflictual coworker relations.

Participation and Coworker Support

Employee participation programs are important for increasing the involvement of workers in complex production systems. The forms of participation are diverse but heightened citizenship appears to result, to a greater or lesser extent, from most forms of increased employee involvement. A question that remains unanswered, however, is the effect of increased participation on relations *among* coworkers. Does participation increase solidarity and mutual support or does it engender a more competitive and conflictual workplace as peers take on supervisory and disciplinary functions previously reserved for management?

Table 8.7 reports patterns of coworker relations across various forms of employee involvement. Some of the contrasts are statistically significant, but few are pronounced or dramatic. The overall pattern suggests that worker solidarity is modestly increased under heightened worker participation. As with citizenship and resistance, the particular form of participation seems to matter less than the contrast between participation and nonparticipation. Settings with no form of participation evidence the lowest levels of solidarity (see also Hodson et al. 1993).

Table 8.7. *Coworker Relations and Worker Participation*

Variables	None	Teams	Formal Input	Partnership	Coop/ ESOP	Significance[a]
Solidarity	−.28	.34	.19	−.04	−.20	.177
Mutual defense	1.92	2.50	2.23	2.47	1.83	.058
Group discipline enforced by workers	1.77	2.82	2.64	2.50	2.44	.027
Group boundaries	3.30	3.83	3.80	3.06	2.71	.033
Friendships on the job	.93	.95	.73	.79	.47	.001
Friendships off the job	.77	1.00	.90	.79	.33	.000
Coworker conflict	−.02	−.05	−.05	.33	−.19	.668
Within group conflict	1.75	2.00	2.08	2.27	1.73	.027
Ethnographies (N)	32	25	20	16	15	

[a] F-test.

An ethnographer studying an automobile factory using Japanese-style production teams argues that workers' experiences in team-based production "lead to an emergent understanding of the gap between company and worker interests. [This] understanding is evident in identification with the team . . . against the company" (Graham 1995:141). Identification with team members can lead to heightened worker solidarity in team production settings.

A further example of high levels of cohesion and group support in a production setting based on team production is provided by an ethnography of deep-sea fishing:

> I allus had a good ol' happy crew. Yes, we were allus a good ol' happy flock. . . . When we finished a voyage we used t' go on a bloody bender. That we did! There used t' be a real beano that day. I never had many fresh chaps in my crew. We were always together, the same chaps. That's the best way t' be. You look after them an' they look after you. (Butcher 1979:104)

Increased employee involvement, including involvement based on team production, appears to increase solidarity among workers. Work groups have long been identified as essential for passing on the "folk wisdom" of production *and* of worker resistance (Jermier 1988; Thompson, William 1983:223). Group-based organizations of work have been identified as "generating both more satisfaction *and* dissatisfaction and more profound changes in expectations and entitlement concerning participation and involvement in the firm [than reorganizations of individual jobs]" (Derber and Schwartz 1983:70). The findings reported here are consistent with these observations. Increased participation appears to increase workers' involvement and concern with their jobs, their coworkers, and their organizations. Increased participation encourages mutual aid and mutual defense. The hypothesis that increased employee involvement in organizations will result in increased worker compliance and erode a critical stance toward management (Burawoy 1985) is thus not supported in the patterns observed in ethnographic accounts of the workplace.

If group solidarity is essential for collective action, as is commonly argued, then the long-term consequences of employee participation may be positive for collective action among workers. Fantasia (1988:128) notes that "the first industrial unions of the CIO in the 1930s were cultivated in the company unionism of the 1920s." It is neither inconceivable, nor inconsistent with the results presented here, that the worker participation schemes of the 2000s may provide a similarly fertile ground for new forms of worker collective action in the next millennium (Freeman and Rogers 1999).

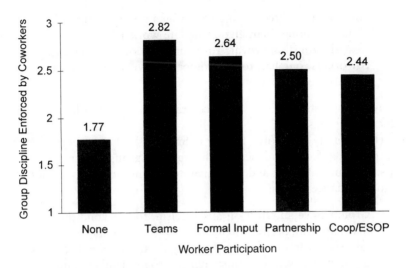

Figure 8.3. Group discipline under various forms of worker participation.

The level of group discipline across production setting differentiated by types of employee participation is displayed graphically in Figure 8.3. The figure shows a clear contrast between settings with and without worker participation. Team production settings evidence the highest levels of group discipline but all forms of participation result in heightened group discipline relative to the absence of participation. Production groups sometimes discipline their members for over zealous work efforts – for overproduction. But, perhaps even more frequently, work groups discipline their members for failing to do their share of the work, thus creating more work for other team members. In such settings, the extensive use of peer pressure results "from the self-interested and quite sensible desire to avoid working even harder than normal" (Rinehart, Hoxley, and Robertson 1997:89). Such self-disciplining activities, however, can also set the stage for an increased awareness of broader concerns facing the work group and the organization.

Working with a short crew is one of the most common sources of extra work. Work groups are thus especially sensitive to absenteeism and tardiness among team members. Strong team pressures to arrive early and begin work on time are reported in an ethnography of clerical work in a Japanese enterprise:

> Promptness was the key to the office. . . . There was a tacit understanding that one would always be on time unless there were extenuating circumstances. Members of a workplace did

not comment directly on a coworker's tardiness but talked about it among themselves. The late worker lost face and was treated with disapproval. To maintain good relations with coworkers, one had to be prompt or have a very good excuse for tardiness. (Lo 1990:41)

Absenteeism and staffing issues are a central concern for workers in team production settings.

An ethnography of a Volvo factory in Sweden similarly reports strong group pressures for attendance. In this factory, groups are responsible for a set amount of work and this generates strong pressures for adherence to attendance norms:

Groups have an effect on absenteeism, too, beyond the drop that naturally occurs when the work becomes more interesting. In one case in the body area, a man in the work group was absent one morning, so group members phoned him at home and said: 'Why aren't you here?' He came in to work that afternoon. (Gyllenhammar 1977:96)

An important contradiction of employee involvement is thus highlighted by the results presented in Table 8.6. Not only is solidarity more common under employee involvement, but so too is infighting. Similar to the situation for professional and craft work, heightened worker participation appears to create an interactionally intense workplace in which both solidarity and conflict are increased. More intense workplace interactions involving both heightened solidarity and conflict can be expected to be an important part of the experience of work life for increasing numbers of employees in the twenty-first century.

Conflict and Tension in Service Work

Service work provides a final setting that we consider in our investigation of coworker relations. Service work is often said to be intense and draining because of the emotional and interactional demands of working with clients (Diamond 1992; Hochschild 1983). Part of this stress results from the pressures that customers place on workers to deliver services (Fine 1996; Frenkel et al. 1999; Leidner 1993). Another stressor is the potentially inauthentic nature of service interactions, which can leave workers feeling alienated from their true emotions and true selves (Erickson and Wharton 1997). The question we wish to address, however, is less about the nature of service work than about the nature of coworker relations given the interactionally demanding nature of the

Table 8.8. *Coworker Relations and Customer Service Work*

Variables	Customer Service	No Customer Contact	Significance[a]
Solidarity	.48	−.06	.092
Mutual defense	2.75	2.14	.055
Coworker conflict	.14	−.02	.580
Between group interference	.75	.41	.037
Ethnographies (N)	13	95	

[a] *t*-test for contrast between two groups.

work involved. Do coworkers provide solidarity and emotional support for facing the demands and stresses of client interactions?

Levels of worker solidarity and coworker conflict across service and nonservice settings are displayed in Table 8.8. The contrasts in coworker relations between service and nonservice work are very modest. Few contrasts are evidenced and several of these are not statistically significant. Nevertheless, a pattern does emerge among these contrasts: Service workers evidence both greater solidarity and greater infighting relative to other workers. This pattern repeats the mix of greater solidarity and greater coworker conflict that we have seen evidenced in other interactionally intense settings, such as those involving professional or craft autonomy and those involving heightened employee involvement. Across diverse situations we observe that greater coworker interaction in the process of work results in increases in both positive *and* negative coworker relations.

An example of high levels of coworker solidarity in a service setting is provided by a study of a cocktail bar (Spradley and Mann 1975:49). The waitresses provide frequent mutual support in the face of difficult work situations. For instance, when a group of eight (potentially rowdy) members of the local college football team come in, "Sue glances at Denise and catches her eye, an instant message of sympathy hidden to everyone else. Sue nods her head at the clock and Denise shakes her head in agreement: 'Its a long time until closing.'"

Solidarity across work groups in a service setting is also noted in an ethnography of a chain restaurant:

> A waitress may . . . decline to offer items that are repeatedly
> sent back to the kitchen, are difficult to stack, take a long
> time to prepare, or annoy the cooks. In this way she saves

herself time, reduces the chances that her customers will be dissatisfied with the food or the wait, and maintains good standing with the kitchen. (Paules 1991:57)

In summary, differences in coworker relations between service and nonservice work are relatively modest and should not be exaggerated. The observed contrasts, however, do conform to a pattern that has emerged regularly in our observations on coworker relations across work settings: Interactionally intense settings appear to produce an increase in both positive and negative aspects of coworker relations.

Coworker Relations across Social Groups

Our primary focus in this chapter has been on how the organization of work influences relations among coworkers. However, it is also important to recognize that social and demographic characteristics of the work force and circumstances external to the organization can also influence coworker relations.

Several aspects of coworker relations of particular importance in the current chapter are evaluated across different social groups and circumstances in Table 8.9. Coworker solidarity and conflict appear to be present at similar levels across work groups with different racial compositions, across time periods, and in the United States and the United Kingdom.

More significant contrasts, however, are evidenced for unionization and gender. Workers in union environments evidence much higher levels of solidarity and mutual defense than are evidenced by workers in nonunion settings. This pattern supports the long acknowledged insight that the power and organizational structure provided by unions are important underpinnings for working-class solidarity and mutual defense (Form 1995; Godard 1992; Parker and Slaughter 1994).

Group solidarity is also strongly differentiated by gender. Work groups with greater male representation have greater solidarity than predominantly female work groups. This gender-based contrast is repeated across solidarity, mutual defense, group leadership, and group discipline. Although female work groups may sometimes exhibit strong group solidarity (Gottfried and Graham 1993; Lamphere 1985), on average they evidence group solidarity and mutual defense much less often than male work groups. Part of the reason for this strong contrast may lie in the more limited attachment of some female workers to the workplace (Borman 1988). That is, significant female labor force marginality may lower average levels of group attachment and solidarity across female

Table 8.9. *Coworker Relations across Social Groups*

Variables	N	Coworker Conflict	Solidarity	Mutual Defense	Group Leadership	Group Discipline
Union	69	.11	.28	2.48	2.11	2.58
Nonunion	33	−.21	−.38	1.71	1.76	2.33
Significance[a]		*.150*	*.002*	*.000*	*.117*	*.371*
Exclusively male (100%)	36	−.20	.39	2.52	2.27	2.77
Some female	17	.36	.08	2.13	2.00	2.60
Gender mixed (25%–75%)	30	−.05	−.18	2.12	1.68	1.85
Mostly female	19	−.05	−.67	1.57	1.50	2.00
Significance[b]		*.697*	*.000*	*.001*	*.003*	*.003*
Majority group (100%)	14	−.39	−.03	2.11	1.80	2.22
Some minority	24	−.27	−.20	1.95	1.87	2.56
Ethnically mixed (25%–75%)	16	.29	.05	1.92	1.91	2.46
Mostly minority	8	−.35	−.05	2.40	1.60	1.50
Significance[b]		*.264*	*.800*	*.763*	*.840*	*.528*
Pre-1975	46	.11	−.12	2.13	1.97	2.19
1975 and after	62	−.08	.10	2.26	1.89	2.58
Significance[a]		*.342*	*.282*	*.489*	*.686*	*.129*
United Kingdom	31	.30	.27	2.43	1.88	2.48
United States	57	−.06	−.04	2.20	1.95	2.47
Significance[a]		*.118*	*.196*	*.291*	*.791*	*.975*

Note: All contrasts that are significant at $p \leq .10$ are in bold type.
[a] *t*-test for contrast between two groups.
[b] F-test for linearity.

work groups thus producing this contrast. Ongoing changes in the position of female workers may encourage the spread of work group attachment and solidarity among female workers in the future, a possibility that suggests the need for further investigation and research (see Adkins 1995).

Conclusions

Our investigation of coworker relations across a wide range of workplace settings suggests that the most significant determinant of both positive and negative coworker relations is the role of management.

Management has the ability to create either a workplace culture of respect and dignity or a culture of disrespect and disorganization. Organizational cultures of respect provide a setting for more positive and cooperative relations among coworkers. Cultures of disrespect erode solidarity and increase infighting among employees. Other organizational characteristics also influence coworker relations, but none rival the power and influence of organizational cultures of respect or disrespect set by management in its relations with employees.

Work organizations that include bilateral input from workers also have an influence on coworker relations. Under bilateral systems of shared input, workers become more involved in workplace decisions. In such interactionally intense settings, solidarity is increased among coworkers as they experience their shared interests through daily interaction. However, conflict also becomes more common as workers experience their divergent interests and the limits of their solidarity. Bilateral systems of work organization include those based on professional and craft autonomy and those based on various forms of worker participation. Service work in which repeated and somewhat artificial interactions with clients can increase work stress are also characterized by a similar pattern of both heightened worker solidarity and increased infighting. In contrast to workplaces involving heightened social interactions, highly rationalized bureaucratic workplaces evidence the lowest levels of solidarity and of coworker interactions of any kind, either conflictual or supportive.

Finally, we have seen that characteristics of the labor force and the external setting can also influence patterns of coworker relations. Unions are essential foundations for achieving heightened worker solidarity because of the power base and organizational resources they provide. Solidarity is also more characteristic of workplaces with largely male work forces. On average, female work forces evidence much lower levels of solidarity. This strong contrast may in part be a reflection of the more marginal employment situation of many female workers and the resulting limits on their commitment and involvement with the workplace, which reduces the observed average level of solidarity for women.

The findings presented in this chapter suggest the possibility that coworker solidarity should be conceptualized differently than it has been in the past. Solidarity appears to be not as much a consequence of conflict with management as a consequence of *positive relations* between workers and managers. Employees are more committed to jobs that provide opportunities for working with dignity and in such settings positive and supportive coworker relations also flourish. The correlation between positive managerial behavior and worker solidarity may also result in part from managers being more careful in their treatment of employees when workers can count on mutual support from their peers.

The findings in this chapter also suggest that we may need to reconceptualize the nature of coworker relations in modern production systems based on team production and heightened employee involvement. This new conceptualization of the contemporary workplace would include a greater role for coworker cohesion and solidarity as foundations for smoothly functioning production systems. Employee involvement, worker solidarity, and positive coworker relations appear to be bound together in a supportive nexus. The findings presented in this chapter thus suggest that managers may want to be careful not to utilize team production systems to undermine independent bases of worker cohesion and solidarity. Such a strategy could have unanticipated negative consequences for the maintenance of the sort of normatively integrated and smoothly functioning workplaces that are essential foundations for effective employee involvement and heightened productivity.

Positive coworker relations are essential for overcoming social aspects of alienation through the establishment of solidarity, mutual defense, group cohesion, and mutual support. However, coworker relations can also be an arena for conflict, competition, and negative experiences. This reality is well known to employees across a wide range of settings. The complex and contradictory nature of coworker relations, unfortunately, has received relatively little attention and been given relatively little weight in the academic literature on the workplace.

The principal challenge to positive and supportive coworker relations occurs in setting where management, through mismanagement or through abusive practices, creates a culture of disrespect and disorganization. Such cultures of managerial disrespect represent a continuing challenge to the goal of working with dignity. The negative coworker relations that result from managerial cultures of disrespect contribute to the disorganized nature of the workplace and serve as an additional limiting factor on their viability, especially in the presence of competing organizations of work based on more competent and organized leadership and greater respect for workers and their rights.

In the next chapter we provide a summary and integration of the analysis presented so far in this book. We focus in particular on several "bottom line" work life experiences with clear consequences for working with dignity, including job satisfaction, creativity, and meaning in work.

Part III

The Future of Dignity

9

Worker Dignity and Well-Being

In prior chapters, we examined how a range of workplace challenges and opportunities influence resistance, citizenship, and relations among coworkers. These challenges and opportunities include mismanagement and abuse, assembly versus nonassembly work, professional and craft autonomy, and employee participation. In this chapter we present an integrated overview of these influences and explore their combined influence on the dignity and well-being of employees. The experiences of job satisfaction, creativity, and meaning in work will serve as touchstones for evaluating the quest for dignity in the contemporary workplace.

The integrated, multivariate models presented in this chapter suggest that the greatest impediment to dignity and to the quality of work life in contemporary organizations is management abuse and disorganization. This impediment is offset by compelling evidence that suggests that workers have a strong and abiding desire to participate meaningfully in work. This desire is manifest through widespread citizenship activities and enthusiasm for a wide range of bilateral involvements in workplace decisions.

A Synthesis

Our focus in this book is on the quest for dignity and on the creation of a world where dignity at work is possible for all. Working with dignity ultimately requires the right to participate actively in all aspects of work life, through both formal and informal means. Dignity rests on the opportunity to exercise agency – to operate purposively and effectively in one's environment. For this reason we have focused on the active behaviors of resistance, citizenship, and coworker relations. Dignity, however, depends not just on agency but also on the *realization* of specific goals that define the lived experience of work. These goals are in essence the "bottom line" for employees. They include job satisfaction, a liveable pace of work, and creativity and meaning in work.

237

The daily experience of job satisfaction is central among these goals, but well-being depends on more than just job satisfaction. One can be satisfied with one's job if the work is relatively easy and nondemanding. Fulfillment at work requires more than just the experience of being satisfied in this minimal sense. People rely on the workplace as a primary arena for realization of meaning and creativity in their daily lives. Fulfillment at work entails more than having a positive attitude toward a job. Dignity at work also requires a sense of fulfillment, growth and development – a realization of one's human potential (Bandura 1995; Marx 1971). Consideration of these aspects of work life is essential if we are to appreciate fully the meaning of working with dignity.

Dignity and well-being require the opportunity to contribute productively and meaningfully to the ongoing activity of the organization (Organ 1988; Schnake 1991). Worker citizenship is essential for fully realized dignity and well-being. But the attainment of workers' well-being through participation requires more than just contributing to organizational goals as these are handed down by management. Well-being also requires that these goals include basic respect for employees and their needs. In order to ensure that an organization's goals support the well-being of its employees, it is thus essential that employees have bilateral input into the organization's goals so that these goals are not determined solely by management fiat (Thompson, Paul 1983).

Conversely, the attainment of employees' goals is essential if organizations are to reach their highest possible productivity. Unrealized human potential is the greatest impediment to organizational advancement (Drucker 1993; Pfeffer 1998). It is imperative that organizations develop mechanisms for facilitating employee involvement, dignity, and well-being in the broadest sense.

Figure 9.1 presents the basic causal model underlying the analysis presented in this chapter. Workplace challenges to dignity, including such denials of dignity as management abuse and disorganization, influence coworker relations, worker resistance and citizenship, and worker dignity and well-being. Coworker relations and worker resistance and citizenship represent mediating factors that condition the influence of workplace challenges on worker dignity and well-being. The inclusion of these factors in the model allows the role of worker agency in determining work life experiences to be fully incorporated on an equal footing with other more structural factors.

Worker Agency

Most social science theories of the workplace conceptualize workers as if they were anesthetized patients on an examination table. Workers are

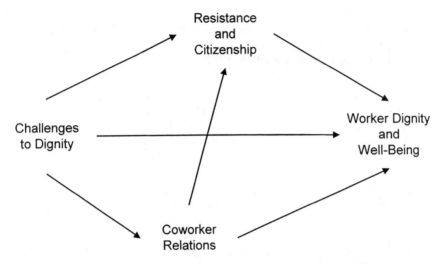

Figure 9.1. Conceptual model of worker dignity and well-being.

conceptualized either as objects to be manipulated by management initiated motivational schemes or as reactive beings whose behavior and consciousness are determined by capitalist social structures or by resistance to those structures. The recognition of workers' autonomous behaviors is typically limited either to a condemnation of footdragging (for those with a management viewpoint) or a glorification of resistance (for those with a more radical viewpoint).

Workers, however, are active on their own terms and are motivated by their own agendas. These agendas are much more diverse than those theoretically allowed by management theory or by radical social science theory. Workers' agendas include compliance and resistance as well as autonomous creative efforts to structure their work lives on their own terms. We have seen in the chapters of this book that the struggle for bilateral participation in the workplace is a central focus for workers. But workers' struggles can also include conflict and strife with coworkers as well as with management.

Workers do not leave their human creativity behind when they enter the workplace. A brief look behind the scenes at any workplace reveals an intricate and multifaceted world of highly creative and purposive activity (Homans 1950; Mars and Nicod 1984; Van Maanen 1998). Unfortunately, contemporary theories of the workplace provide little guidance in understanding workers' autonomous and creative activities. This is equally true of management theories ranging from scientific management to human relations (Argyle 1989; Mayo 1945) as it is of radical theories that focus on the structural determination (or overde-termination) of workers' actions and consciousness (Braverman 1974; Poulantzas 1975).

Those theories that do include a role for workers' autonomous actions typically understand workers' behaviors only within narrow theoretical straitjackets. From the management viewpoint, workers are seen as engaged in output restriction and footdragging (Crozier 1964). Even research more sympathetic to workers has been constrained by a focus on productivity as a central problematic (Ditton 1976). From a radical perspective, workers' behaviors are forced into a theoretical straight-jacket of acquiescence ("false consciousness") or noble resistance to capitalist control of the workplace (Thompson and Ackroyd 1995).

These visions cast workers' actions within very narrow theoretical constraints that have limited and distorted our understanding of workers' true behaviors and motivations. Over time, these limitations have led to a restricted set of questions being asked about workers: How are workers controlled by management and when and how do they resist this control? Other, more diverse questions and issues have been left unexplored.

Some contemporary researchers do argue for a more active view of the worker, but even this vision is typically a constrained one. For example, Burawoy (1979) argues that workers are centrally concerned with "making out" on the shop floor, by which he means devising a way to meet production goals without completely exhausting themselves in the process. Burawoy also argues, however, that contemporary industrial relations are based on hegemonic control of the economic and political relations of production by the capitalist class. Thus, workers' efforts to make out operate within the overriding "logic of the capitalist system" (see also Beynon 1975). Such theories accept as absolute and unalterable the image of the capitalist logic of mass production as constituting a setting in which workers' creative efforts make little or no difference. Thus, even the small range of creative activity allowed workers in these models is rendered theoretically inconsequential.

An alternative view put forward in this book is that workers' goals cannot be reduced to the single dimension of struggle between capital and labor over control of the labor process. Rather, workers' activities are highly diverse and are not easily reducible to any single dimension, including resistance to managerial control. Workers' goals also include engaging in purposive and productive activity and establishing positive relations with coworkers.

We have found in the chapters of this book that workers are neither passive objects of manipulation nor intransigent resisters of every man-agement and organizational goal. The question before us therefore becomes: "How do workers pursue dignity at work and under what structural constraints?" The answers to this question provide important insights into the nature of the contemporary workplace that have been theoretically underdeveloped by prior accounts.

Analysis Plan

In the middle chapters of this book we focused on particular determinants of resistance, citizenship, and coworker relations in order to explore these topics in depth. In this chapter we use multivariate techniques to examine the various determinants as they act in concert. This strategy allows us to examine the simultaneous influence of multiple factors in determining resistance, citizenship, and coworker relations and in shaping the realization of dignity at work. Using this strategy, we are able to differentiate between more and less consequential factors.

The variables and models presented in the following sections have been selected for theoretical relevance, statistical significance, and parsimony. Only workplace characteristics that have effects on worker resistance, citizenship, or well-being that are statistically significant at or above the .05 level have been retained.

The analysis proceeds in two stages. First, we present a unified multivariate model of coworker conflict, resistance, and citizenship. Next, we predict several aspects of worker dignity and well-being as dependent variables using the same model with the addition of coworker conflict, resistance, and citizenship as intervening measures of worker agency.

Infighting, Resistance, and Citizenship

We evaluate a multivariate model of coworker conflict, resistance, and citizenship using data that represent the accumulated ethnographic record of observations in organizations in Table 9.1. Evaluation of this model allows us to identify the main structural determinants of patterns of worker agency in organizations. The model includes management incompetence as well as three alternative strategies for organizing work tasks: bureaucratic, professional, and team-based systems. Coworker infighting is also included in the model. Finally, three controls are included: percent female and percent minority in the work group and a measure of geographic location contrasting the United Kingdom with the United States.

Coworker conflict is well predicted by the basic model with 17 percent explained variance and with statistical significance at the .014 level. The model is even more effective as a predictor of resistance and citizenship.

Table 9.1. *Regression of Worker Infighting, Resistance, and Citizenship on Workplace Characteristics*

Variables	Coworker Conflict	Resistance	Citizenship
Mismanagement	.371^a	.412^a	−.326^a
Bureaucratic	.080	.174^c	.011
Professional	.047	−.135^d	.226^b
Team organization	.044	−.019	.283^a
Coworker conflict	—	.259^b	−.051
Percent female in work group	−.118	.063	.062
Percent minority in work group	.101	.066	−.139^d
United Kingdom	.185^d	.138^d	−.158^d
R^2	.168^c	.426^a	.389^a
N	101	105	108

Notes: Table reports standardized regression coefficients. Statistical significance denoted by: a = p ≤ .001; b = p ≤ .01; c = p ≤ .05; d = p ≤ .10 (two-tailed *t*-tests).

The explained variance is high, 43 percent and 39 percent respectively, and the model is statistically significant at the .001 level for both resistance and citizenship.

Mismanagement is the strongest predictor of all three aspects of worker agency – infighting, resistance, and citizenship. Mismanagement is the sole significant predictor of coworker infighting – a finding anticipated in the more detailed analysis of coworker relations presented in Chapter 8. Resistance and citizenship are also heavily influenced by mismanagement but have other determinants as well.

Worker resistance in the form of gossip, backbiting, and character assassination in a situation of chronic mismanagement is reported in an ethnography of a British apparel factory:

> There was no suggestion from the women in John's department that management had either the right or the ability to manage. Instead, the women were constantly critical of management. They asked, 'When are they going to manage? After all, it's what they get paid for and it's a darn sight more than we get.' The [lead workers] especially, were very critical of management:
>
> *Gracie* The trouble with this place is we never know what's happening and it's my bet that management don't know either. . . .
>
> *Jessie* Either we've got no work or there's a bloody panic on here. I ask you, what do management do with their time? I

reckon I could do better myself than this lot. This place never
runs smoothly. . . .

    Edna I agree, they tell you one thing, you get ready to do it
and then it doesn't arrive. We could do better ourselves, I
don't know what this lot get paid for. (Westwood
1984:25–26)

An employee in a paper products plant similarly expresses frustration
with his supervisor for blatant incompetence: "Anthony doesn't do
nothing. Take it from me, . . . that man doesn't know nothing from
nothing about this department. . . . A good thing he doesn't do nothing
because every time he does come in and do something, it just [messes]
somebody up" (Kusterer 1978:39). Mismanagement is extremely aggravating to employees and seriously undermines their enthusiasm for work
and their vision of the workplace as a productive environment where
they can meaningfully invest their time and energy.

Several other workplace factors beyond mismanagement also influence
worker resistance. Bureaucratic workplaces engender greater resistance
from employees, and professional settings produce less resistance.
Infighting among coworkers also encourages higher levels of resistance
toward management. This pattern repeats the convergence we have
repeatedly observed between hostile relations among coworkers and
hostile labor–management relations.

Mismanagement also has a highly corrosive effect on worker citizenship. Other workplace characteristics, however, also influence citizenship. Professional settings and team production settings generate higher
levels of citizenship than other settings – effects that are almost as large
as the negative effect of mismanagement. An example of citizenship and
extra effort in a team setting is provided by an ethnography of a Norwegian merchant marine:

Everyone understood his job. Everyone was doing his job.
This is the true test of any working community – how well
they do their jobs, and how effectively their skills come into
play, how easily they work with each other in their
cooperative endeavor. . . . 'We all agreed on this training
system before we signed on to the ship,' Johansen said. 'We all
agreed to do this extra work. If we didn't agree, we could
have turned it down and then gone aboard a different ship.'
(Schrank 1983:60)

Chronic infighting also has a negative effect on employee citizenship.
Although this effect is not statistically significant, it is in the expected
direction. An example of how coworker conflict and competition can
lead to reduced peer training and cooperation is provided by an ethnography of a metal parts factory:

> As the shop euphemism puts it, one doesn't have to 'show
> everything' to the new employee. Hostility between trainer
> and trainee may be particularly severe when the newcomer
> poses some threat to the incumbent. . . . Antagonism of trainer
> for trainee may also appear when the trainee threatens to
> eliminate the incumbent's overtime. George, a lathe operator,
> had been working a twelve-hour day for some time and
> wanted to keep it that way. He was an old hand, and his
> fellow operators considered him to be the best lathe operator
> in the shop. Every time he was asked to break someone in on
> his machine, he made sure that they would sooner or later be
> disqualified. There was nothing management could do except
> continue the overtime – they needed George too badly.
> (Burawoy 1979:102)

Ethnographies of workplaces in the United Kingdom suggest greater resistance and less citizenship than ethnographies of workplaces outside the British Isles (see Cheng and Kalleberg 1996; Willis 1977). These two effects, however, are only modestly statistically significant at the .10 level. The strategy of "playing dumb" in a British factory is illustrated by an ethnography of an electrical components factory: "Jeff always says that he can fiddle any ratefixer. You know that when he is being time studied he measures every tube from the drawing although he really knows all the sizes by heart" (Lupton 1963:144). Work avoidance is also commonly reported in ethnographies of British workplaces. A study of work in a British food processing plant provides a good illustration:

> We do three-quarters of an hour packing and three-quarters of
> an hour loading and then have three-quarters of an hour off. I
> mean it's just something that we have arranged ourselves. . . .
> [Also] we are meant to have three or four men [on the job]
> when we go into the other end of the shed but we cut that
> down to two men. We said, 'two men there' and the other
> two men are in having a cup of tea. (Nichols and Beynon
> 1977:135)

Such patterns of workplace resistance are commonplace in Great Britain and appear to represent part of the cultural wisdom of the British worker: "Workers who restrict their output, who 'malinger' at work, frequently justify themselves by their need to regulate the supply of labour. 'If we all worked flat out it would be dead simple what would happen. Half of us would be outside on the stones with our cards in our hands'" (Beynon 1975:133).

Percent minority in the work force also has a negative effect on citizenship, although this effect too is only statistically significant at the .10

level. An ethnography of a piston ring factory in the United States in which the work force is about half white and half African-American provides an example of relatively low levels of citizenship:

> When asked in casual conversation what they thought of their jobs, workers nearly universally responded, 'It's a job.' With such an attitude about their jobs and work time, it is hardly surprising that most workers have reduced motivation to do a particularly good job or to work hard. Nor is it surprising that workers try to make free time for themselves so they can hide. [An older black worker] talked about how hard it was in these times for him and his wife, who also worked, to make ends meet. 'No poor man ever got rich working. . . .' In manifest appreciation of his feelings for his job, he paced himself in each task. Between tasks he hid on the edges of the plant and rested a half-hour. He wasn't lazy, you could see that from how he worked when he wasn't resting. He just gave his job exactly the effort it deserved. (Pfeffer 1979:80)

Ethnographic accounts of occasionally reduced citizenship among minority work forces suggest that the marginality of the job is a decisive determinant of reduced effort. An ethnography of domestic workers in South Africa reports: "Many of the domestic workers in the Eastern Cape sample expressed a deep sense of hopelessness and despondency about their own lives" (Cock 1989:17). Even highly motivated workers find enthusiasm hard to maintain when they are stuck in marginal employment.

Percent female in the work group has no statistically significant effect on coworker conflict, resistance, or citizenship. This null finding is consistent with much of the evidence reported in prior chapters. Although women more often occupy marginal employment positions than do men, men and women seem to experience and respond to work life experiences similarly in matters pertaining to the quest for dignity. As we have seen in the examples provided of citizenship and resistance in male and female work forces, the particular styles may differ between men and women, but the responses to denials of dignity are equally vigorous. When it comes to defending dignity at work, men and women appear to live in parallel universes rather than separate ones.

Many challenges to dignity that we have examined in previous chapters are not included in the unified model. The variables retained in the model are both theoretically and statistically significant. For instance, managerial abuse does not appear in the model. Mismanagement and abuse are highly correlated and it is difficult to statistically untangle their closely related effects on resistance and citizenship. Abuse is not statistically significant as a predictor of resistance or citizenship when mismanagement is included in the fully specified model. The insignificance of abuse in the model also results from the close relationship of abuse with other variables that do appear in the model: bureaucracy, professional organization, and team-based organization. These variables account for much of the relationship of management abuse with citizenship and resistance leaving it with little unique effect. In other words, abuse is in part a reflection of various approaches to the organization of work, which either allow or prevent abuse. Mismanagement operates in a more independent fashion serving to worsen the organizational climate across a wide range of workplaces, regardless of the manner in which work is organized. Therefore, although abuse does not appear directly in the model, its affects are still realized as consequences of organizational forms that encourage or impede abuse. As we have seen in prior chapters, the organizational forms most likely to generate abuse are unilateral managerial control and supervisory fiat.

Solidarity is also not included in the summary model, although coworker conflict is included. The reason again lies in the more independent and far ranging role of coworker conflict and in the close association of solidarity with other factors that are included in the model.

In summary, the principal determinant of coworker conflict is mismanagement. Mismanagement and coworker infighting in turn are principal determinants of resistance and citizenship. The closely related phenomena of managerial abuse and worker solidarity, however, could be substituted for mismanagement and infighting and the model would not be dramatically altered. Bureaucratic, professional, and team organizations of work also have significant effects on resistance and citizenship.

Dignity and Well-Being

Worker well-being has a great many facets, only a few of which can be explored here. The facets of worker well-being that organizational ethnographies most frequently highlight are job satisfaction, the pace of work, and creativity and meaningfulness in work. Based on the descriptions provided in the ethnographic accounts, we coded the average level of job satisfaction for each work setting into one of five categories: very low, moderately low, average, high, or very high. Pace was coded as easy, average, difficult, or brutal. Creativity was coded as none, little, average, or high. Meaningful work was coded as meaningless, somewhat meaningful, or fulfilling.

Table 9.2. *Regression of Worker Well-Being on Workplace Characteristics and Worker Agency*

Variables	Job Satisfaction	Pace	Creativity	Meaningful
Mismanagement	$-.197^c$	$.342^b$	.084	.032
Bureaucratic	$-.022$	.014	.126	.026
Professional	.071	.095	$.209^c$	.050
Team organization	.126	$-.079$	$.188^d$	$-.010$
Coworker conflict	$.172^c$	.053	.146	.046
Resistance	$-.231^c$	$-.388^b$	$-.063$	$-.203^d$
Citizenship	$.424^a$	$-.097$	$.378^a$	$.499^a$
Percent female in work group	.064	.017	$-.133$	$-.149$
Percent minority in work group	.036	.045	.013	$-.018$
United Kingdom	$-.043$	$-.027$	.083	.061
R^2	$.533^a$	$.167^d$	$.355^a$	$.401^a$
N	101	100	102	93

Notes: Table reports standardized regression coefficients. Statistical significance denoted by: $a = p \leq .001$; $b = p \leq .01$; $c = p \leq .05$; $d = p \leq .10$ (two-tailed t-tests).

The analysis of job satisfaction, pace, creativity, and meaningfulness of work as indicators of worker well-being is presented in Table 9.2. This table reports the regression of each of these four variables on the integrated model developed in Table 9.1. Infighting, resistance, and citizenship as indicators of worker agency are also included in the model.

The equations for job satisfaction, creativity, and meaningfulness of work are statistically significant at the .001 level with explained variances of 53 percent, 36 percent, and 40 percent, respectively. These high levels of statistical significance and explained variance indicate that the model effectively predicts these three aspects of worker well-being.

The strongest determinants of worker well-being are mismanagement and worker resistance and citizenship. Mismanagement and resistance by workers erode worker well-being and dignity. Conversely, citizenship is associated with increased worker well-being and dignity and has the strongest direct effects of any variable in the model.

The model does not predict the pace of work as effectively as the other aspects of worker well-being. The explained variance is only 17 percent and the equation is significant only at the .10 level. The reason for the limited ability of the model to predict pace may lie in part in the difficulty of measuring the pace of work across settings in a consistent manner. In some workplaces, pace implies quick physical movements, in others it implies a rapid series of interactions with clients, and in others it implies the rapid handling of data or ideas. The specific determinants of pace, nevertheless, closely parallel those for the other aspects of worker well-being. Mismanagement, for instance, is associated with a rapid pace of work. This finding suggests that inefficient managers attempt to force employees to work harder and faster as a substitute for more substantial and lasting improvements in the organization of work – changes that would require more effort, thought, and creativity from management. Similarly, resistance reduces pace suggesting that workers are sometimes able to set limits on excessive expectations about the pace of work through individual and collective forms of resistance.

An example of the corrosive effects of mismanagement and cronyism on job satisfaction and employee morale is provided by an ethnography of work in French insurance companies: "The fear of favoritism seems to be very widespread. 'There are a lot of people around here who are out to make it any way they can. There are secret payoffs'" (Crozier 1964:111).

Opportunities to engage in citizenship activities and to act in a productive manner, in contrast, are the most powerful positive contributors to worker well-being. Gouldner's classic ethnography of underground miners provides an example of the positive consequences of high levels of citizenship for satisfaction and pride in work: "As one mine mechanic very proudly stated, 'Last week, when they had the cave-in, I worked seventeen hours straight. *But that was an emergency, and everybody helps out then'*" (Gouldner 1964:141; emphasis in original). Conversely, low levels of citizenship contribute to low morale as illustrated in the following excerpt from an ethnography of temporary clerical work: "The temps were bound together by nothing more than a mutual distaste for the job. . . . This lack of integration can lead to confusion and ill-feeling" (McNally 1979:168, 170).

Other determinants of worker dignity and well-being have more modest or indirect effects. Team organization of work, for instance, has a positive effect on creativity at work, although this effect is statistically significant only at the .10 level. An example of a team organization of work as a foundation for increased creativity is provided by an ethnography of firefighters:

> A line man advancing a hose into a building anticipates the length of the line to the fire, when to put on the mask, and when and how to attack the fire. . . . The individual melds his techniques with those of others and thereby both exploits and advances the canon of technique performance. (McCarl 1985:170)

Graphic displays of the model of worker dignity and well-being evaluated for job satisfaction, creativity, and meaning in work are presented in Figures 9.2 through 9.4. The coefficients in these figures are taken from Tables 9.1 and 9.2. The logic of each model follows the scheme presented in Figure 9.1: Workplace challenges and opportunities lead to worker dignity and well-being but this process is mediated by worker agency as expressed through coworker relations, resistance, and citizenship. These models allow us to examine in more detail both the direct and indirect determinants of worker dignity and well-being.

Job Satisfaction

Figure 9.2 displays the determinants of job satisfaction as a key indicator of worker dignity and well-being. Mismanagement influences all subsequent variables in the model and is the only workplace characteristic with multiple effects. The central, and highly negative, role of poor management in determining job satisfaction is clearly highlighted in this model. Mismanagement increases coworker conflict and worker resistance, and it erodes citizenship and job satisfaction. Its effects on infighting, resistance, and citizenship, which are themselves important determinants of job satisfaction, further compound mismanagement's negative effect on job satisfaction.

The strong role of mismanagement in generating worker resistance produces one of the strongest relationships observed in the model. The destructive consequences of mismanagement are clearly evidenced in an ethnography of a Hungarian tractor factory. In this factory, the workers resent the supervisors who set their piece rates and distribute work. There is a sense that the supervisors have no real skills and that they abuse their positions. In response, the workers slow the pace of work whenever the opportunity arises:

> In a burst of rage, a young worker who turned a semi-automatic lathe said to me: 'That lot, what they do, I mean what they *really* do, could be done just as well by an unskilled labourer, all on his own. . . . They are emperors here. They hold us all in their hands. They dole out favours as they feel like it. . . .'
> The worker [however] has some tricks of his own. The best is to follow the technical instructions, and make the machine run at the speed indicated. He also observes the safety regulations: he doesn't touch the table while the machine turns; he tightens all the bolts into their nuts; he sweeps up the swarf after each piece. (Haraszti 1978:86, 128)

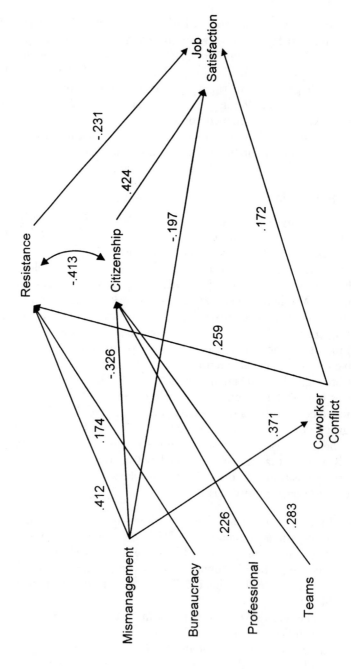

Figure 9.2. Job satisfaction. (Figure reports only paths significant at the .05 level.)

Mismanagement also erodes employee citizenship, as well as sparking resistance. An example of worker citizenship in response to good managerial leadership is provided by an ethnography of inland fishing. The ethnographer reports on the pride, extra effort, and citizenship of workers in response to new nets provided by the owner:

> We set these ten boxes of new nets, and I'm telling you, man, I never seen so many saugers in my life. Jesus, them nets was just full of them. Man, they just come up and look like a blanket coming up with saugers. Half the day I'd pick up the nets, and the other half of the day picking the fish out. (Lloyd and Mullen 1990:62–63)

Other workplace characteristics besides mismanagement have more limited and partial effects on worker dignity and well-being. Bureaucratic organizations of work increase resistance. Conversely, professional occupations and team organizations of work produce greater citizenship. None of these workplace characteristics, however, has a direct effect on job satisfaction. The effects of these additional workplace characteristics on resistance and citizenship are also smaller than are those of mismanagement.

The largest of these effects is that of team organizations of work on citizenship. An ethnography of deep-sea fishing reports on the cohesiveness and positive work environment of the close-knit crews of the ships of a tuna fleet: "A familial role identification appears to take place in stable crew settings. This seems to be a reasonable correlate of the tendency to view the ship as "home" [and includes] the desire to conduct operations in a cooperative egalitarian atmosphere with minimal clashes over decisions and authority" (Orbach 1977:168). Similarly, an ethnography of a Swedish automobile assembly factory reports on the positive consequences of moving to a team-based production system: "There were some benefits. Most of the employees felt they understood the overall process a little better, and had more tolerance for their colleagues when they learned that the other jobs were not as easy as they thought. Improved contact with fellow workers sometimes led one person spontaneously to help another" (Gyllenhammar 1977:90).

Coworker conflict has important and somewhat contradictory consequences for worker dignity and well-being. Infighting increases resistance and thus indirectly erodes job satisfaction because of the negative relationship between resistance and job satisfaction. Coworker infighting, however, has a positive direct effect on job satisfaction. This positive relationship is somewhat surprising on first consideration. Coworker infighting may be positively related to job satisfaction because both are part of a matrix of intense interactions. Interactionally intense work situations may generate both high levels of infighting and high levels of satisfaction and self-realization.

Resistance decreases job satisfaction and citizenship increases it. These are the two strongest direct effects on job satisfaction. This pattern of effects is reminiscent of Herzberg's (1966) two-factor theory of job satisfaction that stresses both positive aspects, or "motivators," and negative aspects, or "hygienics." In the current model, citizenship serves as an important positive motivator of job satisfaction and resistance as an important inhibiting factor.

The strong positive effect of citizenship on job satisfaction generates the largest coefficient in the job satisfaction model. An example of the positive effects of citizenship activities on job satisfaction and meaning in work is provided by an ethnography of inland fishing:

> [The work] also has an . . . aesthetic side, through which the quality of work can be judged and the pleasure in cooperation and good work can be expressed. Bob Bodi and Martin Hosko, who worked together for many years out of Toledo, recalled their subtle cooperation:
>
> BB: 'We got to know each other so good that Martin didn't have to tell me what he was going to do. I knew what he was going to do, and he knew what I was going to do.'
>
> MH: 'I made a little motion, and he knew what that motion meant. Just a little nudge with the hand, and he knew exactly what to do.' (Lloyd and Mullen 1990:11)

In summary, job satisfaction has four direct determinants: mismanagement and all three aspects of worker agency – infighting, resistance, and citizenship. The other workplace characteristics are also important for job satisfaction but their effects are indirect and operate only through their influence on worker agency. For example, bureaucracy increases resistance, and professional and team settings increase citizenship, and thus indirectly influence job satisfaction through their effects on resistance and citizenship.

Creativity

Turning to creativity, we see many similar but also some different patterns at work. Figure 9.3 summarizes the influences on creativity at work as an indicator of self-fulfillment, dignity, and well-being. The left-hand part of the model predicating the three aspects of worker agency is identical to the previous model presented in Figure 9.2; only the right-hand components predicating creativity are different.

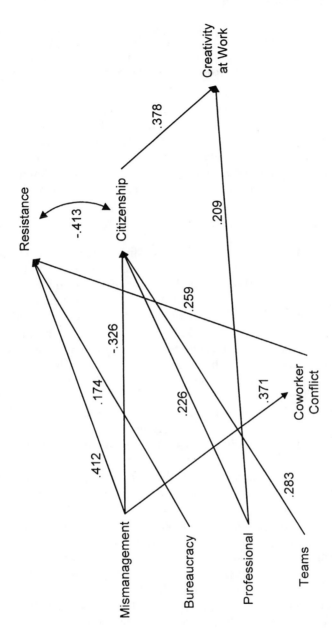

Figure 9.3. Creativity at work. (Figure reports only paths significant at the .05 level.)

The strongest determinant of creativity at work is the opportunity to engage in citizenship behaviors – exactly the same pattern as for job satisfaction. Creativity, however, has fewer additional causes. Mismanagement, resistance, and infighting do not directly influence creativity at work as they do job satisfaction. Mismanagement has a large influence on creativity, but this influence is realized indirectly through mismanagement's negative effects on all three aspects of worker agency. Professional settings, conversely, encourage greater creativity at work. The positive effect of professional settings on creativity at work rests on the training, the deep knowledge base, and the substantial autonomy of professionals to decide how best to do their work (Friedson 1994).

Meaningful Work

Turning to meaningfulness in work as a final aspect of worker dignity and well-being, we again see similar patterns emerging with a few new twists. Figure 9.4 displays the model of worker well-being evaluated for meaningful work. Meaningful work has fewer direct determinants than either job satisfaction or creativity at work. Worker citizenship has a direct effect on meaningful work, as it also has on job satisfaction and creativity. In the case of meaningful work, however, citizenship is the only direct determinant. This is also the strongest relationship in the model suggesting that the other determinants influence the meaningfulness of work primarily through their influence on citizenship. Mismanagement again has a central role in this regard; it influences each of the three aspects of worker agency and through these negative influences has a large cumulative negative effect on the meaningfulness of work.

To summarize the results of our analysis, worker agency has a powerful and multifaceted role in determining worker dignity and well-being. The effects of organizational determinants are largely realized through and mediated by their influence on worker agency. Only mismanagement has direct (and highly negative) effects on worker dignity and well-being. Mismanagement has additional negative indirect effects on worker well-being through its suppression of positive aspects of worker agency.

Other aspects of work life outside of mismanagement and worker agency have more partial and indirect effects on worker dignity and well-being. These include positive effects of professional and team organizations of work and negative effects of bureaucracy. These effects are important in particular settings and for particular aspects of worker well-being. The central roles of mismanagement and worker agency as key determinants of the quality of work life and worker dignity, however, are clearly highlighted by the results presented here.

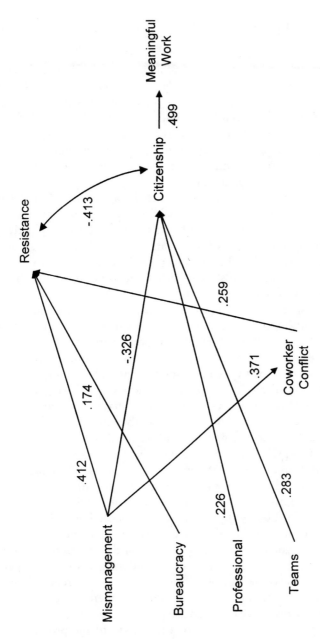

Figure 9.4. Meaningful work. (Figure reports only paths significant at the .05 level.)

Conclusions

The integrated models evaluated in this chapter clearly signal the role of mismanagement as a central obstacle to working with dignity. The negative effects of mismanagement on dignity operate both directly through undermining worker well-being and indirectly through undercutting positive aspects of worker agency. In contrast to the negative role of mismanagement, the most significant positive determinant of worker well-being is the opportunity to exercise citizenship in one's daily work life. This latter finding highlights the reality that employees are eager to be active and positive participants in their organizations and that they do so with enthusiasm whenever the situation allows. This reservoir of positive citizenship is a potentially powerful force for productivity and for improving the quality of work life across a broad range of workplaces. Unfortunately, the organizational foundations for increased worker agency and citizenship are often underdeveloped and this potential frequently goes underutilized.

Several aspects of organizational structure are also important for worker dignity, agency, and well-being. Bureaucracy has a negative effect on dignity at work through extreme rationalization and overregimentation. Various forms of bilateral participation, by contrast, have positive effects on working with dignity. Professional and team organizations of work are particularly important contributors to working with dignity. These bilateral forms of work organization have the potential to allow both greater employee autonomy over daily work decisions and greater employee input into larger-scale organizational strategies.

The guiding principle of management is to increase the profitability of the organization. Toward this goal, managers seek to increase their control over the manner in which the organization conducts itself. Control and power, however, can also become ends in themselves and power is easily abused by those who hold it. Powerful actors seem inevitably to believe that their decisions are best and that their goals should be everyone's goals. The efficiency of the production process and the quality of the product are only secondary goals for management – they are means to the end, which is profit. If outsourcing, downsizing, environmental dumping, discrimination, or undercutting the health and safety of the work force can increase profits faster or easier than increasing the efficiency of operations or the quality of the product, then the choice for management is clear. Profit is the touchstone and all other considerations are only obstacles or opportunities toward that goal.

Workers have a different orientation. They have an abiding interest in the efficiency of production and in the quality of the product because their own well-being and the quality of their daily lives at work depend on efficiency and quality. Increasing the efficiency of production and the quality of the product is their principal, and often sole, avenue for ensuring organizational success and the continuation of their own jobs. In addition, meaning and satisfaction in work are grounded in doing quality work. Workers resist oppression and abuse from management, but as the results presented in this book clearly show, resistance comes at a cost in terms of satisfaction and meaning in work. Employees prefer to act positively at the workplace and do so whenever the workplace situation allows positive action.

An additional contribution that employees make to organizational efficiency is through bilateralism. Bilateral input from employees creates a channel for workers' voices to be heard in defense of quality, efficiency, and dignity. Bilateralism also undermines unilateral management rule and the resulting bending of organizational goals to short-term profit in preference to quality and efficiency. Bilateralism, which can occur through professional or craft organizations of work, through teams, or through a range of participative arrangements, is as essential ingredient for long-term organizational vitality.

One key factor influencing the future of work is the rising educational base of the labor force and the increasing knowledge requirements of industry (Bell 1973; Touraine 1971). The insights provided by ethnographic studies of organizational life, however, suggest that the future of the workplace will also be determined by other factors in addition to the rise of a knowledge-based society (Drucker 1993). The expansion of knowledge is important, but a positive future for postindustrial society also requires an expansion of the power of employees to accompany their greater knowledge. An expansion of the power of workers is necessary if their greater knowledge is to be put effectively to use to increase productivity. Increased worker power is essential if society is to reach its fullest productive capacity. In this process, management's unilateral rule must be curtailed to allow room for a greater voice for the knowledge, insights, and concerns of workers. In essence, workers are ready to take their place as full cocontributors to production. The impediment at this point is the reluctance of management to relinquish its historic power to rule the industrial enterprise by unilateral fiat (Rogers and Streeck 1995).

A true sharing of managerial power may seem fanciful to some, but there are many reasons to believe that it is also inevitable. Unconstrained managerial power leads to mismanagement and abuse. These consequences significantly impede advances in productive capacity. Mismanagement and abuse also stimulate worker infighting and resistance and undermine worker citizenship. Unilateral management power therefore creates its own limits, and in so doing it creates the conditions for its own demise.

Workers face many challenges at the beginning of the twenty-first century. Perhaps the greatest of these is a continuation of unilateral managerial power, rule by supervisory fiat, and accompanying mismanagement and abuse. Important opportunities are also available, however. Central among these is the movement toward greater employee participation. This movement is to some extent inevitable because of the increasing education and skills of workers and because of workers' increasingly central role in realizing the highest levels of organizational efficiency and productivity. The unleashing of the productive capabilities of the work force at this time in history represents an unprecedented opportunity to increase organizational productivity *and* worker dignity and well-being across a wide range of settings.

What is needed in the current context is for management to find a new vision of its role as a shared partner in power. This role should include a commitment to act in a manner worthy of worker trust and enthusiasm. Employees cannot be expected to trust management because an organizational consultant says productive organizations must be based on trust. Employees will only trust management and become willing and eager participants in work life when management *acts* in such a way as to earn their trust by respecting employees' rights, interests, and dignity. What is needed in the workplace of the twenty-first century is a clearer commitment to management citizenship behavior as a foundation for employee citizenship. In the final chapter of this book we explore these themes and the future of dignity at work in greater detail.

10

Dignity, Agency, and the Future of Work

The quest for working with dignity faces many challenges and many opportunities. The main challenge to working with dignity is the continuation of unilateral management power in many sectors of the economy and resulting patterns of mismanagement and abuse. Mismanagement and abuse spark resistance, undermine worker citizenship, creativity, and self-realization in work, and promote infighting among employees, all of which erode dignity, productivity, and well-being for employees and for society at large. But important opportunities for increased dignity at work are available at this time as well. The central opportunity for increasing dignity at work rests squarely on the necessity for modern systems of production to incorporate greater employee participation in order to run efficiently. This necessity sets the stage for greater worker power and for increased dignity at work.

Workers want to participate and contribute in the workplace, but they are too often prevented from doing so by unilateral management power, mismanagement, and abuse. The continuation of unilateral managerial power in the face of an increased need for employee involvement and worker empowerment is the core contradiction in the contemporary organization of work. In order for workers and organizations to take advantage of increased opportunities for productivity and for working with dignity, workers must exercise greater agency and bilateral power in the workplace (Grint 1991:135).

What Have We Learned?

In this book we have offered many insights about working with dignity. In the following sections, we review the core findings. We also offer some thoughts on the implication of these findings for social science theory and for the future of work.

259

Mismanagement and Abuse

Mismanagement, abuse, and supervisory fiat are principal contributors to worker resistance and are equally corrosive of worker citizenship. Mismanagement, abuse, and supervisory fiat also increase infighting among workers and undermine the foundations for solidarity and mutual assistance. Across a wide range of workplaces, employees are interested in taking pride in their work and gaining meaning from it. Mismanagement and abuse, however, rob them of this opportunity. Employees cannot take pride in their work or be expected to give extra effort when they face abuse or when those in control have made it impossible to work effectively.

Worker resistance and the lack of worker citizenship in abusive and poorly managed workplaces act as limiting factors on the viability of such workplaces, but squandered opportunities for worker cooperation has not eliminated such workplaces. Nor does it appear likely that mismanagement and abuse will disappear at any time in the foreseeable future. The continued prevalence of mismanagement and abuse in the workplace at the beginning of the third millennium poses one of the most significant challenges to creating a humane workplace in which all workers can find dignity and meaning in work.

Assembly Work

Overwork and exploitation associated with the extreme rationalization of production in repetitive assembly work lead to some of the most alienating working conditions in modern economies. Workers experience reduced freedom of movement, a steady and grinding pace, and have less skill, autonomy, creativity, and meaning in their work. These alienating conditions lead to resistance against work and against management. Workers are particularly likely to quit or to have high rates of absenteeism.

Nonassembly work, however, also produces many forms of resistance. Employees appear to rely on resistance as a bargaining tactic in all workplaces, not just in those typified by repetitive assembly work. In addition, the ability of assembly workers to engage in some forms of resistance, such as procedure sabotage, making out, or making up games, may actually be less than that of nonassembly workers. The tightly scripted job tasks typical of assembly work limit opportunities for some forms of resistance, and opportunities to resist are equally as important as motivations to resist.

The aspect of assembly work that stands out most strongly in ethnographic descriptions is its strong suppression of citizenship behaviors. Virtually every form of employee citizenship is reduced in assembly work. This strong reduction in voluntary positive actions on the part of employees may be the greatest failing of rationalized assembly work. Management may have succeeded in getting a fast pace of work from assembly workers, but effective production requires more than grudging adherence to requirements. In the modern economy with its increasingly sophisticated production systems, efficiency also requires significant initiative on the part of employees. Opportunities for worker initiative are largely squandered in highly rationalized forms of assembly work.

The undermining of worker initiative and citizenship by rationalized assembly work is an important limiting factor on the continued viability of this form of work organization. Worker initiative is increasingly required for successful production, even in repetitive assembly work.

Professional and Craft Autonomy

Professional and craft employees, in contrast, take great pride in their work and display high levels of citizenship across a variety of dimensions that contribute to the overall efficiency of production. Professional and craft employees differ, however, in important ways. Craft workers resist management and management directives on a regular basis. In terms of conflict with management, subversion of particular managers, and creation of alternative status hierarchies, craft workers offer more resistance to management directives than any other occupational group. It appears that craft workers use the power provided by their unique skills to redefine the workplace on their own terms and to resist subordination to management demands and agendas. Professionals, in contrast, exhibit less resistance than any other occupational category. The sharp divergence in resistance behaviors between professional and craft workers is particularly surprising in light of strong similarities between these groups in terms of skill, autonomy, and citizenship.

The fact that professionals work very hard and without resistance helps explains why they are so often looked upon favorably by management (Barley and Orr 1997). Hard work in the absence of a culture of resistance, however, also helps explain why so many professional employees report working excessively long hours. If professional workers continue to be "trusted employees" who rarely if ever resist management directives, the future for professionals may well be characterized by continuing overwork and excessive hours (Hochschild 1997; Schor 1992).

Employee Participation

Employee participation is here to stay and will only increase in the future to include more and more workers. The dynamics leading to greater employee participation include more complex production technologies, increased educational levels, and heightened demands for involvement.

Increased employee participation results in significant improvements in the quality of work life across a wide range of organizations. Employee involvement is associated with increased skills and autonomy, reduced mismanagement and abuse, and greater pride and citizenship at work. These positive transformations of the workplace create new opportunities for rewarding work lives for an increasing proportion of the labor force.

Under participatory forms of production the work group takes on an increased role in organizing production and in negotiating and enforcing work standards. Under participatory systems management runs a heightened risk of being defined as inefficient or inept – as restricting the development of productive capacity (Wolf 1995). Worker concerns and worker resistance in participatory settings are easily displaced from shop floor production issues to what have traditionally been management prerogatives (Rogers and Streeck 1995).

In theory, organizational goals become workers' goals in participatory settings. When employees are encouraged to identify with the fate of the company, however, they implicitly gain the right to be concerned with broader company policies. These new rights can generate increased concern with managerial choices and with managerial competence. Greater involvement in and closer scrutiny of organizational procedures and decisions can sensitize employees to mismanagement in ways that exclusion from these decisions never did. Participatory practices at the workplace thus create many possibilities for heightened worker power that have yet to be fully realized. Economic miracles should not be expected from employee participation. Greater employee involvement can, however, make important contributions to productivity. Current employee involvement programs are in all likelihood the precursors to new systems of industrial relations that will become increasingly common in the twenty-first century.

Coworker Relations

Coworker relations are a central and even defining experience for many employees in their daily work lives. Coworker relations can be key contributors to both positive and negative workplace experiences. Workplace settings where management, through abusive practices or through mismanagement, creates a culture of disrespect and disorganization are a key impediment to positive and supportive coworker relations. The negative coworker relations that result from organizational cultures of disrespect contribute to the disorganized and abusive nature of such workplaces and further limit their viability.

Organizations of work based on bilateral input from workers have their own unique patterns of coworker relations. Under bilateral systems of shared input, employees become more involved in workplace decisions. In such interactionally intense settings, solidarity is increased as workers experience their shared interests through daily interaction. Conflict, however, also becomes more common as workers also experience their divergent interests and the limits of their solidarity. The workplace of the future will in all likelihood be characterized by increasing interaction among employees as they individually and collectively work to solve ongoing problems of production. Such workplace arrangements can be expected to result in an intensification of both positive and negative coworker relations.

Gender, Race, and Nation

Labor force and national characteristics appear to be less determinant influences on worker agency and on working with dignity than organizational characteristics of work that span demographic and national differences. Percent female in the work group does not have statistically significant effects on either resistance or citizenship in the summary models presented in Chapter 9. The limited effect of gender on worker agency is consistent with much of the evidence reported in prior chapters. Men and women seem to experience and respond to the workplace similarly in matters pertaining to the quest for dignity. The particular styles in which men and women engage in agency at work may differ, but responses to violations of dignity are equally vigorous for both men and women. When it comes to defending dignity at work, men and women seem to travel parallel paths (Acker 1990; Cockburn 1985). Women, however, occupy marginal employment positions more often than do men. Employment marginality thus represents a special challenge to working with dignity for many female employees.

Ethnographic accounts frequently report reduced citizenship among minority work forces. Many of the jobs held by minorities are significantly marginalized, and marginality reduces citizenship. In equivalent jobs, minority employees, like female employees, respond to violations of dignity in a manner highly similar to majority workers.

Workplaces in the United Kingdom evidence greater worker resistance and less citizenship than workplaces outside the British Isles. Such patterns of resistance appear to reflect deeply rooted cultural beliefs on the part of the British working class that management will eliminate jobs and speed up work given the slightest opportunity. Two centuries of industrial capitalism have provided a historically and culturally based memory for the British working class that provides a powerful lens through which contemporary industrial relations are seen and understood. The ability of British workers and British managers to develop more cooperative arrangements is an important challenge as the United Kingdom moves into the twenty-first century (Hill 1991).

Theoretical Implications

Working with dignity is essential for the realization of one's full humanity. We have defined dignity as entailing inherent and earned aspects. Abuse and chronic disorganization undermine one's inherent dignity at work. Earned dignity is realized through creative and meaningful productive activities. Working with dignity requires both protection from abuse and the opportunity to realize one's human potential through creative activity. In order to defend their dignity, workers exercise agency as active, purposive human beings. As the place where we spend the better part of our days and years, the workplace is a central, and essential, location for the realization of human agency and dignity in contemporary society.

Agency is essential for the attainment of dignity, but certain realized outcomes are essential too. Agency is not enough – agency must result in the achievement of specific goals if dignity is to be realized. The essential goals of worker agency in the contemporary workplace are the creation and enforcement of norms that provide protection from mismanagement and abuse and the creation of bilateral structures of participation that provide opportunities for the realization of purposive and productive activity. The concepts of *agency* and *workplace norms* are essential theoretical underpinnings for our understanding of working with dignity.

Worker Agency

The struggle for control is a central concern in the workplace. However, this struggle rarely takes place as a head-on clash between management and labor. Trade unions and political parties representing employees are key organizational bases of power in this struggle and they are essential for helping to achieve a balance of power in the battle for dignity at work. But the daily battle for dignity is also won or lost in the office suite and on the shop floor. Much of the daily battle for dignity at work is waged by individual workers and small groups of workers against managers and supervisors and also against other employees and groups of employees. These struggles are often highly symbolic in nature with gossip and character assassination playing central roles. One of the most noteworthy insights from the ethnographic literature on the workplace is the diffuse nature of the struggle between capital and labor. The struggle is characterized less by major battles than by chronic running skirmishes.

The first and most crucial goal for workers is to establish a positive and supportive context within which to work. In this sense, the concept of worker agency we have developed comes full circle on Frederick Taylor and scientific management: The independent normative order that Taylor sought to destroy is conceptualized in a model of the workplace based on worker agency as an essential precondition for productive activity (Fine 1984; Littler and Salaman 1984). Workers' struggles are often the decisive factor in highlighting the contradictions and limitations of an existing organization of production and forcing the development of new, more humane, and more efficient ways of organizing work.

Conflicts between employees and managers are often subtle, but they are also pervasive, and they have important consequences. These consequences vary between different work settings and this diversity generates dynamics that help drive the ebb and flow of the fortunes of various groups of employees. The abilities of different groups of workers to engage in autonomous, self-defining activity at the workplace is an important key to understanding their changing fortunes and the relative successes of their struggles to work with dignity.

Technology, organizational structure, and workplace culture all influence the likely outcome of workers' efforts to structure the workplace in a way compatible with their needs (Fantasia 1988; Shaiken 1984). New technologies can limit employee control through heightened surveillance and centralized management information systems (Beniger 1986; Marx 1999). But new technologies can also give workers greater power by creating a worker monopoly on the ability to understand and control the new equipment. Similarly, new organizational forms relying on team-based responsibility can rob workers of their autonomy through increased management manipulation (Parker and Slaughter 1994). Alternately, work groups can increase employee power through heightening communication among workers and providing a context for the emergence of group solidarity. Workplace cultures can increase fragmentation and competition, or they can provide a context in which the work group becomes central to one's identity and provides a lasting attachment based on solidarity and mutual aid (Fantasia 1988).

What would our leading theories of the workplace look like if they took worker agency and the negotiated nature of work life more fully into account? Several changes would be demanded of our theories in order for them to conceptualize adequately the workplace as it exists day-to-day as a locus of the lived experience of work.

In order to understand workplace behaviors we need a theoretical model of the worker that is neither anesthetized nor limited to resisting management strategies of control. Such a model must include central roles for pride in work and for the struggle to create autonomous spheres of activity. Autonomous activity is an essential requirement both for workers and for the viability and vitality of organizations. Among the most noteworthy and recurrent observations reported in organizational ethnographies are the enduring positive orientations of workers toward their work and their unceasing efforts to take pride and make meaning out of even the most mundane tasks. Prevailing theories of the workplace, however, too often treat workers' autonomous actions either as a disruption to be eliminated or as theoretically inconsequential.

Employees are active and creative human beings. No industrial regime can completely deny them this and survive, and this is truer today than ever before. The struggle over the specifics of the effort bargain and the details of work practices is thus the lifeblood of organizations. Our theories need to give greater weight to the ongoing activities of workers to cocreate their own environments. Workers' power rests on their "practical autonomy" – the necessity that employees' creative and autonomous contributions be solicited if the ongoing business of the enterprise is to be achieved (Friedman 1977; Wardell 1992). Workers' contributions are realized through both their individual and collective activities. The analysis of workers' practical autonomy, its varieties, and its antecedents and consequences is a vast, little explored, and yet centrally important concern for a fully developed sociology of work.

We must also give greater weight to the significance of subtle forms of worker resistance in our theories of social stratification and social change. Perhaps we should put aside such questions as: "Why are workers not more class conscious?" and begin to ask: "What are the current patterns of workplace resistance among workers?" and "Where are these patterns of resistance taking workers?" Workers' behaviors of resistance cannot be ignored on the grounds that they do not meet the criterion of "class consciousness." Daily workplace skirmishes have fundamental consequences for altering the terrain on which employees and employers meet for their initial, most intimate, and most lasting confrontation.

In order to understand the workplace as a genuinely *social* setting we also need to give at least as much theoretical attention to the work group and to informal social control through gossip and infighting as to management agendas and resistance to these agendas. Training by peers is a central mechanism through which skills and knowledge are developed, reproduced, and shared. Definitions of appropriate directions and levels of effort are also essentially collective in nature (Becker et al. 1961; Cherry 1974). An adequate model of worker agency will have to rely more on emergent collective meanings and behaviors than on free-floating individual attitudes such as "job satisfaction" and "job commitment" (Fisher 1980; Hodson 1991).

Much controversy surrounds current transformations of work involving increased participation and greater organizational flexibility. Many researchers sympathetic to the cause of employees decry the potentially manipulative content of many current changes (Parker and Slaughter 1994; Rothschild and Russell 1986; Vallas and Beck 1996). The specifics of these programs are being actively negotiated in workplaces around the world on a daily basis. The outcome of these negotiations will depend to an important extent on small-scale actions of compliance, resistance, and creativity among workers. In order to understand these changes and the directions in which they are taking the workplace, we must seek a greater understanding of workplace behaviors as workers experience work, not as we project our theoretical agendas and concepts onto it.

The study of worker agency must centrally involve the analysis of *both* resistance and citizenship. Resistance will always occur in the workplace as employees distance themselves from management agendas that are abusive or ill-considered (Kunda 1992). But citizenship is also pervasive in the workplace. Indeed, the ethnographic evidence analyzed in this book suggests that citizenship may be a better barometer of the quality of work life than resistance. Resistance will always take place in the workplace, but citizenship is more variable and contingent. Heightened employee citizenship is contingent on creating a more humane and liveable workplace: Workers give or withhold citizenship in a fashion that closely parallels their experience of respect and dignity in the workplace. Employees want to be good citizens, but they can do so only when the workplace allows them to act with citizenship and still maintain their dignity while being treated with respect.

Twenty-first Century Organizational Norms

Agency alone is not sufficient for dignity; working with dignity also requires the creation of a workplace with certain realized goals. The realization of specific objectives in how work is organized is essential for the full realization of dignity at work. Chief among these objectives is the creation of a workplace with norms for management behavior that include respect for employees' rights and facilitate the maintenance of a coherent and viable system of production. In other words, dignity at work also depends on management meeting its end of the bargain. If employees are to participate positively in the workplace through citizenship activities, so too must management. The establishment and enforcement of norms defining and insisting on management citizenship is essential for working with dignity.

Greater attention to management citizenship behavior may resolve some ambiguities for workplace theories in understanding and predicting worker behavior. Workers are most likely to resist when management fails to live up to basic workplace norms – norms that support worker dignity and a productive environment. The lack of a normative script for management behavior represents a significant impediment to workers' consent to active participation in production. Disrespectful, disorganized, and chaotic workplaces engender worker resistance. In contrast, worker citizenship is supported in workplaces that are coherently organized and in which employees are treated with dignity and respect. Citizenship is further increased by significant levels of worker control such as those evidenced in professional and craft settings and in settings with significant employee involvement.

Management citizenship is a crucial variable in the explanation of worker behavior, but management citizenship has been largely overlooked in contemporary theories of the workplace. A key finding of the analysis presented in this book is that worker resistance and citizenship depend centrally on the level of adherence by organizations to basic normative standards concerning work and employment.

The current proliferation of diverse varieties of flexible accumulation (strategic management) could also effectively be conceptualized in terms of adherence to different normative orders (Appelbaum and Batt 1994; Vallas and Beck 1996). Some organizational normative orders include respect for workers' rights and dignity, and others are oblivious to such concerns. By developing theories that include a normative conceptualization of work life, the bargaining over these different normative structures can become an important object of theoretical and empirical investigation, as can the analysis of whether or not these bargains are fulfilled after they are made. Where such normative structures are present, employee involvement and worker dignity become realizable possibilities. In the absence of such normative structures, employee involvement and worker dignity have an uncertain future (Kochan and Osterman 1994).

The Classics Revisited

Karl Marx helped us see that human beings have a drive to be productive members of society in order to realize their true "species-being." Emile Durkheim warned us that such goals would not be realizable under extreme divisions of labor unless new normative orders were developed to regulate the market. Weber worried that none of this would be possible because of the rationalization of power within administrative structures.

These insights are the building blocks of contemporary social science theory. In this book, I have sought to apply and extend these ideas to the contemporary workplace, a setting that is much different than the one first studied by Marx, Durkheim, and Weber. Probably the most central change is the increased importance of employees of all occupations and trades for the success of organizations. Workers are much more educated and skilled than in the past and their contributions are increasingly central to the success of organizations. Organizations rely on these skills in developing and operating ever more complex and sophisticated production systems that require greater individual skill and greater coordination between teams of workers. These complex systems make organizations increasingly dependent on the individual and collective good will and citizenship of employees.

What is centrally different today from the beginning of modern industrial society is the greater importance and potential power of workers. Employment may still be "at will" in many settings, but extra effort and high-level skills are absolutely essential for organizational success and will only become more important in coming decades. These changes do not mean that workers have won the battle for dignity and respect in the workplace. They do mean, however, that workers have important new tools with which to demand greater dignity and respect at work. Working with dignity will not come automatically with new skills, but workers today, to a greater extent than at any time in history, have important new tools they can use in their struggle for dignity at work.

Implications for Organizations

If the greater productivity and increased dignity promised by new worker skills and increased employee involvement are to be realized, organizational cultures of mismanagement and abuse must be replaced by organizational cultures that respect workers' rights and contributions. The longstanding tradition of unilateral management power must be replaced by bilateral systems of power in which workers' voices can be heard. Workers' voices must be heard on issues directly related to the technical aspects of production. But equally important, workers' voices must also be heard regarding broader issues if a culture of respect for workers' rights is to be established in the workplace. Such a culture of respect is essential if workers are to fully support new programs for increasing productivity based on increased effort and citizenship on their part.

The process of developing new organizational norms and cultures of respect will necessitate increased employee participation in the workplace. This participation can occur through professional responsibility, craft autonomy, or any of a variety of forms of worker participation, depending on the specifics of each organizational setting. The specifics of the choices among these options do matter, but what is important is the widespread movement toward a variety of forms of bilateral employee involvement in the workplace.

Team-based production systems have been among the most widely discussed forms of employee involvement in recent decades. The analysis presented in this book suggests that team-based production systems exert a positive influence on the workplace and are associated with increased agency for workers, increased dignity, and increased well-being. However, team-based production systems are not unique in this regard and are only one of a range of forms of participation that produce similar positive results. In addition, many team-based production systems incorporate manipulative aspects that are meant to undermine and limit employee involvement by substituting team-based participation for collective forms of participation based on unions and collective bargaining (Grenier 1988; Parker and Slaughter 1994). As part of a package of increased participation, based on a variety of forms of employee involvement, team production systems offer significant potential contributions to the workplace of the future both in terms of productivity and in terms of dignity. As a substitute for unions as an independent voice for workers, however, they may actually have negative implications for dignity at work.

What is centrally needed in the contemporary workplace are norms encouraging greater citizenship on the part of *all* stakeholders – employees, managers, and owners. A future based on heightened organizational productivity and increased worker dignity requires that all actors in the workplace subscribe to norms respecting the rights and contributions of employees. Creating such a workplace is a goal that we can all support and many tools and building blocks are already available. The path is open before us if we have the will to take it.

Ethnographies as Data

The arguments and findings we have presented in this book concerning the importance of dignity at work have been based on the systematic analysis of the body of ethnographic data on organizations. As with any source of information, ethnographies have both strengths and limitations.

Strengths

The analysis presented in this book combines qualitative data with quantitative analysis to test hypotheses about contemporary developments in the world of work. The method combines in-depth observation with the analytic power of statistical analysis (Zetka and Walsh 1994:43). The systematic analysis of ethnographic accounts attempts to combine the strengths of qualitative and quantitative approaches. I have tried to draw conclusions based on these analyses that are sufficiently well developed so that they can be debated, cross-examined, and cross-validated.

The methods used in this book add the rigor of explicit comparison groups and controls to qualitative field observations. Evaluation of a broader range of cases significantly increases the variation available for analysis. An additional positive outcome of the methods used for this analysis has been the ability to suggest new constructs about the world of work. The concept of management citizenship behavior that has emerged from the analysis as a key determinant of dignity and meaning at work is a case in point. The importance of coworker infighting has also emerged as a central concern in studying the contemporary world of work. Neither of these concepts has previously held as central a place in the study of work life as the current analysis suggests they should hold.

Limitations

The analysis of ethnographic field observations of the workplace faces certain limitations because of the nature of the data and the available cases to be analyzed. Categorization and coding can result in the loss of some of the richness of the original observations. The data used will be less detailed and less sensitive than the data presented in individual cases.

The set of cases studied is also not a random sample of all possible organizations. Inferential statistics are inappropriate for generalizing from this population to the broader population of all organizations. Generalizations from the analysis must therefore be made with caution. Support for the credibility of the findings depends in part on their consistency with prior theory and research.

Not all topics can be covered in a single volume. Many topics only touched on briefly in the current volume warrant further analysis. Gender differences in patterns of employee behavior are one such important topic for future research. A rich literature on gender differences as they relate to work has developed in recent decades that has transcended prior debates about differences in workplace attitudes and preferences between men and women. These studies have shown that women are far from passive recipients of managerial directives and they have their own workplace cultures of resistance and citizenship (Kesselman 1990; Paules 1991; Williams 1989; Yount 1991). Future studies are needed to investigate the specific areas in which women's cultures of resistance and citizenship overlap with, and diverge from, those of male employees.

Work life is intimately connected with family life and with leisure (Biggart 1989; Hochschild 1997; Schor 1998). The interaction between work life, family life, and leisure is an important concern for both male and female employees. Concerns arising from family life and leisure interests influence strategies of resistance at the workplace in ways that are likely to vary across cultures and historical periods, as well as between the sexes (see Cock 1989; Grenier 1988; Paules 1991; Rollins 1985). These interactions involving work, family, and leisure highlight important areas that deserve additional attention in a fully developed model of worker agency and the defense of dignity.

A New Window on the Workplace

As with all methods, the systematic analysis of ethnographic accounts of the workplace is best utilized as part of an ongoing research dialogue involving contributions from a variety of methods. The study of the workplace has traditionally relied on three principal sources of data: surveys, government statistics, and field observation. The systematic analysis of ethnographic accounts that had been used previously only in a case study format provides new opportunities for social science analysis of the workplace.

The study of the workplace is an intellectually vital field in part because it builds on many different research traditions and methods of data collection. If the concepts of dignity and agency at the workplace are to be further developed, it will be important to engage in that exploration using a variety of research methods. There is no reason why questions such as, "Why and under what conditions do you work more (or less) than 100 percent?" and "Does your organization respect the following list of worker rights?" cannot replace, "How satisfied are you with your job?" Survey methodologies could provide an important source of methodological triangulation to validate and extend the current findings on the antecedents, consequences, and correlates of worker agency, management citizenship, and dignity at work.

It is desirable that social scientists develop theories and methods for studying the workplace that are equally as creative as workers' daily behaviors of resistance and citizenship. Such theories and methods are essential if we are to do justice to the lives of those whom we study.

Conclusions

The struggles of employees of all occupations and trades to work with dignity that are reported in the ethnographic accounts analyzed in this book have been both poignant and inspiring. In their work lives people exercise tremendous creativity, good will, and citizenship in trying to make meaningful lives for themselves at work. Organizations of work that are to prosper in the highly competitive global economy of the twenty-first century must incorporate a central role for worker initiative and worker dignity.

The nineteenth century promise to be freed from drudgery at work was not realized in the twentieth century, but it may be in the twenty-first. Mechanization and automation have eliminated a great deal of grueling physical labor. However, significant denials of dignity remain in the workplace. Chief among these are mismanagement and abuse. The elimination of these and the development of twenty-first century workplace norms that demand management citizenship as an accompaniment to worker citizenship may set the stage for realization of the promise of work with dignity.

References

Abbott, Andrew. 1988. *The System of Professions*. Chicago: University of Chicago Press.

Abbott, Andrew. 1992. "From Causes to Events: Notes on Narrative Positivism." *Sociological Methods and Research* 20,4 (May):428–55.

Acker, Joan. 1990. "Hierarchies, Jobs, Bodies: A Theory of Gendered Organizations." *Gender and Society* 4:139–58.

Ackers, Peter, Chris Smith, and Paul Smith (editors). 1996. *The New Workplace and Trade Unionism*. London: Routledge.

Adler, Paul S. and Bryan Borys. 1996. "Two Types of Bureaucracy: Enabling and Coercive." *Administrative Science Quarterly* 41,1 (March):61–89.

Adkins, Lisa. 1995. *Gendered Work*. Buckingham, England: Open University Press.

Amenta, Edwin. 1998. *Bold Relief: Institutional Politics and the Origins of Modern American Social Policy*. Princeton, NJ: Princeton University Press.

Aminzade, Ronald. 1984. "Capitalist Industrialization and Patterns of Industrial Protest: A Comparative Urban Study of Nineteenth-Century France." *American Sociological Review* 49:437–53.

Aminzade, Ronald. 1993. *Ballots and Barricades*. Princeton, NJ: Princeton University Press.

Appelbaum, Eileen R. and Rosemary Batt. 1994. *The New American Workplace*. Ithaca, NY: Industrial and Labor Relations Press.

Applebaum, Herbert. 1981. *Royal Blue: The Culture of Construction Workers*. New York: Holt.

Argyle, Michael. 1989. *The Social Psychology of Work*. Harmondsworth, England: Penguin.

Armstrong, Peter. 1989. "Management, Labour Process and Agency." *Work, Employment and Society* 3:307–22.

Babb, Sarah. 1996. "'A True American System of Finance': Frame Resonance in the U.S. Labor Movement, 1866 to 1886." *American Sociological Review* 61:1033–52.

Bandura, Albert. 1995. "Exercise of Personal and Collective Efficacy in Changing Societies." In *Self-Efficacy in Changing Societies* edited by Albert Bandura, pp. 1–45. New York: Cambridge University Press.

Barbash, Jack. 1984. *The Elements of Industrial Relations*. Madison: University of Wisconsin Press.

Barker, James R. 1999. *The Discipline of Teamwork: Participation and Concertive Control*. Thousand Oaks, CA: Sage.

Barley, Stephen R. and Gideon Kunda. 1992. "Design and Devotion: Surges of Rational and Normative Ideologies of Control in Managerial Discourse." *Administrative Science Quarterly* 37,3 (September):363–99.

Barley, Stephen R. and Julian E. Orr (editors). 1997. *Between Craft and Science: Technical Work in U.S. Settings*. Ithaca, NY: Cornell University Press.

Barnard, Chester I. 1950. *The Functions of the Executive*. Cambridge, MA: Harvard University Press.

Baron, James, N. Devreaux Jennings, and Frank Dobbin. 1988. "Mission Control? The Development of Personnel Systems in U.S. Industry." *American Sociological Review* 53(4):497–514.

Barry, Herbert, III and Alice Schlegel (editors). 1980. *Cross-Cultural Samples and Codes*. Pittsburgh, PA: University of Pittsburgh Press.

Batstone, Eric. 1984. *Working Order*. Oxford, England: Basil Blackwell.

Becker, Howard S., Blanche Geer, Everett C. Hughes, and Anselm L. Strauss. 1961. *Boys in White*. Chicago: University of Chicago Press.

Bell, Daniel. 1973. *The Coming of Post-Industrial Society*. New York: Basic.

Bendix, Reinhard. 1960. *Max Weber: An Intellectual Portrait*. Garden City, NY: Doubleday.

Beniger, James R. 1986. *The Control Revolution: Technological and Economic Origins of the Information Society*. Cambridge, MA: Harvard University Press.

Bensman, Joseph and Israel Gerver. 1963. "Crime and Punishment in the Factory." *American Sociological Review* 28,4 (August):588–98.

Bernard, H. Russell and G. W. Ryan. 1998. "Textual Analysis: Qualitative and Quantitative Methods." In *Handbook of Methods in Cultural Anthropology* edited by H. R. Bernard, pp. 595–646. Walnut Creek, CA: Altamira.

Besser, Terry L. 1996. *Team Toyota: Transplanting the Toyota Culture to the Camry Plant in Kentucky*. Albany, NY: State University of New York Press.

Beynon, Huw. 1975. *Working for Ford*. East Ardsley, England: E.P. Publishing.

Bierstedt, Robert. 1963. *The Social Order*, 2d ed. New York: McGraw Hill.

Biggart, Nicole. 1989. *Charismatic Capitalism: Direct Selling Organizations in America*. Chicago: University of Chicago Press.

Blauner, Robert. 1964. *Alienation and Freedom*. Chicago: University of Chicago Press.

Bond, Doug, J. Craig Jenkins, Charles L. Taylor, and Kurt Schock. 1997. "Mapping Mass Political Conflict and Civil Society: Issues and Prospects for the Automated Development of Event Data." *Journal of Conflict Resolution* 41,4 (August):533–79.

Borman, Kathryn M. 1988. "Playing on the Job in Adolescent Work Settings." *Anthropology and Education Quarterly* 19,2 (June):163–81.

Bosk, Charles L. 1979. *Forgive and Remember*. Chicago: University of Chicago Press.

Bosk, Charles L. 1992. *All God's Mistakes: Genetic Counseling in a Pediatric Hospital*. Chicago: University of Chicago Press.

Bottomore, T. B. 1963. *Karl Marx: Early Writings*. New York: McGraw-Hill.

Bradley, Keith, Saul Estrin, and Simon Taylor. 1990. "Employee Ownership and Company Performance." *Industrial Relations* 29,3 (Fall):385–402.

Brant, Clare and Yun Lee Too (editors). 1994. *Rethinking Sexual Harassment*. London: Pluto.

Braverman, Harry. 1974. *Labor and Monopoly Capital: The Degradation of Work in the Twentieth Century*. New York: Monthly Review.

Breaugh, James A. and Alene S. Becker. 1987. "Further Examination of the Work Autonomy Scales." *Human Relations* 40:381–400.

Brecher, Jeremy. 1972. *Strike!* Boston: South End.

Bridges, William P. and Wayne J. Villemez. 1994. *The Employment Relationship: Causes and Consequences of Modern Personnel Administration*. New York: Plenum.

Burawoy, Michael. 1979. *Manufacturing Consent*. Chicago: University of Chicago Press.

Burawoy, Michael. 1985. *The Politics of Production*. London: New Left Books.

Burawoy, Michael. 1991. "The Extended Case Study Method." In *Ethnography Unbound* edited by Michael Burawoy et al., pp. 271–90. Berkeley: University of California Press.

Burris, Beverly H. 1983. *No Room at the Top*. New York: Praeger.

Burris, Beverly H. 1993. *Technocracy at Work*. Albany, NY: State University of New York Press.

Butcher, David. 1979. *The Driftermen*. Reading, England: Tops'l Books.

Butcher, David. 1980. *The Trawlermen*. Reading, England: Tops'l Books.

Cappelli, Peter, Laurie Bassi, Harry Katz, David Knoke, Paul Osterman, and Michael Useem. 1997. *Change at Work*. New York: Oxford University Press.

Casey, Catherine. 1995. *Work, Self and Society: After Industrialization*. London: Routledge.

Cassell, Joan. 1991. *Expected Miracles: Surgeons at Work*. Philadelphia: Temple University Press.

Castel, R. 1996. "Work and Usefulness to the World." *International Labour Review* 135,6:615–22.

Cavendish, Ruth. 1982. *Women on the Line*. Boston: Routledge and Kegan Paul.

Chelte, Anthony F., Peter Hess, Russell Fanelli, and William P. Ferris. 1989. "Corporate Culture as an Impediment to Employee Involvement." *Work and Occupations* 16,2 (May):153–64.

Cheng, Y. and Arne L. Kalleberg. 1996. "Employee Job Performance in Britain and the United States." *Sociology* 30,1 (February):115–29.

Cherry, Mike. 1974. *On High Steel: The Education of an Ironworker*. New York: Quadrangle.

Chetkovich, Carol. 1997. *Real Heat: Gender and Race in the Urban Fire Service*. New Brunswick, NJ: Rutgers University Press.

Chinoy, Ely. 1955. *Automobile Workers and the American Dream*. New York: Doubleday.

Clawson, Dan and Richard Fantasia. 1983. "Beyond Burawoy: The Dialectics of Conflict and Consent on the Shop Floor." *Theory and Society* 12:671–80.

Cock, Jacklyn. 1989. *Maids and Madams: Domestic Workers under Apartheid.* London: Women's Press.

Cockburn, Cynthia. 1985. *Machinery of Dominance: Women, Men and Technical Know-How.* London: Pluto.

Cockburn, Cynthia. 1991. *In the Way of Women.* Basingstoke, England: Macmillan.

Cole, Robert E. 1989. *Strategies for Learning: Small-Group Activities in American, Japanese, and Swedish Industry.* Berkeley: University of California Press.

Collinson, David L. 1988. " 'Engineering Humor': Masculinity, Joking and Conflict in Shop-floor Relations." *Organization Studies* 9,2:181–99.

Collinson, David L. 1994. "Strategies of Resistance: Power, Knowledge and Subjectivity in the Workplace." In *Resistance and Power in Organizations* edited by J. M. Jermier, D. Knights, and W. Nord, pp. 25–68. London: Routledge.

Collinson, David L. and Jeff Hearn (editors). 1996. *Men as Managers, Managers as Men.* London: Sage.

Constable, Nicole. 1997. *Maid to Order in Hong Kong: Stories of Filipina Workers.* Ithaca, NY: Cornell University Press.

Cook, Thomas. 1992. *Meta-Analysis for Explanation.* New York: Russell Sage.

Cooke, William N. 1990. "Factors Influencing the Effect of Joint Union-Management Programs on Employee-Supervisor Relations." *Industrial and Labor Relations Review* 43,5 (July):587–603.

Cooley, Charles H. 1922. *Human Nature and the Social Order.* New York: Scribners.

Cornfield, Daniel B. 1989. *Becoming a Mighty Voice: Conflict and Change in the United Furniture Workers of America.* New York: Russell Sage Foundation.

Cornfield, Daniel B. 1991. "The U.S. Labor Movement: Its Development and Impact on Social Inequality and Politics." In *Annual Review of Sociology*, Volume 17 edited by W. R. Scott and J. Blake, pp. 27–49. Palo Alto, CA: Annual Reviews.

Creighton, Sean and Randy Hodson. 1997. "Whose Side Are They On? Technical Workers and Management Ideology." In *Between Craft and Science: Technical Work in U.S. Settings* edited by S. R. Barley and J. E. Orr, pp. 82–97. Ithaca, NY: Cornell University Press.

Cress, Daniel M. and David A. Snow. 1996. "Mobilization at the Margins: Resources, Benefactors, and the Viability of Homeless Social Movement Organizations." *American Sociological Review* 61:1089–109.

Cressey, Peter. 1985. *Just Managing: Authority and Democracy in Industry.* Philadelphia: Open University Press.

Crompton, Rosemary and Fiona Harris. 1998. "Gender Relations and Employment: The Impact of Occupation." *Work, Employment and Society* 12: 297–315.

Cross, Michael. 1985. *Towards the Flexible Craftsman.* London: The Technical Change Center.

Crozier, Michel. 1964. *The Bureaucratic Phenomenon.* Chicago: University of Chicago Press.

Crozier, Michel. 1971. *The World of the Office Worker*. Chicago: University of Chicago Press.

Dalton, M. 1959. *Men Who Manage*. New York: John Wiley & Sons.

De Coster, Stacy, Sara Beth Estes and Charles W. Mueller. 1999. "Routine Activities and Sexual Harassment in the Workplace." *Work and Occupations* 26,2 (February):21–49.

Delbridge, Rick. 1998. *Life on the Line in Contemporary Manufacturing*. Oxford: Oxford University Press.

Della Fave, L. Richard. 1980. "The Meek Shall Not Inherit the Earth: Self-Evaluation and the Legitimacy of Stratification." *American Sociological Review* 45 (December):955–71.

de Man, Henri. 1929. *Joy in Work*. Translated by Eden Paul and Cedar Paul. London: George Allen and Unwin.

Derber, Charles and William Schwartz. 1983. "Toward a Theory of Worker Participation." *Sociological Inquiry* 53 (Winter):61–78.

Derrida, Jacques. 1992. "The Law of the Genre." In *Acts of Literature* edited by D. Attridge, pp. 221–52. London: Routledge.

Diamond, Timothy. 1992. *Making Gray Gold: Narratives of Nursing Home Care*. Chicago: University of Chicago Press.

DiFazio, William. 1985. *Longshoremen: Community and Resistance on the Brooklyn Waterfront*. South Hadley, MA: Bergin and Garvey.

Dill, Bonnie Thornton. 1994. *Across the Boundaries of Race and Class: An Exploration of Work and Family among Black Female Domestic Servants*. New York: Garland.

Ditton, J. 1976. "Moral Horror versus Folk Terror: Output Restriction, Class, and the Social Organization of Exploitation." *Sociological Review* 24: 519–44.

Dobbin, Frank, John R. Sutton, John W. Meyer, and W. Richard Scott. 1993. "Equal Opportunity Law and the Construction of Internal Labor Markets." *American Journal of Sociology* 99,2 (September):396–427.

Dohse, Knuth, Ulrich Jurgens, and Thomas Malsch. 1985. "From 'Fordism' to 'Toyotism'? The Social Organization of the Labor Process in the Japanese Automobile Factory." *Politics and Society* 14,2:115–45.

Dore, Ronald. 1973. *British Factory – Japanese Factory: The Origins of National Diversity in Industrial Relations*. Berkeley: University of California Press.

Doucouliagos, Chris. 1995. "Worker Participation and Productivity in Labor-Managed and Participatory Capitalist Firms." *Industrial and Labor Relations Review* 49,1 (October):58–77.

Drucker, Peter F. 1993. *Post-Capitalist Society*. New York: Harper Collins.

Dunlop, John T. 1958. *Industrial Relations Systems*. Carbondale, IL: Southern Illinois University Press.

Durkheim, Emile. 1984 [1933]. *The Division of Labor in Society*. Translated by W. D. Halls. New York: Free Press.

Eaton, Adrienne E. 1994. "The Survival of Employee Participation Programs in Unionized Settings." *Industrial and Labor Relations Review* 47,3 (April):371–89.

Eaton, Adrienne E., Michael E. Gordon and Jeffrey H. Keefe. 1992. "The Impact of Quality of Work Life Programs and Grievance System Effectiveness on Union Commitment." *Industrial and Labor Relations Review* 45,3 (April):591–604.

Edelman, Lauren B. 1990. "Legal Environments and Organizational Governance: The Expansion of Due Process in the American Workplace." *American Journal of Sociology* 95,6 (May):1401–40.

Edwards, Paul K. 1991. "Workers are Working Harder: Effort and Shop-Floor Relations in the 1980s." *British Journal of Industrial Relations* 29,4 (December):593–601.

Edwards, Paul K. 1992a. "Industrial Conflict: Themes and Issues in Recent Research." *British Journal of Industrial Relations* 30,3 (September): 361–404.

Edwards, Paul K. 1992b. "Comparative Industrial Relations: The Contribution of the Ethnographic Tradition." *Relation Industrielles-Industrial Relations* 47,3 (Summer):411–38.

Edwards, Paul K. 1995. *Industrial Relations: Theory and Practice in Britain.* Oxford: Basil Blackwell.

Edwards, Paul K. and Hugh Scullion. 1982. *The Social Organization of Industrial Conflict.* Oxford: Basil Blackwell.

Edwards, Richard C. 1979. *Contested Terrain.* New York: Basic Books.

Edwards, Richard C. 1993. *Rights at Work: Employment Relation in the Post-Union Era.* Washington, DC: Brookings Institute.

Eisenberg, Susan. 1998. *We'll Call You if We Need You: Experiences of Women Working Construction.* Ithaca, NY: Industrial and Labor Relations Press.

Eisenhardt, Kathleen M. 1989. "Building Theories from Case Study Research." *Academy of Management Review* 14,4:532–50.

Elden, J. Maxwell. 1981. "Political Efficacy at Work." *American Political Science Review* 75,1 (March):43–58.

Elger, Tony and Chris Smith. 1998. "Exit, Voice and 'Mandate': Management Strategies and Labour Practices of Japanese Firms in Britain." *British Journal of Industrial Relations* 36,2:185–207.

Ember, Carol R. and David Levinson. 1991. "The Substantive Contributions of Worldwide Cross-Cultural Studies Using Secondary Data." *Behavior Science Research* 25:79–140.

Endo, Koshi. 1994. "*Satei* (Personal Assessment) and Interworker Competition in Japanese Firms." *Industrial Relations* 33,1 (January):70–82.

Engels, Frederick. 1971 [1845]. *The Conditions of the Working Class in England.* Oxford: Basil Blackwell.

England, Paula. 1992. *Comparable Worth: Theories and Evidence.* New York: Aldine de Gruyter.

Erickson, Rebecca J. and Amy S. Wharton. 1997. "Inauthenticity and Depression: Assessing the Consequences of Interactive Service Work." *Work and Occupations* 24,2 (May):188–213.

Etzioni, Amitai. 1961. *A Comparative Analysis of Complex Organizations.* New York: Free Press.

Ezzamel, Mahmoud and Hugh Willmott. 1998. "Accounting for Teamwork: A Critical Study of Group-based Systems of Organizational Control." *Administrative Science Quarterly* 43,2 (June):358–96.

Fantasia, Rick. 1988. *Cultures of Solidarity*. Berkeley: University of California Press.

Fantasia, Rick, Dan Clawson, and Gregory Graham. 1988. "A Critical View of Worker Participation in American Industry." *Work and Occupations* 15,4 (November):468–88.

Farh, Jiing-Lin, P. Christopher Earley, and Shu-Chi Lin. 1997. "Impetus for Action: A Cultural Analysis of Justice and Organizational Citizenship Behavior in Chinese Society." *Administrative Science Quarterly* 42: 421–44.

Feagin, Joe R. 1991. "The Continuing Significance of Race: Antiblack Discrimination in Public Places." *American Sociological Review* 56,1 (February): 101–16.

Feagin, Joe R., Anthony M. Orum and Gideon Sjoberg (editors). 1991. *A Case for the Case Study*. Chapel Hill, NC: University of North Carolina Press.

Fennell, Mary L. and Jeffrey A. Alexander. 1993. "Perspectives on Organizational Change in the U.S. Medical Care Sector." In *Annual Review of Sociology*, Volume 19 edited by J. Blake and J. Hagen, pp. 89–112. Palo Alto, CA: Annual Reviews.

Ferman, Louis A., Michele Hoyman, and Joel Cutcher-Gershenfeld. 1990. "Joint Union-Management Training Programs." In *New Developments in Worker Training* edited by L. A. Ferman, M. Hoyman, J. Cutcher-Gershenfeld and E. J. Savoie, pp. 157–89. Madison, WI: University of Wisconsin, Industrial Relations Research Association.

Ferner, Anthony and Richard Hyman (editors). 1992. *Changing Industrial Relations in Europe*, 2d ed. Oxford: Blackwell.

Fernie, Sue and David Metcalf. 1995. "Participation, Contingent Pay, Representation and Workplace Performance: Evidence from Great Britain." *British Journal of Industrial Relations* 33,3 (September):379–415.

Festinger, Leon. 1957. *A Theory of Cognitive Dissonance*. Stanford, CA: Stanford University Press.

Fine, Gary Alan. 1984. "Negotiated Orders and Organizational Cultures." In *The Annual Review of Sociology*, Volume 10 edited by R. H. Turner and J. F. Short, Jr., pp. 239–62. Palo Alto, CA: Annual Reviews.

Fine, Gary Alan. 1996. *Kitchens: The Culture of Restaurant Work*. Berkeley: University of California Press.

Fink, Deborah. 1998. *Cutting into the Meatpacking Line*. Chapel Hill, NC: University of North Carolina Press.

Finlay, William. 1988. *Work on the Waterfront: Worker Power and Technological Change in a West Coast Port*. Philadelphia: Temple University Press.

Fisher, C. D. 1980. "On the Dubious Wisdom of Expecting Job Satisfaction to Correlate with Performance." *Academy of Management Review* 5:607–12.

Foner, Nancy. 1994. *The Caregiving Dilemma: Work in an American Nursing Home*. Berkeley: University of California Press.

Form, William H. 1973. "The Internal Stratification of the Working Class: System Involvements of Auto Workers in Four Nations." *American Sociological Review* 38:697–711.

Form, William H. 1987. "On the Degradation of Skills." In *Annual Review of Sociology*, Volume 13 edited by W. R. Scott and J. F. Short, Jr., pp. 29–47. Palo Alto, CA: Annual Reviews.

Form, William H. 1995. *Segmented Labor, Fractured Politics*. New York: Plenum.

Foucault, Michel. 1988. *Politics, Philosophy, Culture: Interviews and Other Writings*. New York: Routledge.

Frankl, Viktor E. 1963. *Man's Search for Meaning*. New York: Washington Square.

Franzosi, Roberto. 1990. "Strategies for the Prevention, Detection, and Correction of Measurement Error in Data Collected from Textual Sources." *Sociological Methods and Research* 18,4 (May):442–72.

Franzosi, Roberto. 1995. *The Puzzle of Strikes*. Cambridge, England: Cambridge University Press.

Franzosi, Roberto. 2000. *From Words to Numbers: Narrative as Data*. Cambridge, England: Cambridge University Press.

Freeman, Richard B. (editor). 1994. *Working Under Different Rules*. New York: Russell Sage.

Freeman, Richard B. and James L. Medoff. 1984. *What Do Unions Do?* New York: Basic.

Freeman, Richard B. and Joel Rogers. 1999. *What Workers Want*. Ithaca, NY: Industrial and Labor Relations Press.

Frenkel, Steve, Marek Korczynski, Leigh Donoghue and Karen Shire. 1995. "Reconstituting Work: Trends Towards Knowledge Work and Info-normative Control." *Work, Employment and Society* 9,4 (December):773–96.

Frenkel, Stephen J., Marek Korczynski, Karen A. Shire and May Tam. 1999. *On the Front Line: Organization of Work in the Information Economy*. Ithaca, NY: Industrial and Labor Relations Press.

Friedland, William H. 1971. *Migrant: Agricultural Workers in America's Northeast*. New York: Holt, Rinehart and Winston.

Friedman, Andrew L. 1977. *Industry and Labor: Class Struggle at Work and Monopoly Capitalism*. London: Macmillan.

Friedman, Andrew L. 1987. "The Means of Management Control and Labour Process Theory: A Critical Note on Storey." *Sociology* 21,2:287–94.

Friedson, Eliot. 1994. *Professionalism Reborn: Theory, Prophecy and Change*. Chicago: University of Chicago Press.

Fromm, Erich. 1966. *Marx's Concept of Man*. New York: F. Ungar.

Fruin, W. Mark. 1997. *Knowledge Works: Managing Intellectual Capital at Toshiba*. New York: Oxford University Press.

Fucini, Joseph and Suzy Fucini. 1990. *Working for the Japanese: Inside Mazda's American Auto Plant*. New York: Free Press.

Gabarro, John J. 1987. "The Development of Working Relationships." In *Handbook of Organizational Behavior* edited by J. W. Lorsch, pp. 172–89. Englewood Cliffs, NJ: Prentice-Hall.

282   *References*

Galbraith, John Kenneth. 1986. "Behind the Wall." *The New York Review of Books* April 10:11–13.

Gamson, William A. 1975. *The Strategy of Social Protest*. Belmont, CA: Wadsworth.

Gamst, Frederick C. 1980. *The Hoghead: An Industrial Ethnology of the Locomotive Engineer*. New York: Holt Rinehart and Winston.

Gannage, Charlene. 1995. "Union Women in the Garment Industry Respond to New Managerial Strategies." *Canadian Journal of Sociology* 20,4:469–95.

Garson, Barbara. 1988. *The Electronic Sweatshop*. London: Penguin.

Genovese, Eugene D. 1974. *Roll, Jordon, Roll: The World the Slaves Made*. New York: Pantheon.

Giroux, Henry A. 1983. *Theory and Resistance in Education*. New York: Bergin and Garvey.

Glazer, Myron Peretz and Penina Migdal Glazer. 1989. *The Whistleblowers: Exposing Corruption in Government and Industry*. New York: Basic Books.

Glenday, Daniel. 1995. "What Has Work Done to the Working Class? A Comparison of Workers and Production Technologies." *British Journal of Sociology* 46,3 (September):473–98.

Godard, John. 1992. "Strikes as Collective Voice: A Behavioral Analysis of Strike Activity." *Industrial and Labor Relations Review* 46:161–75.

Goffee, Robert. 1981. "Incorporation and Conflict: A Case Study of Subcontracting in the Coal Industry." *Sociological Review* 29:475–97.

Goldthorpe, John H., David Lockwood, Frank Bechhofer, and Jennifer Platt. 1968. *The Affluent Worker: Industrial Attitudes and Behavior*. Cambridge, England: Cambridge University Press.

Gottfried, Heidi and Laurie Graham. 1993. "Constructing Difference: The Making of Gendered Subcultures in a Japanese Automobile Assembly Plant." *Sociology* 27,4 (November):611–28.

Gouldner, Alwin W. 1964. *Patterns of Industrial Bureaucracy*. New York: Free Press.

Graham, Laurie. 1995. *On the Line at Subaru-Isuzu*. Ithaca, NY: Industrial and Labor Relations Press.

Gramsci, Antonio. 1971. *Prison Notebooks*. Edited and translated by Quintin Hoare and Geoffrey Nowell Smith. New York: International Publishers.

Granfield, Robert. 1992. *Making Elite Lawyers: Visions of Law at Harvard and Beyond*. New York: Routledge.

Granovetter, Marc. 1985. "Economic Action and Social Structure: The Problem of Embeddedness." *American Journal of Sociology* 91,3 (November):481–510.

Green, Gary S. 1997. *Occupational Crime*, 2nd ed. Chicago: Nelson-Hall.

Greenberg, Edward S. 1986. *Workplace Democracy*. Ithaca, NY: Cornell University Press.

Grenier, Guillermo J. 1988. *Inhuman Relations: Quality Circles and Anti-Unionism in American Industry*. Philadelphia: Temple University Press.

Grenier, Guillermo J. and Raymond L. Hogler. 1991. "Labor Law and Managerial Ideology: Employee Participation as a Social Control System." *Work and Occupations* 18,3 (August):313–33.

Griffin, Larry J. 1993. "Narratives, Event-Structure Analysis, and Causal Interpretation in Historical Sociology." *American Journal of Sociology* 98,5 (March):1094–133.

Griffith, David. 1993. *Jones's Minimal: Low-Wage Labor in the United States.* Albany, NY: State University of New York Press.

Grint, Keith. 1991. *The Sociology of Work.* Cambridge, England: Basil Blackwell.

Griswold, Wendy. 1992. "The Writing on the Mud Wall: Nigerian Novels and the Imaginary Village." *American Sociological Review* 57:709–24.

Guba, Egon G. and Yvonna S. Lincoln. 1994. "Competing Paradigms in Qualitative Research." In *Handbook of Qualitative Research* edited by N. K. Denzin and Y. S. Lincoln, pp. 105–17. Thousand Oaks, CA: Sage.

Gwartney-Gibbs, Patricia A. and Denise H. Lach. 1991. "Workplace Dispute Resolution and Gender Inequality." *Negotiation Journal* 7,2 (April): 187–200.

Gyllenhammar, Pehr G. 1977. *People at Work.* Reading, MA: Addison-Wesley.

Haas, Jack. 1972. "Binging: Educational Control among High Steel Ironworkers." *American Behavioral Scientist* 16,1 (September–October): 27–34.

Haas, Jack and William Shaffir. 1987. *Becoming Doctors: The Adoption of a Cloak of Competence.* Greenwich, CT: JAI Press.

Hackman, Richard (editor). 1990. *Groups that Work (and Those That Don't).* San Francisco: Jossey-Bass.

Hakim, Catherine. 1996. *Key Issues in Women's Work.* London: Athlone.

Halle, David. 1984. *America's Working Man.* Chicago: University of Chicago Press.

Hammersley, Martyn. 1992. *What's Wrong with Ethnography?* New York: Routledge.

Hammersley, Martyn. 1997. "Qualitative Data Archiving: Some Reflections on Its Prospects and Problems." *Sociology* 31,1 (February):131–42.

Hamper, Ben. 1991. *Rivethead: Tales from the Assembly Line.* New York: Warner.

Haraszti, Miklos. 1978. *A Worker in a Worker's State.* New York: Universe.

Harris, Rosemary. 1987. *Power and Powerlessness in Industry.* London: Tavistock.

Harrison, Bennett. 1994. *Lean and Mean: The Changing Landscape of Corporate Power in the Age of Flexibility.* New York: Basic Books.

Haydu, Jeffrey. 1988. *Between Craft and Class.* Berkeley: University of California Press.

Heckscher, Charles and Anne Donnellon (editors). 1994. *The Post-Bureaucratic Organization.* Thousand Oaks, CA: Sage.

Henson, Kevin D. 1996. *Just a Temp.* Philadelphia: Temple University Press.

Herzberg, Frederick. 1966. *Work and the Nature of Man.* Cleveland, OH: World Publishers.

Hill, Stephen. 1991. "Why Quality Circles Failed but Total Quality Management Might Succeed." *British Journal of Industrial Relations* 29,4 (December):541–68.

Hirschman, Albert O. 1970. *Exit, Voice, and Loyalty: Responses to Decline in Firms, Organizations and States.* Cambridge, MA: Harvard University Press.

Hirszowicz, Maria. 1982. *Industrial Sociology.* New York: St. Martin's.

Hochschild, Arlie. 1983. *The Managed Heard: Commercialization of Human Feeling.* Berkeley: University of California Press.

Hochschild, Arlie. 1997. *The Time Bind: When Work Becomes Home and Home Becomes Work.* New York: Metropolitan Books.

Hodson, Randy. 1989. "Gender Differences in Job Satisfaction: Why Aren't Women Workers More Dissatisfied?" *Sociological Quarterly* 30:385–99.

Hodson, Randy. 1991. "Good Soldiers, Smooth Operators, and Saboteurs: A Model of Workplace Behaviors." *Work and Occupations* 18,3 (August):271–90.

Hodson, Randy. 1995. "Worker Resistance: An Underdeveloped Concept in the Sociology of Work." *Economic and Industrial Democracy* 16:79–110.

Hodson, Randy. 1996. "Dignity in the Workplace Under Participative Management: Alienation and Freedom Revisited." *American Sociological Review* 61,5 (August):719–38.

Hodson, Randy. 1997. "Group Relations at Work: Coworker Solidarity, Conflict, and Relations with Management." *Work and Occupations* 24,4 (November):426–52.

Hodson, Randy. 1998a. "Pride in Task Completion and of Organizational Citizenship Behaviour: Evidence from the Ethnographic Literature." *Work and Stress* 12,4 (December):307–21.

Hodson, Randy. 1998b. "Organizational Ethnographies: An Underutilized Resource in the Sociology of Work." *Social Forces* 76:1173–208.

Hodson, Randy. 1999a. *Analyzing Documentary Accounts.* Quantitative Applications in the Social Sciences, #128. Thousand Oaks, CA: Sage.

Hodson, Randy. 1999b. "Organizational Anomie and Worker Consent." *Work and Occupations* 26,3 (August):293–324.

Hodson, Randy. 1999c. "Management Citizenship Behavior: A New Concept and an Empirical Test." *Social Problems* 46,3 (August):460–78.

Hodson, Randy (editor). 2000. *Research in the Sociology of Work, Volume 8: Marginality.* Greenwich, CT: JAI Press.

Hodson, Randy and Teresa A. Sullivan. 1995. *The Social Organization of Work,* 2d ed. Belmont, CA: Wadsworth.

Hodson, Randy, Sandy Welsh, Sabine Rieble, Cheryl Sorenson Jamison and Sean Creighton. 1993. "Is Worker Solidarity Undermined by Autonomy and Participation? Patterns from the Ethnographic Literature." *American Sociological Review* 58,3 (June):398–416.

Hollinger, Richard C. and John P. Clark. 1983. *Theft by Employees.* Lexington, MA: D.C. Heath.

Homans, George. 1950. *The Human Group.* New York: Harcourt, Brace and World.

Hsiung, Ping-Chun. 1996. *Living Rooms as Factories: Class, Gender and the Satellite Factory System in Taiwan.* Philadelphia: Temple University Press.

Hughes, Everett C. 1958. *Men and Their Work.* Glencoe, IL: The Free Press.

Hunter, Kathryn M. 1991. *Doctor's Stories: The Narrative Structure of Medical Knowledge*. Princeton, NJ: Princeton University Press.

Hurlbert, Jeanne S. 1991. "Social Networks, Social Circles, and Job Satisfaction." *Work and Occupations* 18,4 (November):415–30.

Jackall, Robert. 1978. *Workers in a Labyrinth: Jobs and Survival in a Bank Bureaucracy*. Montclair, NJ: Allanheld and Osmun.

Jackall, Robert. 1988. *Moral Mazes: The World of Corporate Managers*. New York: Oxford University Press.

Jackson, Robert Max. 1984. *The Formation of Craft Labor Markets*. Orlando, FL: Academic Press.

Jackson, Susan E. and Marian N. Ruderman. 1995. *Diversity in Work Teams*. Washington, DC: American Psychological Association.

Jermier, John M. 1988. "Sabotage at Work." In *Research in the Sociology of Organizations*, Volume 6 edited by N. DiTomaso, pp. 101–35. Greenwich, CT: JAI Press.

Jermier, John M., David Knights, and Walter Nord (editors). 1995. *Resistance and Power in Organizations*. London, England: Routledge.

Juravich, Tom. 1985. *Chaos on the Shop Floor*. Philadelphia: Temple University Press.

Juravich, Tom and Kate Bronfenbrenner. 1999. *Ravenswood: The Steelworkers' Victory and the Revival of American Labor*. Ithaca, NY: Industrial and Labor Relations Press.

Kamata, Satoshi. 1982. *Japan in the Passing Lane*. Translated by Tatsuru Akimoto. New York: Pantheon.

Kanter, Rosabeth Moss. 1977. *Men and Women of the Corporation*. New York: Basic Books.

Kapferer, Bruce. 1972. *Strategy and Transaction in an African Factory*. Manchester, England: Manchester University Press.

Karoshi National Defense Counsel. 1990. *Karoshi: When the "Corporate Warrior" Dies*. Tokyo: Mado-Sha.

Keef, Stephen P. 1998. "The Causal Association Between Employee Share Ownership and Attitudes." *British Journal of Industrial Relations* 36,1 (March):73–82.

Keller, Berndt K. 1995. "Emerging Models of Worker Participation and Representation." *British Journal of Industrial Relations* 33,3 (September): 317–27.

Kelly, John and Caroline Kelly. 1991. "'Them and Us': Social Psychology and 'The New Industrial Relations.'" *British Journal of Industrial Relations* 29,1 (March):25–48.

Kelly, Michael P. 1980. *White-Collar Proletariat*. London: Routledge and Kegan Paul.

Kelly, Michael P. 1990. "The Engineering Dimension." *International Journal of Sociology and Social Policy* 10,1:28–46.

Kesselman, Amy. 1990. *Fleeting Opportunities: Women Shipyard Workers in Portland and Vancouver During WWII and Reconversion*. Albany, NY: State University of New York Press.

Kimberly, John R. 1976. "Organizational Size and the Structuralist Perspective." *Administrative Science Quarterly* 21 (December):571–97.

Klein, Janice A. 1991. "A Reexamination of Autonomy in Light of New Manufacturing Practices." *Human Relations* 44,1:21–38.

Kochan, Thomas A., Harry C. Katz, and Robert B. McKersie. 1994. *The Transformation of American Industrial Relations*. New York: Basic Books.

Kochan, Thomas A., Harry C. Katz, and Nancy R. Mower. 1984. *Worker Participation and American Unions*. Kalamazoo, MI: W.E. Upjohn Institute for Employment Research.

Kochan, Thomas A. and Paul Osterman. 1994. *The Mutual Gains Enterprise*. Boston: Harvard Business School Press.

Kohn, Melvin L. and Carmi Schooler. 1983. *Work and Personality*. Norwood, NJ: Ablex.

Kolb, Deborah M. and Jean M. Bartunek. 1992. *Hidden Conflict in Organizations*. Newbury Park, CA: Sage.

Kolchin, Peter. 1978. "The Process of Confrontation: Patterns of Resistance to Bondage in Nineteenth-Century Russia and the United States." *Journal of Social History* 11,4 (Summer):457–90.

Koskinen, Ilpo. 1999. *Managerial Evaluations at the Workplace*. Dissertation, Department of Sociology, University of Helsinki, Finland.

Krecker, Margaret L. 1995. "From the 'Instinct of Workmanship' to 'Gift Exchange': Employment Contracts, Social Relations of Trust, and the Meaning of Work." In *Research in the Sociology of Work, Volume 5: The Meaning of Work* edited by R. L. Simpson and I. H. Simpson, pp. 105–33. Greenwich, CT: JAI Press.

Kunda, Gideon. 1992. *Engineering Culture: Control and Commitment in a High-Tech Corporation*. Philadelphia: Temple University Press.

Kusterer, Kenneth. 1978. *Know-How on the Job: The Important Working Knowledge of 'Unskilled' Workers*. Boulder, CO: Westview.

Lamont, Michele. 2000. *The World in Moral Order: Working Men Evaluate Immigrants, Blacks, the Poor and the Upper Half*. New York: Oxford University Press.

Lamphere, Louise. 1985. "Bringing the Family to Work: Women's Culture on the Shop Floor." *Feminist Studies* 11,3 (Fall):519–40.

Langford, Tom. 1996. "Effects of Strike Participation on the Political Consciousness of Canadian Postal Workers." *Industrial Relations* 51: 563–82.

Lebell, Sharon. 1994. *A Manual for Living*. San Francisco: Harper Collins.

Lecher, Wolfgang and Stefan Rüb. 1999. "The Constitution of European Works Councils: From Information Forum to Social Actor?" *European Journal of Industrial Relations* 5:7–25.

Lee, Ching Kwan. 1998. *Gender and the South China Miracle: Two Worlds of Factory Women*. Berkeley: University of California Press.

Lee, Thomas W. 1999. *Using Qualitative Methods in Organizational Research*. Thousand Oaks, CA: Sage.

Lee-Treweek, Geraldine. 1997. "Women, Resistance and Care: An Ethnographic Study of Nursing Work." *Work, Employment and Society* 11:47–64.

Leicht, Kevin. 1989. "Unions, Plants, Jobs and Workers: An Analysis of Union Satisfaction and Participation." *Sociological Quarterly* 30,2 (Summer): 331–62.

Leicht, Kevin T. and Mary Fennell. 1997. "The Changing Organizational Context of Professional Work." In *Annual Review of Sociology*, Volume 23 edited by J. Hagan and K. S. Cook, pp. 307–28. Palo Alto, CA: Annual Reviews.

Leidner, Robin. 1993. *Fast Food and Fast Talk: Service Work and the Routinization of Everyday Life*. Berkeley: University of California Press.

LeMasters, E. E. 1975. *Blue Collar Aristocrats*. Madison, WI: University of Wisconsin Press.

LeRoy, Greg. 1987. "Mismanagement: Labor's Rightful Cause." *Labor Studies Journal* 6,1 (Spring):1–11.

Levine, David I. 1995. *Reinventing the Workplace: How Business and Employees Can Both Win*. Washington, DC: Brookings Institute.

Levinson, Daniel J. 1959. "Role, Personality, and Social Structure in the Organizational Setting." *Journal of Abnormal and Social Psychology* 58:170–80.

Levinson, David. 1989. "The Human Relations Area Files." *Reference Services Review* 17:83–90.

Levinson, David and Martin Malone. 1980. *Toward Explaining Human Culture*. New Haven, CT: Human Relations Areas Files.

Lewis, Michael. 1993. "Self-conscious Emotions: Embarrassment, Pride, Shame, and Guilt." In *Handbook of Emotions* edited by M. Lewis and J. Haviland, pp. 563–73. New York: Guilford.

Lieberson, Stanley. 1991. "Small *N*'s and Big Conclusions: An Examination of the Reasoning in Comparative Studies Based on a Small Number of Cases." *Social Forces* 70,2:307–20.

Lillrank, Paul and Noriaki Kano. 1989. *Continuous Improvement: Quality Circles in Japanese Industry*. Ann Arbor: University of Michigan Center for Japanese Studies.

Lincoln, James R. and Arne L. Kalleberg. 1990. *Culture, Control, and Commitment*. New York: Cambridge University Press.

Lindenfeld, Frank and Joyce Rothschild-Whitt (editors). 1982. *Workplace Democracy and Social Change*. Boston: Horizons.

Linhart, Robert. 1981. *The Assembly Line*. Translated by Margaret Crosland. Amherst, MA: University of Massachusetts Press.

Lipset, Seymour Martin, Martin A. Trow, and James S. Coleman. 1956. *Union Democracy*. Glencoe, IL: Free Press.

Littek, Wolfgang and Tony Charles (editors). 1995. *The New Division of Labour: Emerging Forms of Work Organisation in International Perspective*. Berlin: Walter de Gruyter.

Littler, Craig R. and Graeme Salaman. 1984. *Class at Work: The Design, Allocation and Control of Jobs*. London: Batsford.

Lloyd, Timothy C. and Patrick B. Mullen. 1990. *Lake Erie Fishermen: Work Identity and Tradition*. Urbana, IL: University of Illinois Press.

Lo, Jeannie. 1990. *Office Ladies/Factory Women: Life and Work at a Japanese Factory*. Armonk, NY: M. E. Sharpe.

Lofland, John. 1996. *Social Movements Organizations*. New York: Aldine de Gruyter.

Lorenz, Edward H. 1992. "Trust and the Flexible Firm: International Comparisons." *Industrial Relations* 31,3 (Fall):455–72.

Loscocco, Karyn A. 1990. "Reactions to Blue-collar Work: A Comparison of Women and Men." *Work and Occupations* 17,2 (May):152–77.

Lupton, Tom. 1963. *On the Shop Floor: Two Studies of Workshop Organization and Output*. Oxford, England: Pergamon.

MacLeod, Jay. 1995. *Ain't No Makin' It*. Boulder, CO: Westview.

Marcuse, Herbert. 1991. *One-Dimensional Man: Studies in the Ideology of Advanced Industrial Society*. Boston: Beacon.

Marks, Abigail, Patricia Findlay, James Hine, Alan McKinlay, and Paul Thompson. 1998. "The Politics of Partnership? Innovation in Employment Relations in the Scottish Spirits Industry." *British Journal of Industrial Relations* 36,2 (June):209–26.

Mars, Gerald. 1982. *Cheats at Work*. London: Unwin.

Mars, Gerald and Michael Nicod. 1984. *The World of Waiters*. London: George Allen and Unwin.

Marsh, Robert M. 1992. "The Difference Between Participation and Power in Japanese Factories." *Industrial and Labor Relations Review* 45,2 (January):250–57.

Marshall, Alfred. 1958. *Economics of Industry*. London: Macmillan.

Martin, Susan Ehrlich. 1980. *Breaking and Entering: Policewomen on Patrol*. Berkeley: University of California Press.

Marx, Gary T. 1999. "Measuring Everything That Moves: The New Surveillance at Work." In *Research in the Sociology of Work, Volume 8: Deviance in the Workplace* edited by Ida Harper Simpson and Richard L. Simpson, pp. 165–89. Greenwich, CT: JAI Press.

Marx, Karl. 1971 [1844]. *The Economic and Philosophic Manuscripts of 1844*. In *Karl Marx* edited by Z. A. Jordon. London: Michael Joseph.

Marx, Karl. 1967 [1887]. *Capital, Volume 1*. New York: International Publishers.

Maslow, Abraham H. 1970. *Motivation and Personality*. New York: Harper and Row.

May, Tim. 1999. "From Banana Time to Just-in-Time: Power and Resistance at Work." *Sociology* 33,4 (November):767–83.

Mayer, J. P. 1956. *Max Weber and German Politics*, 2nd ed. London: Faber and Faber.

Mayo, Elton. 1945. *The Social Problems of an Industrial Civilization*. Cambridge, MA: Harvard University Press.

McCarl, Robert. 1985. *The District of Columbia's Fire Fighters' Project: A Case Study in Occupational Folklife*. Washington, DC: Smithsonian Institution Press.

McCarthy, John D., Clark McPhail, and Jackie Smith. 1996. "Images of Protest." *American Sociological Review* 61:478–99.

McKinlay, Alan and Ken Starkey. 1997. *Foucault, Management and Organisation*. London: Sage.

McNally, Fiona. 1979. *Women for Hire*. New York: St. Martin's.

Meiksins, Peter and Chris Smith. 1993. "Organizing Engineering Work." *Work and Occupations* 20,2 (May):123–46.

Mendez, Jennifer Bickham. 1998. "Of Mops and Maids: Contradictions and Continuities in Bureaucratized Domestic Work." *Social Problems* 45,1 (February):114–35.

Meyer, Marshall W. and Lynne G. Zucker. 1989. *Permanently Failing Organizations*. Newbury Park, CA: Sage.

Meyer, Michael J. and W. A. Parent. 1992. *The Constitution of Rights: Human Dignity and American Values*. Ithaca, NY: Cornell University Press.

Milkman, Ruth. 1997. *Farewell to the Factory: Auto Workers in the Late Twentieth Century*. Berkeley: University of California Press.

Miller, Gale. 1991. *Enforcing the Work Ethic: Rhetoric and Everyday Life in a Work Incentive Program*. Albany, NY: State University of New York Press.

Millman, Marcia. 1976. *The Unkindest Cut: Life in the Backrooms of Medicine*. New York: Morrow.

Molstad, Clark. 1986. "Choosing and Coping with Boring Work." *Urban Life* 15,2 (July):215–36.

Molstad, Clark. 1988. "Control strategies used by industrial brewery workers: Work avoidance, impression management and solidarity." *Human Organization* 47,4:354–60.

Montgomery, David. 1979. *Workers' Control in America*. Cambridge, England: Cambridge University Press.

Montgomery, David. 1987. *The Fall of the House of Labor*. Cambridge, England: Cambridge University Press.

Moos, Rudolf H. 1986. "Work as a Human Context." In *Psychology and Work* edited by M. Pallak and R. Perloff, pp. 9–48. Washington, DC: American Psychological Association.

Morrill, Calvin. 1995. *The Executive Way: Conflict Management in Corporations*. Chicago: University of Chicago Press.

Morrill, Calvin and Gary Alan Fine. 1997. "Ethnographic Contributions to Organizational Sociology." *Sociological Methods and Research* 25,4: 424–51.

Mortimer, Jeylan T. and Jon Lorence. 1989. "Satisfaction and Involvement: Disentangling a Deceptively Simple Relationship." *Social Psychology Quarterly* 52,4:249–65.

Mueller, Carol. 1997. "International Press Coverage of East German Protest Events, 1989." *American Sociological Review* 62,5 (October):820–32.

Mueller, Charles W., E. Marcia Boyer, James L. Price and Roderick D. Iverson. 1994. "Employee Attachment and Noncoercive Conditions of Work." *Work and Occupations* 21:179–212.

Naroll, Raoul, Gary L. Michik, and Frada Naroll. 1980. "Holocultural Research Methods." In *Handbook of Cross-Cultural Research, Volume 2: Methodology* edited by H. C. Triandis and J. W. Berry, pp. 479–521. Boston: Allyn and Bacon.

Nichols, Theo and Huw Beynon. 1977. *Living with Capitalism: Class Relations and the Modern Factory*. London: Routledge.

Nonet, Philippe. 1969. *Administrative Justice: Advocacy and Change in a Governmental Agency*. New York: Russell Sage.

Olzak, Susan. 1989. "Analysis of Events in the Study of Collective Action." In *Annual Review of Sociology*, Volume 15 edited by W. R. Scott and J. Blake, pp. 119–41. Palo Alto, CA: Annual Reviews.

Orbach, Michael. 1977. *Hunters, Seamen and Entrepreneurs*. Berkeley: University of California Press.

Organ, Dennis W. 1988. *Organizational Citizenship Behavior*. Lexington, MA: D.C. Heath.

Orr, Julian. 1996. *Talking about Machines: An Ethnography of a Modern Job*. Ithaca, NY: Cornell University Press.

Ortiz, Luis. 1998. "Union Response to Teamwork: The Case of Opel Spain." *Industrial Relations Journal* 29:42–57.

Osterman, Paul. 1994. "How Common is Workplace Transformation and Who Adopts It?" *Industrial and Labor Relations Review* 47,2 (January):173–88.

Ouchi, William. 1981. *Theory Z*. Reading, MA: Addison-Wesley.

Palm, Goran. 1977. *The Flight from Work*. Cambridge, England: Cambridge University Press.

Paludi, Michele (editor). 1991. *Working 9 to 5: Women, Men, Sex, and Power*. Albany, NY: State University of New York Press.

Parker, Mike and Jane Slaughter. 1994. *Working Smart: A Union Guide to Participation Programs and Reengineering*. Detroit, MI: Labor Notes.

Paules, Greta Foff. 1991. *Dishing it Out: Power and Resistance among Waitresses in a New Jersey Restaurant*. Philadelphia: Temple University Press.

Pavalko, Ronald M. 1988. *Sociology of Occupations and Professions*, 2d ed. Itasca, IL: Peacock.

Pendleton, Andrew, Nicholas Wilson, and Mike Wright. 1998. "The Perception and Effects of Share Ownership: Empirical Evidence from Employee Buy-Outs." *British Journal of Industrial Relations* 36,1 (March):99–123.

Perrolle, Judith A. 1986. "Intellectual Assembly Lines: The Rationalization of Managerial, Professional, and Technical Work." *Computers and Social Sciences* 2:111–21.

Perrow, Charles. 1986. *Complex Organizations: A Critical Essay*, 3d ed. Glenview, IL: Scott, Foresman.

Perrucci, Robert. 1994. *Japanese Auto Transplants in the Heartland*. Hawthorn, NY: Aldine.

Perry, Stewart E. 1978. *San Francisco Scavengers: Dirty Work and the Pride of Ownership*. Berkeley: University of California Press.

Pfeffer, Jeffrey. 1998. *The Human Equation: Building Profits by Putting People First*. Boston: Harvard Business School Press.

Pfeffer, Richard M. 1979. *Working for Capitalism*. New York: Columbia University Press.

Pierce, Jennifer L. 1995. *Gender Trials: Emotional Lives in Contemporary Law Firms*. Berkeley: University of California Press.

Pilcher, William W. 1972. *The Portland Longshoremen: A Dispersed Urban Community*. New York: Holt, Rinehart, and Winston.

Pollard, Sidney. 1965. *The Genesis of Modern Management*. London: Edward Arnold.

Pollert, Anna. 1981. *Girls, Wives, Factory Lives*. London: MacMillan.

Pollert, Anna. 1996. "Gender and Class Revisited." *Sociology* 30:639–59.

Porter, Sam. 1993. "Critical Realist Ethnography." *Sociology* 27,4 (November):591–609.

Poulantzas, Nicos. 1975. *Classes in Contemporary Capitalism*. London: New Left Books.

Power-Waters, Brian. 1980. *Margin for Error? None*. Chestertown, MD: Pierce.

Rabinow, Paul. 1996. *Making PCR: A Story of Biotechnology*. Chicago: University of Chicago Press.

Ragin, Charles. 1987. *The Comparative Method*. Berkeley: University of California Press.

Ragin, Charles and Howard Becker (editors). 1992. *What is a Case? Exploring the Foundations of Social Inquiry*. Cambridge, England: Cambridge University Press.

Ramsay, Robert A. 1966. *Managers and Men: Adventures in Industry*. Sydney: Ure Smith.

Ray, Carol Axtell. 1986. "Corporate Culture: The Last Frontier of Control." *Journal of Management Studies* 23,3 (May):285–97.

Reed, Michael I. 1988. "The Problem of Human Agency in Organizational Analysis." *Organizational Studies* 9:33–46.

Reich, Robert B. 1992. *The Work of Nations*. New York: Vintage.

Reskin, Barbara and Irene Padavic. 1994. *Women and Men at Work*. Thousand Oaks, CA: Pine Forge.

Rifkin, Jeremy. 1994. *The End of Work: The Decline of the Global Labor Force and the Dawn of the Post-Market Era*. New York: Putnam.

Rinehart, James, Christopher Huxley, and David Robertson. 1997. *Just Another Car Factory? Lean Production and Its Discontents*. Ithaca, NY: Cornell University Press.

Ritzer, George. 1993. *The McDonaldization of Society*. Newbury Park, CA: Pine Forge.

Roberson, James E. 1998. *Japanese Working Class Lives: An Ethnographic Study of Factory Workers*. London: Routledge.

Roberts, Glenda S. 1994. *Staying on the Line: Blue-Collar Women in Contemporary Japan*. Honolulu: University of Hawaii Press.

Roethlisberger, F. J. and William J. Dickson. 1939. *Management and the Worker*. Cambridge, MA: Harvard University Press.

Rogers, Carl R. 1961. *On Becoming A Person: A Therapist's View of Psychotherapy*. Boston: Houghton Mifflin.

Rogers, Everett M. and Judith K. Larsen. 1984. *Silicon Valley Fever*. New York: Basic Books.

Rogers, Joel and Wolfgang Streeck. 1995. *Works Councils: Consultation, Representation, and Cooperation in Industrial Relations*. Chicago: University of Chicago Press.

Rollins, Judith. 1985. *Between Women: Domestics and Their Employers.* Philadelphia: Temple University Press.

Romero, Mary. 1992. *Maid in the U.S.A.* New York: Routledge.

Roscigno, Vincent and William Danaher. 2001. "Social Movement Culture and Media: The Case of Radio and Worker Insurgency, 1929–1934." *American Sociological Review* 66,1 (February):21–48.

Rothman, Robert A. 1998. *Working: Sociological Perspectives*, 2d ed. Upper Saddle River, NJ: Prentice Hall.

Rothschild, Joyce and Terance D. Miethe. 1999. "Whistle-Blower Disclosure and Management Retaliation." *Work and Occupations* 26,1 (February):107–28.

Rothschild, Joyce and Marjukka Ollilainen. 1999. "Obscuring But Not Reducing Managerial Control: Does TQM Measure up to Democracy Standards?" *Economic and Industrial Democracy* 20:583–624.

Rothschild, Joyce and Raymond Russell. 1986. "Alternatives to Bureaucracy: Democratic Participation in the Economy." In *Annual Review of Sociology*, Volume 12 edited by R. H. Turner and J. F. Short, pp. 307–28. Palo Alto, CA: Annual Reviews.

Roy, Donald. 1954. "Efficiency and 'The Fix': Informal Intergroup Relations in a Piecework Machine Shop." *American Journal of Sociology* 60:255–66.

Roy, Donald. 1958. "'Banana Time': Job Satisfaction and Informal Interaction." *Human Organization* 18:158–68.

Rubinstein, Jonathan. 1973. *City Police.* New York: Farrar, Straus and Giroux.

Russell, Raymond. 1993. "Organizational Theories of the Labor-Managed Firm: Arguments and Evidence." In *Research in the Sociology of Organizations*, Volume 11 edited by S. B. Bacharach, pp. 1–32. Greenwich, CT: JAI Press.

Russell, Raymond and Veljko Rus (editors). 1991. *International Handbook of Participation in Organizations, Volume 2: Ownership and Participation.* Oxford: Oxford University Press.

Rutten, Rosanne. 1982. *Women Workers of Hacienda Milagros.* Amsterdam: Universiteit van Amsterdam.

Sabel, Charles F. 1982. *Work and Politics: The Division of Labor in Industry.* Cambridge, England: Cambridge University.

Santino, Jack. 1989. *Miles of Smiles, Years of Struggle: Stories of Black Pullman Porters.* Urbana, IL: University of Illinois Press.

Savage, Charles H., Jr. and George F. F. Lombard. 1986. *Sons of the Machine.* Cambridge, MA: MIT Press.

Sayles, Leonard R. 1958. *Behavior of Industrial Work Groups.* New York: John Wiley & Sons.

Scheff, Thomas J. 1990. "Socialization of Emotions: Pride and Shame as Causal Agents." In *Research Agendas in the Sociology of Emotions* edited by T. D. Kemper, pp. 281–304. Albany, NY: State University of New York Press.

Schnake, Mel. 1991. "Organizational Citizenship." *Human Relations* 44,7:735–59.

Schor, Juliet B. 1992. *The Overworked American.* New York: Basic Books.

Schor, Juliet B. 1998. *The Overspent American.* New York: Basic Books.

Schrank, Robert. 1983. *Industrial Democracy at Sea: Authority and Democracy on a Norwegian Freighter.* Cambridge, MA: MIT Press.

Schwartzman, Helen B. 1993. *Ethnography in Organizations.* Qualitative Research Methods Series #27. Newbury Park, CA: Sage.

Scott, James C. 1985. *Weapons of the Weak: Everyday Forms of Peasant Resistance.* New Haven, CT: Yale University Press.

Scott, James C. 1990. *Domination and the Arts of Resistance.* New Haven, CT: Yale University Press.

Scott, W. Richard. 1998. *Organizations: Rational, Natural, and Open Systems,* 4th ed. Englewood Cliffs, NJ: Prentice-Hall.

Seider, Maynard. 1984. *A Year in the Life of a Factory.* San Pedro, CA: Singlejack.

Selznick, Philip. 1992. *The Moral Commonwealth: Social Theory and the Promise of Community.* Berkeley: University of California Press.

Sewell, Graham and Barry Wilkinson. 1992. "'Someone to Watch Over Me': Surveillance, Discipline and the Just-in-Time Labour Process." *Sociology* 26,2 (May):271–89.

Sexton, Patricia Cayo. 1981. *The New Nightingales: Hospital Workers, Unions, New Women's Issues.* New York: Enquiry.

Shaiken, Harley. 1984. *Work Transformed: Automation and Labor in the Computer Age.* New York: Holt, Rinehart, and Winston.

Shapiro, Gilbert and John Markoff. 1997. *Revolutionary Demands: A Content Analysis of the Cahiers de Doleances of 1789.* Stanford, CA: Stanford University Press.

Shostak, Arthur B. 1991. *Robust Unionism.* Ithaca, NY: Industrial and Labor Relations Press.

Silver, Beverly J. 1995. "Labor Unrest and World-Systems Analysis: Premises, Concepts, and Measurement." *Review* 18,1:7–34.

Simonds, Wendy. 1996. *Abortion at Work: Ideology and Practice in a Feminist Clinic.* New Brunswick, NJ: Rutgers University Press.

Simpson, Ida Harper. 1999. "Historical Patterns of Workplace Organization: From Mechanical to Electronic Control and Beyond." *Current Sociology* 47,2 (April):47–75.

Singleton, Royce A., Jr. and Bruce C. Straits. 1999. *Approaches to Social Research,* 3d ed. New York: Oxford University Press.

Smigel, Erwin O. 1969. *The Wall Street Lawyer: Professional Organizational Man?* New York: Free Press.

Smith, Vicki. 1990. *Managing the Corporate Interest: Control and Resistance in an American Bank.* Berkeley: University of California Press.

Smith, Vicki. 1996. "Employee Involvement, Involved Employees: Participative Work Arrangements in a White-Collar Service Occupation." *Social Problems* 43,2 (May):166–79.

Smith, Vicki. 1997. "New Forms of Work Organization." In *Annual Review of Sociology* edited by J. Hagan and K. S. Cook, pp. 315–39. Palo Alto, CA: Annual Reviews.

Smith, Vicki. 2001. "Ethnographies of Work and the Work of Ethnographers." In *Handbook of Ethnography* edited by Paul Atkinson, Amanda Coffey, Sara Delamont, John Lofland, and Lyn H. Lofland, pp. 220–33. Thousand Oaks, CA: Sage.

Sotirin, P. and Heidi Gottfried. 1999. "The Ambivalent Dynamics of Secretarial 'Bitching': Control, Resistance and the Construction of Identity." *Organization* 6,1:57–80.

Spector, Paul E. 1986. "Perceived Control by Employees: A Meta-analysis of Studies Concerning Autonomy and Participation at Work." *Human Relations* 39:1005–16.

Spencer, Charles. 1977. *Blue Collar: An Internal Examination of the Workplace*. Chicago: Lakeside.

Spradley, James P. and Brenda J. Mann. 1975. *The Cocktail Waitress: Woman's Work in a Man's World*. New York: John Wiley & Sons.

Stark, David. 1980. "Class Struggle and the Transformation of the Labor Process." *Theory and Society* 9,1 (January):89–130.

Starkey, Ken and Alan McKinlay. 1994. "Managing for Ford." *Sociology* 28,4 (November):975–90.

Steiger, Thomas L. and William Form. 1991. "The Labor Process in Construction: Control without Bureaucratic and Technological Means?" *Work and Occupations* 18,3 (August):251–70.

Stinchcombe, Arthur L. 1959. "Bureaucratic and Craft Administration of Production." *Administrative Science Quarterly* 4:168–87.

Stryker, Robin. 1996. "Beyond History versus Theory: Strategic Narrative and Sociological Explanation." *Sociological Methods and Research* 23,3 (February):304–52.

Swerdlow, Marian. 1998. *Underground Women: My Four Years as a New York City Subway Conductor*. Philadelphia: Temple University Press.

Tannenbaum, Arnold S. and Robert L. Kahn. 1958. *Participation in Union Locals*. Evanston, IL: Row, Peterson and Company.

Tausky, Curt. 1992. "Work is Desirable/Loathsome: Marx versus Freud." *Work and Occupations* 19,1:3–17.

Tausky, Curt and Anthony F. Chelte. 1991. "Employee Involvement: A Comment on Grenier and Hogler." *Work and Occupations* 18,3:334–42.

Taylor, Frederick W. 1911. *The Principles of Scientific Management*. New York: Harper and Row.

Taylor, Laurie and Paul Walton. 1971. "Industrial Sabotage: Motives and Meanings." In *Images of Deviance* edited by S. Cohen, pp. 219–45. London: Penguin.

Taylor, Verta. 1999. "Gender and Social Movements: Gender Processes in Women's Self-help Movements." *Gender and Society* 13,1 (February):8–33.

Terris, William and John Jones. 1982. "Psychological Factors Related to Employees' Theft in the Convenience Store Industry." *Psychological Reports* 51,3 (December):1219–38.

Thomas, Robert J. 1988. "Quality and Quantity? Worker Participation in the U.S. and Japanese Automobile Industries." In *Technological Change and Workers' Movements* edited by M. Dubofsky, pp. 162–88. Beverly Hills, CA: Sage.

Thomas, Robert J. 1994. *What Machines Can't Do*. Berkeley: University of California Press.

Thompson, E. P. 1974. "Patrician Society, Plebeian Culture." *Journal of Social History* 7,4 (Summer):382–405.

Thompson, E. P. 1978. *The Poverty of Theory and Other Essays*. New York: Monthly Review.

Thompson, Paul. 1983. *The Nature of Work*. London: Macmillan.

Thompson, Paul and Stephen Ackroyd. 1995. "All Quiet on the Workplace Front?" *Sociology* 29,4 (November):615–33.

Thompson, Paul and Chris Warhurst (editors). 1998. *Workplaces of the Future*. Basingstoke, England: Macmillan.

Thompson, William E. 1983. "Hanging Tongues: A Sociological Encounter with the Assembly Line." *Qualitative Sociology* 6,3 (Fall):215–37.

Tilly, Charles. 1981. *As Sociology Meets History*. New York: Academic.

Tilly, Charles. 1998. *Durable Inequalities*. Berkeley: University of California Press.

Tilly, Chris. 1996. *Half a Job: Bad and Good Part-Time Jobs in a Changing Labor Market*. Philadelphia: Temple University Press.

Tobin, Joseph. 1990. "The HRAF as Radical Text?" *Cultural Anthropology* 5,4 (November):473–87.

Touraine, Alain. 1971. *The Post-Industrial Society*. New York: Random House.

Traweek, Sharon. 1988. *Beamtimes and Lifetimes: The World of High Energy Physics*. Cambridge, MA: Harvard University Press.

Tsui, Anne S., Jone L. Pearce, Lyman W. Porter, and Angela M. Tripoli. 1997. "Alternative Approaches to the Employee-Organization Relationship: Does Investment in Employees Pay Off?" *Academy of Management Journal* 40,5 (October):1089–121.

Tuch, Steven A. and Jack K. Martin. 1991. "Race in the Workplace: Black/White Differences in the Sources of Job Satisfaction." *Sociological Quarterly* 32,1 (February):103–16.

Tucker, James. 1993. "Everyday Forms of Employee Resistance." *Sociological Forum* 8,1:25–45.

Tucker, James. 1999. *The Therapeutic Corporation*. New York: Oxford University Press.

Turner, Steve. 1980. *Night Shift in a Pickle Factory*. San Pedro, CA: Singlejack.

Vallas, Steven P. 1987. "The Labor Process as a Source of Class Consciousness" *Sociological Forum* 2,2 (Spring):251–73.

Vallas, Steven P. 1999. "Rethinking Post-Fordism: The Meaning of Workplace Flexibility." *Sociological Theory* 17,1 (March):68–101.

Vallas, Steven P. and John P. Beck. 1996. "The Transformation of Work Revisited: The Limits of Flexibility in American Manufacturing." *Social Problems* 43,3 (August):339–61.

Van Maanen, John (editor). 1998. *Qualitative Studies in Organizations*. Thousand Oaks, CA: Sage.

Van Maanen, John and Stephen R. Barley. 1984. "Occupational Communities: Culture and Control in Organizations." In *Research in Organizational Behavior*, Volume 6 edited by B. M. Staw and L. L. Cummings, pp. 287–365. Greenwich, CT: JAI Press.

Vaughan, Diane. 1983. *Controlling Unlawful Organizational Behavior*. Chicago: University of Chicago Press.

Vaughan, Diane. 1996. *The Challenger Launch Decision: Risky Technology, Culture, and Deviance at NASA*. Chicago: University of Chicago Press.

Veblen, Thorstein. 1914. *The Instinct of Workmanship and the State of the Industrial Arts*. New York: Macmillan.

Vecsey, George. 1974. *One Sunset a Week: The Story of a Coal Miner*. New York: E.P. Dutton.

Vredenburgh, D. and Y. Brender. 1998. "The Hierarchical Abuse of Power in Work Organizations." *Journal of Business Ethics* 17,12 (September): 1337–47.

Wajcman, Judy. 1983. *Women in Control: Dilemmas of a Workers Co-operative*. New York: St. Martin's.

Walker, Charles R. 1957. *Toward the Automatic Factory: A Case Study of Men and Machines*. New Haven, CT: Yale University Press.

Walker, Charles R. and Robert H. Guest. 1952. *The Man on the Assembly Line*. Cambridge, MA: Harvard University Press.

Walker, Charles R., Robert H. Guest, and Arthur N. Turner. 1956. *The Foreman on the Assembly Line*. Cambridge, MA: Harvard University Press.

Walsh, John P. and Shu-fen Tseng. 1998. "The Effects of Job Characteristics on Active Effort at Work." *Work and Occupations* 25,1 (February):74–96.

Walton, J. 1992. "Making the Theoretical Case." In *What is a Case? Exploring the Foundations of Social Inquiry* edited by C. Ragin and H. Becker, pp. 121–37. Cambridge, England: Cambridge University Press.

Walton, Richard E. and J. Richard Hackman. 1986. "Groups under Contrasting Management Strategies." In *Designing Effective Work Groups* edited by Paul S. Goodman and Associates, pp. 168–201. San Francisco: Jossey Bass.

Wardell, Mark. 1992. "Changing Organizational Forms: From the Bottom-up." In *Rethinking Organizations: New Directions in Organizational Theory and Analysis* edited by M. L. Reed and M. Hughes, pp. 144–65. London: Sage.

Watson, Tony. 1994. *In Search of Management*. London: Routledge.

Webb, Mike and Gerry Palmer. 1998. "Evading Surveillance and Making Time: An Ethnographic View of the Japanese Factory Floor in Britain." *British Journal of Industrial Relations* 36,4 (December):611–27.

Weber, Robert P. 1990. *Basic Content Analysis*, 2nd ed. Quantitative Applications in the Social Sciences, #49. Newbury Park, CA: Sage.

Weber, Max. 1947. *The Theory of Social and Economic Organization*. Translated by A. M. Henderson and Talcott Parsons. New York: Free Press.

Weber, Max. 1968. *Economy and Society*. Edited by Guenther Roth and Claus Wittich. New York: Bedminster.

Wedderburn, Dorothy and Rosemary Crompton. 1972. *Workers' Attitudes and Technology*. Cambridge, England: Cambridge University Press.

Weick, Karl A. 1985. "Systematic Observational Methods." In *The Handbook of Social Psychology* edited by G. Lindzey and E. Aronson, pp. 567–634. New York: Random House.

Weinstein, Deena. 1979. *Bureaucratic Opposition*. New York: Pergamon.

Wellman, David. 1995. *The Union Makes Us Strong: Radical Unionism on the San Francisco Waterfront.* Cambridge, England: Cambridge University Press.

Welsh, Sandy and A. Nierobisz. 1997. "How Prevalent is Sexual Harassment?" *Canadian Journal of Sociology* 22,4 (Fall):505–22.

Westwood, Sallie. 1984. *All Day, Every Day: Factory and Family in the Making of Women's Lives.* London: Pluto.

Whalley, Peter. 1991. "Negotiating The Boundaries of Engineering: Professionals, Managers and Manual Work." *Research in the Sociology of Organizations* 8:191–215.

Whalley, Peter and Stephen R. Barley. 1997. "Technical Work in the Division of Labor." In *Between Craft and Science: Technical Work in U.S. Settings* edited by S. R. Barley and J. E. Orr, pp. 23–52. Ithaca, NY: Cornell University Press.

Wharton, Amy and James N. Baron. 1987. "So Happy Together? The Impact of Gender Segregation on Men at Work." *American Sociological Review* 52:574–87.

Whyte, William Foot, Tove H. Hammer, and Christopher B. Meek. 1983. *Worker Participation and Ownership: Cooperative Strategies for Strengthening Local Economics.* Ithaca, NY: Industrial and Labor Relations Press.

Wilensky, H. L. 1964. "The Professionalization of Everybody?" *American Journal of Sociology* 70:137–58.

Wilkinson, Adrian, Graham Godfrey, and Mick Marchington. 1997. "Bouquets, Brickbats and Blinkers: Total Quality Management and Employee Involvement in Practice." *Organization Studies* 18:799–820.

Williams, Bruce B. 1987. *Black Workers in an Industrial Suburb.* New Brunswick, NJ: Rutgers University Press.

Williams, Christine L. 1989. *Gender Differences at Work: Women and Men in Nontraditional Occupations.* Berkeley: University of California Press.

Williams, Claire. 1981. *Open Cut: The Working Class in an Australian Mining Town.* Boston, MA: Allen and Unwin.

Willis, Paul. 1977. *Learning to Labor: How Working Class Kids Get Working Class Jobs.* New York: Columbia University Press.

Wolf, Harald. 1995. "Introduction." *International Journal of Political Economy* (special issue on *Democracy at Work?*) 25,3 (Fall):3–19.

Womack, James, Daniel Jones, and Daniel Roos. 1990. *The Machine That Changed the World.* New York: Rawson Associates.

Wright, Erik O. 1997. *Class Counts: Comparative Studies in Class Analysis.* New York: Cambridge University Press.

Wuthnow, Robert and Wesley Shrum. 1983. "Knowledge Workers as a 'New Class': Structural and Ideological Convergence among Professional-Technical Workers and Managers." *Work and Occupations* 10,4:471–87.

Yount, Kristen R. 1991. "Ladies, Flirts, and Tomboys: Strategies for Managing Sexual Harassment in an Underground Coal Mine." *Journal of Contemporary Ethnography* 19,4 (January):396–422.

Zald, Mayer N. and Michael A. Berger. 1978. "Social Movements in Organizations." *American Journal of Sociology* 83,4 (January):823–61.

Zander, Alvin and Warwick Armstrong. 1972. "Working for Group Pride in a Slipper Factory." *Journal of Applied Social Psychology* 2,4:293–307.

Zetka, James R., Jr. and John P. Walsh. 1994. "A Qualitative Protocol for Studying Technological Change in the Labor Process." *Bulletin de Methodologie Sociologique* 45:37–73.

Zuboff, Shoshanna. 1988. *In the Age of the Smart Machine*. New York: Basic Books.

Zussman, Robert. 1985. *Mechanics of the Middle Class: Work and Politics among American Engineers*. Berkeley: University of California Press.

Zussman, Robert. 1992. *Intensive Care: Medical Ethics and the Medical Profession*. Chicago: University of Chicago Press.

Appendix A: A Brief History of the Workplace Ethnography (W.E.) Project

As a student of the workplace I have long been an avid reader of organizational ethnographies. The research project that inspired this book began when I read a number of especially interesting organizational ethnographies during a sabbatical year. I was impressed by the insights the ethnographies offered about work life. It was also apparent that the authors had taken great care to describe a standard and reasonably comprehensive set of workplace characteristics and concerns in addition to their focal issues. Tom Juravich's *Chaos on the Shop Floor* (1985) stands out as an exemplar in the genre. Based on these readings, I decided to pursue a project of systematically coding workplace ethnographies. The goal of this project was to take advantage of the in-depth observations offered by workplace ethnographies while simultaneously providing a framework for identifying repeated patterns and relationships.

Selecting the Cases

The first step was to select the cases to be analyzed. With the help of a research assistant, I examined thousands of case studies in a two-phase procedure to locate appropriate book-length ethnographies. First, likely titles were generated by computer-assisted searches of archives, perusal of the bibliographies of ethnographies already located, and searching the library shelves in the immediate area of previously identified ethnographies. We screened titles using on-line computer archives, book reviews, or direct examination of the books selected from the shelves. Repeated application of these procedures constitutes what we believe was an exhaustive search – eventually our pursuit of new leads produced only titles already considered. We excluded cases that used primarily archival or survey data for their analysis rather than ethnographic observation. This selection process yielded a pool of 365 books as potential candidates for inclusion.

During the second phase of selection, we examined each book directly. The criteria for inclusion were: (1) the book had to be based on direct ethnographic methods of observation over a period of at least six months; (2) the observations had to be of a single organization; and (3) the book had to focus on at least one specific group of workers – an assembly line, a typing pool, a project group, or some other identifiable work group. The requirements of an ethnographic

299

method and a focus on a specific work group were necessary in order to limit the pool to cases with the depth of observation needed to reliably ascertain the many aspects of workplace relations in which we were interested. The focus on a single organization was necessary to produce measures of the organizational characteristics that we hypothesized to be the determinants of workplace relations.

Of the 365 books, 84 were retained as appropriate for analysis and 281 were rejected. Of those rejected, over 200 were excluded because they reported on an occupation as a whole rather that on a particular group of workers in a specific organization. These studies generally failed to provide reliable measures of either work group relations or their organizational contexts.

About twenty-five additional books were excluded because they reported on industries as a whole rather than on specific organizations. These studies generally lacked good first-hand information on worker–management and coworker relations. Fifteen books met the three criteria for inclusion but were either so short or so loosely written that accurate, complete information could not be ascertained. Thirteen books were excluded because they focused primarily on a specific job redesign program. Again, these books did not provide adequate information to code many of the variables in which we were interested. Eleven books were community studies, often of a factory town. These studies were typically based on observing and interviewing people and families outside of work, and not inside the workplace. As a result, these books generally did not provide adequate organizational or labor process information. Eight books were excluded because they focused on a particular strike or collective action and included little material on the nature of work or the labor process. Six books were excluded because they concerned plant closings and the resulting stresses and dislocations. These books also provided little material on the nature of work or on workplace relations prior to the shutdown. Seven books were excluded because they were company histories or executive biographies and contained little information on the actual work taking place in the organization.

In all cases we examined each book carefully to see if it met the three criteria for inclusion. In some cases, a book was relatively weak on one criterion, but the depth of its material in other areas allowed its inclusion. Thus, we sometimes included a book with a fairly broad occupational focus if it had excellent ethnographic material on the organization and the labor process in several occupations. For example, a book might contain information about both assembly workers and machinists. When coding material from such a book, we determined which occupational category was the major focus and coded only material about that occupation. In some books the data allowed the coding of two cases. For example, we coded two cases from a book reporting on a cocktail lounge – one for waitresses and one for managers (see Spradley and Mann 1975). Gouldner's (1964) *Patterns of Industrial Bureaucracy* also generated two cases – one for underground miners and one for workers in the gypsum board factory. We coded multiple cases from twelve books. We included ethnographies based on observations in several organizations if descriptions of the work process were particularly strong. Such books were included only if the organizations were similar and were discussed in detail. We coded organizational characteristics for these cases from a composite.

Application of the above criteria generated 108 cases from the 86 published ethnographies. We believe these cases constitute the population of book-length English language ethnographies that provide relatively complete information on a single workplace and on an identifiable work group within that workplace. The ethnographies are listed in Appendix B. Other organizational ethnographies that were not included or that were published subsequent to the coding are also used in parts of the analysis as sources of additional quotes and insights.

Coding the Ethnographies

A team of four researchers – the author and three advanced graduate students, developed the coding instrument for the ethnographies. We first developed a list of relevant concepts and preliminary response categories. Next, over a period of six months, eight selected ethnographies were read and coded by each of the four team members. After each ethnography was coded, we discussed our respective codings to decide on the retention or removal of items and develop new response categories and coding protocols. Our goal was to create an instrument that could be completed for every ethnography with high reliability by trained interviewers.

The ethnographies were read and coded by the same team of four researchers and by the eight members of a graduate research practicum. All coders were trained on a common ethnography and met twice weekly as a group to discuss problems and questions. Coders recorded up to three page numbers identifying the passages used for coding each variable. If multiple instances of a behavior were found, the coder was instructed to review all previous passages cited, reconcile inconsistencies between the passages, and record the best answer, along with all relevant page numbers. Coders were instructed to look for behavioral indicators or specific descriptions for each variable coded and not to rely on ethnographers' summary statements or evaluations (Weber 1990).

After completing a book, the primary coder was debriefed by a member of the research staff to check the accuracy of the codings. At this time, the codings were reviewed in detail. One book was selected as a reliability check and coded independently by three reviewers. The correlations between these different codings indicate a relatively high degree of reliability (average intercorrelation = .79). Validity checks indicate that the ethnographies evidence no distinct patterns of findings based on theoretical orientation or other ethnographer characteristics. Similarly, no differences between coders are observed based on statistical analysis of possible coder effects (see Hodson 1998b).

Not all ethnographies discuss every topic resulting in missing data for some measures. Workplace ethnographies, however, typically have a somewhat stylized format. This format can be traced jointly to the work of cultural anthropologists and industrial sociologists. The format includes mandatory coverage of a fixed set of topics including organizational characteristics, worker characteristics, management style, coworker relations, and sociotechnical relations. This standard format allows data from the ethnographies to be coded without generating a data set with large areas of missing data. Scales summarizing available data are developed for key concepts to further lessen the impact of missing data. See Hodson (1999a) for a more complete discussion of the methodological issues involved in coding data from ethnographic and other documentary accounts.

Appendix B: Workplace Ethnography
Data Set

Applebaum, Herbert. 1981. *Royal Blue, the Culture of Construction Workers.* New York: Holt.

Beynon, Huw. 1972. *Perceptions of Work: Variations Within a Factory.* Cambridge: Cambridge University Press.

Beynon, Huw. 1975. *Working for Ford.* East Ardsley, England: E.P. Publishing.

Biggart, Nicole. 1989. *Charismatic Capitalism: Direct Selling Organizations in America.* Chicago: University of Chicago Press.

Bosk, Charles. 1979. *Forgive and Remember.* Chicago: University of Chicago Press.

Burawoy, Michael. 1979. *Manufacturing Consent.* Chicago: University of Chicago Press.

Burris, Beverly H. 1983. *No Room at the Top: Underemployment and Alienation in the Corporation.* New York: Praeger.

Butcher, David. 1979. *The Driftermen.* Reading, England: Tops'l Books.

Butcher, David. 1980. *The Trawlermen.* Reading, England: Tops'l Books.

Cavendish, Ruth. 1982. *Women on the Line.* Boston: Routledge and Kegan Paul.

Cherry, Mike. 1974. *On High Steel: The Education of an Ironworker.* New York: Quadrangle.

Chinoy, Ely. 1955. *Automobile Workers and the American Dream.* Garden City, NY: Doubleday.

Cock, Jacklyn. 1989. *Maids and Madams: Domestic Workers under Apartheid.* London: Women's Press.

Cressey, Peter. 1985. *Just Managing: Authority and Democracy in Industry.* Philadelphia: Open University Press.

Crozier, Michel. 1971. *The World of the Office Worker* (translated by David Landau). Chicago: University of Chicago Press.

Dalton, Melville. 1959. *Men Who Manage.* New York: Wiley.

DiFazio, William. 1985. *Longshoremen: Community and Resistance on the Brooklyn Waterfront.* South Hadley, MA: Bergin & Garvey.

Finlay, William. 1988. *Work on the Waterfront: Worker Power and Technological Change in a West Coast Port.* Philadelphia: Temple University Press.

Foster, Charles. 1969. *Building with Men.* London: Tavistock.

Friedland, William H. 1971. *Migrant: Agricultural Workers in America's Northeast.* New York: Holt, Rinehart and Winston.

303

Gamst, Frederick C. 1980. *The Hoghead: An Industrial Ethnology of the Locomotive Engineer*. New York: Holt, Rinehart and Winston.

Gouldner, Alwin. 1964. *Patterns of Industrial Bureaucracy*. New York: Free Press.

Greenberg, Edward S. 1986. *Workplace Democracy*. Ithaca, NY: Cornell University Press.

Grenier, Guillermo J. 1988. *Inhuman Relations: Quality Circles and Anti-Unionism in American Industry*. Philadelphia: Temple University Press.

Gyllenhammar, Pehr G. 1977. *People at Work*. Reading, MA.: Addison-Wesley.

Haas, Jack and William Shaffir. 1987. *Becoming Doctors: The Adoption of a Cloak of Competence*. Greenwich, CT: JAI Press.

Halle, David. 1984. *America's Working Man*. Chicago: University of Chicago Press.

Hamper, Ben. 1991. *Rivethead: Tales from the Assembly Line*. New York: Warner.

Haraszti, Miklos. 1978. *A Worker in a Worker's State*. New York: Universe Books.

Harris, Rosemary. 1987. *Power and Powerlessness in Industry*. London: Tavistock.

Hill, Stephen. 1976. *The Dockers: Class and Tradition in London*. London: Heinemann.

House, J. D. 1977. *Contemporary Entrepreneurs: The Sociology of Residential Real Estate Agents*. Westport, CT: Greenwood Press.

Huws, Ursula. 1984. *The Homeworkers' New Technology and the Changing Location of White Collar Work*. London: Low Pay Unit.

Jackall, Robert. 1978. *Workers in a Labyrinth: Jobs and Survival in a Bank Bureaucracy*. Montclair, NJ: Allanheld and Osmun.

Johnson, Paula J. (ed). 1988. *Working the Water: The Commercial Fisheries of Maryland's Patuxent River*. Charlottesville, VA: Calvert Marine Museum and the University Press of Virginia.

Juravich, Tom. 1985. *Chaos on the Shop Floor: A Worker's View of Quality, Productivity, and Management*. Philadelphia: Temple University Press.

Kamata, Satoshi. 1982. *Japan in the Passing Lane* (translated by Tatsuru Akimoto). New York: Pantheon Books.

Kanter, Rosabeth Moss. 1977. *Men and Women of the Corporation*. New York: Basic Books.

Kapferer, Bruce. 1972. *Strategy and Transaction in an African Factory: African Workers and Indian Management in a Zambian Town*. Manchester, England: Manchester University Press.

Kesselman, Amy. 1990. *Fleeting Opportunities: Women Shipyard Workers in Portland and Vancouver During WWII and Reconversion*. Albany, NY: SUNY Press.

Kunda, Gideon. 1992. *Engineering Culture: Control and Commitment in a High-Tech Corporation*. Philadelphia: Temple University Press.

Kusterer, Kenneth. 1978. *Know-How on the Job: The Important Working Knowledge of "Unskilled" Workers*. Boulder, CO: Westview.

Linhart, Robert. 1981. *The Assembly Line*. Amherst: University of Massachusetts Press.

Lloyd, Timothy C. and Patrick B. Mullen. 1990. *Lake Erie Fishermen: Work Identity and Tradition*. Urbana, IL: University of Illinois Press.

Lo, Jeannie. 1990. *Office Ladies/Factory Women: Life and Work at a Japanese Factory*. Armonk, NY: M.E. Sharpe, Inc.

Lupton, Tom. 1963. *On the Shop Floor: Two Studies of Workshop Organization and Output*. New York: Pergamon Press.

Mars, Gerald and Michael Nicod. 1984. *The World of Waiters*. London: George Allen and Unwin.

Martin, Susan Ehrlich. 1980. *Breaking and Entering: Policewomen on Patrol*. Berkeley: University of California Press.

McCarl, Robert. 1985. *The District of Columbia's Fire Fighters' Project: A Case Study in Occupational Folklife*. Washington, DC: Smithsonian Institution Press.

McNally, Fiona. 1979. *Women for Hire*. New York: St. Martin.

Mers, Gilbert. 1988. *Working the Waterfront: The Ups and Downs of a Rebel Longshoreman*. Austin: University of Texas Press.

Millman, Marcia. 1976. *The Unkindest Cut: Life in the Backrooms of Medicine*. New York: Morrow.

Nichols, Theo. 1977. *Living with Capitalism: Class Relations and the Modern Factory*. London: Routledge.

Orbach, Michael. 1977. *Hunters, Seamen and Entrepreneurs*. Berkeley: University of California Press.

Palm, Goran. 1977. *The Flight from Work*. Cambridge: Cambridge University Press.

Paules, Greta Foff. 1991. *Dishing it Out: Power and Resistance among Waitresses in a New Jersey Restaurant*. Philadelphia: Temple University Press.

Perry, Stewart E. 1978. *San Francisco Scavengers: Dirty Work and the Pride of Ownership*. Berkeley: University of California Press.

Pfeffer, Richard M. 1979. *Working for Capitalism*. New York: Columbia University Press.

Pilcher, William W. 1972. *The Portland Longshoremen: A Dispersed Urban Community*. New York: Holt, Rinehart and Winston.

Pine, Vanderlyn R. 1965. *Caretaker of the Dead: The American Funeral Director*. New York: Irvington.

Pollert, Anna. 1981. *Girls, Wives, Factory Lives*. London: MacMillan.

Power-Waters, Brian. 1980. *Margin for Error? None*. Chestertown, MD: Pierce.

Rollins, Judith. 1985. *Between Women: Domestics and Their Employers*. Philadelphia: Temple University Press.

Rubinstein, Jonathan. 1973. *City Police*. New York: Farrar, Straus and Giroux.

Rutten, Rosanne. 1982. *Women Workers of Hacienda Milagros*. Amsterdam: Universiteit van Amsterdam.

Santino, Jack. 1989. *Miles of Smiles, Years of Struggle: Stories of Black Pullman Porters*. Urbana, IL: University of Illinois Press.

Savage, Charles H., Jr. and George F. F. Lombard. 1986. *Sons of the Machine*. Cambridge, MA: MIT Press.

Schrank, Robert. 1983. *Industrial Democracy at Sea: Authority and Democracy on a Norwegian Freighter*. Cambridge, MA: MIT Press.

Seider, Maynard, 1984. *A Year in the Life of a Factory*. San Pedro, CA: Singlejack Books.

Smigel, Erwin O. 1969. *The Wall Street Lawyer: Professional Organizational Man?* New York: Free Press.

Smith, Vicki. 1990. *Managing in the Corporate Interest: Control and Resistance in an American Bank*. Berkeley: University of California Press.

Spencer, Charles. 1977. *Blue Collar: An Internal Examination of the Workplace*. Chicago: Lakeside Press.

Spradley, James P. and Brenda J. Mann. 1975. *The Cocktail Waitress: Woman's Work in a Man's World*. New York: Wiley.

Turner, Steve. 1980. *Night Shift in a Pickle Factory*. San Pedro, CA: Singlejack Books.

Vecsey, George. 1974. *One Sunset a Week: The Story of a Coal Miner*. New York: E.P. Dutton.

Wajcman, Judy. 1983. *Women in Control: Dilemmas of a Workers' Co-operative*. New York: St. Martin's Press.

Walker, Charles R. [1977] 1957. *Toward the Automatic Factory: A Case Study of Men and Machines*. New Haven, CT: Yale University Press.

Walker, Charles R., Robert H. Guest, and Arthur N. Turner. [1987] 1956. *The Foreman on the Assembly Line*. Cambridge, MA: Harvard University Press.

Walker, Charles R. and Robert H. Guest. 1952. *The Man on the Assembly Line*. Cambridge, MA: Harvard University Press.

Wedderburn, Dorothy. 1972. *Workers' Attitudes and Technology*. Cambridge: Cambridge University Press.

Westwood, Sallie. 1982. *All Day, Every Day: Factory and Family in the Making of Women's Lives*. London: Pluto Press.

Williams, Bruce B. 1987. *Black Workers in an Industrial Suburb: The Struggle Against Discrimination*. New Brunswick, NJ: Rutgers University Press.

Williams, Claire. 1981. *Open Cut: The Working Class in an Australian Mining Town*. Boston: Allen and Unwin.

Wolcott, Harry F. 1973. *The Man in the Principal's Office*. New York: Holt, Rinehart and Winston.

Appendix C: Supplemental Tables

Table 1. *Resistance Scale*

Variables	Factor Loadings
Effort bargain	.545
Absenteeism	.605
Withhold enthusiasm	.672
Work avoidance	.787
Playing dumb	.662
Machine sabotage	.520
Procedure sabotage	.660
Social sabotage	.805
Subvert particular manager	.696

Notes: First eigenvalue = 4.01; second eigenvalue = 1.09; Cronbach's alpha = .84. Average number of variables available for scale construction = 6.06.

Table 2. *Citizenship Scale*

Variables	Factor Loadings
Cooperation	.791
Commitment to organizational goals	.648
Pride in work	.761
Extra effort	.760
Extra time	.672
Peer training	.537

Notes: First eigenvalue = 2.94; second eigenvalue = .87; Cronbach's alpha = .79. Average number of variables available for scale construction = 5.24.

307

Table 3. *Management Abuse Scale*

Variables	Factor Loadings
Abuse	.666
Firings	.586
Job security	.756
Layoffs	.613
Reduced hours	.521
On-the-job training	.563

Notes: First eigenvalue = 2.32; second eigenvalue = .93; Cronbach's alpha = .68. Average number of variables available for scale construction = 4.91.

Table 4. *Mismanagement Scale*

Variables	Factor Loadings
Organization of production	.831
Leadership	.815
Communication	.680
Repair	.615

Notes: First eigenvalue = 2.20; second eigenvalue = .80; Cronbach's alpha = .72. Average number of variables available for scale construction = 3.53.

Table 5. *Worker Solidarity Scale*

Variables	Factor Loadings
Mutual defense	.808
Cohesion	.739
Group leadership	.775
Group discipline enforced by workers	.806

Notes: First eigenvalue = 2.45; second eigenvalue = .70; Cronbach's alpha = .79. Average number of variables available for scale construction = 3.02.

Table 6. *Coworker Conflict Scale*

Variables	Factor Loadings
Within group conflict	.594
Within group gossip	.625
Within group interference	.682
Between group conflict	.685
Between group gossip	.722
Between group interference	.614

Notes: First eigenvalue = 2.58; second eigenvalue = 1.20; Cronbach's alpha = .73. Average number of variables available for scale construction = 3.71.

Index

Abbott, Andrew, 13, 31, 37, 57, 141, 159, 160
absenteeism: and assembly work, 125–6; as form of resistance, 62–3, 104; and time trends, 138; and work groups, 227–8
abuse: citizenship and resistance as responses to, 99–105, 113; continued prevalence of, 114; coworkers as source of, 200; and denials of dignity at work, 19, 35–6, 74–5; and Durkheim on exploitation of workers, 26; and employee involvement, 39, 185–6; and future of work, 260; history of, 83–7; in professional and craft settings, 37–8, 147–8; and quest for dignity in work, 5–7; and workplace norms, 91–9. *See also* physical abuse; verbal abuse
Acker, Joan, 263
Ackers, Peter, 38, 43, 103
Ackroyd, Stephen, 39, 138, 197, 240
Adkins, Lisa, 96, 231
Adler, Paul S., 92
advertising, and overwork, 36
agency: concept of in social sciences, 41; definition of, 16; and future of work, 264–7; and requirements for dignity in work, 238–41; workers and social structures, 50
agricultural work, 167
Alexander, Jeffrey A., 165
alienation: and coworker relations, 233; and employee participation, 196; and Marx on dignity in work, 22, 23–5; and organizational size, 161, 162t
Amenta, Edwin, 40
American exceptionalism, 112
Aminzade, Ronald, 48, 131
anomie, and Durkheim on dignity in work, 25–7, 49
anthropology: and Human Relations Area Files, 54–5; and organizational ethnographies, 301–2
Appelbaum, Eileen R., 32, 38, 171, 172, 173, 176, 268
Applebaum, Herbert, 66, 72–3, 102, 126, 153, 158, 207–8, 212–13, 224
Argyle, Michael, 239
Armstrong, Peter, 50
Armstrong, Warwick, 208

assembly lines: and coworker relations, 220–2; and future of work, 260–1; and overwork, 8, 75–6, 115–39
automobile industry: and alienation, 164; and assembly work, 120, 126–7; and employee involvement, 38, 39, 79, 182–5, 186, 188, 189, 226, 228; and joint union-management programs, 178–9; and mismanagement, 106; and outside ownership, 163; and resistance, 63, 64, 100–1, 104–5; and scientific management, 116; and social group differences, 166; and work intensification, 118
autonomy: and assembly work, 121–2; and coworker relations, 222–5; and denials of dignity at work, 19–20, 36–8; and employee participation, 183; and methods of analysis, 72–3; of professional and craft workers, 76–7, 140–70; and quest for dignity in work, 10–13; and theoretical concepts, 46–7

Bandura, Albert, 45, 142, 238
banking industry, 5, 13–16, 18, 98, 211, 215–16
Barbash, Jack, 92
Barker, James R., 39, 80, 175
Barley, Stephen R., 16, 143, 169, 173, 261
Barnard, Chester, 31–2, 68, 93, 173
Baron, James N., 77, 205
Barry, Herbert, III, 55
Bartunek, Jean M., 202
Batstone, Eric, 93
Batt, Rosemary, 32, 38, 171, 172, 173, 176, 268
Beck, John P., 198, 267, 268
Becker, Alene S., 121, 141
Becker, Howard S., 52, 267
Bell, Daniel, 257
Bendix, Reinhard, 28
Beniger, James R., 265
Bensman, Joseph, 87
Berger, Michael A., 42
Bernard, H. Russell, 52
Besser, Terry L., 177
Beynon, Huw, 64, 88, 106, 122, 127, 136, 161, 166, 244
Bierstedt, Robert, 91

311